THIRD EDITION

Concise Introduction to Tonal Harmony

THIRD EDITION

Concise Introduction to Tonal Harmony

L. POUNDIE BURSTEIN

Graduate Center and Hunter College

City University of New York

JOSEPH N. STRAUS

Graduate Center

City University of New York

W. W. NORTON & COMPANY

Independent Publishers Since 1923

W. W. Norton & Company has been independent since its founding in 1923, when William Warder Norton and Mary D. Herter Norton first published lectures delivered at the People's Institute, the adult education division of New York City's Cooper Union. The firm soon expanded its program beyond the Institute, publishing books by celebrated academics from America and abroad. By midcentury, the two major pillars of Norton's publishing program—trade books and college texts—were firmly established. In the 1950s, the Norton family transferred control of the company to its employees, and today—with a staff of five hundred and hundreds of trade, college, and professional titles published each year—W. W. Norton & Company stands as the largest and oldest publishing house owned wholly by its employees.

....

Editor: Chris Freitag
Project Editor: Meg Wilhoite
Assistant Editor: Julie Kocsis
Manuscript Editor: Jodi Beder
Managing Editor, College: Marian Johnson
Managing Editor, College Digital Media: Kim Yi
Production Manager: Karen Romano
Proofreader: Debra Nichols
Media Editor: Steve Hoge
Media Associate Editor: Ellie Shirocky
Marketing Manager, Music: Trevor Penland
Design Director: Rubina Yeh
Design: Juan Paolo Francisco
Permissions Associate: Patricia Wong
Composition: Amnet
Music Engraving: David Botwinik, Willow Graphics, London N3 2BN
Manufacturing: Transcontinental, Beauceville, QC

Permission to use copyrighted material is included in the credits section of this book, which begins on page C-1.

ISBN: 978-1-324-07261-4

W. W. Norton & Company, Inc., 500 Fifth Avenue, New York, NY 10110-0017
wwnorton.com
W. W. Norton & Company, Ltd., 15 Carlisle Street, London WID 3BS

1 2 3 4 5 6 7 8 9 0

Contents in Brief

Contents

Part Four Chromatic Harmony 225

Preface

Successfully used by thousands of students at hundreds of schools in its first edition, *Concise Introduction to Tonal Harmony* represents a tested, concise approach to the tonal harmony textbook. Rather than a sprawling, encyclopedic compendium, this is a guidebook to the most important things that students need to know. Our text introduces all the topics typically covered in the undergraduate theory sequence—fundamentals, diatonic and chromatic harmony, form, and post-tonal theory—but it approaches each topic with focus and concision. No frills and no nonsense—just the essentials. When it comes to textbooks, less can be more, and this is a text that students will be able to read and comprehend, freeing up class time for enriching activities.

Online resources offer yet another way to make class time more efficient. This third edition features new tutorials for the post-tonal chapters, in addition to the materials authored by our colleagues who have made extensive use of online tools in their own classrooms—Anna Gawboy (Ohio State University) and Inessa Bazayev (Louisiana State University)—to improve upon the best set of online resources for music theory available today. Accompanying each chapter, students will find innovative Know It? Show It! activities. Interactive video tutorials and adaptive online quizzes help students understand the content of the chapter and prepare them for the workbook assignments.

FEATURES

- Each carefully crafted chapter is just a few pages long and isolates a particular harmony and the voice-leading issues associated with it. Students quickly grasp the essential concepts, and instructors have the flexibility to teach chapters in a different order from the one that appears in the text.

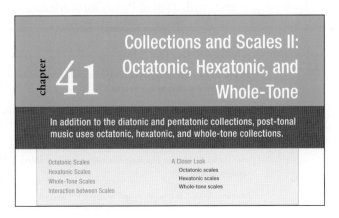

chapter

41 Collections and Scales II: Octatonic, Hexatonic, and Whole-Tone

In addition to the diatonic and pentatonic collections, post-tonal music uses octatonic, hexatonic, and whole-tone collections.

Octatonic Scales
Hexatonic Scales
Whole-Tone Scales
Interaction between Scales

A Closer Look
Octatonic scales
Hexatonic scales
Whole-tone scales

- Explanations are concise and clearly worded, with key terms in bold. In the ebook, students can tap on or mouse over boldface terms to reveal definitions.

- Concepts are illustrated with short musical examples, carefully selected to illustrate the topic at hand and to expose students to diverse composers and works. Annotations draw attention to key features of each example. Extended versions of nearly every brief musical example appear in the ebook, offering opportunities for additional study.

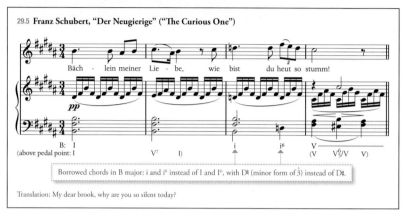

29.5 **Franz Schubert, "Der Neugierige" ("The Curious One")**

Bäch - lein meiner Lie - be, wie bist du heut so stumm!

B: I   V⁷   I)   i   i⁶   V   V⁶₅/V   V)
(above pedal point: I   (V

Borrowed chords in B major: i and i⁶ instead of I and I⁶, with D♮ (minor form of 3̂) instead of D♯.

Translation: My dear brook, why are you so silent today?

- Musical examples provide models of correct usage, but they also anticipate mistakes, showing students common errors and how to avoid them.

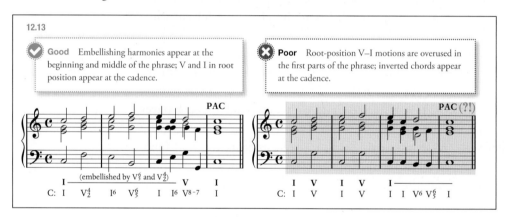

12.13

✓ **Good** Embellishing harmonies appear at the beginning and middle of the phrase; V and I in root position appear at the cadence.

✗ **Poor** Root-position V–I motions are overused in the first parts of the phrase; inverted chords appear at the cadence.

PAC

PAC (?!)

I   (embellished by V⁶₃ and V⁴₂)   V   I
C: I   V⁴₂   I⁶   V⁶₃   I   I⁶   V⁸⁻⁷   I

I   V   I   V   I
C: I   V   I   V   I   I   V⁶   V⁶₃   I

- Each chapter ends with a list of Points for Review.

POINTS FOR REVIEW

- Depending on the qualities of the thirds and fifths they contain, triads may be diminished, minor, major, or augmented.

- Triads may appear in three positions: root position ($\frac{5}{3}$, root in bass), first inversion ($\frac{6}{3}$, third in bass), or second inversion ($\frac{6}{4}$, fifth in bass).

- Roman numerals combined with figures (stacks of Arabic numbers) identify the root (as a scale degree in a major or minor scale), quality, and inversion of a triad or seventh chord.

- In minor keys, $\hat{7}$ is usually raised to make $V^{(7)}$ and $vii^{\circ(7)}$.

- Chapters close with a Test Yourself activity, to ensure that students understand the concepts discussed. Answers appear in the back of the printed text or can be revealed in the ebook.

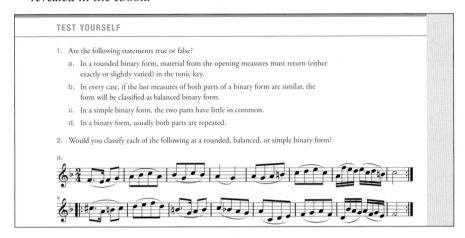

- The accompanying workbook, which is available both in print and in printable digital format, offers instructors a wide range of exercises to choose from in assembling assignments for theory classes. Error detection, chord spelling, figured bass and Roman numeral realization, composition, harmonization, and analysis exercises appear throughout the workbook, at all levels of difficulty. Review questions invite students to explain key concepts and processes in their own words.
- An Instructor's Edition of the workbook offers sample solutions to workbook exercises.

ONLINE RESOURCES

The Norton Illumine Ebook, included with every copy of the text, allows students to read on a wide variety of devices. Special ebook enhancements include:

- Links to **recordings** of every musical example in the text, making listening easier than ever.
- **Extended musical examples**, allowing students to see and hear longer versions of the short excerpts that appear in the text. These examples, which feature both notated music and recordings, can even be used instead of an anthology.
- **Closer Look** features, which go into more detail about less common or exceptional uses of the harmonies discussed in the text.
- **Check Your Understanding** questions at the end of each section to check in on student comprehension as they read through the ebook.
- **New** to the third edition is a **test bank** of nearly 1,000 questions written by Inessa Bazayev. All questions can be selected and edited in the Norton Testmaker program, accessed from the instructor's resource page. These tests can be deployed through learning management systems.

Concise Introduction to Tonal Harmony also features Know It? Show It! pedagogy, which is designed to develop students' skills and prepare them to complete workbook exercises.

- As they read the chapter, students watch short **video tutorials**, created by Anna Gawboy and keyed to each topic discussed in the text. Tutorials show students how to work through the problems they will encounter in their homework assignments. Each video tutorial includes interactive exercises, making it possible for students to practice skills as they view the tutorials and for instructors to assign tutorials and receive a completion grade for each student. New to this edition are a set of tutorials focusing on the post-tonal chapters, created by Joe Straus and produced by Scott Miller.

- Carefully graduated **adaptive online quizzes** by Inessa Bazayev, powered by Norton's InQuizitive system, deepen students' understanding and demonstrate mastery of the material. InQuizitive asks students questions until they've demonstrated that they understand the chapter material. When students have trouble, tailored feedback points them back to the book. And once students complete the activity, rich data about their performance can be reported to campus learning management systems. InQuizitive includes additional questions giving students even more opportunity to practice skills.

With **Total Access**, all students who purchase a new book—regardless of format—will receive access to all the media, including the Norton Illumine Ebook and Know It? Show It! pedagogy.

WHAT'S NEW IN THE THIRD EDITION?

With the help of feedback from dozens of instructors who have used this book with their students, we've thoroughly revised *Concise Introduction to Tonal Harmony* to make it more useful for professors and students.

- The repertoire of music in the text and workbook has been considerably revised. The number of examples from historically underrepresented composers has nearly trebled, to around 450, and they now comprise nearly one-half of the selections used. This continues our commitment to a basic principle: The musical languages of tonality and post-tonality are not the property of an elite group of canonical "master" composers; rather, they are a widely shared basis for creating music, employed by a remarkable diversity of composers over a very long period.

- Interactive tutorials are now available for nearly every chapter, including the six of the seven chapters at the end devoted to post-tonal music and its theory. Each tutorial includes an opportunity for students to use the skill discussed in the tutorial. Tutorials can be assigned, with a completion grade reported to campus learning management systems.

- The third edition takes full advantage of the new Norton Illumine Ebook platform. Each chapter's embedded Check Your Understanding questions with rich answer-specific feedback help to guide student reading and reinforce key concepts; many questions feature embedded notation. The Norton Illumine Ebook also features embedded audio clips for all of the musical examples.

- New to the third edition: Norton Testmaker question bank by Inessa Bazayev (Louisiana State University). Nearly 1,000 questions, many including notation and audio, to create tests administered through campus learning management systems.

- Each chapter's InQuizitive activity has been refreshed with questions that include new musical examples and notation exercises, crafted by Alyssa Barna (University of Minnesota).

ACKNOWLEDGMENTS

A book of this kind is not possible without feedback and insight from many, many people. For the first and second edition, scores of instructors—and, in some cases, their students—from across the United States and Canada offered us suggestions, encouragement, and constructive criticism.

For the third edition, the following instructors commented on our revision plan and we are grateful for their contributions: Alyssa Barna (University of Minnesota Twin Cities), Anita Bonkowski (University of Victoria), Christopher Brandt (Graceland University), Karl Braunschweig (Wayne State University), Frank Chiou (Ohio Wesleyan University), Rebecca Doran Eaton (Texas State University), Christopher Ellis (Faith Baptist Bible College), Laura Emmery (Emory University), Jon-Tomas Godin (Brandon University), Amanda Gunderson (Lycoming College), Timothy Howard (California State University, Northridge), Ivana Ilic (Emory University), Samantha Inman (Stephen F. Austin State University), Adam Kolek (Rowan University), Peter Lea (University of Missouri), Bonnie McLarty (University of Missouri), Will Peebles (Western Carolina University), Jesse Pierson (Front Range Community College), and Jennifer Russell (Northern Arizona University).

At W. W. Norton, an editorial dream team turned our vision of a concise introduction to tonal harmony into a tangible (and virtual) reality. Two former editors, Maribeth Payne and Justin Hoffman (a brilliant music theorist in his own right) helped us to conceive the project and guide it to publication. Our editor for the third edition, Christopher Freitag, worked with an experienced and capable team, including Meg Wilhoite, David Botwinik, Karen Romano, Juan Paolo Francisco, Steve Hoge, Julie Kocsis, Mica Clausen, Trevor Penland, Patricia Wong, and Ellie Shirocky, and Emma Daughtery. We benefitted from their professionalism and expertise in countless ways, large and small, and we are deeply grateful to all of them. Steven Beck assembled the musicians that perform on many of the recordings that accompany this text, and

Lon Kaiser provided expertly crafted digital recordings for the remainder. We also had assistance from two of our talented doctoral students at the CUNY Graduate Center: Scott Miller and Matt Sandahl.

NOTE TO INSTRUCTORS

Many of the examples in this text focus on four-part harmony exercises—and the problems that students encounter in completing them. That a certain feature is labeled in an example as "poor" does not mean that it is poor in an aesthetic sense, or something that never appears in music, but that it is inappropriate within the context of harmony exercises, which reinforce the norms of tonal practice and increase sensitivity to underlying smooth and independent voice leading. We encourage instructors to dive more deeply into how these principles play out in real music, whether using the extended examples in the ebook or examples of their own choosing.

one

Fundamentals

chapter 0

Notation of Pitch and Rhythm

Musical notation conveys information about pitch (high and low) and rhythm (long and short).

The Staff	Eighth notes and sixteenth notes
Notating Pitches	Dots and ties
Treble clef	Rests
Bass clef	Simple Meter
Grand staff	Compound Meter
Semitones and whole tones	A Closer Look
Accidentals	C clefs
Rhythmic Durations	Triplets
Quarter notes, half notes, and whole notes	

THE STAFF

Music is written on a five-line **staff**. **Pitches**—specific points on the continuum of audible sound—are represented by notes written on the lines and spaces of the staff. As notes go higher on the staff the pitches ascend, and as notes go lower the pitches descend.

0.1

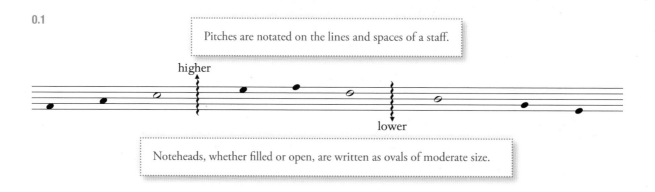

Pitches are notated on the lines and spaces of a staff.

higher

lower

Noteheads, whether filled or open, are written as ovals of moderate size.

Pitches that are too high or too low for the staff are written on **ledger lines** (temporary extensions of the staff).

0.2

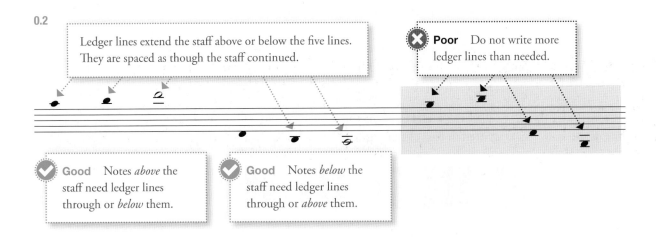

Ledger lines extend the staff above or below the five lines. They are spaced as though the staff continued.

⊗ **Poor** Do not write more ledger lines than needed.

✓ **Good** Notes *above* the staff need ledger lines through or *below* them.

✓ **Good** Notes *below* the staff need ledger lines through or *above* them.

NOTATING PITCHES

TREBLE CLEF

Musicians use letters from A to G to identify the notes on the white keys of the piano. As a point of reference, the C in the middle of the piano keyboard is called **middle C**. A **clef** associates lines and spaces on the staff with specific pitches. The **treble clef** (𝄞, also called the **G clef**), assigns the G above middle C to the second line of the staff.

0.3

The treble clef associates particular lines and spaces on the staff with white keys on the piano.

A B C D E F G A B C D E F G A B C D E

middle C

The G clef is a stylized letter G: it encircles the second line of the staff and identifies it as G.

As pitches ascend or descend, the letter names repeat once every eight notes, or **octave**.

0.4

Starting on any note, and including the starting point, moving eight notes in either direction takes you back to your starting point.

BASS CLEF

The **bass clef** (𝄢, also called the **F clef**) assigns the F below middle C to the fourth line of the staff. Notes written in bass clef are usually lower than those in treble clef.

0.5

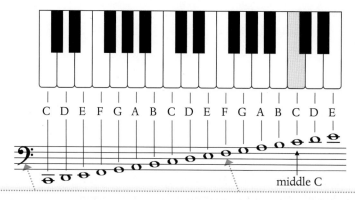

The F clef is a stylized letter F: it is centered on the fourth line of the staff and identifies it as F.

GRAND STAFF

One staff in treble clef and one staff in bass clef may be combined in a **grand staff**.

0.6

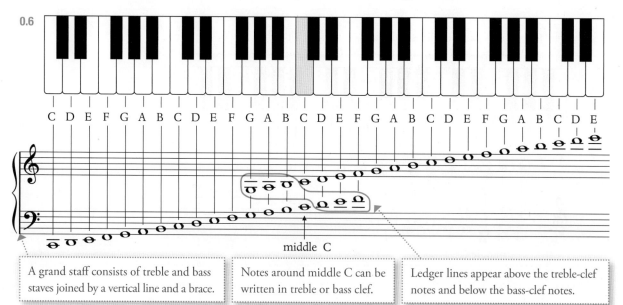

A grand staff consists of treble and bass staves joined by a vertical line and a brace.

Notes around middle C can be written in treble or bass clef.

Ledger lines appear above the treble-clef notes and below the bass-clef notes.

SEMITONES AND WHOLE TONES

A **semitone** is the smallest possible space between two notes. Any two adjacent keys on the piano keyboard comprise a semitone, and there are twelve semitones in the octave. Two semitones make up a **whole tone**. Among the white keys, E–F and B–C are separated by a semitone. All other pairs of white keys are a whole tone apart; they are separated by a black key.

0.7

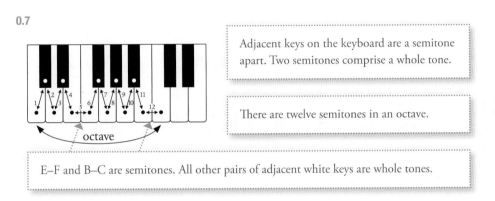

Adjacent keys on the keyboard are a semitone apart. Two semitones comprise a whole tone.

There are twelve semitones in an octave.

E–F and B–C are semitones. All other pairs of adjacent white keys are whole tones.

ACCIDENTALS

Accidentals are used to raise or lower pitches by a semitone: a **sharp** sign (♯) raises a pitch by one semitone; a **flat** sign (♭) lowers a pitch by one semitone. D♭, for example, is a semitone below D, and F♯ is a semitone above F. Pitches may have more than one name (different names for the same pitch are **enharmonic equivalents**).

0.8

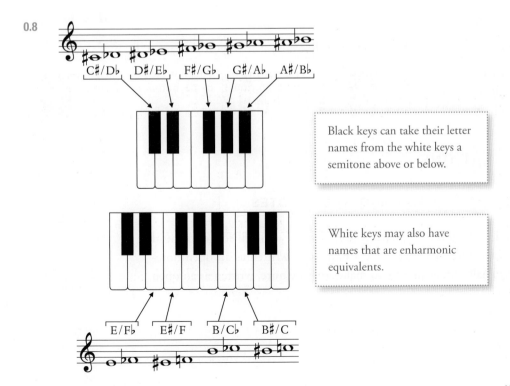

Black keys can take their letter names from the white keys a semitone above or below.

White keys may also have names that are enharmonic equivalents.

On the staff, accidentals are written *before* the note, but when you say (or write) the name of a note, the accidental comes *after* the letter name, as in "F-sharp" or "G-flat." A note that is neither sharp nor flat is **natural**, and is identified by a natural sign (♮). Most often, the natural sign is used to cancel a previous sharp or flat. For example, C♮ tells you that the C is no longer sharp or flat, but has been restored to its usual unmodified state.

0.9

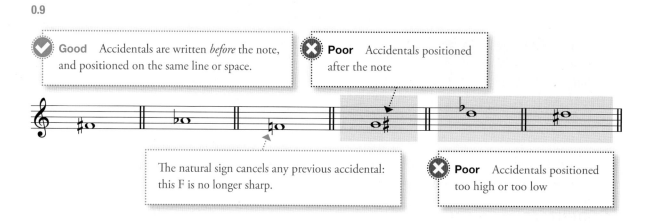

It is also possible to raise a note by two semitones using a **double sharp** sign (𝄪) or to lower a note by two semitones using a **double flat** sign (𝄫).

0.10

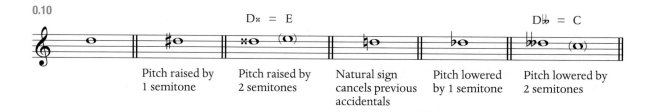

| D𝄪 = E | | | | D𝄫 = C |
| Pitch raised by 1 semitone | Pitch raised by 2 semitones | Natural sign cancels previous accidentals | Pitch lowered by 1 semitone | Pitch lowered by 2 semitones |

RHYTHMIC DURATIONS

QUARTER NOTES, HALF NOTES, AND WHOLE NOTES

The basic unit of musical duration is a **quarter note**, written with a filled-in notehead and a stem. Two quarter notes together make a **half note**, written as an open notehead with a stem. Two half notes combine to make a **whole note**, written as an open notehead with no stem.

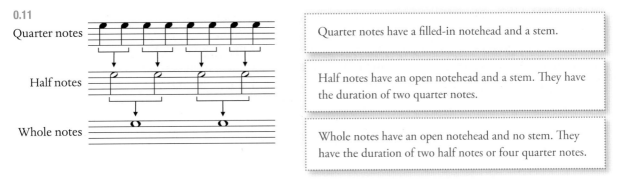

0.11

Quarter notes

Half notes

Whole notes

Quarter notes have a filled-in notehead and a stem.

Half notes have an open notehead and a stem. They have the duration of two quarter notes.

Whole notes have an open notehead and no stem. They have the duration of two half notes or four quarter notes.

When writing quarter notes and half notes, make the stem an octave in length. When the note is on or below the second space of the staff, the stem goes to the right and points up. When the note is on or above the third line of the staff, the stem goes to the left and points down.

0.12

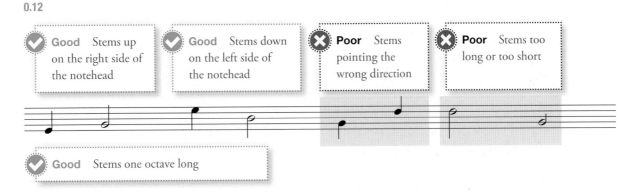

Good Stems up on the right side of the notehead

Good Stems down on the left side of the notehead

Poor Stems pointing the wrong direction

Poor Stems too long or too short

Good Stems one octave long

EIGHTH NOTES AND SIXTEENTH NOTES

Just as quarter notes can be combined to create longer durations, they can be divided to create shorter ones. A quarter note can be divided into two **eighth notes**, each written with a filled-in notehead and a stem with a **flag**. When two eighth notes occur together as a pair, join them with a **beam** instead of using flags. An eighth note can be divided into two **sixteenth notes**, each written as a filled-in notehead with a double flag or, in pairs or groups of four, joined together with a double beam. (Further subdivisions—thirty-second notes and sixty-fourth notes—are also possible.)

0.13

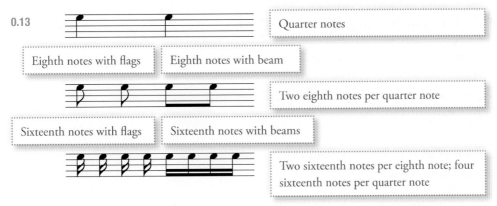

Quarter notes

Eighth notes with flags   Eighth notes with beam

Two eighth notes per quarter note

Sixteenth notes with flags   Sixteenth notes with beams

Two sixteenth notes per eighth note; four sixteenth notes per quarter note

DOTS AND TIES

So far, all of the durations that we have considered involve halving or doubling the quarter note. We can create additional rhythmic values by using the **augmentation dot**. A dot placed directly after a note increases the duration of that note by one half.

0.14

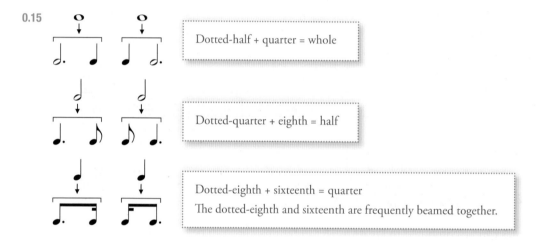

Dotted rhythms often divide a duration into two unequal parts.

0.15

Dotted-half + quarter = whole	
Dotted-quarter + eighth = half	
Dotted-eighth + sixteenth = quarter The dotted-eighth and sixteenth are frequently beamed together.	

Still more rhythmic values become available with **ties**. A tie connecting two notes combines them into a single duration.

0.16

A tie combines two notes into a single duration.

RESTS

A **rest** indicates a duration of silence. Rests can correspond to any rhythmic value. They are written in the middle of the staff.

0.17

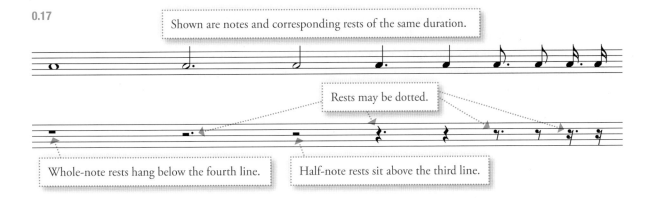

Shown are notes and corresponding rests of the same duration.

Rests may be dotted.

Whole-note rests hang below the fourth line.

Half-note rests sit above the third line.

SIMPLE METER

Meter involves three or more coordinated layers of regular pulsations (repeated rhythmic values). The pulsations in the middle layer are called **beats**. The beats may be divided by the lower layer into two or three parts (**divisions**). The beats may be grouped by the upper layer into groups of two, three, or four beats. These groupings are notated as **measures** (or bars) separated by **barlines**. The first beat of each measure is relatively accented and is called the **downbeat**.

0.18

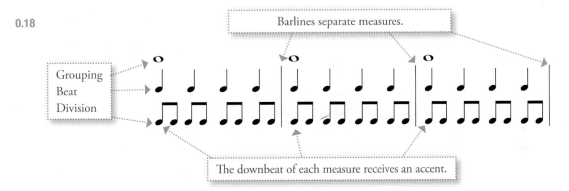

Barlines separate measures.

Grouping
Beat
Division

The downbeat of each measure receives an accent.

The **time signature** provides information about the beat, its grouping into measures, and its divisions. It consists of two stacked numbers. The bottom number determines the note value of each beat. In **simple meters**, where the beat is divided into two parts, the quarter note—indicated by a 4 at the bottom of the time signature—is the most common beat, but eighth notes (8) and half notes (2) can also function as the beat. The top number of a time signature determines the number of beats in each measure. In simple meters, this number is 2, 3, or 4.

0.19

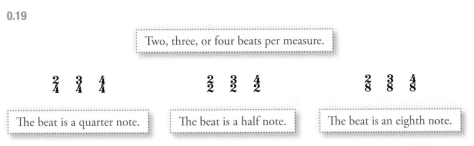

Two, three, or four beats per measure.

The beat is a quarter note.

The beat is a half note.

The beat is an eighth note.

If there are four beats per measure, a 4 appears at the top of the time signature, and the meter is **quadruple**. For quadruple simple meters, the most common time signature is 𝄴, which indicates four quarter notes per measure. 𝄴 is sometimes called "common time" and labeled **C**.

0.20

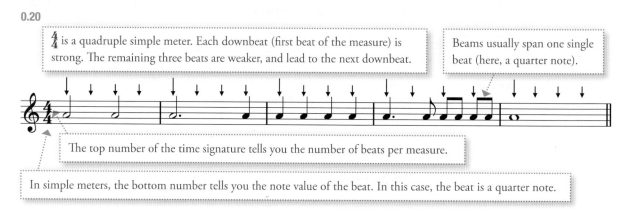

If there are three beats per measure, a 3 appears at the top of the time signature and the meter is **triple**.

0.21

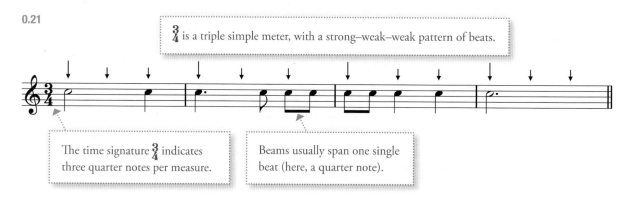

Duple meters have two beats per measure.

0.22

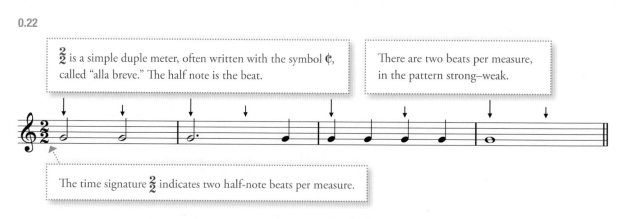

COMPOUND METER

In simple meters, the beat is divided into *two parts*: quarter-note beats contain two eighth notes, half-note beats contain two quarter notes, and eighth-note beats contain two sixteenth notes. In **compound meters**, the beat is divided into *three parts*, and the beat itself is a dotted note. Because the bottom number of a time signature cannot show a dotted beat unit, compound time signatures show instead the divisions of the beat. If the bottom number of a compound time signature is 8, the beat will be a dotted-quarter note, which is three eighth notes grouped together. Other beat units are also possible: a dotted-half note can be divided into three quarter notes (4), or a dotted-eighth note into three sixteenths (16).

The top number of a compound meter signature is 6, 9, or 12 and shows the number of *beat divisions* in each measure. Divide by three to find the number of beats in each measure. Like simple meters, compound meters may be duple (6 in the time signature), triple (9), or quadruple (12).

0.23

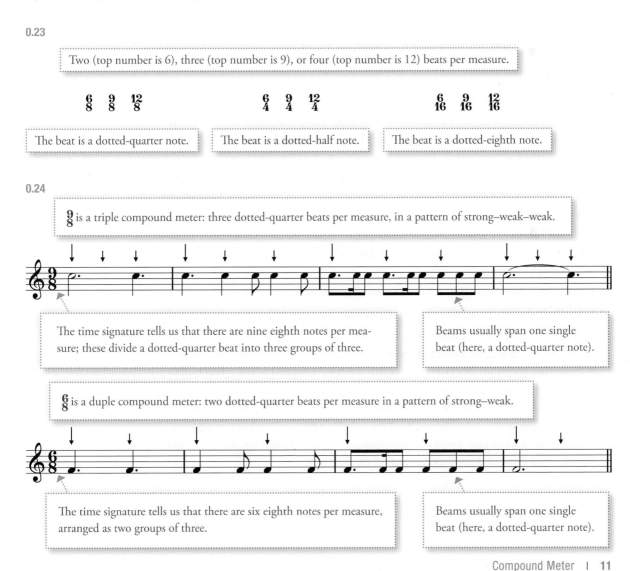

SUMMARY OF PRINCIPAL METERS

	NOTE VALUE OF THE BEAT	DUPLE (2 BEATS PER MEASURE)	TRIPLE (3 BEATS PER MEASURE)	QUADRUPLE (4 BEATS PER MEASURE)
Simple	Half note	$\frac{2}{2}$ or ¢	$\frac{3}{2}$	$\frac{4}{2}$
Simple	Quarter note	$\frac{2}{4}$	$\frac{3}{4}$	$\frac{4}{4}$ or C
Simple	Eighth note	$\frac{2}{8}$	$\frac{3}{8}$	$\frac{4}{8}$
Compound	Dotted-half note	$\frac{6}{4}$	$\frac{9}{4}$	$\frac{12}{4}$
Compound	Dotted-quarter note	$\frac{6}{8}$	$\frac{9}{8}$	$\frac{12}{8}$
Compound	Dotted-eighth note	$\frac{6}{16}$	$\frac{9}{16}$	$\frac{12}{16}$

 For more on notation, see A Closer Look.

POINTS FOR REVIEW

- Pitches are written on the lines and spaces of the five-line staff.
- Clefs determine the location of pitches on the staff. The most commonly used clefs are the treble clef (second line = G above middle C) and the bass clef (fourth line = F below middle C).
- Accidentals (sharps and flats) raise or lower pitches by a semitone. Less commonly, double sharps and double flats raise or lower pitches by two semitones. Naturals are neither sharp nor flat.
- The most common durational value is the quarter note. The other common values—whole notes, half notes, eighth notes, and sixteenth notes—are made by combining or dividing quarter notes.
- An augmentation dot increases the duration of a note by half.
- A tie combines two notes into a single duration.
- In simple meters, the beat unit divides into two parts. The top number of a simple time signature is 2, 3, or 4 and indicates the number of beats per measure. The bottom number shows the beat unit (8 = eighth note; 4 = quarter note; 2 = half note).
- Compound meters have a dotted note as the beat, which divides into three parts. The top number of a compound time signature is 6, 9, or 12 and indicates the number of beat divisions; divide by three to find the number of beats. The bottom number indicates the unit of beat divisions (16 = sixteenth note; 8 = eighth note; 4 = quarter note); group three of them together to find the beat unit.

1. Identify each note.

2. Write a note that is enharmonically equivalent to each given note.

3. Insert barlines to create complete measures in the indicated time signatures.

4. There are blank spots in some of these measures (indicated by arrows). Fill them in by inserting a single note of the proper duration.

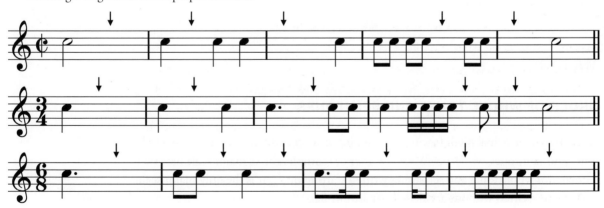

chapter 1

Scales

Major and minor scales are the basic building blocks of tonal music.

Major Scale
Order of whole tones and semitones
Scale degrees
Transposition
Minor Scales
Natural minor scale
Harmonic minor scale
Ascending melodic minor scale

Key Signatures for Major Keys
Circle of fifths
Key Signatures for Minor Keys
Circle of fifths
Relative and Parallel Keys
Relative keys
Parallel keys

A **scale** is a collection of notes, organized around a central, **tonic** pitch and used as the basis for a musical composition. Scales are typically written in ascending order within an octave. There are two scales commonly used in tonal music: major and minor. In both major and minor scales, each of the seven letter names (A, B, C, D, E, F, and G) occurs only once and none is omitted. Major and minor scales thus contain seven different notes, although the first note is generally written again an octave higher at the end.

MAJOR SCALE

ORDER OF WHOLE TONES AND SEMITONES

Built above a principal pitch (the tonic), a **major scale** consists of a sequence of whole tones and semitones: W–W–S–W–W–W–S. For example, the C major scale uses that sequence of whole tones and semitones written starting on C. It is the only major scale that can be written without accidentals (sharps or flats).

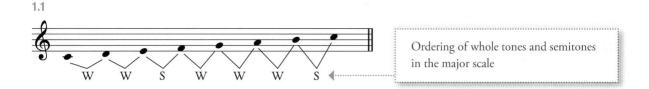

1.1

Ordering of whole tones and semitones in the major scale

SCALE DEGREES

The notes of the scale, known as **scale degrees**, can be identified either with traditional **scale-degree names** or with **scale-degree numbers**, written beneath a caret sign (ˆ). The first scale degree, for instance, is known either as tonic or as $\hat{1}$. The two semitones of the major scale may be found between $\hat{3}$ and $\hat{4}$ and between $\hat{7}$ and $\hat{8}$.

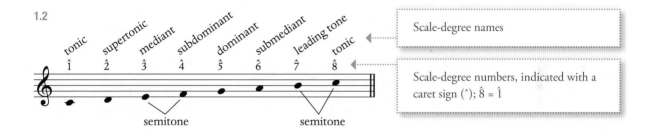

1.2

Scale-degree names

Scale-degree numbers, indicated with a caret sign (ˆ); $\hat{8} = \hat{1}$

TRANSPOSITION

The C major scale can be **transposed** to any of the remaining eleven notes. Some of the notes will have to be altered with sharps or flats, however, to preserve C major's pattern of whole tones and semitones.

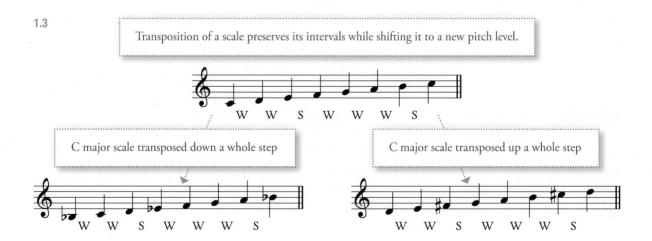

1.3

Transposition of a scale preserves its intervals while shifting it to a new pitch level.

C major scale transposed down a whole step

C major scale transposed up a whole step

MINOR SCALES

NATURAL MINOR SCALE

The **minor scale** (sometimes called the **natural minor scale**) has a different arrangement of semitones and whole tones than the major scale. The minor scale has semitones between $\hat{2}$ and $\hat{3}$ and between $\hat{5}$ and $\hat{6}$, while the major scale has semitones between $\hat{3}$ and $\hat{4}$ and between $\hat{7}$ and $\hat{8}$.

1.4

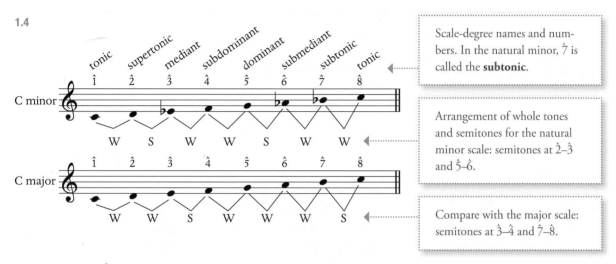

Scale-degree names and numbers. In the natural minor, $\hat{7}$ is called the **subtonic**.

Arrangement of whole tones and semitones for the natural minor scale: semitones at $\hat{2}$–$\hat{3}$ and $\hat{5}$–$\hat{6}$.

Compare with the major scale: semitones at $\hat{3}$–$\hat{4}$ and $\hat{7}$–$\hat{8}$.

Note that $\hat{7}$ in natural minor is called the subtonic rather than the leading tone. Because the subtonic is a whole tone rather than a semitone below $\hat{1}$, it lacks a sense of directed movement toward the tonic.

HARMONIC MINOR SCALE

The subtonic is often raised by one semitone, turning it into a leading tone. Depending on the scale, raising the subtonic to a leading tone may require a natural (if the subtonic is flat), a sharp (if the subtonic is natural), or a double sharp (if the subtonic is sharp). The scale that results from raising $\hat{7}$ is called **harmonic minor**.

1.5

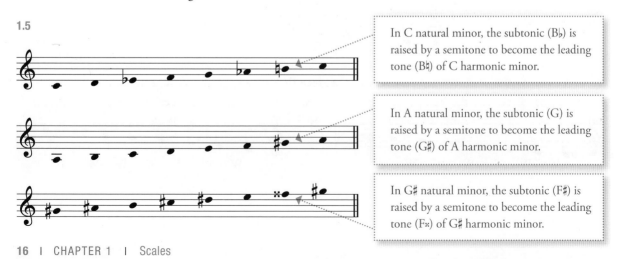

In C natural minor, the subtonic (B♭) is raised by a semitone to become the leading tone (B♮) of C harmonic minor.

In A natural minor, the subtonic (G) is raised by a semitone to become the leading tone (G♯) of A harmonic minor.

In G♯ natural minor, the subtonic (F♯) is raised by a semitone to become the leading tone (F𝄪) of G♯ harmonic minor.

In the harmonic minor scale, there are semitones between $\hat{2}$ and $\hat{3}$ and between $\hat{5}$ and $\hat{6}$ (as in natural minor), as well as between $\hat{7}$ and $\hat{8}$ (as in major, but not natural minor). There is also a gap, spanning three semitones, between $\hat{6}$ and $\hat{7}$. This gap is called an **augmented second** (see Chapter 2).

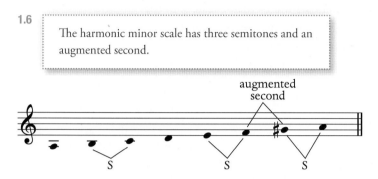

1.6 The harmonic minor scale has three semitones and an augmented second.

ASCENDING MELODIC MINOR SCALE

Sometimes, the gap between $\hat{6}$ and $\hat{7}$ in the harmonic minor scale is smoothed out by also raising $\hat{6}$. Note that $\hat{6}$ is typically raised only in conjunction with $\hat{7}$. Raising both $\hat{6}$ and $\hat{7}$ creates a second variant of the minor scale called **ascending melodic minor**. Like natural minor, the ascending melodic minor scale contains only two semitones: $\hat{2}$–$\hat{3}$ and $\hat{7}$–$\hat{8}$. Melodic minor is particularly suitable for singing or playing a melody that ascends to the tonic. Like raised $\hat{7}$, raised $\hat{6}$ always requires an accidental: if $\hat{6}$ in natural minor is flat, it must be made natural; if it is natural, it must be made sharp; if it is sharp, it must be made double sharp.

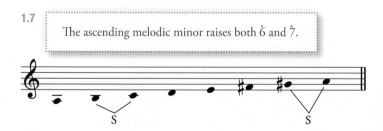

1.7 The ascending melodic minor raises both $\hat{6}$ and $\hat{7}$.

A final variant of the minor scale is called **descending melodic minor**. When descending melodically, the upward tendencies of raised $\hat{6}$ and $\hat{7}$ may no longer be musically desirable. Therefore, when descending, $\hat{6}$ and $\hat{7}$ revert to their natural minor form. As a result, the descending melodic minor is identical to natural minor.

KEY SIGNATURES FOR MAJOR KEYS

CIRCLE OF FIFTHS

A piece or passage that makes consistent reference to a particular major or minor scale is said to be in that **key**. So, for example, music that uses the B♭ major scale is in the key of B♭ major and music that uses the E minor scale is in the key of E minor. The sharps and flats (accidentals) needed for a major scale (or major key) can be conveniently summarized in a **key signature**, written directly after the clef at the beginning of each line of a musical staff.

1.8

With each counterclockwise move around the circle (e.g., C–F), the tonic pitch descends five steps and one flat is added to the key signature (or one sharp is taken away).

With each clockwise move around the circle (e.g., C–G), the tonic pitch ascends five steps and one sharp is added to the key signature (or one flat is taken away).

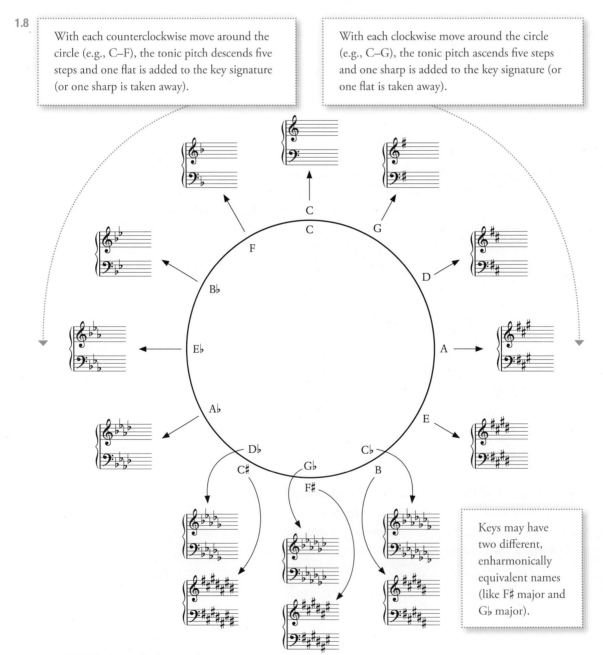

Keys may have two different, enharmonically equivalent names (like F♯ major and G♭ major).

The key signature directs performers to consistently perform notes with sharps or flats, unless they are canceled by another accidental. Transposing a scale up five steps adds one sharp to the key signature (or removes one flat). Transposing a scale down five steps adds one flat to the key signature (or removes one sharp). As a result, all of the major key signatures can be arranged around a **circle of fifths**.

The accidentals in the key signature must be written in the correct position on the staff and in the proper order. The order in which sharps and flats are written follows the circle of fifths. Sharps move clockwise from F♯: F♯–C♯–G♯–D♯–A♯–E♯–B♯. Flats move counterclockwise from B♭: B♭–E♭–A♭–D♭–G♭–C♭–F♭.

1.9

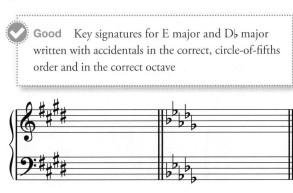

✓ **Good** Key signatures for E major and D♭ major written with accidentals in the correct, circle-of-fifths order and in the correct octave

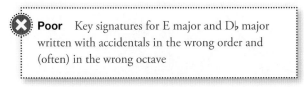

✗ **Poor** Key signatures for E major and D♭ major written with accidentals in the wrong order and (often) in the wrong octave

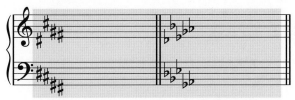

KEY SIGNATURES FOR MINOR KEYS

CIRCLE OF FIFTHS

As with the major scale, the natural minor scale (and its variants) can be transposed to start on any of the twelve notes. As with major, the circle of fifths can show the accidentals needed to write minor scales (or minor keys) gathered into a key signature. (The illustration uses a common shorthand of lowercase letters to represent minor keys.)

With each counterclockwise move around the circle, the tonic pitch descends five steps and one flat is added to the key signature (or one sharp is taken away).

With each clockwise move around the circle, the tonic pitch ascends five steps and one sharp is added to the key signature (or one flat is taken away).

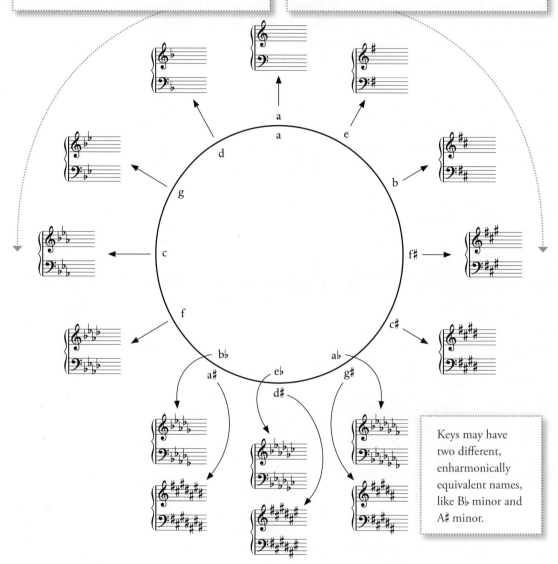

Keys may have two different, enharmonically equivalent names, like B♭ minor and A♯ minor.

When writing a minor key signature, use only the accidentals from the natural minor. This is the basic form of the minor scale—the others (harmonic minor and ascending melodic minor) are variants that result from altering $\hat{7}$ or both $\hat{6}$ and $\hat{7}$.

RELATIVE AND PARALLEL KEYS

RELATIVE KEYS

Major and minor keys with the same key signature are called **relative keys**. For example, G major and E minor both use the same seven notes (the only accidental is F♯), but each starts on a different note.

1.11

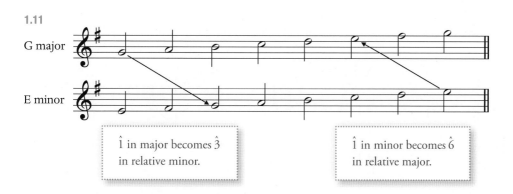

$\hat{1}$ in major becomes $\hat{3}$ in relative minor.

$\hat{1}$ in minor becomes $\hat{6}$ in relative major.

A double circle of fifths can show all of the relative major and minor keys and the key signature they share.

1.12

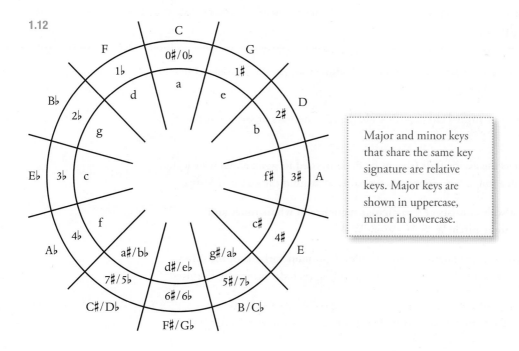

Major and minor keys that share the same key signature are relative keys. Major keys are shown in uppercase, minor in lowercase.

PARALLEL KEYS

Major and minor keys that share the same tonic are called **parallel keys**. Looking back to the double circle of fifths, if you start on a minor key and move three fifths clockwise, you will find its parallel major, and if you start on a major key and move three fifths counterclockwise you will find its parallel minor. Although their key signatures are different (unlike relative keys), parallel keys share not only $\hat{1}$, but also $\hat{2}$, $\hat{4}$, and $\hat{5}$. Indeed, they differ only in $\hat{3}$, $\hat{6}$, and $\hat{7}$.

1.13

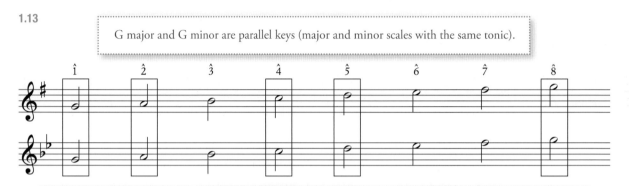

G major and G minor are parallel keys (major and minor scales with the same tonic).

Parallel keys have the same $\hat{1}$, $\hat{2}$, $\hat{4}$, and $\hat{5}$. Scale degrees $\hat{3}$, $\hat{6}$, and $\hat{7}$ are a semitone lower in the parallel minor.

POINTS FOR REVIEW

- A major scale consists of a particular sequence of whole tones and semitones above a tonic pitch: W–W–S–W–W–W–S.

- Scale degrees can be identified either with scale-degree numbers or with traditional names.

- A key signature lists the accidentals (sharps or flats) needed to write a major or minor scale beginning on a tonic. Key signatures are ordered around the circle of fifths.

- The natural minor scale consists of a particular sequence of whole tones and semitones above a tonic pitch: W–S–W–W–S–W–W.

- Minor key signatures refer to natural minor scales. Common variants of the minor scale are harmonic minor (with raised $\hat{7}$) and ascending melodic minor (with raised $\hat{6}$ and $\hat{7}$).

- Relative keys have the same key signature. Parallel keys have the same tonic ($\hat{1}$).

1. Write scales as indicated. Use appropriate accidentals (do not use key signatures).

A major

F minor (natural)

B minor (ascending melodic)

G♯ minor (harmonic)

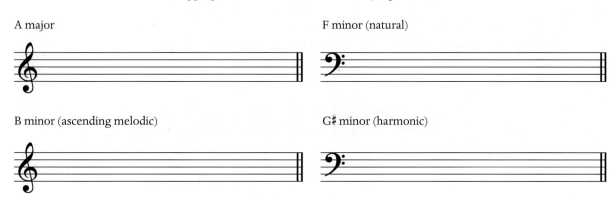

2. Given the name of a major or minor scale and a scale-degree number, write the appropriate note.

F major: 4̂   F♯ minor: 6̂   G minor: 7̂   A♭ major: 3̂   D minor: 6̂   E major: 5̂
            (natural minor) (harmonic minor)   (ascending
                                                            melodic minor)

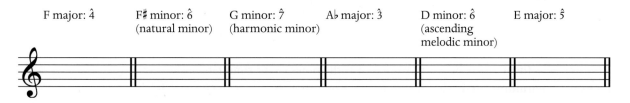

3. Write key signatures for these keys.

B minor   E♭ major   F minor   E minor   F♯ major   D minor

4. Name the two keys, one major and one minor, represented by each of these key signatures. Use uppercase to indicate the major key, lowercase for minor.

_____   _____   _____   _____   _____   _____

chapter 2

Intervals

Intervals measure the size and quality of the distance between notes.

Interval Size
Simple and Compound Intervals
Interval Quality
  Major and minor intervals (seconds, thirds, sixths, sevenths)
  Perfect intervals (unisons, fourths, fifths, octaves)

Interval inversion
Natural (white-key) intervals
Enharmonic intervals
Consonant and Dissonant Intervals
Intervals in a Key
A Closer Look
  Intervals in a key

An **interval** is the distance between two notes. If the notes occur simultaneously, the interval is a **harmonic interval**; if the notes occur one after the other, the interval is a **melodic interval**.

2.1

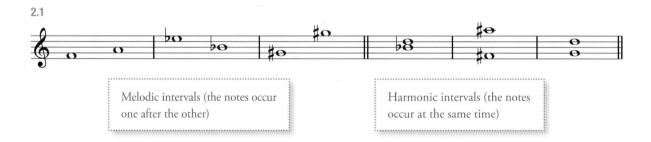

Melodic intervals (the notes occur one after the other)

Harmonic intervals (the notes occur at the same time)

INTERVAL SIZE

The size of an interval is the number of letter names it spans, counting either up or down (including the first note in the count). To determine the size of an interval, ignore any accidentals.

SIZE	NUMBER OF STEPS (LETTER NAMES) SPANNED	EXAMPLES
Unison	1 (C–C)	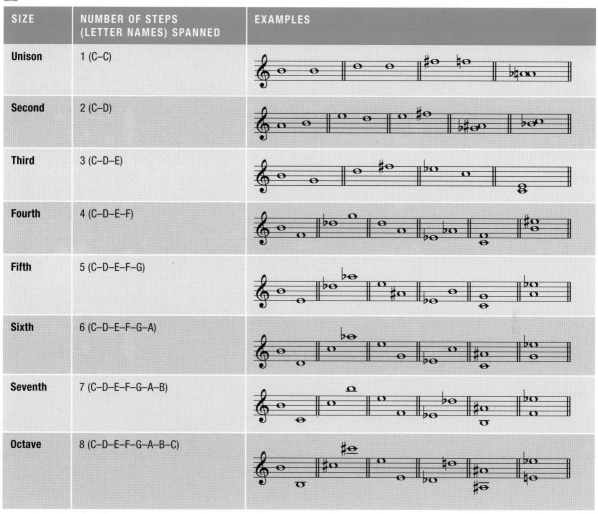
Second	2 (C–D)	
Third	3 (C–D–E)	
Fourth	4 (C–D–E–F)	
Fifth	5 (C–D–E–F–G)	
Sixth	6 (C–D–E–F–G–A)	
Seventh	7 (C–D–E–F–G–A–B)	
Octave	8 (C–D–E–F–G–A–B–C)	

SIMPLE AND COMPOUND INTERVALS

Intervals smaller than an octave are **simple intervals**. Intervals larger than an octave are **compound intervals**; they contain a simple interval plus one or more octaves. You can identify a compound interval as you do a simple interval, by counting the total number of letter names it contains. Alternatively, compound intervals may be identified by the simple interval they contain, ignoring any extra octaves. When adding an octave to a simple interval, the arithmetic will look a little odd. For example, a second plus an octave is a ninth, not a tenth. That is because we are counting scale steps, not measuring distances.

SIMPLE NAME (STEPS)	EXAMPLE	COMPOUND NAME (STEPS)	EXAMPLE
Second (2)		Ninth (9 = 2 + 8)	9th / 2nd + 8ve
Third (3)		Tenth (10 = 3 + 8)	10th / 3rd + 8ve
Fourth (4)		Eleventh (11 = 4 + 8)	11th / 4th + 8ve
Fifth (5)		Twelfth (12 = 5 + 8)	12th / 5th + 8ve
Sixth (6)		Thirteenth (13 = 6 + 8)	13th / 6th + 8ve
Seventh (7)		Fourteenth (14 = 7 + 8)	14th / 7th + 8ve

INTERVAL QUALITY

MAJOR AND MINOR INTERVALS (SECONDS, THIRDS, SIXTHS, SEVENTHS)

Intervals of the same numerical size may vary in **quality** depending on how many semitones they contain. Seconds, thirds, sixths, and sevenths are usually **minor** (smaller) or **major** (larger) in quality. If a minor interval shrinks by a semitone, it becomes **diminished**; if a major interval expands by a semitone, it becomes **augmented**. Note that the same thing is true of the equivalent compound intervals. For instance, a ninth (compound second) may be diminished, minor, major, or augmented.

2.4

DIMINISHED (d)	MINOR (m)	MAJOR (M)	AUGMENTED (A)
smaller ←			→ larger

We focus on seconds and thirds.

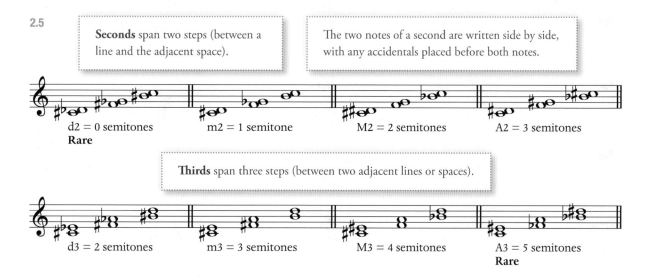

2.5

Seconds span two steps (between a line and the adjacent space).

The two notes of a second are written side by side, with any accidentals placed before both notes.

d2 = 0 semitones
Rare
m2 = 1 semitone
M2 = 2 semitones
A2 = 3 semitones

Thirds span three steps (between two adjacent lines or spaces).

d3 = 2 semitones
m3 = 3 semitones
M3 = 4 semitones
A3 = 5 semitones
Rare

PERFECT INTERVALS (UNISONS, FOURTHS, FIFTHS, OCTAVES)

Unisons, fourths, fifths, and octaves and their compounds are usually **perfect** (*they may never be minor or major*). If they shrink by a semitone, they become diminished; if they expand by a semitone, they become augmented.

2.6

DIMINISHED (d)	PERFECT (P)	AUGMENTED (A)
smaller ←		→ larger

We focus on fourths and fifths.

2.7

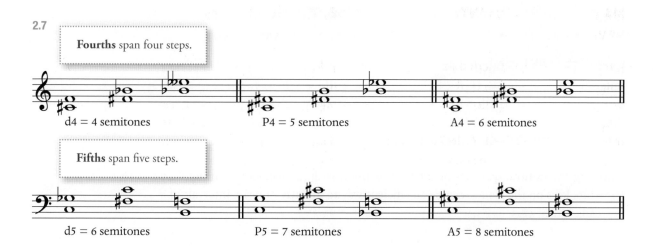

Fourths span four steps.

d4 = 4 semitones
P4 = 5 semitones
A4 = 6 semitones

Fifths span five steps.

d5 = 6 semitones
P5 = 7 semitones
A5 = 8 semitones

INTERVAL INVERSION

If you divide an octave into two smaller intervals, the two intervals are related by **inversion**.

2.8

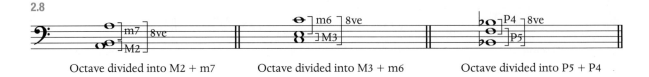

Octave divided into M2 + m7   Octave divided into M3 + m6   Octave divided into P5 + P4

To invert an interval, either shift the lower note up an octave, or the upper note down an octave, so that the two notes reverse position.

2.9

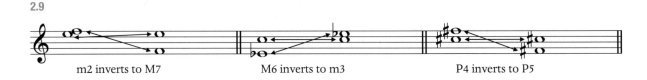

m2 inverts to M7   M6 inverts to m3   P4 inverts to P5

When intervals are inverted, their size and quality change in predictable ways.

2.10

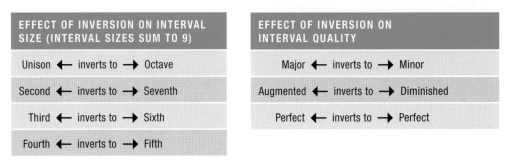

EFFECT OF INVERSION ON INTERVAL SIZE (INTERVAL SIZES SUM TO 9)
Unison ← inverts to → Octave
Second ← inverts to → Seventh
Third ← inverts to → Sixth
Fourth ← inverts to → Fifth

EFFECT OF INVERSION ON INTERVAL QUALITY
Major ← inverts to → Minor
Augmented ← inverts to → Diminished
Perfect ← inverts to → Perfect

NATURAL (WHITE-KEY) INTERVALS

Knowing the **natural** qualities of intervals—written without accidentals, using only the white keys on the piano—can be an efficient way to identify or write intervals of a particular quality.

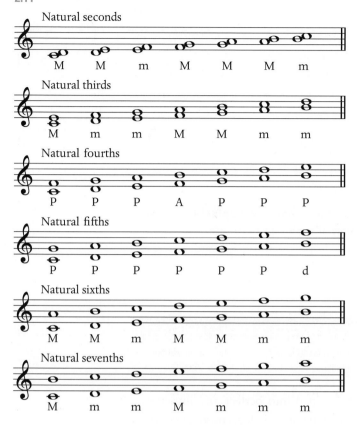

Adding a sharp to the upper note of an interval, or a flat to the lower note, causes the interval to expand. Conversely, adding a flat to the upper note, or a sharp to the lower note, causes the interval to contract.

2.12

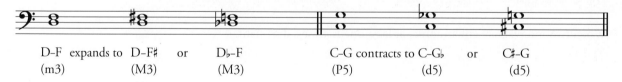

ENHARMONIC INTERVALS

Intervals of different sizes (spanning a different number of letter names) but that contain the same number of semitones are **enharmonic**. For example, A6 and m7—one a sixth and the other a seventh—both span 10 semitones.

2.13

Enharmonic intervals include the same number of semitones but span a different number of scale steps.

Size and quality:	A2	m3	M3	d4	d5	A4	M6	d7	A6	m7
Semitones:	3	3	4	4	6	6	9	9	10	10

CONSONANT AND DISSONANT INTERVALS

Music treats intervals as either consonant or dissonant. **Consonant intervals** are relatively stable—they appear at beginnings and especially endings of phrases and pieces. **Dissonant intervals** are relatively unstable—they propel the music forward.

2.14

CONSONANT INTERVALS	DISSONANT INTERVALS	PERFECT FOURTH
Perfect unisons, fifths, and octaves; major and minor thirds and sixths	Seconds and sevenths; all diminished and augmented intervals	Consonant or dissonant, depending on context

The consonant intervals are often further divided into perfect and imperfect consonances. This distinction will be important later, because perfect consonances can be approached only in certain ways (see Chapter 5).

2.15

PERFECT CONSONANCES	IMPERFECT CONSONANCES
Perfect unisons, perfect fifths, perfect octaves	Major and minor thirds and sixths

When two intervals are enharmonic, at least one is always dissonant.

INTERVALS IN A KEY

In major keys, the intervals above the tonic are all major or perfect.

2.16

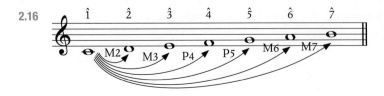

This information can be useful in calculating the quality of intervals. Imagine that the lowest note of an interval is the tonic of a major scale, and compare the upper note to the degrees of the scale.

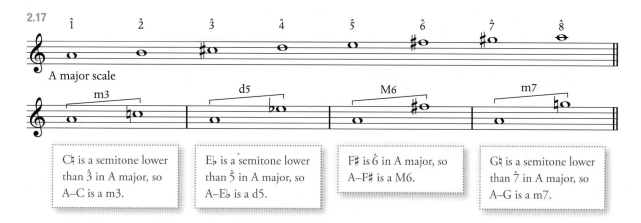

2.17

A major scale

C♯ is a semitone lower than 3̂ in A major, so A–C♮ is a m3.

E♭ is a semitone lower than 5̂ in A major, so A–E♭ is a d5.

F♯ is 6̂ in A major, so A–F♯ is a M6.

G♯ is a semitone lower than 7̂ in A major, so A–G♮ is a m7.

In the natural minor scale, the intervals formed above the tonic are minor and perfect, except for the major second between 1̂ and 2̂.

2.18

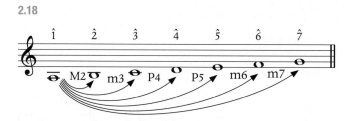

🔍 To learn about intervals in a key, see A Closer Look.

POINTS FOR REVIEW

- **The size of an interval is the number of letter names it spans, irrespective of accidentals.**

- **Intervals smaller than an octave are simple intervals. Intervals larger than an octave are compound intervals, because they contain a simple interval plus one or more octaves.**

- **Seconds, thirds, sixths, sevenths, and their compounds may be diminished, minor, major, or augmented.**

- **Fourths, fifths, octaves, and their compounds may be diminished, perfect, or augmented.**

- **Dividing the octave in two smaller parts produces two intervals related by inversion. Intervals related by inversion have sizes that sum to 9 (like seconds and sevenths, thirds and sixths, and fourths and fifths) and qualities that are related in predictable ways (diminished becomes augmented and vice versa; minor becomes major and vice versa; perfect remains perfect).**

- **Enharmonic intervals contain the same number of semitones but have different names.**

- **Major and minor thirds and sixths are consonant (imperfect consonances), as are perfect fifths and octaves (perfect consonances). Seconds, sevenths, and all augmented and diminished intervals are dissonant. The perfect fourth may be consonant or dissonant depending on context.**

- **Intervals may be calculated with reference either to the natural (white-key) intervals or the major scale of which the interval's lowest note is the tonic.**

- **A major scale has only major and perfect intervals above the tonic. A minor scale has mostly minor and perfect intervals above the tonic.**

TEST YOURSELF

1. Identify these intervals by numerical size and quality (d = diminished; m = minor; M = major; P = perfect; A = augmented). If the interval is larger than an octave (compound), give its simple size and quality.

2. Write the requested interval above the given note.

M3   d7   P5   P8   m6   M7   P4   m7

3. Name the notes and the interval between these pairs of scale degrees (ascending from the first to the second):

   a. F major: $\hat{2}$-$\hat{6}$
   b. B♭ major: $\hat{4}$-$\hat{7}$
   c. E major: $\hat{1}$-$\hat{6}$
   d. D major: $\hat{3}$-$\hat{5}$

4. Name the notes and interval between these pairs of scale degrees (ascending from the first to the second):

   a. G♯ minor: $\hat{2}$-$\hat{6}$ (natural minor)
   b. B♭ minor: $\hat{7}$-$\hat{6}$ (harmonic minor)
   c. D minor: $\hat{1}$-$\hat{5}$
   d. C♯ minor: $\hat{4}$-$\hat{7}$ (harmonic minor)

3   Triads and Seventh Chords

Triads and seventh chords are the basic harmonies of most Western music.

TRIADS

TRIAD CONSTRUCTION

A **triad** consists of three different pitches: a fifth divided into two thirds, or two thirds stacked to make a fifth. Triads can appear on three consecutive lines or spaces on the staff. When a triad is stacked in thirds, the lowest note is the **root**, the middle note is the **third**, and the highest note is the **fifth**.

3.1

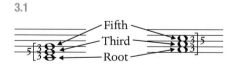

TRIAD QUALITIES

Triads are classified by **quality**: depending on the qualities of the thirds and fifths they contain, triads may be **diminished**, **minor**, **major**, or **augmented**. Refer to a triad by its name and quality, for example, C♯ major triad or D minor triad.

3.2

> **Chord symbols** identify the root and quality of a triad. Diminished triads are indicated with a degree symbol (°) after the root, minor triads with a lowercase m, and augmented triads with a plus sign (⁺). Major triads are indicated with just their root.

NATURAL (WHITE-KEY) TRIADS

Knowing the **natural triads**—without accidentals—can be helpful in identifying triad quality.

3.3

> Every triad uses one of these seven groups of letter names: CEG, DFA, EGB, FAC, GBD, ACE, BDF.

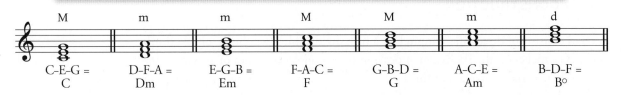

3.4

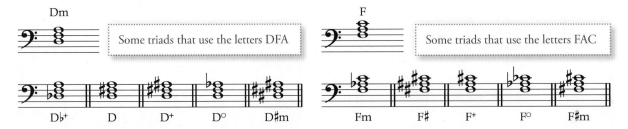

To spell a triad, start with a white-key triad and, if necessary, add an accidental to match the root requested. Then check the intervals of the triad, adding accidentals as needed for the proper quality of the third and the fifth.

Task: **Write an E major triad (E).**

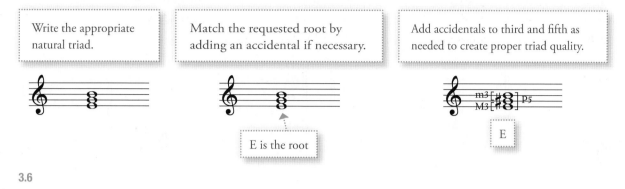

| Write the appropriate natural triad. | Match the requested root by adding an accidental if necessary. | Add accidentals to third and fifth as needed to create proper triad quality. |

E is the root

E

3.6

Task: **Write a G♯ minor triad (G♯m).**

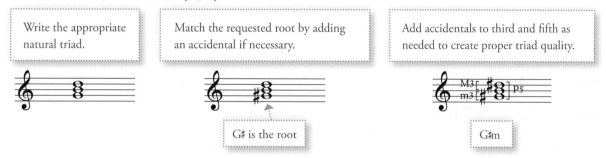

| Write the appropriate natural triad. | Match the requested root by adding an accidental if necessary. | Add accidentals to third and fifth as needed to create proper triad quality. |

G♯ is the root

G♯m

TRIADS IN INVERSION

Triads can be arranged in a variety of ways, from three notes played with one hand at the piano to being spread out over an entire orchestra. However they are arranged, the lowest-sounding note of a triad is called the **bass**; any one of a triad's three notes can sound in the bass. The bass note of a triad determines its **position**. When the root of a triad is in the bass, the triad is in **root position**. When the third of a triad is in the bass, the triad is in **first inversion**. When the fifth of a triad is in the bass, the triad is in **second inversion**. It does not matter which notes are on the top or in the middle of the chord: the position is determined solely by the bass.

3.7

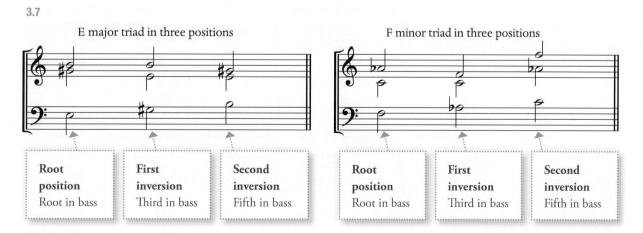

E major triad in three positions   F minor triad in three positions

| **Root position** Root in bass | **First inversion** Third in bass | **Second inversion** Fifth in bass | **Root position** Root in bass | **First inversion** Third in bass | **Second inversion** Fifth in bass |

Triad positions are commonly labeled with a stack of two Arabic numbers, or a **figure**: $\frac{5}{3}$ = root position; $\frac{6}{3}$ = first inversion; $\frac{6}{4}$ = second inversion. These numbers correspond to the intervals formed above the lowest-sounding note.

3.8

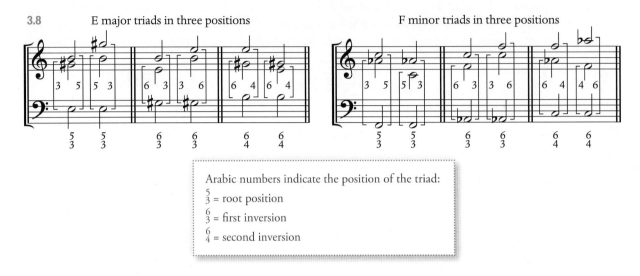

E major triads in three positions — F minor triads in three positions

Arabic numbers indicate the position of the triad:

$\frac{5}{3}$ = root position

$\frac{6}{3}$ = first inversion

$\frac{6}{4}$ = second inversion

TRIADS IN MAJOR AND MINOR KEYS

ROMAN NUMERALS

Within a major or minor key, **Roman numerals**—corresponding to the scale degree of the root—identify triads. Major triads are indicated with uppercase Roman numerals; lowercase Roman numerals indicate minor triads; and lowercase Roman numerals followed by a degree symbol (○) indicate diminished triads. (Augmented triads require accidentals and occur only under special, rare conditions.)

3.9

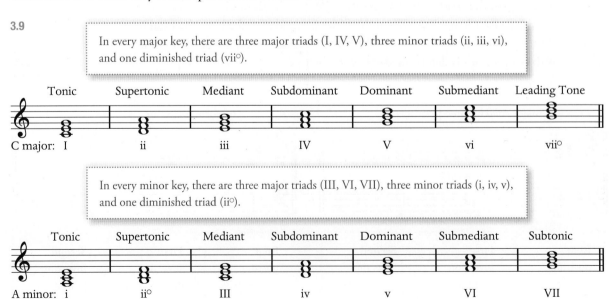

In every major key, there are three major triads (I, IV, V), three minor triads (ii, iii, vi), and one diminished triad (vii○).

In every minor key, there are three major triads (III, VI, VII), three minor triads (i, iv, v), and one diminished triad (ii○).

In minor keys, the dominant and subtonic harmonies are usually modified with raised $\hat{7}$ from the harmonic minor scale, creating a leading tone (a semitone below the tonic). (The raised $\hat{7}$ is not ordinarily used in the III triad.)

3.10

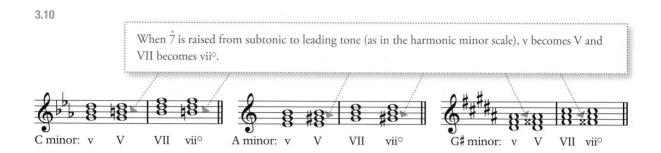

When $\hat{7}$ is raised from subtonic to leading tone (as in the harmonic minor scale), v becomes V and VII becomes vii°.

C minor: v   V   VII   vii°   A minor: v   V   VII   vii°   G♯ minor: v   V   VII   vii°

ROMAN NUMERALS AND INVERSIONS

A Roman numeral can be combined with a figure that consists of Arabic numbers to show the root, quality, and position of a triad.

3.11

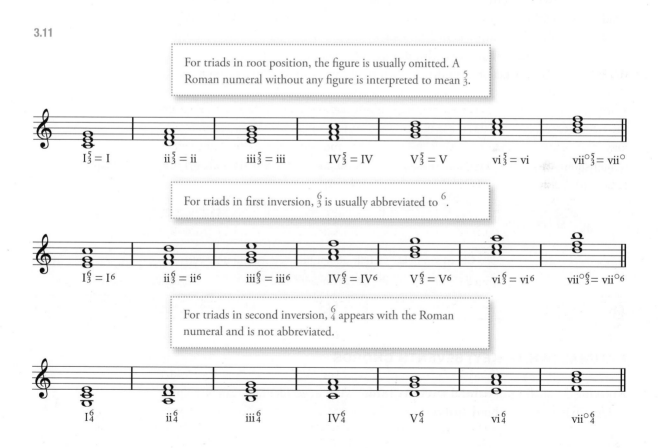

For triads in root position, the figure is usually omitted. A Roman numeral without any figure is interpreted to mean $\frac{5}{3}$.

$I\frac{5}{3}=I$ $ii\frac{5}{3}=ii$ $iii\frac{5}{3}=iii$ $IV\frac{5}{3}=IV$ $V\frac{5}{3}=V$ $vi\frac{5}{3}=vi$ $vii°\frac{5}{3}=vii°$

For triads in first inversion, $\frac{6}{3}$ is usually abbreviated to ^{6}.

$I\frac{6}{3}=I^6$ $ii\frac{6}{3}=ii^6$ $iii\frac{6}{3}=iii^6$ $IV\frac{6}{3}=IV^6$ $V\frac{6}{3}=V^6$ $vi\frac{6}{3}=vi^6$ $vii°\frac{6}{3}=vii°^6$

For triads in second inversion, $\frac{6}{4}$ appears with the Roman numeral and is not abbreviated.

$I\frac{6}{4}$ $ii\frac{6}{4}$ $iii\frac{6}{4}$ $IV\frac{6}{4}$ $V\frac{6}{4}$ $vi\frac{6}{4}$ $vii°\frac{6}{4}$

SEVENTH CHORDS

SEVENTH-CHORD CONSTRUCTION

A **seventh chord** can be understood as either a triad plus a seventh over its root or a triad with an additional third stacked on top of its fifth. Seventh chords are written on four consecutive staff lines or four consecutive spaces. When a seventh chord is stacked in thirds, the lowest note is called the root, followed by the **third**, the **fifth**, and the **seventh**.

3.12
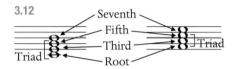

SEVENTH-CHORD QUALITIES

Like triads, seventh chords are classified by **quality**. Depending on the qualities of the triads and sevenths they contain, seventh chords may be **fully diminished** (diminished triad + diminished seventh), **half-diminished** (diminished triad + minor seventh), **minor** (minor triad + minor seventh), **dominant** (major triad + minor seventh), or **major** (major triad + major seventh). As with triads, you can refer to a seventh chord by its root and quality.

3.13
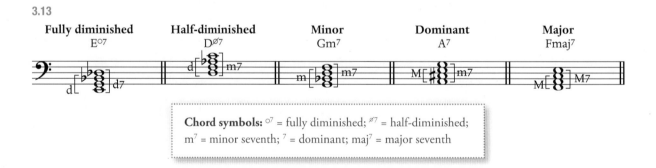

NATURAL (WHITE-KEY) SEVENTH CHORDS

Knowing the qualities of **natural seventh chords**—without accidentals—can be helpful in identifying seventh-chord quality.

Every seventh chord uses one of these seven groups of letter names: CEGB, DFAC, EGBD, FACE, GBDF, ACEG, BDFA.

Major	Minor	Minor	Major	Dominant	Minor	Half-Diminished
C–E–G–B = Cmaj⁷	D–F–A–C = Dm⁷	E–G–B–D = Em⁷	F–A–C–E = Fmaj⁷	G–B–D–F = G⁷	A–C–E–G = Am⁷	B–D–F–A = Bø⁷

3.15

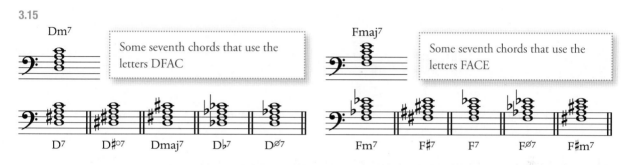

Some seventh chords that use the letters DFAC

Some seventh chords that use the letters FACE

Dm⁷   D⁷   D♯°⁷   Dmaj⁷   D♭⁷   Dø⁷

Fmaj⁷   Fm⁷   F♯⁷   F⁷   Fø⁷   F♯m⁷

To spell a seventh chord, start with a white-key seventh chord and, if necessary, add an accidental to match the root requested. Then check the intervals of the seventh chord, adding accidentals as needed for the proper quality of third, fifth, and seventh.

3.16

Task: **Write an E♭ major seventh chord (E♭maj⁷).**

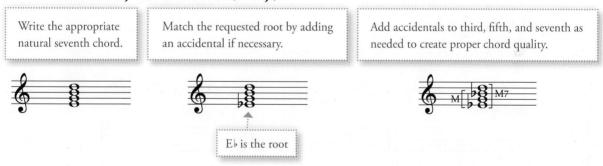

Write the appropriate natural seventh chord.

Match the requested root by adding an accidental if necessary.

Add accidentals to third, fifth, and seventh as needed to create proper chord quality.

E♭ is the root

3.17

Task: **Write a G♯ half-diminished seventh chord (G♯ø⁷).**

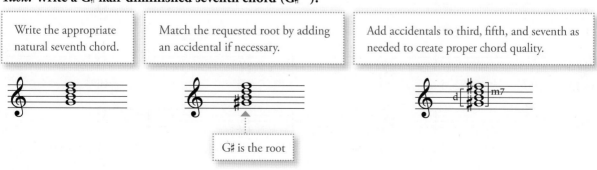

Write the appropriate natural seventh chord.

Match the requested root by adding an accidental if necessary.

Add accidentals to third, fifth, and seventh as needed to create proper chord quality.

G♯ is the root

SEVENTH CHORDS IN INVERSION

Like triads, seventh chords can appear in inversion as well as root position; any of the four notes of a seventh chord can sound in the bass. A figure (stack of three Arabic numbers) is used to identify these inversions: $\frac{7}{5}$ = root position; $\frac{6}{5}$ = first inversion; $\frac{6}{4}$ = second inversion; $\frac{6}{4}$ = third inversion.

3.18

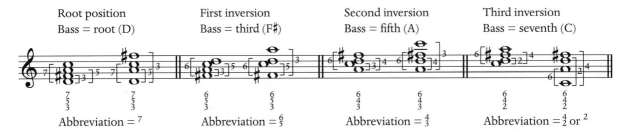

SEVENTH CHORDS IN MAJOR AND MINOR KEYS

ROMAN NUMERALS AND INVERSIONS

For seventh chords as for triads, a combination of a Roman numeral and a figure indicates the root, quality, and position (major seventh chords and dominant seventh chords are shown the same way, with an uppercase Roman numeral followed by the number 7). Seventh chords built on $\hat{2}$, $\hat{4}$, $\hat{5}$, and $\hat{7}$ are more common than those on $\hat{1}$, $\hat{3}$, or $\hat{6}$.

3.19

In every major key, ii^7 is minor, IV^7 is major, V^7 is dominant, and $vii^{\varnothing7}$ is half-diminished.

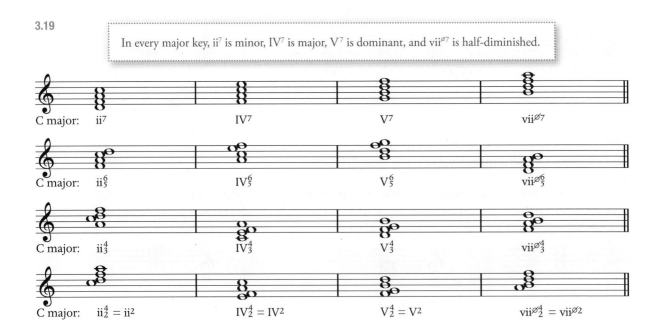

3.20

In every minor key, ii⁰⁷ is half-diminished, and iv⁷ is minor. The seventh chords on $\hat{5}$ and $\hat{7}$ usually use the raised $\hat{7}$, the leading tone, from the harmonic minor scale; thus V⁷ is dominant, and vii°⁷ is fully diminished.

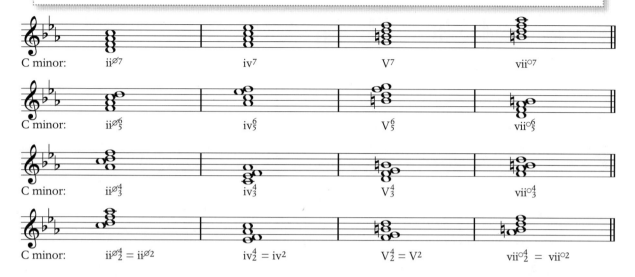

C minor: ii⁰⁷   iv⁷   V⁷   vii°⁷

C minor: ii⁰⁶₅   iv⁶₅   V⁶₅   vii°⁶₅

C minor: ii⁰⁴₃   iv⁴₃   V⁴₃   vii°⁴₃

C minor: ii⁰⁴₂ = ii⁰²   iv⁴₂ = iv²   V⁴₂ = V²   vii°⁴₂ = vii°²

POINTS FOR REVIEW

- Depending on the qualities of the thirds and fifths they contain, triads may be diminished, minor, major, or augmented.

- Triads may appear in three positions: root position ($\frac{5}{3}$, root in bass), first inversion ($\frac{6}{3}$, third in bass), or second inversion ($\frac{6}{4}$, fifth in bass).

- Roman numerals combined with figures (stacks of Arabic numbers) identify the root (as a scale degree in a major or minor scale), quality, and inversion of a triad or seventh chord.

- In minor keys, $\hat{7}$ is usually raised to make V⁽⁷⁾ and vii°⁽⁷⁾.

- Depending on the qualities of the triads and sevenths they contain, seventh chords may be fully diminished, half-diminished, minor, dominant, or major.

- Seventh chords may appear in four positions: root position (⁷, root in bass), first inversion ($\frac{6}{5}$, third in bass), second inversion ($\frac{4}{3}$, fifth in bass), or third inversion ($\frac{4}{2}$ or ², seventh in bass).

TEST YOURSELF

1. Identify each triad with its root and quality.

_____ _____ _____ _____ _____

2. Write each triad in root position.

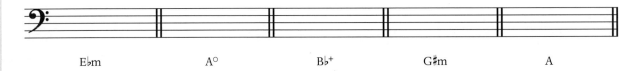

E♭m   A°   B♭+   G♯m   A

3. Identify each seventh chord with its root and quality.

_____ _____ _____ _____ _____

4. Write each seventh chord in root position.

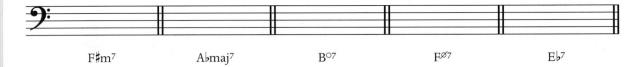

F♯m⁷   A♭maj⁷   B°⁷   F⌀⁷   E♭⁷

5. Use a Roman numeral with a figure to identify each triad or seventh chord in the key indicated.

D minor: B♭ major: F minor: E major: E♭ major:

6. Write each triad or seventh chord in the key indicated. Use accidentals rather than key signatures.

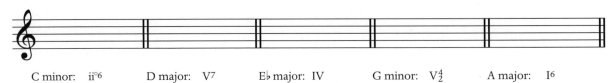

C minor: ii°⁶   D major: V⁷   E♭ major: IV   G minor: V⁴₂   A major: I⁶

part two

Overview of Harmony and Voice Leading

chapter 4

Four-Part Harmony

Four-part harmony is an important model for tonal music.

Writing Chords in Four Parts
Formats for Writing Four-Part Harmony
   SATB format
   Keyboard format
Realizing Roman Numerals in Four-Part Harmony
   Determining the correct notes
   Doubling

Tendency tones (leading tones and chordal dissonance)
Realizing Figured Bass
   Determining the correct notes
   Abbreviated figures
   Accidentals in figured bass

WRITING CHORDS IN FOUR PARTS

Four-part harmony is often used to illustrate principles of tonal music. In four-part harmony, each chord uses four notes, with the same basic rhythm in all four parts, as in a typical hymn.

4.1 Alice Nevin, "Elsie" (hymn)

A standard four-part harmony setting includes four notes in each chord. All four voices share the same basic rhythm.

Four-part harmony is useful as a model for harmonic practices found in settings that are more elaborate as well, and it forms the basis of most traditional exercises in tonal harmony.

FORMATS FOR WRITING FOUR-PART HARMONY

Four-part writing is traditionally studied in either of two formats: SATB (chorale) format or keyboard format.

SATB FORMAT

Four-part harmony is typically notated in **SATB (or chorale) format**, for a vocal choir consisting of a soprano, alto, tenor, and bass. In SATB format, the soprano and alto parts are written on the treble staff and the tenor and bass parts on the bass staff. On each staff, the upper part (soprano or tenor) is written with stems up and the lower part (alto or bass) with stems down.

4.2

Good Soprano and tenor are always stemmed upward; alto and bass are always stemmed downward.

Poor No matter how high or low the notes are, soprano and tenor should never be stemmed downward; alto and bass should never be stemmed upward.

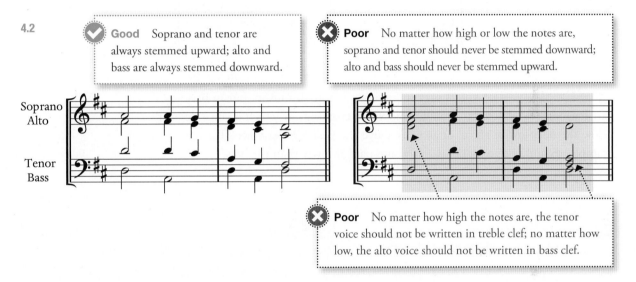

Poor No matter how high the notes are, the tenor voice should not be written in treble clef; no matter how low, the alto voice should not be written in bass clef.

Range   Each voice in SATB writing remains within a specified **range**, so that the notes are not too high or too low to be sung comfortably by singers in a standard choir.

4.3

Soprano   Alto   Tenor   Bass

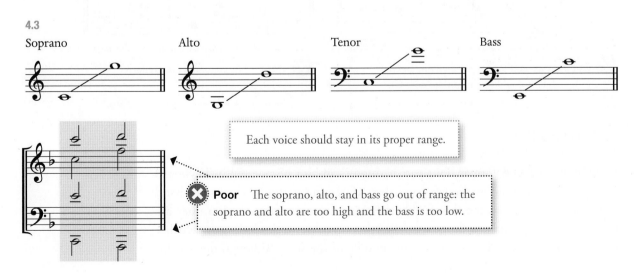

Each voice should stay in its proper range.

Poor The soprano, alto, and bass go out of range: the soprano and alto are too high and the bass is too low.

Spacing   Every chord should have a proper **spacing**; the notes of adjacent upper parts (soprano + alto; alto + tenor) should never be more than an octave apart. The tenor and bass can be more than an octave apart.

4.4

Good   Pitches are within proper range; and alto and soprano are always within an octave of each other, as are tenor and alto.

Poor   Pitches of the alto and tenor are more than an octave apart in the first chord, as are the pitches of the soprano and alto in the second chord.

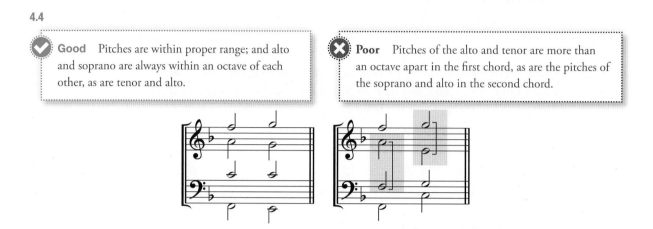

Voice Crossing   Two voices may sing the same note in unison, but in basic four-part harmony exercises you should avoid **voice crossing**, in which a voice descends below the next lowest voice, or ascends above the next highest voice. The tenor, for example, should not go higher than the alto part or lower than the bass.

4.5

Good   Alto and soprano sing the same pitch (notated with two side-by-side whole notes).

Poor   Voice crossing: the last two notes in the alto are lower than the last two notes in the tenor.

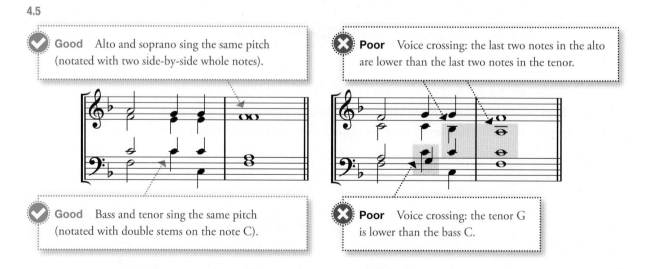

Good   Bass and tenor sing the same pitch (notated with double stems on the note C).

Poor   Voice crossing: the tenor G is lower than the bass C.

KEYBOARD FORMAT

In addition to SATB format, four-part harmony can also be notated in **keyboard format**, with one note in the left hand (bass clef) against three in the right hand (treble clef). As long as the three treble-clef voices have the same rhythm, they are notated on a single stem, with the stem direction up or down depending on whether most of the notes are above or below the middle of the staff. Although notated for performance on a piano or other keyboard instrument, the four notes of each chord in keyboard format are nonetheless regarded as distinct voices that often are referred to as soprano, alto, tenor, and bass. Thus when two of the upper voices are on the same pitch, the notehead may be written twice.

4.6

In the second chord, both soprano and alto are on E.

Keyboard notation: one voice is in bass clef, three voices are in treble.

When an interval of a second appears within a chord, one of the notes is written on the side of the stem opposite the others; the upper note of the second is always placed on the right side of the stem.

4.7

Good   Because of the harmonic second between G and F, G is on the opposite side of the stem from F and B.

Poor   G and F are crammed together, making them hard to read.

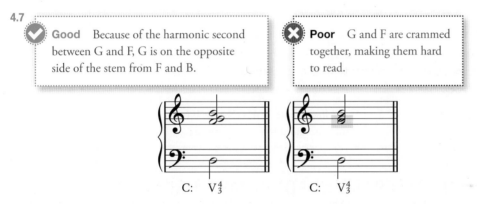

If one of the upper voices has a rhythm different from the others within the same chord, it is stemmed separately and in the opposite direction.

4.8

Good   On beats 1 and 2, the alto has two quarter notes while the soprano and tenor each have a half note; these rhythms are stemmed in opposite directions.

Poor   Different rhythms are stemmed together, which is visually confusing and even ambiguous. On the third beat it is unclear which are quarter notes and which are eighths.

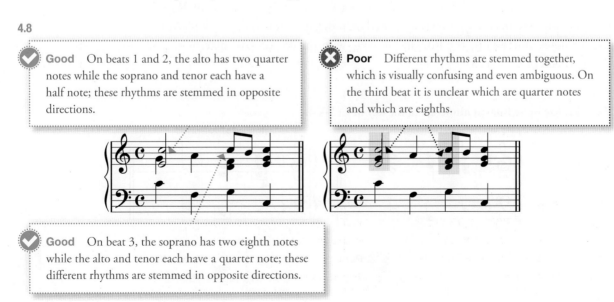

Good   On beat 3, the soprano has two eighth notes while the alto and tenor each have a quarter note; these different rhythms are stemmed in opposite directions.

Spacing   In standard keyboard format, the upper three voices (soprano, alto, and tenor) are placed within an octave so that they can be comfortably played by the right hand alone.

4.9

> ✓ **Good**   The top three voices are spaced within an octave.

> ✗ **Poor**   The tenor and soprano voices are more than an octave apart.

Inversions   A chord's inversion is always determined by its lowest note, *not* by the lowest note in the treble part. Keep this in mind when writing for keyboard, where the lowest note of the right hand is not the same as the lowest note of the chord.

4.10

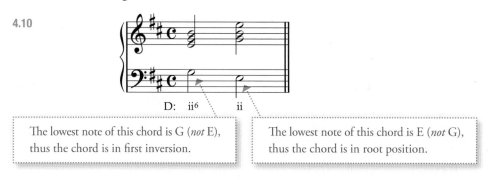

> The lowest note of this chord is G (*not* E), thus the chord is in first inversion.

> The lowest note of this chord is E (*not* G), thus the chord is in root position.

REALIZING ROMAN NUMERALS IN FOUR-PART HARMONY

DETERMINING THE CORRECT NOTES

In studying four-part harmony, you often are asked to **realize** a series of Roman numerals—that is, to compose a passage based on indicated chords. Each chord should use the notes indicated by the Roman numeral, with the correct bass determined by the inversion of the chord.

4.11

Task: **Realize these Roman numerals in the key of C: I–V–I.**

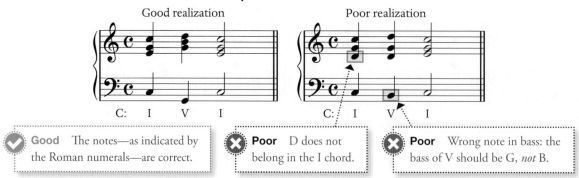

> ✓ **Good**   The notes—as indicated by the Roman numerals—are correct.

> ✗ **Poor**   D does not belong in the I chord.

> ✗ **Poor**   Wrong note in bass: the bass of V should be G, *not* B.

In minor keys, $\hat{7}$ is most often raised to create a leading tone. Depending on the key signature, this requires a natural, sharp, or double sharp.

4.12

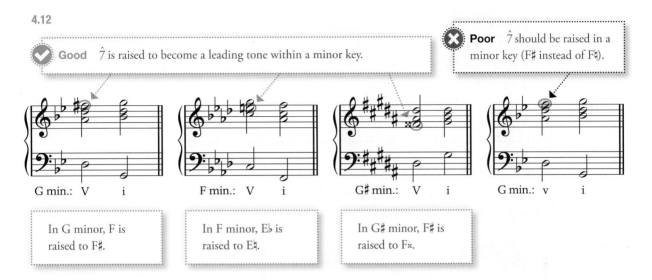

Good $\hat{7}$ is raised to become a leading tone within a minor key.

Poor $\hat{7}$ should be raised in a minor key (F♯ instead of F♮).

G min.: V   i

F min.: V   i

G♯ min.: V   i

G min.: v   i

In G minor, F is raised to F♯.

In F minor, E♭ is raised to E♮.

In G♯ minor, F♯ is raised to F𝄪.

DOUBLING

When three notes of a triad are distributed among four voices, one of the notes must be **doubled**—that is, it appears in two different voices (regardless of octave) at the same time. Since seventh chords have four different notes, they do not require any doubling.

4.13

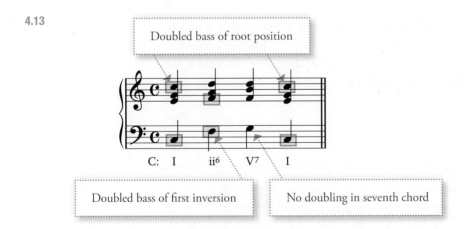

Doubled bass of root position

C: I   ii⁶   V⁷   I

Doubled bass of first inversion

No doubling in seventh chord

It usually is preferable to double the *bass* of root-position and second-inversion triads. In first-inversion triads, you can usually double any note.

4.14

Task: **Write a IV chord in E major. Since IV in E has the notes A–C♯–E (with A in the bass), some possible answers are:**

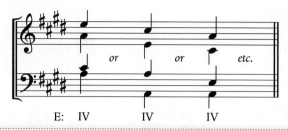

E: IV   IV   IV

> The note A (the bass of the chord) is doubled; there are two A's in each chord.

4.15

Task: **Write a i⁶ chord in F minor. Some possible answers are:**

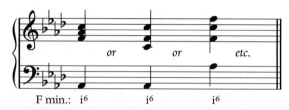

F min.:   i⁶   i⁶   i⁶

> Note: In a first-inversion chord, usually any note (root, third, or fifth) may be doubled.

TENDENCY TONES (LEADING TONES AND CHORDAL DISSONANCE)

In four-part harmony, you should never double **tendency tones**, that is, notes that need to move stepwise either up or down. Doubling such tones leads to part-writing errors (see Chapter 5). One such tendency tone is the leading tone: because it has a strong tendency to move up by step, it should not be doubled.

4.16

> In A♭ major, the leading tone ($\hat{7}$) is G. Since it is a tendency tone, it may *not* be doubled.

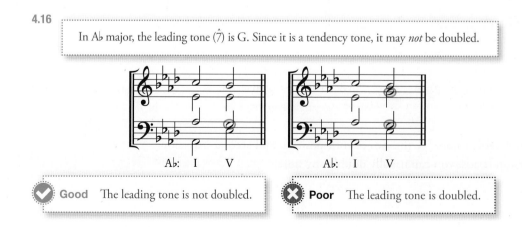

A♭:   I   V   A♭:   I   V

✅ **Good**   The leading tone is not doubled.

❌ **Poor**   The leading tone is doubled.

Another type of tendency tone is a **chordal dissonance**, which is a dissonant member of a chord, such as the seventh of a seventh chord. A chordal dissonance has a strong tendency to resolve down by step, and thus may not be doubled.

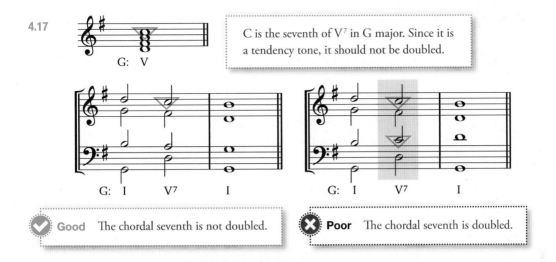

4.17

G: V

C is the seventh of V^7 in G major. Since it is a tendency tone, it should not be doubled.

G: I V^7 I

G: I V^7 I

✓ **Good**   The chordal seventh is not doubled.

✗ **Poor**   The chordal seventh is doubled.

REALIZING FIGURED BASS

DETERMINING THE CORRECT NOTES

In addition to Roman numerals, you will often be asked to realize chord progressions from a **figured bass**. Figured bass uses numerals to designate the upper notes of chords by indicating the intervals above the bass notes. Thus, for instance, the figure $\frac{5}{3}$ indicates the upper notes of the chord should be a fifth and a third (or their compound equivalents) above the bass. When you see an accidental preceding a figure, alter the note as indicated. The guidelines for doubling are the same in realizing a figured bass as they are for realizing Roman numerals.

4.18

Task: **Realize this figured bass in SATB format.**
Some possible answers are:

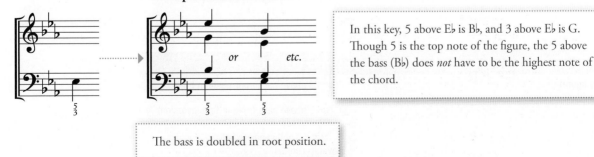

or   etc.

In this key, 5 above E♭ is B♭, and 3 above E♭ is G. Though 5 is the top note of the figure, the 5 above the bass (B♭) does *not* have to be the highest note of the chord.

The bass is doubled in root position.

4.19

Task: **Realize this figured bass in keyboard format.**

Some possible answers are:

> 6 above G is E, and 3 above G is B. These notes can appear in any register. Because the chord is in first inversion, any note can be doubled.

As you saw in Chapter 3, these figures may also designate chord inversions. Thus in most cases you can find the notes of a chord by using the figured bass to determine the inversion.

4.20

Task: **Realize this figured bass in keyboard format, determining the notes by using chord inversion.**

Some possible answers are:

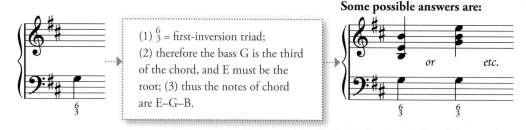

(1) ⁶₃ = first-inversion triad; (2) therefore the bass G is the third of the chord, and E must be the root; (3) thus the notes of chord are E–G–B.

Notice that both of the methods described above for finding the notes of figured bass produce the same results. However, it is not always possible to realize a figured bass by first finding the root of the chord. Especially with more complex figures, the chord may need to be determined by the intervals above the bass.

ABBREVIATED FIGURES

As you saw in Chapter 3, the most common figures are abbreviated. You should memorize these abbreviations. The most common figured bass abbreviations are given below (others are discussed in Chapter 3 and later chapters).

4.21

FIGURE ABBREVIATION ...	STANDS FOR ...	WHICH INDICATES ...
(no figure)	$\begin{smallmatrix}5\\3\end{smallmatrix}$	5 and 3 above bass (root-position triad)
6	$\begin{smallmatrix}6\\3\end{smallmatrix}$	6 and 3 above bass (triad in first inversion)
7	$\begin{smallmatrix}7\\5\\3\end{smallmatrix}$	7, 5, and 3 above bass (root-position seventh chord)

4.22

This figured bass: is an abbreviated form of this:

ACCIDENTALS IN FIGURED BASS

An accidental alone, with no number following it, applies to the third above the bass.

4.23

FIGURE ABBREVIATION . . .	STANDS FOR . . .	WHICH INDICATES . . .
♯	$\begin{smallmatrix}5\\\sharp3\end{smallmatrix}$	5 and ♯3 above bass
♭	$\begin{smallmatrix}5\\\flat3\end{smallmatrix}$	5 and ♭3 above bass
$\begin{smallmatrix}6\\\sharp\end{smallmatrix}$	$\begin{smallmatrix}6\\\sharp3\end{smallmatrix}$	6 and ♯3 above bass
$\begin{smallmatrix}7\\\natural\end{smallmatrix}$	$\begin{smallmatrix}7\\5\\\natural3\end{smallmatrix}$	7, 5, and ♮3 above bass

4.24

This figured bass: is an abbreviated form of this:

4.25

Task: **Realize the figured bass in keyboard format.**

Some possible answers are:

or   etc.

(1) $\begin{smallmatrix}7\\\sharp\end{smallmatrix}$ is an abbreviated form of $\begin{smallmatrix}7\\5\\\sharp3\end{smallmatrix}$; (2) thus the notes in the chord above D are C, A, and F♯.

POINTS FOR REVIEW

- **Four-part harmony exercises are traditionally notated in either SATB or keyboard format; strict guidelines govern each of these formats.**

- **Parts written in SATB format should be singable, with the notes for each of the voices (soprano, alto, tenor, bass) lying within an appropriate range.**

- In SATB format, the notes of the soprano and alto should be within an octave of each other, as should notes of the tenor and alto.

- In keyboard format, the top three notes should fall within an octave (the tenor and soprano should not be more than an octave apart).

- A note is doubled if it appears in two different voices.

- Tendency tones—such as leading tones and chordal dissonances—may *not* be doubled.

- In minor keys, the seventh scale degree ($\hat{7}$) is usually raised by a half step (with a sharp, natural, or double sharp) to create a leading tone.

- Roman numerals indicate the root of the chord, with figures further indicating the chord's inversion; figured bass indicates the intervals that appear above a given bass note.

- Often figured bass symbols are abbreviated.

TEST YOURSELF

1. The following questions refer to the SATB chord below:
   a. Which voice is too high?
   b. Which pair of voices are too far apart?
   c. Which note is stemmed incorrectly?
   d. Which note is doubled: root, third, or fifth?
   e. Assume that this key is B♭ major. Label the chord with the appropriate Roman numeral and figures to indicate its inversion.

2. Which of these figured bass realizations (a–e) are correct?

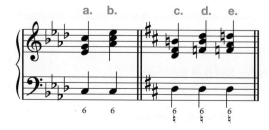

5

Voice Leading

When moving from one harmony to the next, voices ideally move slowly and independently.

Moving between Harmonies (Voice Leading)
  Harmonic progression
  Steps and leaps
Kinds of Motion
  Motion between intervals
  Motion between pairs of intervals in four-part harmony
	Voice Leading in Four-Part Harmony
	  Parallel octaves and fifths
	  The leading tone
	  Chordal sevenths
	  Approaching perfect intervals in similar motion
	A Closer Look
	  Voice crossing and overlap

MOVING BETWEEN HARMONIES (VOICE LEADING)

HARMONIC PROGRESSION

In tonal music, a chord is understood to move to the one that follows, so that a series of chords form a **harmonic progression** or **chord progression**. When one chord moves to another, each note in the first chord moves to a note in the next. In four-part harmony, this creates four separate melodic lines, called voices.

5.1

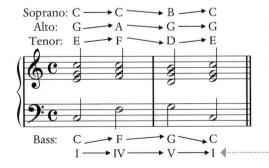

Chords don't simply succeed one another: each chord *progresses* to the next, with each of the four voices forming a separate melodic line.

Roman numerals identify the harmonic progression: I–IV–V–I.

The manner in which the notes and intervals of each chord move to the next is called **voice leading**. The guidelines for voice leading in four-part harmony exercises help develop sensitivity to the way in which individual notes move between chords in an underlying smooth and independent manner, with particular attention paid to tendency tones. Naturally, guidelines for exercises tend to be stricter than actual musical practice, where the artistic contexts often give rise to exceptions (or seeming exceptions).

STEPS AND LEAPS

In four-part harmony exercises, the three upper voices (soprano, alto, and tenor) should move smoothly, mostly with small melodic intervals. Usually, upper voices either stay on the same note or move by step or third, and they never use leaps greater than a sixth. The bass line, on the other hand, frequently uses melodic leaps.

5.2

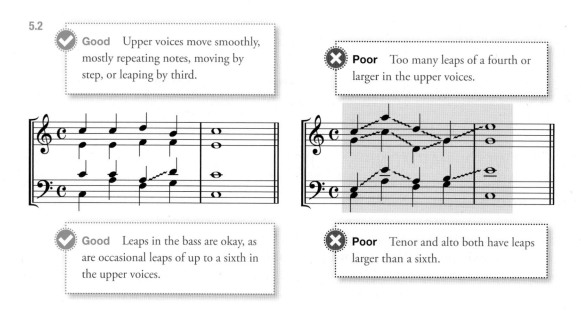

Good Upper voices move smoothly, mostly repeating notes, moving by step, or leaping by third.

Poor Too many leaps of a fourth or larger in the upper voices.

Good Leaps in the bass are okay, as are occasional leaps of up to a sixth in the upper voices.

Poor Tenor and alto both have leaps larger than a sixth.

5.3 **Ann Bartholomew, "Hodderson" (hymn)**

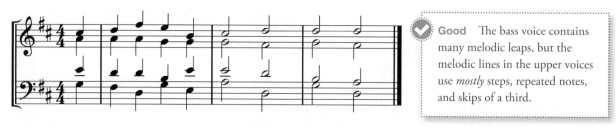

Good The bass voice contains many melodic leaps, but the melodic lines in the upper voices use *mostly* steps, repeated notes, and skips of a third.

When a chord repeats or is sustained, on the other hand, melodic leaps in one or more of the upper voices are not a problem. These leaps are called **chord skips**.

5.4

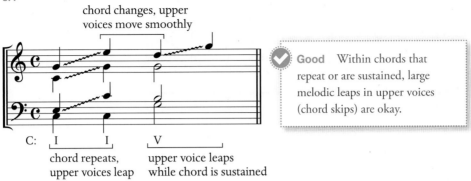

chord changes, upper voices move smoothly

Good Within chords that repeat or are sustained, large melodic leaps in upper voices (chord skips) are okay.

chord repeats, upper voices leap

upper voice leaps while chord is sustained

5.5 John W. Work Jr., "Calvary"   **5.6 Emma Moody, "God Is Love"**

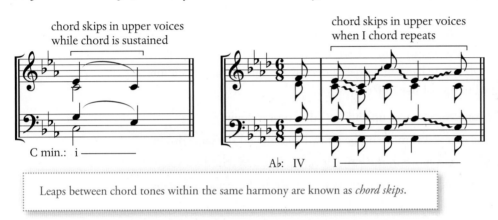

chord skips in upper voices while chord is sustained

chord skips in upper voices when I chord repeats

Leaps between chord tones within the same harmony are known as *chord skips*.

Although melodic leaps are common in the bass, even there you should avoid leaps greater than an octave or leaps of a seventh. Furthermore, melodic augmented intervals (including the augmented second) should not appear in any voice.

5.7

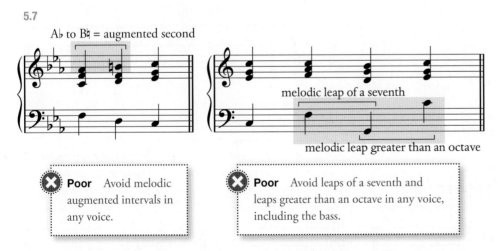

A♭ to B♮ = augmented second

melodic leap of a seventh

melodic leap greater than an octave

Poor Avoid melodic augmented intervals in any voice.

Poor Avoid leaps of a seventh and leaps greater than an octave in any voice, including the bass.

Also, avoid approaching a leading tone with an *ascending* melodic leap of more than a third, since this would sound too strident for a harmony exercise.

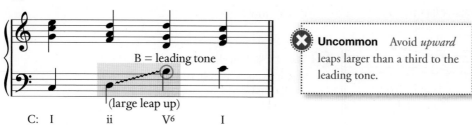

B = leading tone

(large leap up)

C: I   ii   V⁶   I

Uncommon Avoid *upward* leaps larger than a third to the leading tone.

KINDS OF MOTION

MOTION BETWEEN INTERVALS

Instead of thinking about all four voices at once, it can be helpful to think about them in pairs, like soprano + alto, or soprano + bass. For each pair of voices, you should think about the intervals formed and how these intervals are approached. Each interval may be approached in one of five different ways:

1. **Contrary motion**: one voice moves up and the other moves down.
2. **Parallel motion**: the two voices move in the same direction and the same distance.
3. **Similar motion**: the voices move in the same direction but different distances.
4. **Oblique motion**: one voice remains on the same note while the other moves up or down.
5. **Stationary motion**: both voices remain on the same note.

5.9

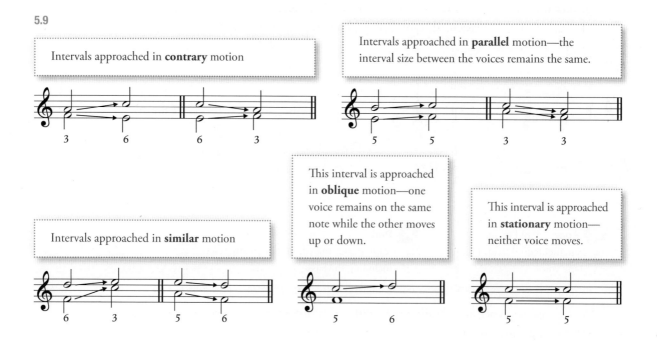

Intervals approached in **contrary** motion

Intervals approached in **parallel** motion—the interval size between the voices remains the same.

3   6   6   3

5   5   3   3

Intervals approached in **similar** motion

This interval is approached in **oblique** motion—one voice remains on the same note while the other moves up or down.

This interval is approached in **stationary** motion—neither voice moves.

6   3   5   6

5   6

5   5

Note that in parallel motion the interval size stays the same, but the interval quality might change. Thus, for instance, a minor third may move in parallel motion to a major third.

5.10

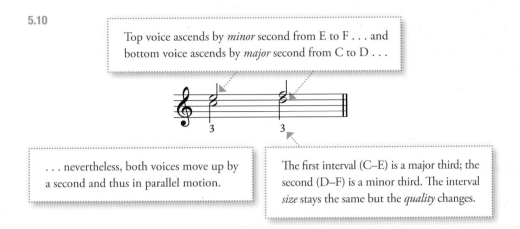

Top voice ascends by *minor* second from E to F . . . and bottom voice ascends by *major* second from C to D . . .

. . . nevertheless, both voices move up by a second and thus in parallel motion.

The first interval (C–E) is a major third; the second (D–F) is a minor third. The interval *size* stays the same but the *quality* changes.

MOTION BETWEEN PAIRS OF INTERVALS IN FOUR-PART HARMONY

The voice leading from one chord to another in four-part harmony can be understood as involving a number of simultaneous motions between pairs of voices.

5.11

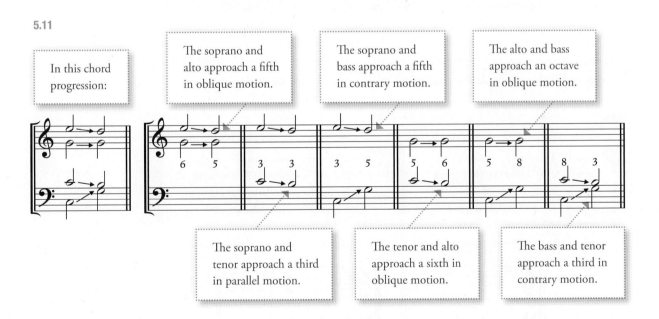

In this chord progression:

The soprano and alto approach a fifth in oblique motion.

The soprano and bass approach a fifth in contrary motion.

The alto and bass approach an octave in oblique motion.

The soprano and tenor approach a third in parallel motion.

The tenor and alto approach a sixth in oblique motion.

The bass and tenor approach a third in contrary motion.

VOICE LEADING IN FOUR-PART HARMONY

The most important voice-leading rules for harmony involve (1) approaching perfect intervals and (2) treatment of tendency tones, such as leading tones and chordal sevenths.

PARALLEL OCTAVES AND FIFTHS

A perfect interval—such as a perfect octave, a perfect fifth, or a perfect unison—may *not* be approached in parallel motion, since this would counteract the independence of the voices. This prohibition applies to compound as well as to simple octaves and fifths. Approaching an octave in parallel motion produces **parallel octaves**; approaching a perfect fifth produces **parallel fifths**; approaching a unison produces **parallel unisons**.

5.12

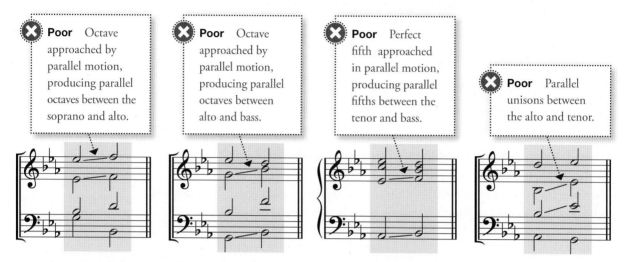

⊗ Poor Octave approached by parallel motion, producing parallel octaves between the soprano and alto.

⊗ Poor Octave approached by parallel motion, producing parallel octaves between alto and bass.

⊗ Poor Perfect fifth approached in parallel motion, producing parallel fifths between the tenor and bass.

⊗ Poor Parallel unisons between the alto and tenor.

At times something that at first looks like faulty parallel fifths or octaves actually arises between two *different* pairs of voices, and therefore is unproblematic. Also, octaves and fifths approached in stationary motion are always allowed.

5.13

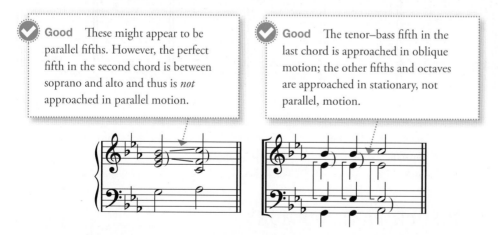

✓ Good These might appear to be parallel fifths. However, the perfect fifth in the second chord is between soprano and alto and thus is *not* approached in parallel motion.

✓ Good The tenor–bass fifth in the last chord is approached in oblique motion; the other fifths and octaves are approached in stationary, not parallel, motion.

You may move from a perfect fifth to a diminished fifth, since this does not entail approaching a *perfect* interval in parallel motion. On the other hand, you may not move from a diminished fifth to a perfect fifth (except in special cases that will be discussed in Chapter 13), since this would involve approaching a perfect interval in parallel motion.

5.14

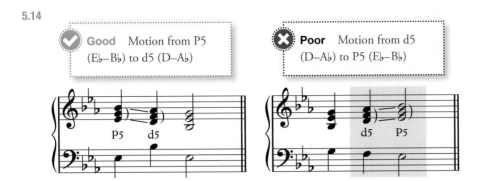

THE LEADING TONE

The leading tone (that is, $\hat{7}$ in major keys or raised $\hat{7}$ in minor keys) has a strong tendency to lead up to the tonic. If the leading tone appears in an outer (bass or soprano) voice in one chord and the tonic appears in the following chord, the voice with the leading tone must resolve up to the tonic.

5.15

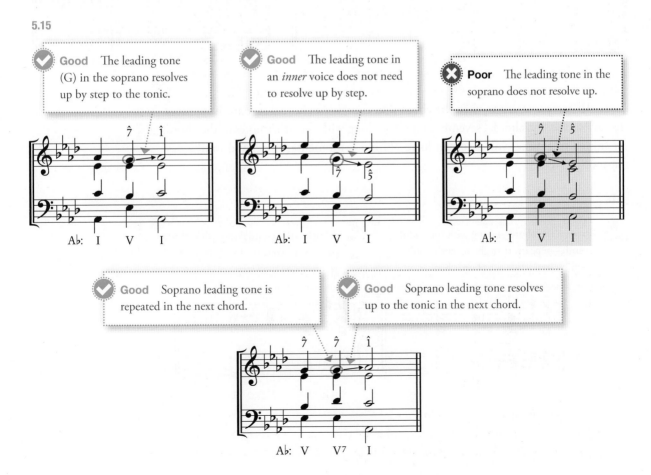

5.16 R. Nathaniel Dett, "Let Us Cheer the Weary Traveler"

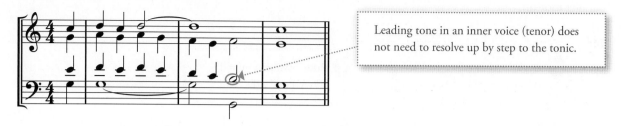

Leading tone in an inner voice (tenor) does not need to resolve up by step to the tonic.

CHORDAL SEVENTHS

Dissonant tones, including especially the **chordal seventh**, have a strong melodic tendency to resolve *down* by step, even if they appear in an inner voice.

5.17

✓ **Good** The chordal seventh (C, the seventh of D⁷) resolves down by step, in both the top voice and an inner voice.

✗ **Poor** The chordal seventh moves up instead of resolving down.

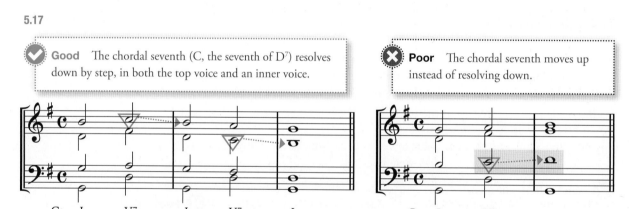

An exception arises when the chord that contains a chordal seventh is repeated. In such a case, the chordal seventh is repeated along with the other notes of the chords or shifted to another voice, so that its resolution is momentarily delayed until a new harmony enters.

5.18

✓ **Good** The chord—along with the chordal seventh—repeats, then the seventh resolves down by step when the chord changes.

✓ **Good** The chordal seventh is shifted to another voice and register, then resolves down by step.

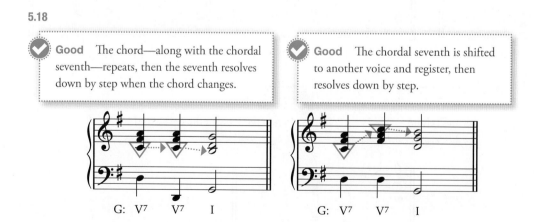

5.19 Dmitry Bortniansky, "We praise Thee, the Lord" (hymn)

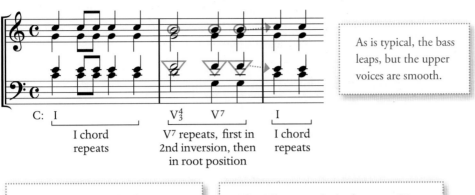

C: I   V$\frac{4}{3}$ V^7 I

I chord
repeats

V^7 repeats, first in
2nd inversion, then
in root position

I chord
repeats

As is typical, the bass
leaps, but the upper
voices are smooth.

With repeated chords, there are no
parallel fifths or octaves, but rather
stationary fifths and octaves.

After V^7 repeats, the leading tone (B)
resolves up and the chordal seventh (F)
resolves down.

APPROACHING PERFECT INTERVALS IN SIMILAR MOTION

Approaching a perfect interval in similar motion is far less objectionable than
approaching one in parallel motion. However, you should avoid approaching a perfect
octave or fifth between the outer voices (that is, the bass and soprano voices) in similar
motion *unless the soprano voice moves by step*. A perfect octave approached in similar
motion creates **similar octaves** (or hidden octaves or direct octaves). A perfect fifth
approached in similar motion creates **similar fifths** (or hidden fifths or direct fifths).

5.20

Good The octave D–D is
approached in similar motion, with
the soprano moving by step.

Poor Similar octaves: the octave
D–D is approached in similar motion
in the *outer* voices, with the soprano
moving by *leap*.

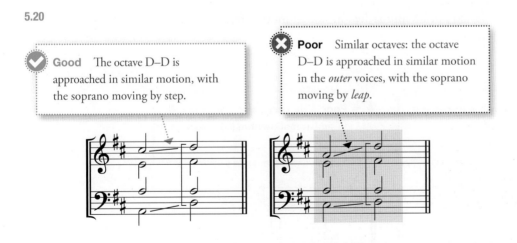

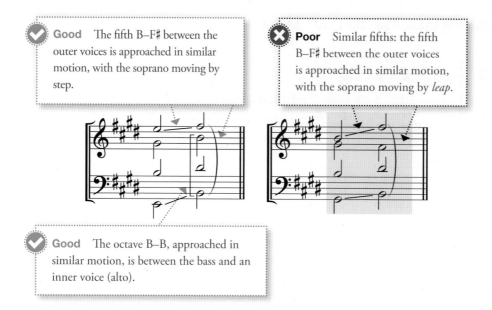

> ✓ **Good**   The fifth B–F♯ between the outer voices is approached in similar motion, with the soprano moving by step.

> ✗ **Poor**   Similar fifths: the fifth B–F♯ between the outer voices is approached in similar motion, with the soprano moving by *leap*.

> ✓ **Good**   The octave B–B, approached in similar motion, is between the bass and an inner voice (alto).

Also, a perfect unison between any two upper voices should not be approached in similar motion.

5.21

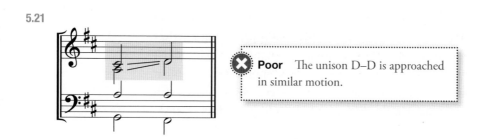

> ✗ **Poor**   The unison D–D is approached in similar motion.

Finally, an octave should not be approached in similar motion from a dissonant interval of a seventh or second.

5.22

> ✗ **Poor**   The octave F–F is approached in similar motion from a seventh (A–G).

> ✗ **Poor**   The octave F–F is approached in similar motion from a (compound) second (G–A).

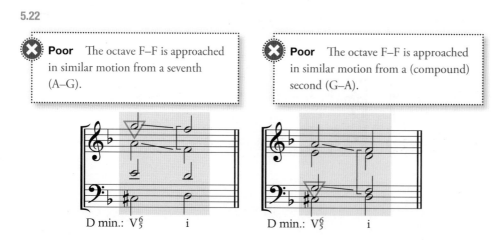

🔍 To learn about voice crossing and overlap, see A Closer Look.

- **Guidelines for melodic lines in four-part harmony**
  - The melodic motion in the upper three voices of four-part harmony should be mostly smooth.
  - In all voices, avoid augmented intervals, leaps larger than a third ascending to a leading tone, leaps of a seventh, and leaps greater than an octave.

- **Guidelines for voice leading in four-part harmony**
  - **Types of motion between intervals**: Intervals between pairs of voices may be approached in contrary motion (one voice moves up, the other down), parallel motion (voices move in the same direction and the same distance), similar motion (voices move in the same direction but different distances), oblique motion (only one voice moves), or stationary motion (neither voice moves).
  - **Perfect intervals**: Do not approach a perfect octave, fifth, or unison in parallel motion.
  - **Leading tones**: A leading tone ($\hat{7}$) in an outer voice must either repeat or resolve up to the tonic ($\hat{8}$).
  - **Chordal sevenths**: Chordal sevenths must resolve down by step, or be repeated from one chord to the next before resolving down by step.
  - **Similar motion to octaves and unisons**: (a) Do not approach an octave in similar motion between the bass and soprano unless the soprano moves by step; (b) do not approach a unison in similar motion; (c) do not lead from a dissonance to an octave in similar motion.

TEST YOURSELF

1. Which of these excerpts uses melodic lines that are more typical of standard four-part harmony, and why?

a.

b.

2. Label the type of motion in each pair of intervals below: contrary, parallel, similar, oblique, or stationary.

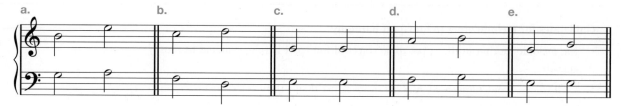

3. Which of the pairs of chords below involve faulty parallel motion?

4. Identify the leading tones in each of the two progressions below. Identify any chordal sevenths. Then fill in the missing notes.

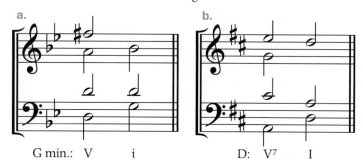

G min.: V   i   D: V⁷   I

5. Mark the incorrect instances of parallel or similar motion to a perfect interval, and explain the problem.

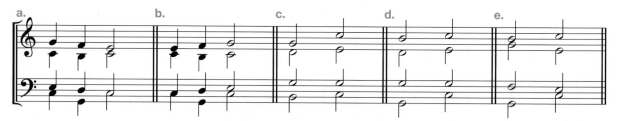

6. Label how each interval in the following is approached: P (parallel), C (contrary), O (oblique), SIM (similar), STA (stationary).

Luís Álvares Pinto, "Lições de Solfejo 2"

chapter

6 Harmonic Progression

Harmonies in tonal music follow conventional progressions.

Beginning and Ending Phrases	Harmonizing Melodies
Authentic and half cadences	Matching chords to the melody
Perfect and imperfect authentic cadences	Voice leading
Functions and Harmonic Patterns	Conventional harmonic progressions
T–D–T (Tonic–Dominant–Tonic)	
T–S–D–T (Tonic–Subdominant–Dominant–Tonic)	

Chords follow one another in typical patterns that create a sense of harmonic tension and resolution. Though these patterns vary from one style to another, conventional harmonic successions are vital to most music.

BEGINNING AND ENDING PHRASES

AUTHENTIC AND HALF CADENCES

A **phrase** is the basic unit of tonal music, akin to a sentence in language. Phrase beginnings and endings are crucial harmonic events. Typically, phrases begin with a root-position I triad. Even more standard is the harmonic setting at the end of the phrase, or the **cadence**. Phrases almost always conclude with either a root-position V or V^7 chord leading to root-position I (or i), or with a root-position V. A cadence consisting of V or V^7 moving to I (or i) is an **authentic cadence** (**AC**); a cadence ending with a V triad is a **half cadence** (**HC**). Because they end on a stable tonic harmony, authentic cadences generally sound more conclusive than half cadences.

6.1 W. A. Mozart, Clarinet Quintet in A, K. 581, iv

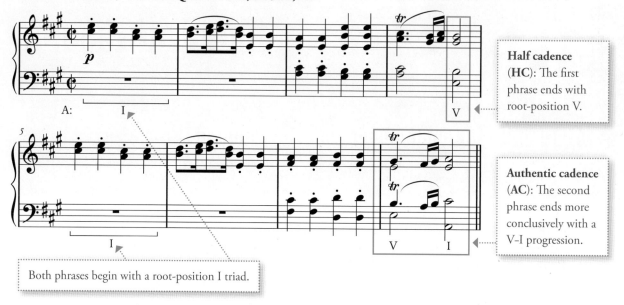

Half cadence (**HC**): The first phrase ends with root-position V.

Authentic cadence (**AC**): The second phrase ends more conclusively with a V–I progression.

Both phrases begin with a root-position I triad.

PERFECT AND IMPERFECT AUTHENTIC CADENCES

Authentic cadences are further categorized by the final note in the melody. An authentic cadence that ends with $\hat{1}$ in the melody is a **perfect authentic cadence** (**PAC**). An authentic cadence that ends with $\hat{3}$ or $\hat{5}$ in the melody is an **imperfect authentic cadence** (**IAC**). Perfect authentic cadences tend to sound more conclusive than imperfect authentic cadences.

6.2 Wilhelmine von Troschke und Rosenwerth, Thema con Variazioni

Imperfect authentic cadence (**IAC**): The first phrase ends with V⁷–I, and with $\hat{3}$ in the melody.

Perfect authentic cadence (**PAC**): The second phrase ends with V⁷–I, and with $\hat{1}$ in the melody.

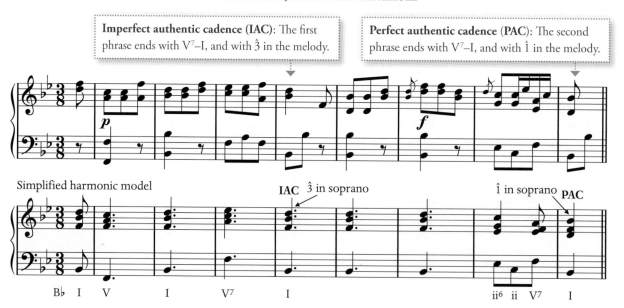

As you will see later, there are some other types of cadences; nevertheless, the HC, PAC, and IAC are by far the most common. Also, it should be noted that harmonies alone do not determine where cadences occur: cadences appear only at the ends of phrases, which are determined not only by the chords that are used, but also by the rhythm and melody.

FUNCTIONS AND HARMONIC PATTERNS

Compared to the beginning and end, the middle of a phrase offers a wider variety of harmonic possibilities. Choosing the proper order for chords in the middle of phrases can be challenging, and will be a primary focus of Parts 3 and 4. As you will see, each chord fits into one of a few **functions**, either **Tonic**, **Dominant**, or **Subdominant**. You already know the terms tonic, subdominant, and dominant to apply to I, IV, and V, but the *categories* of **T**onic, **D**ominant, and **S**ubdominant include more than these three chords. These basic categories in turn help determine the order in which chords progress.

T–D–T (TONIC–DOMINANT–TONIC)

A particularly common pattern involves a stable **T**onic chord moving to an unstable **D**ominant and then back to a **T**onic (**T–D–T**). The **T**onic chord in the **T–D–T** progression must be a triad (not a seventh chord), and it can be in root position or (especially if it appears in the middle of a phrase) first inversion (I^6); it may *not* appear as a second-inversion chord (I_4^6), since I_4^6 is an unstable harmony. The **D**ominant chord may be V, V^7, or (especially if it appears in the middle of a phrase) an inversion (like V^6 or V_2^4), as well as other similar harmonies that will be discussed in Part 3.

6.3 **The Tonic–Dominant–Tonic pattern**

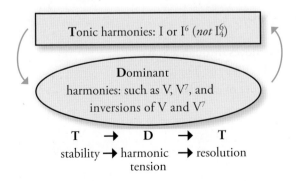

Tonic harmonies: I or I^6 (*not* I_4^6)

Dominant harmonies: such as V, V^7, and inversions of V and V^7

T → D → T

stability → harmonic tension → resolution

6.4

SOME EXAMPLES OF CHORD PROGRESSIONS THAT FOLLOW THE T–D–T PATTERN:			
I–V–I	I–V^7–I	I–V^6–I	I–V$^4_3$–I^6
T–D–T	**T–D–T**	**T–D–T**	**T–D–T**

Within the **T-D-T** pattern, a chord may repeat or move to another chord within the same category before progressing onward.

6.5

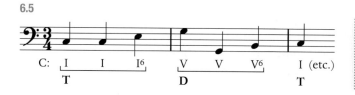

> Two or more **Tonic** chords may appear in a row; two or more **Dominant** chords may appear in a row.

6.6 **Lowell Mason, "Ariel" (hymn)**

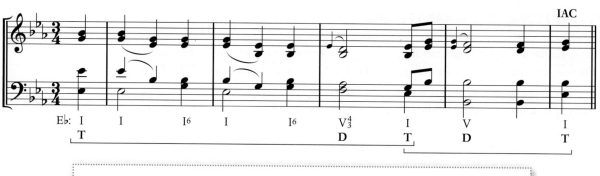

> The chord progressions in this excerpt follow the standard **Tonic–Dominant–Tonic** pattern.

T–S–D–T (TONIC–SUBDOMINANT–DOMINANT–TONIC)

Another standard harmonic pattern involves a **Tonic** chord that moves through a **Sub-dominant** chord to a **Dominant** and back to a **Tonic** (**T-S-D-T**). Like the **Tonic** and **Dominant** categories, the **Subdominant** category includes a number of chords: IV, ii^6, and other chords to be discussed later.

6.7 The Tonic–Subdominant–Dominant–Tonic pattern

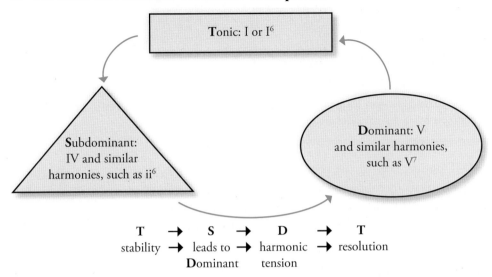

$T \rightarrow S \rightarrow D \rightarrow T$

stability → leads to → harmonic → resolution
Dominant   tension

6.8

SOME EXAMPLES OF CHORD PROGRESSIONS THAT FOLLOW THE T–S–D–T PATTERN:				
I–IV–V–I	I–ii⁶–V⁷–I	I–IV–V$_3^4$–I	I–ii⁶–V–I⁶	I–ii⁶–V⁶–I
T–S–D–T	T–S–D–T	T–S–D–T	T–S–D–T	T–S–D–T

A **S**ubdominant chord may repeat or be followed by another **S**ubdominant chord before progressing to a **D**ominant.

6.9

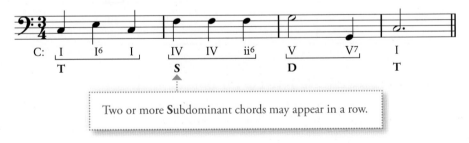

Two or more **S**ubdominant chords may appear in a row.

Although a **S**ubdominant often leads to a **D**ominant, the reverse is *not* true: in four-part harmony, it is very unusual for a **D**ominant to move to a **S**ubdominant, as in I–V–IV–I or I–V⁷–ii⁶–I.

6.10

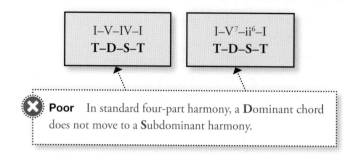

I–V–IV–I	I–V⁷–ii⁶–I
T–D–S–T	**T–D–S–T**

❌ **Poor** In standard four-part harmony, a **D**ominant chord does not move to a **S**ubdominant harmony.

T-D-T and **T-S-D-T** do not exhaust the possibilities for harmonic progressions. For instance, another particularly common chord progression is I–IV–I (**T**onic–**S**ubdominant–**T**onic, see Chapter 16). Nonetheless, the harmonic structure of most tonal music may be understood as a series of **T-D-T** and **T-S-D-T** patterns.

6.11 Ludwig van Beethoven, Variations in G, WoO 77

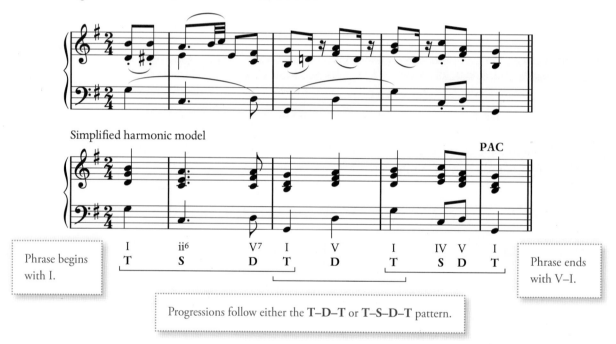

Simplified harmonic model

PAC

Phrase begins with I.

| I | ii⁶ | V⁷ | I | V | I | IV | V | I |
| T | S | D | T | D | T | S | D | T |

Progressions follow either the **T–D–T** or **T–S–D–T** pattern.

Phrase ends with V–I.

HARMONIZING MELODIES

One way to enhance your understanding of harmonic progressions is to **harmonize** melodies. When harmonizing a melody, you are given a melody with a simple rhythm and directed to supply a harmony for every note (or almost every note), using standard voice-leading and harmonic procedures.

- Begin by identifying the key and determining the scale degrees of the melody in that key.

- Then locate the cadences and determine a proper bass line and Roman numerals for the cadences.
- Finally, determine the Roman numerals and bass line for the rest of the harmonies.

Strategies for developing the skills for harmonizing melodies are discussed in detail starting in Part 3. In each case, the chords chosen for the harmonization must include the notes found in the melody, allowing for good voice leading and harmonic progressions.

6.12

Task: **Harmonize this melody by providing a bass line and Roman numerals.**

MATCHING CHORDS TO THE MELODY

In harmonizing a melody, you must make sure that each note belongs to the chord chosen to harmonize it.

6.13

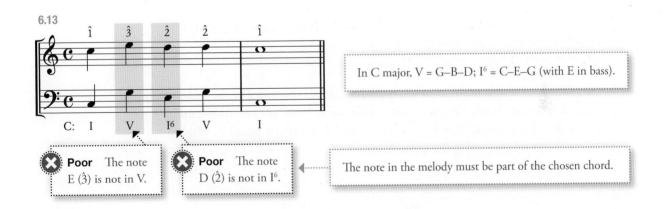

In C major, V = G–B–D; I⁶ = C–E–G (with E in bass).

Poor The note E ($\hat{3}$) is not in V.

Poor The note D ($\hat{2}$) is not in I⁶.

The note in the melody must be part of the chosen chord.

VOICE LEADING

In harmonizing a melody, you should follow voice-leading and chord construction guidelines, such as avoiding parallel fifths and avoiding doubled leading tones.

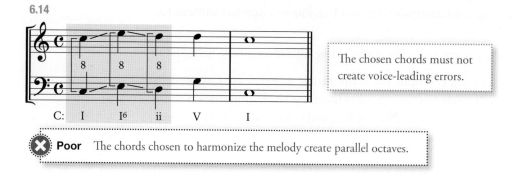

The chosen chords must not create voice-leading errors.

❌ **Poor**   The chords chosen to harmonize the melody create parallel octaves.

CONVENTIONAL HARMONIC PROGRESSIONS

Finally, the harmonization should follow conventional harmonic progressions, using patterns such as **T–D–T** or **T–S–D–T** and ending each phrase with a cadence.

6.15

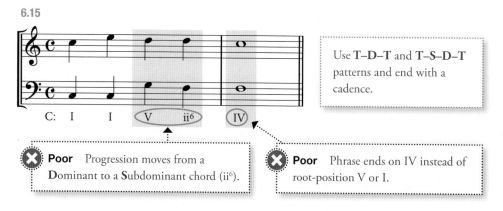

Use **T–D–T** and **T–S–D–T** patterns and end with a cadence.

❌ **Poor**   Progression moves from a **D**ominant to a **S**ubdominant chord (ii⁶).

❌ **Poor**   Phrase ends on IV instead of root-position V or I.

The following harmonization of the melody is good: the notes of the melody appear in each of the chords chosen to harmonize them, there are no voice-leading errors, and the chord progression follows conventional harmonic practice, with an appropriate chord progression at the cadence.

6.16

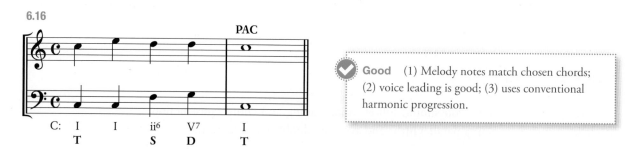

✅ **Good**   (1) Melody notes match chosen chords; (2) voice leading is good; (3) uses conventional harmonic progression.

After choosing the harmonies and writing the bass line, you can fill in the inner voices, paying attention to chord construction (see Chapter 4) and voice leading (see Chapter 5).

6.17

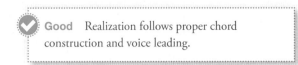

> ✓ **Good**   Realization follows proper chord construction and voice leading.

POINTS FOR REVIEW

- **Phrases most often begin with a root-position I chord and end either with a cadence on a root-position V or with a cadence on a root-position I preceded by root-position V (or V^7).**

- **A cadence ending on a root-position V is a half cadence (HC).**

- **A cadence that ends V–I or V^7–I is an authentic cadence (AC). An authentic cadence that ends with $\hat{1}$ in the soprano is a perfect authentic cadence (PAC); an authentic cadence that ends with $\hat{3}$ or $\hat{5}$ in the melody is an imperfect authentic cadence (IAC).**

- **The ordering of harmonies within a phrase follows conventional progressions, including Tonic–Dominant–Tonic (T–D–T) and Tonic–Subdominant–Dominant–Tonic (T–S–D–T).**

- **Chords in the Tonic category are I and I^6; chords in the Dominant category include V, V^7, and inversions of V and V^7; chords in the Subdominant category include IV and ii^6.**

- **In a good melody harmonization, the chord chosen for each note of the melody should include the melody note, conform to voice-leading guidelines, and result in a chord progression that follows the conventions of harmony.**

TEST YOURSELF

1. In the following examples, do the phrases (each ending is marked by a fermata) end with a PAC, IAC, or HC?

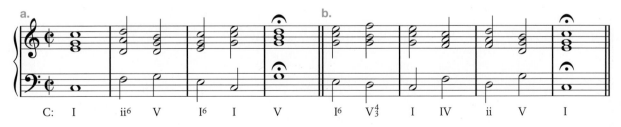

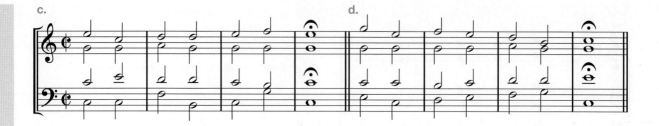

c. **d.**

2. Why are the following phrase endings (indicated by fermatas) not conventional cadences?

D: I   ii^6 V   I^6 I   V$^6_5$ I   V$^4_3$ I^6 IV   ii   V$^4_3$ I

3. Which of the following are **T**onic–**D**ominant–**T**onic chord progressions, which are **T**onic–**S**ubdominant–**D**ominant–**T**onic progressions, and which are neither?

   a. I–V–I   **b.** I–I–V–V^6–I   **c.** I–V–IV–I   **d.** I–ii^6–V–I

4. Which of the following are good harmonizations of the given melodies? If the harmonization is not good, what is the problem with it?

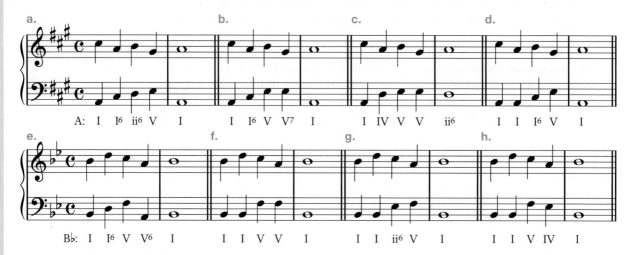

a. A: I   I^6 ii^6 V   I   **b.** I   I^6 V   V^7 I   **c.** I   IV   V   V   ii^6 **d.** I   I   I^6 V   I

e. B♭: I   I^6 V   V^6 I   **f.** I   I   V   V   I   **g.** I   I   ii^6 V   I   **h.** I   I   V   IV   I

chapter 7

Melodic Elaboration

The voice leading of a composition may often be understood as an elaboration of an underlying four-part framework.

Arpeggiation
Octave Doubling
Embellishing Tones
  Approaching and leaving embellishing tones
  Accented and unaccented embellishing tones
  Passing tones

Neighbor tones
Suspensions
Other Embellishments
A Closer Look
  Upper, lower, and double neighbors
  Types of incomplete neighbors

Four-part harmony may be elaborated with doubling, arpeggiation, and embellishment by non-chord tones. To better understand the underlying harmonies of a composition, it is helpful to relate its notes to a basic four-part model.

ARPEGGIATION

Four separate voices are not needed to imply four-voice harmony. Instead of sounding at the same time, some (or all) of the chord tones may be **arpeggiated** with **chord skips** (leaps from one chord tone to another). To determine the underlying harmony in such a case, imagine the notes as if they were played simultaneously. Furthermore, when only one or two notes of a chord are present, often the chord's missing notes may be understood as implied by the context.

7.1 Louise Farrenc, Etude Op. 50, No. 4

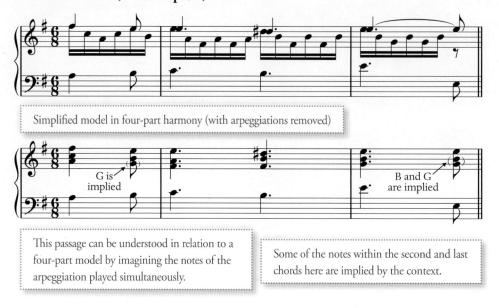

Simplified model in four-part harmony (with arpeggiations removed)

G is implied

B and G are implied

This passage can be understood in relation to a four-part model by imagining the notes of the arpeggiation played simultaneously.

Some of the notes within the second and last chords here are implied by the context.

OCTAVE DOUBLING

Any voice of a four-part texture may be **doubled** in octaves throughout, resulting in what appears to be a five-voice texture. These octave doublings simply enrich the underlying four-part texture so as to create a fuller sound, however, and are thus not considered forbidden parallel octaves.

7.2 Johanna Kinkel, "Hymnus in Coena Domini"

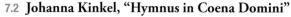

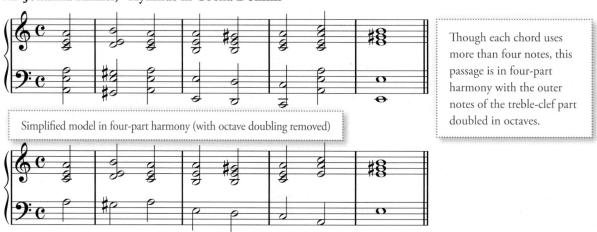

Though each chord uses more than four notes, this passage is in four-part harmony with the outer notes of the treble-clef part doubled in octaves.

Simplified model in four-part harmony (with octave doubling removed)

EMBELLISHING TONES

Chord tones also may be decorated by notes that do not belong to the harmony. In identifying the underlying harmony, these **embellishing tones** may be ignored.

7.3 Theophania Cecil, "Evening Hymn"

G: I   ii$^6_5$ V^8——^{7} I   IV^6 V   I

> Embellishing tones (highlighted by triangles) decorate the notes of the harmony.

> Simplified harmonic model (with embellishing tones removed)

G: I   ii$^6_5$ V^8—^{7} I   IV^6 V   I

APPROACHING AND LEAVING EMBELLISHING TONES

Embellishing tones are classified by how they are approached and left—by step, leap, or common tone.

7.4

Approached by step and left by step

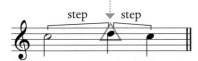

Approached by step and left by leap

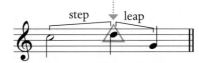

Approached by common tone and left by step

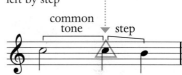

ACCENTED AND UNACCENTED EMBELLISHING TONES

Embellishing tones are also classified as either **accented** or **unaccented**. An unaccented embellishing tone appears after the arrival of the chord, on a weaker beat or part of the beat. In contrast, an accented embellishing tone appears at the very start of the chord.

7.5 J. S. Bach, Chorale 256

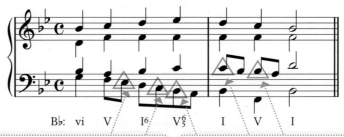

B♭: vi   V   I^6 V$^6_5$ I   V   I

> Unaccented embellishing tones appear after the start of the chord and on a weak part of the beat.

> Accented embellishing tones appear at the onset of the chord.

PASSING TONES

The most common type of embellishing tone is a **passing tone** (PT). Passing tones fill in the space between two different chord tones with stepwise motion. A passing tone is thus always approached and left by step in the same direction.

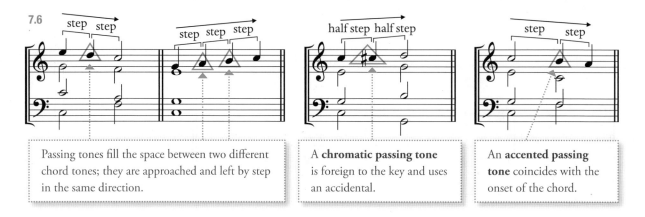

7.6

Passing tones fill the space between two different chord tones; they are approached and left by step in the same direction.

A **chromatic passing tone** is foreign to the key and uses an accidental.

An **accented passing tone** coincides with the onset of the chord.

NEIGHBOR TONES

Unlike the passing tone, which moves between two different chord tones, the **neighbor tone** (NT) decorates a single tone. Accordingly, a neighbor tone departs from a chord tone by step and returns to the same tone by step in the opposite direction.

7.7   **upper neighbor**   **lower neighbor**

Neighbor tones are approached and left by step in opposite directions, decorating a single tone.

A **chromatic neighbor tone** uses an accidental and is both approached and left by half step.

Accented neighbor tone

SUSPENSIONS

Another common type of embellishing tone is the **suspension** (SUS). A suspension is an accented embellishing tone that is approached by common tone from a note of the previous chord. A suspension resolves *down* by step.

7.8

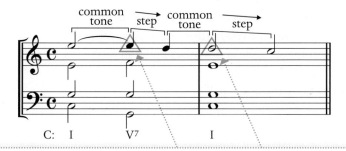

Suspensions are accented dissonances, approached by common tone from a note of the previous chord and resolving *down* by step. Suspended notes may be either tied or restruck.

7.9 J. H. Knecht, "Herzlich tut mich verlangen"

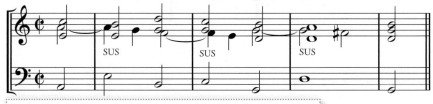

The underlying chord progression here is decorated with suspensions.

Simplified harmonic model (with embellishing tones removed)

OTHER EMBELLISHMENTS

Other embellishing tones are found less frequently. These include the **incomplete neighbor tone** (INT), which is an embellishing tone that is either approached by step and left by leap, or approached by leap and left by step.

7.10

An incomplete neighbor tone may be approached by step and left by leap . . .

. . . or approached by leap and left by step.

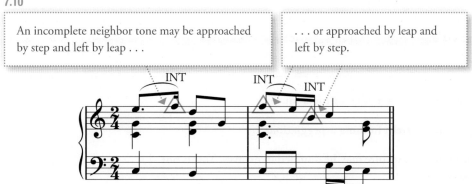

Still rarer are the **anticipation** (ANT), an unaccented non-chord tone that is approached by step and left by common tone; and the **retardation** (RET), an accented embellishing tone that is approached by common tone and resolves up by step.

7.11 R. Nathaniel Dett, "Let de heaven light shine on me"

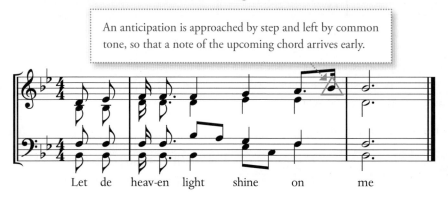

An anticipation is approached by step and left by common tone, so that a note of the upcoming chord arrives early.

Let de heav-en light shine on me

7.12 Lucille Grétry, *Le mariage d'Antonio*, Act I, scene ii

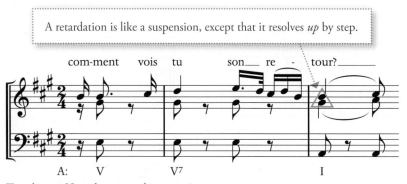

A retardation is like a suspension, except that it resolves *up* by step.

com-ment vois tu son re - tour?

A: V   V7   I

Translation: How do you see his return?

🔍 For more on neighbor tones, see A Closer Look.

POINTS FOR REVIEW

- **Four-part harmony is often used as a model for tonal music.**

- **Chord tones may appear successively, forming arpeggiations.**

- **One or more voices in a four-part texture may be doubled in octaves. This is not considered a voice-leading error.**

- Chord tones may be decorated by embellishing tones. These embellishing tones are classified by how they are approached and left (by step, leap, or common tone—up or down), as well as whether they are accented or unaccented.

- The most common embellishing tones are the passing tone (PT), neighbor tone (NT), and suspension (SUS).

passing tone
- links two different tones
- approached and left by step in the same direction
- may be accented or unaccented

neighbor tone
- decorates a single tone
- approached and left by step in opposite directions
- may be accented or unaccented

suspension
- must be accented
- approached by common tone, then resolves down by step
- may be either tied or restruck

- Less common embellishing tones include the incomplete neighbor tone (INT), anticipation, and retardation.

incomplete neighbor tone
- either approached by step and left by leap, or approached by leap and left by step

anticipation
- decorates a single tone
- approached by step and left by common tone
- must be unaccented

retardation
- must be accented
- approached by common tone, then resolves up by step

TEST YOURSELF

1. Label the Roman numerals of this excerpt. How might this be understood to represent four parts?

C: ___   ___   ___   ___

2. For the examples below, label how each embellishing tone (marked by a triangle) is approached and left: by step, leap, or common tone.

approached by: _____   _____   _____   _____   _____   _____   _____

left by: _____   _____   _____   _____   _____   _____   _____

3. For the examples below, label each embellishing tone (marked by a triangle) as either accented or unaccented. Then identify whether it is a PT (passing tone), NT (neighbor tone), SUS (suspension), ANT (anticipation), RET (retardation), or INT (incomplete neighbor tone).

accented or unaccented? _____   _____   _____   _____

type of embellishment: _____   _____   _____   _____

accented or unaccented? _____   _____   _____   _____

type of embellishment: _____   _____   _____   _____

8

Species Counterpoint

Species counterpoint involves writing a new melody to sound with a given melody.

First Species
Second Species
Fourth Species

A Closer Look
Strategies for writing species counterpoint

Species counterpoint is a traditional way to learn voice leading, especially the use of dissonant embellishing tones and the treatment of perfect consonances. In species counterpoint, you are given a melody in whole notes, called a **cantus firmus**, and asked to write a melody to go with it. There are five *species* in this method, each defining the rhythmic values and embellishing tones you may use in the added melody:

- whole notes and no dissonance in first species;
- half notes and dissonant passing or neighboring tones in second species;
- quarter notes and dissonant passing or neighboring tones in third species;
- half notes tied across the barline and dissonant suspensions in fourth species;
- and a free combination of all the previous possibilities in fifth species.

In what follows, we will discuss only first, second, and fourth species, and we will be concerned only with melodies composed above the cantus firmus.

FIRST SPECIES

In **first-species counterpoint**, a new melody in whole notes is written against the cantus firmus (CF), using only consonant intervals between the melodies. To help keep track of the intervals, label them between the staves, and put a box around any perfect intervals—they require special treatment.

Counterpoint starts on $\hat{1}$, an octave above the cantus.

Counterpoint moves mostly by step and has a single melodic high point in the middle.

Counterpoint ends $\hat{7}$–$\hat{8}$, while the cantus firmus ends $\hat{2}$–$\hat{1}$. Scale-degree $\hat{7}$ is raised to leading tone in minor.

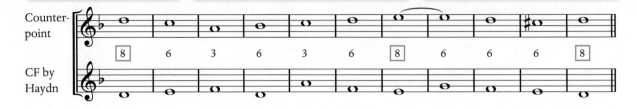

Only consonant intervals are used between the melodies, mostly imperfect consonances (thirds and sixths).

Perfect consonances (boxed) are approached in contrary or oblique motion, never in similar or parallel motion.

8.2

Counterpoint starts on $\hat{5}$, a fifth above the cantus.

Counterpoint moves mostly by step, with a large leap to the melodic high point followed by a long stepwise descent.

Counterpoint ends $\hat{7}$–$\hat{8}$, while the cantus firmus ends $\hat{2}$–$\hat{1}$. Scale-degree $\hat{7}$ is raised in minor.

Only consonant intervals are used between the melodies, mostly imperfect consonances (thirds and sixths).

Perfect consonances (boxed) are approached in contrary or oblique motion, never in similar or parallel motion.

As you write first-species counterpoint, follow these guidelines:

1. *Rhythm*: Use whole notes only.

2. *Beginning and ending*: Start the counterpoint a fifth or an octave above the cantus; conclude it with $\hat{7}$–$\hat{8}$ (in minor, raising the subtonic to leading tone). The cantus firmus always ends $\hat{2}$–$\hat{1}$, so the last two intervals between the melodies will always be 6–8 (a sixth expanding to an octave).

3. *Harmonic intervals*:

   • Use only consonances.

   • Major or minor thirds and sixths should predominate; perfect fifths and octaves appear less frequently.

   • Dissonances, including seconds, sevenths, and augmented or diminished intervals, are forbidden. (Beware the diminished fifth between $\hat{7}$ and $\hat{4}$!)

- The perfect fourth is considered a dissonance when writing in two parts and is forbidden.
- Unisons are also forbidden.

4. *Approaching perfect intervals*: Approach perfect fifths and octaves in contrary motion (one voice moves up while the other moves down) or oblique motion (one voice stays on the same note while the other moves). Perfect intervals may not be approached by parallel motion (both voices move in the same direction by the same interval) or similar motion (both voices move in the same direction but by different intervals).

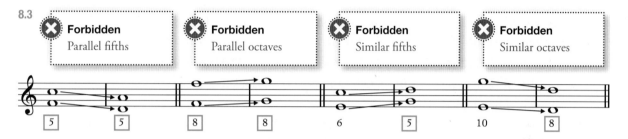

8.3

5. *Melody*:

- Like the cantus firmus, the counterpoint should have a single melodic climax or high point (which must not be the leading tone).
- The counterpoint should move mostly by step, punctuated by leaps, which are often followed by stepwise motion in the opposite direction.
- The counterpoint must remain above the cantus firmus (voice crossing is not permitted).
- The counterpoint may contain a single pair of tied notes.
- Leaps by augmented second, diminished fifth, augmented fourth, and seventh are not permitted. In minor, raise $\hat{6}$ if necessary to avoid the augmented second.
- Do not use any accidentals, other than raised $\hat{7}$ or raised $\hat{6}$ and $\hat{7}$ at the very end of a minor-key counterpoint. Do not write chromatic semitones (like B♭–B♮).

8.4

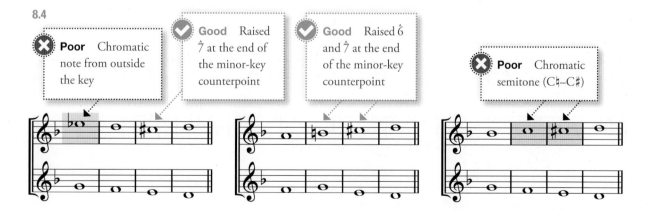

SECOND SPECIES

Second-species melodies are written in half notes, so there are two notes in the counterpoint for each whole note in the cantus firmus.

- Dissonant intervals may be used, but only on the unaccented second half of the measure and when the dissonant note is both approached and left by step: you may not leap into or out of a dissonance.

- As a result, every dissonance is either a passing tone (connecting two consonant tones a third apart) or a neighbor tone (stepping away from and back to a consonant tone).

- As in first species, fifths and octaves on the downbeats must be approached in contrary motion (never in similar or parallel motion).

- Perfect consonances on downbeats and all dissonances require special treatment (in exercises, place dissonant intervals in triangles and perfect consonances in boxes).

- Unisons are permitted on weak beats.

8.5 Cantus firmus by W. A. Mozart, second-species counterpoint by Barbara Ployer*

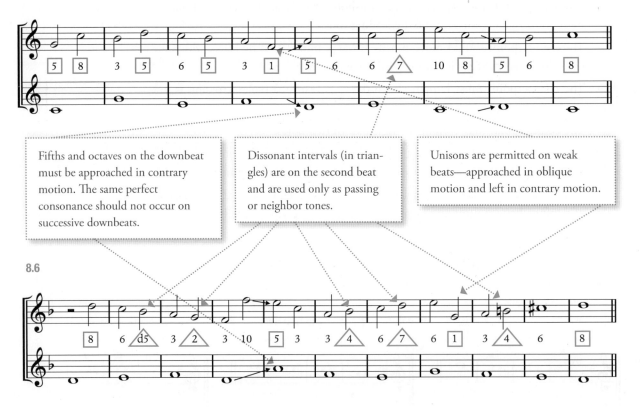

Fifths and octaves on the downbeat must be approached in contrary motion. The same perfect consonance should not occur on successive downbeats.

Dissonant intervals (in triangles) are on the second beat and are used only as passing or neighbor tones.

Unisons are permitted on weak beats—approached in oblique motion and left in contrary motion.

8.6

* Mozart's student

Here are guidelines for writing second-species counterpoint:

1. *Rhythm*:
   - Use half notes throughout, with only these exceptions:
     - the first measure may begin with a half-note rest;
     - the second-to-last measure may contain a whole note;
     - the last measure must be a whole note.
   - Do not repeat or tie notes.

2. *Beginning and ending*:
   - The first note must be $\hat{5}$ or $\hat{8}$ (a fifth or octave above the cantus firmus).
   - The second-to-last note must be $\hat{7}$ (raised in minor; $\hat{6}$ may also have to be raised to avoid a melodic augmented second).
   - The final note must be an octave above the cantus.
   - As in first species, the last two intervals between the melodies will always be 6–8 (a sixth expanding to an octave).

8.7

The first measure may contain either two half notes or a half-note rest plus a half note. The first note must be either $\hat{5}$ or $\hat{8}$.

The second-to-last measure may contain two half notes or a whole note. The last two notes must be $\hat{7}$–$\hat{8}$. Between the melodies, a sixth expands to an octave.

Dissonances (in triangles) are on the second half of the measure and are used only as passing or neighboring tones.

3. *Intervals between the voices*:
   - The first half note of every measure must be consonant.
   - The second half note may be either consonant or dissonant.
   - If it is dissonant, the dissonance must be approached and left by step.
   - Every dissonant note must thus be either a passing tone or a neighboring tone.
   - Unlike dissonant notes, consonant notes may be freely leapt to and away from.
   - Unisons may occur on the second beat, approached by leap and left by step.

4. *Approaching perfect fifths and octaves*: A fifth or octave that appears on the downbeat may not be approached by parallel or similar motion.

8.8

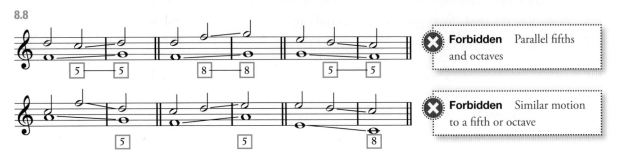

5. Avoid using the same perfect interval (fifth or octave) on two successive downbeats, even when the second one is approached in contrary motion.

8.9

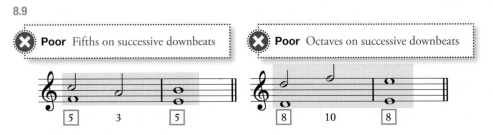

6. *Melody*:

- As in first species, the counterpoint should have a single melodic high point (which must not be the leading tone).
- As in first species, the counterpoint should move mostly by step, punctuated by leaps. Leaps larger than a third generally occur within the measure (from the first to the second half note), rather than across the barline, and are often followed by stepwise motion in the opposite direction from the leap.
- As in first species, do not cross the voices (the melody has to be higher than the cantus); do not leap by diminished fifth, augmented fourth, or seventh; do not use any accidentals other than raised $\hat{7}$ or raised $\hat{6}$ and $\hat{7}$ at the very end of the counterpoint in a minor key; do not write chromatic semitones (like B♭–B♮).
- Unlike in first species, you may not repeat a note.

FOURTH SPECIES

Fourth-species counterpoint is mostly written in pairs of half notes that are tied across the barline. Dissonances may occur only on the *first* half of the measure (the second note of a tied pair) and only with a consonant preparation (the first note of a tied pair) and a resolution down by step to another consonant interval. A strong-beat dissonance like this, with a consonant preparation and a stepwise resolution down, is a **suspension**.

Suspensions are named by the intervals of the dissonant suspension and its resolution: 7–6, for example, refers to a suspended seventh resolving to a sixth. The best dissonant suspensions are 7–6 and 4–3. You may use two or more 7–6 or 4–3 suspensions in a row; in fact, chains of suspensions, pushing the melody downward, are typical of fourth species. A 9–8 suspension is also possible, but you cannot use two (or more) in a row, as that creates a series of parallel octaves separated only by dissonant ninths. (There are also consonant suspensions, like 6–5, but our focus here is on the proper treatment of dissonant suspensions.)

8.10

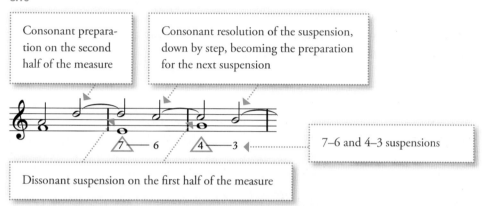

Consonant preparation on the second half of the measure

Consonant resolution of the suspension, down by step, becoming the preparation for the next suspension

7–6 and 4–3 suspensions

Dissonant suspension on the first half of the measure

8.11

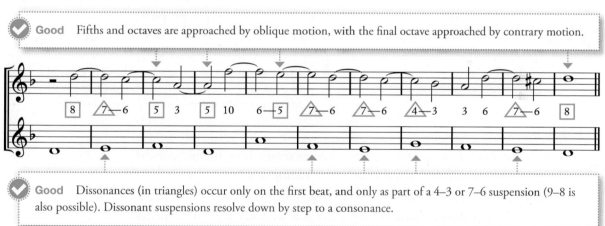

✔ **Good** Fifths and octaves are approached by oblique motion, with the final octave approached by contrary motion.

✔ **Good** Dissonances (in triangles) occur only on the first beat, and only as part of a 4–3 or 7–6 suspension (9–8 is also possible). Dissonant suspensions resolve down by step to a consonance.

Here are guidelines for writing fourth-species counterpoint:

1. *Rhythm*: Use only half notes, except in the first measure, which begins with a half-note rest, and the last measure, which should be a whole note. Generally, the second half note of each measure should be tied to the first half note of the next, but there may occasionally be pairs of non-tied half notes (as in second species).

2. *Beginning and ending*: The first note must be an octave or fifth above the cantus. In the second-to-last measure, a 7–6 suspension resolves to $\hat{7}$ (raised in minor), followed in the last measure by a whole note an octave above the cantus (the same sixth expanding to an octave that ends first and second species).

3. *Intervals between the voices*:

- Dissonances may occur only on the first half of the measure and only as suspensions.
- Consonances that occur on the first beat of the measure may be left either by step or by leap (to another consonance).
- For untied half notes, the rules of second species apply: the second half of the measure may be a dissonant passing or neighboring tone, and the first half of the measure must be a consonance.

4. *Approaching fifths and octaves*: Because voices generally do not move at the same time, motion between them is oblique; there is no restriction on approaching a fifth or octave with oblique motion. If the first half note of a measure is not tied from the previous measure, however, fifths and octaves must be approached in contrary motion (as in second species), not in similar or parallel motion.

8.12

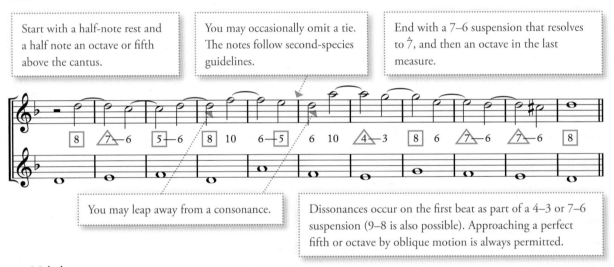

Start with a half-note rest and a half note an octave or fifth above the cantus.

You may occasionally omit a tie. The notes follow second-species guidelines.

End with a 7–6 suspension that resolves to $\hat{7}$, and then an octave in the last measure.

You may leap away from a consonance.

Dissonances occur on the first beat as part of a 4–3 or 7–6 suspension (9–8 is also possible). Approaching a perfect fifth or octave by oblique motion is always permitted.

5. *Melody*:

- As with first and second species, the counterpoint should have a single melodic climax or high point (which should not be the leading tone).
- The counterpoint should move mostly by step, punctuated by leaps. Because suspensions must resolve down by step, there is a tendency for fourth-species counterpoint to move continually downward. Look for opportunities to step or leap up, either by occasionally not tying the half notes across the barline or by placing a consonance on the first beat of the measure (you are always free to leap away from a consonance).
- As in first species, do not cross the voices; do not leap by diminished fifth, augmented fourth, or seventh; do not use any accidentals other than raised $\hat{7}$ or raised $\hat{6}$ and $\hat{7}$ at the very end of the counterpoint in a minor key; do not write chromatic semitones (like B♭–B♮).

 For strategies to write counterpoint, see A Closer Look.

- Species counterpoint is a traditional way of learning about tonal voice leading, especially the proper treatment of dissonance and approaches to perfect fifths and octaves.

- First-species counterpoint involves writing a melody in whole notes against the cantus firmus, also in whole notes. Only consonant intervals are permitted between the parts. Parallel and similar fifths and octaves are prohibited.

- Second-species counterpoint involves writing a melody in half notes against the cantus firmus in whole notes. Dissonant passing and neighboring tones are permitted on the second half of the measure.

- Fourth-species counterpoint involves writing a melody consisting mostly of pairs of half notes tied across the measure. Dissonant suspensions occur on the first half of the measure, prepared by a consonance, and resolved down by step to another consonance.

TEST YOURSELF

- In each of the following species counterpoint exercises, label the intervals. Mark perfect consonances with boxes and dissonances with triangles.

- Errors are marked with arrows. Determine what each error is, and label it in the blank, using the following abbreviations: DIS (impermissible or improperly treated dissonance between the voices); MEL (impermissible melodic interval); PAR or SIM (forbidden parallel or similar motion to a fifth or octave); CHR (impermissible chromaticism); CROSS (voice crossing); START (wrong way to begin); CAD (incorrect cadence).

1. First species

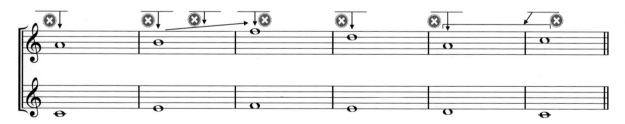

2. Second species

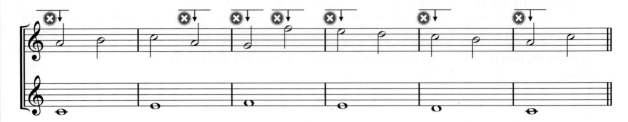

3. Fourth species

part
three

chapter 9 — I and V

The stability of the I triad contrasts with the tension of the V triad.

The Tonic and Dominant Triads
Voice-Leading in Four-Part Harmony
The Leading Tone within the V Chord
Leaps in Upper Voices

Harmonization
A Closer Look
Weak-to-strong chord repetitions

THE TONIC AND DOMINANT TRIADS

The I and V triads in root position are among the most important chords of tonal harmony. The I chord has a **T**onic function and establishes tonal repose. The V chord has a **D**ominant function. It creates a sense of tension, released only when V progresses to I. I and V triads may appear anywhere within a phrase, especially as part of a cadence.

9.1 **Josephine Auernhammer, Variations on a Theme (by Antonio Salieri), Op. 63**

> The I chord is stable, while the V chord creates tension.

Simplified model in four-part harmony

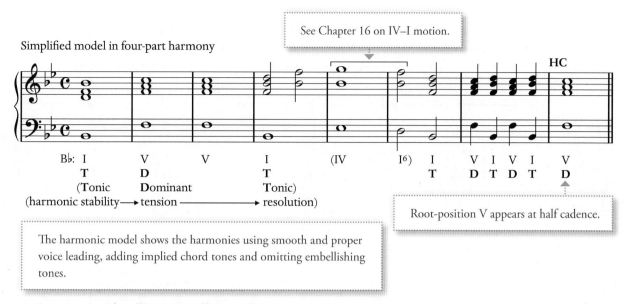

See Chapter 16 on IV–I motion.

HC

Bb: I V V I (IV I⁶) I V I V I V
T D D T T D T D T D
(Tonic Dominant Tonic)
(harmonic stability → tension → resolution)

Root-position V appears at half cadence.

The harmonic model shows the harmonies using smooth and proper voice leading, adding implied chord tones and omitting embellishing tones.

9.2 Ignatius Sancho, "Trip to Dillington"

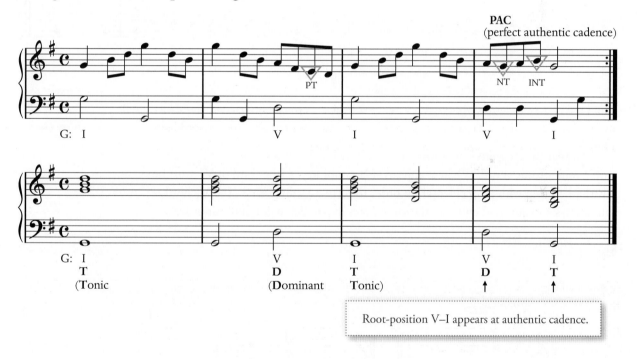

PAC
(perfect authentic cadence)

PT NT INT

G: I V I V I

G: I V I V I
T D T D T
(Tonic (Dominant Tonic) ↑ ↑

Root-position V–I appears at authentic cadence.

VOICE-LEADING IN FOUR-PART HARMONY

In four-part harmony, it is generally best to double the root of a root-position I or V chord. When progressing between I and V, the upper parts (soprano, alto, and tenor) usually either stay on the same note or move to the nearest chord tone.

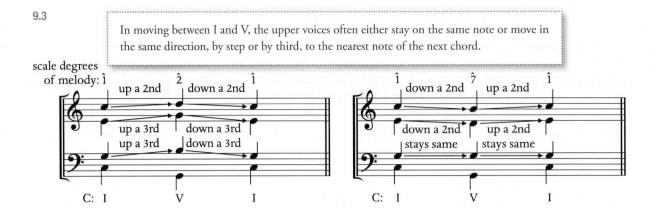

In moving between I and V, the upper voices often either stay on the same note or move in the same direction, by step or by third, to the nearest note of the next chord.

scale degrees of melody: $\hat{1}$ $\hat{2}$ $\hat{1}$ — up a 2nd — down a 2nd — up a 3rd — down a 3rd — up a 3rd — down a 3rd

C: I V I

scale degrees of melody: $\hat{1}$ $\hat{7}$ $\hat{1}$ — down a 2nd — up a 2nd — down a 2nd — up a 2nd — stays same — stays same

C: I V I

9.4 Ludwig van Beethoven, Piano Concerto in E♭, Op. 73, i

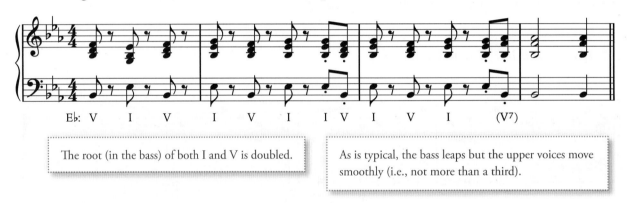

E♭: V I V I V I I V I V I (V⁷)

The root (in the bass) of both I and V is doubled.

As is typical, the bass leaps but the upper voices move smoothly (i.e., not more than a third).

Similar progressions—with the same voice leading—also occur in minor keys, with a minor tonic chord. When V appears in a minor key, $\hat{7}$ (the third of V) must be raised a half step with an accidental, in order to form a leading tone. The V chord is thus always a major triad and uses the same notes in parallel major and minor keys.

In minor keys, use an accidental to raise $\hat{7}$ by a half step. The V chord is thus the same as it would be in the parallel major.

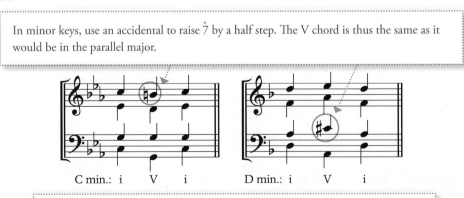

C min.: i V i   D min.: i V i

In a minor key, the tonic triad (i) is minor and the dominant triad (V) is major.

THE LEADING TONE WITHIN THE V CHORD

The V chord includes the leading tone ($\hat{7}$). As noted in Chapter 4, the leading tone is a tendency tone that strives upward. As a result, the leading tone may not be doubled, and if it appears in an outer voice, it must resolve *up* by step to the tonic when V progresses to I.

9.6 **"O give thanks unto the Lord"** (hymn)

> $\hat{7}$ in an outer voice *must* resolve up by step to the tonic, and it also may resolve up to tonic in an inner voice.

9.7

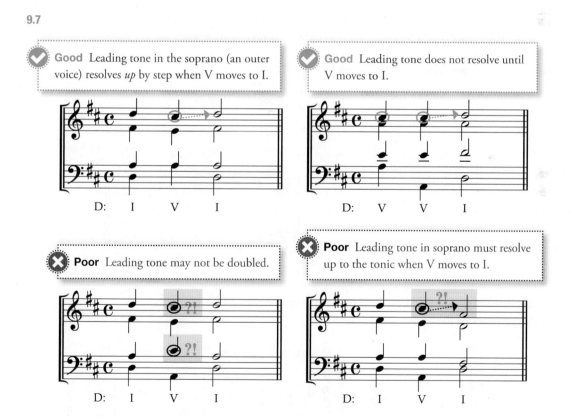

✓ Good Leading tone in the soprano (an outer voice) resolves *up* by step when V moves to I.

✓ Good Leading tone does not resolve until V moves to I.

✕ Poor Leading tone may not be doubled.

✕ Poor Leading tone in soprano must resolve up to the tonic when V moves to I.

However, when it appears in an inner voice (the tenor or alto)—where it is less prominent—the leading tone does not need to resolve up by step.

9.9 Johann Friedrich Doles, "Meine Seele erhebt den Herren"

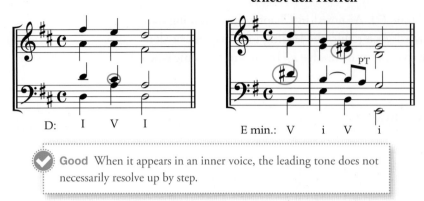

D: I   V   I   E min.: V   i   V   i

> ✓ **Good** When it appears in an inner voice, the leading tone does not necessarily resolve up by step.

LEAPS IN UPPER VOICES

Although the upper voices usually move smoothly when one chord moves to another, they may *occasionally* leap. If you use leaps in the upper voices to progress between I and V, be careful to avoid voice-leading errors, such as parallel octaves and fifths.

9.10 Theophania Cecil, "How Glorious the Lamb"

> The tenor part leaps between I and V, with no parallel fifths or octaves.

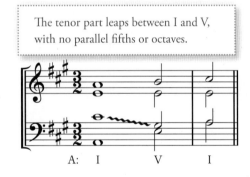

A: I   V   I

9.11

> ✗ **Poor** This example includes too many leaps in the upper voices when I moves to V. The leaps create parallel octaves and fifths.

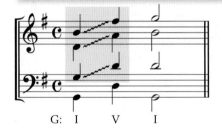

G: I   V   I

Also, when a harmony is repeated or sustained, the upper voices may leap freely between the different notes of the chord.

9.12

9.13 Artemis Johnson, "Wake O my soul"

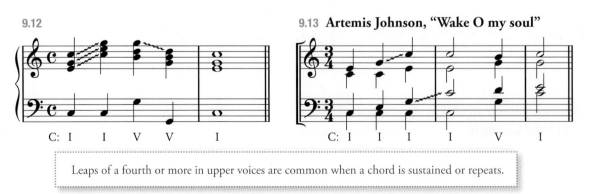

C: I   I   V   V   I   C: I   I   I   I   V   I

> Leaps of a fourth or more in upper voices are common when a chord is sustained or repeats.

HARMONIZATION

Certain melodic patterns may be harmonized with a I–V–I progression. Memorizing some of the more common of these patterns will be helpful in harmonizing melodies.

9.14

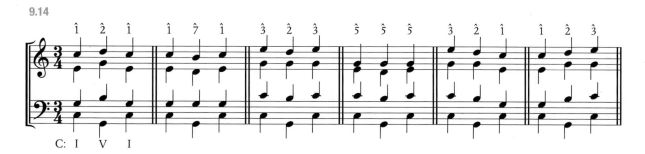

 To learn about weak-to-strong chord repetitions, see A Closer Look

POINTS FOR REVIEW

- The I triad establishes harmonic stability, and the V triad creates harmonic tension. V moving to I creates a sense of resolution.

- In four-part harmony, the root (bass) of root-position I and V triads typically is doubled.

- In I–V and V–I progressions, the upper voices usually move smoothly, with melodic intervals of a third or smaller.

- Do not double the leading tone.

- When the leading tone is in the soprano, it must resolve up by step when V progresses to I.

- In minor keys, $\hat{7}$ must be raised by a half step with an accidental in order to form a leading tone.

- Upper voices may leap freely when a chord repeats.

1. Spell the I and V chords in (a) E♭ major, (b) E major, and (c) E minor.

2. Compare the voice leading in each of the following pairs. Is the voice leading better in (a) or (b)? In (c) or (d)?

   a.   b.   c.   d.

C: I   V   I   I   V   I   A: I   V   I   I   V   I

3. In the excerpt below, complete the chords by filling in the missing notes.

F: I   V   I

4. The following V chords are each missing one accidental. Supply the correct accidentals.

   a.   b.   c.   d.   e.   f.

F♯ min.: V   C min.: V   C♯ min.: V   G♯ min.: V   F min.: V   D min.: V

5. Find the errors in the progressions below.

   a.   b.   c.   d.

G min.: i   V   i   E: I   V   I   A: I   V   I   D: I   V   I

10

The Dominant Seventh Chord: V⁷

V⁷ is a Dominant harmony whose instability is intensified by a dissonant chordal seventh.

V⁷ AND TENDENCY TONES

The root-position V⁷ (the **dominant seventh chord**) functions much like V (the dominant triad), except that V⁷ is less stable and thus resolves more emphatically to I.

10.1 Joseph Haydn, Divertimento, Hob. XVI:1, iii

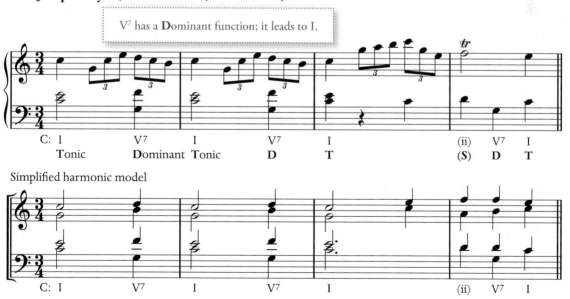

V⁷ has a **D**ominant function; it leads to I.

Simplified harmonic model

V^7 contains two tendency tones that pull in opposite directions: the chordal seventh and the leading tone. Do not confuse these two. The chordal seventh (the seventh of the *chord*) must resolve *down* by step when V^7 moves to I (even if it appears in an inner voice). The leading tone (the seventh degree of the *scale*) tends to resolve *up* by step (though it need not do so if it appears in an inner voice). These two tendency tones are separated by a dissonant diminished fifth or augmented fourth.

10.2

Within V^7, the leading tone (B = $\hat{7}$) pulls upward, the chordal seventh (F = $\hat{4}$) pulls downward.

The chordal seventh of V^7 must resolve down by step even in an inner voice . . .

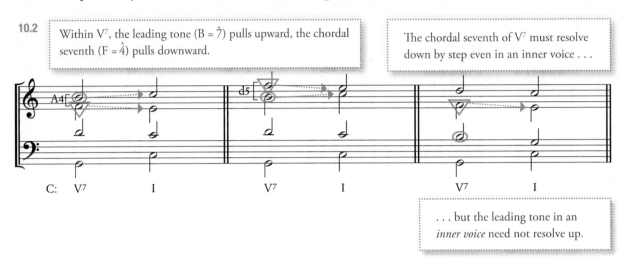

. . . but the leading tone in an *inner voice* need not resolve up.

10.3 Harry T. Burleigh, "My Lawd's a-writin' down time"

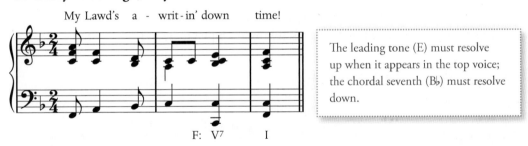

The leading tone (E) must resolve up when it appears in the top voice; the chordal seventh (B♭) must resolve down.

V^7 may also repeat before leading to I. In such a case, the chordal seventh resolves only when V^7 progresses to I.

10.4 Alice Nevin, "He Hides within the Lily"

The leading tone (F♯) does not need to resolve up when it appears in an inner voice, but the chordal seventh (C) must resolve down, even in an inner voice.

10.5 Maria Teresa Agnesi, Keyboard Sonata in E♭

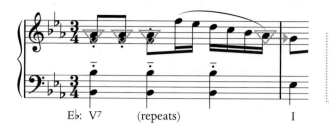

E♭: V⁷ (repeats) I

When two or more V⁷ chords appear in a row, the chordal seventh resolves when V⁷ moves to I.

10.6 Marie-Thérèse-Louise Benaut, Variations on Theme (by N. Dalayrac)

F: I V⁷ I V⁷——— I

Before resolving, the chordal seventh of V⁷ may switch voices while the V⁷ chord is sustained…

10.7 R. Nathaniel Dett, "Roll, Jordan, Roll"

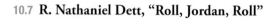

To hear Jor - dan roll.

E♭: I V⁷ V⁷ I

…or when the V⁷ chord repeats.

OMITTING THE FIFTH OF V⁷ OR I IN FOUR-PART HARMONY

In four-part harmony, you may omit the fifth of the chord of either V⁷ or I. Indeed, to avoid voice-leading errors, the fifth must be omitted from one of the chords of a V⁷–I progression when the leading tone appears in the top voice of V⁷.

10.8

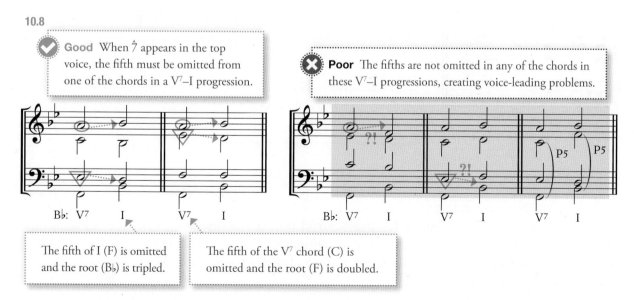

Good When $\hat{7}$ appears in the top voice, the fifth must be omitted from one of the chords in a V⁷–I progression.

Poor The fifths are not omitted in any of the chords in these V⁷–I progressions, creating voice-leading problems.

B♭: V⁷ I V⁷ I

B♭: V⁷ I V⁷ I V⁷ I

The fifth of I (F) is omitted and the root (B♭) is tripled.

The fifth of the V⁷ chord (C) is omitted and the root (F) is doubled.

When the fifth is omitted from V^7, you should double the root of the chord (you may *not* double the leading tone or chordal seventh). When the fifth is omitted from I, you should *triple* the root of the chord.

10.9 Johannes Brahms, "Marias Wallfahrt" ("Mary's Pilgrimage")

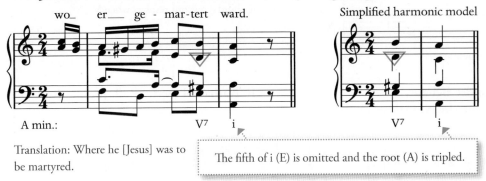

Translation: Where he [Jesus] was to be martyred.

The fifth of i (E) is omitted and the root (A) is tripled.

10.10 Ann S. Mounsey, "Greenland"

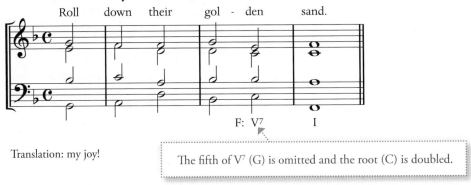

Translation: my joy!

The fifth of V^7 (G) is omitted and the root (C) is doubled.

Although you may omit the fifth of a chord, you should not omit the third, since this creates a hollow-sounding sonority.

10.11

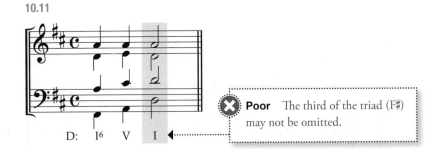

Poor The third of the triad (F♯) may not be omitted.

V TO V^7 (V^{8-7})

If V^7 were to move to V, the chordal dissonance would not resolve; thus a V^7–V progression should be avoided. On the other hand, moving from V to V^7 increases the urgency of the dominant's need to resolve to the tonic. For this reason, the V–V^7 progression is extremely common.

10.12

F: V V⁷ I   V V⁷ I

F: (V⁷ V) I

✓ **Good** V–V⁷ is very common.

✗ **Poor** The seventh of V⁷ does not resolve, thus V⁷–V should be avoided.

10.13 Abby Hutchinson, "Don't stay away"

Don't stay a - way, un - til the judg-ment day.

A: I   V   V⁷   I

V moves to V⁷, then resolves to I.

The succession V–V⁷ is usually labeled simply as a V$^{8-7}$. V$^{8-7}$–I almost always results from a V–I progression decorated by an embellishing tone in an upper voice.

10.14 J. M. Nunes Garcia, Memento II, Kyrie

10.15 Emma Ashford, "Evelyn"

G min.: i   V⁸ – ⁷   i

A: V⁸—⁷   I

In each of these progressions, V$^{8-7}$–I results when a V–I progression is decorated by an embellishing tone. (V$^{8-7}$ means the same thing as V–V⁷.)

In figured bass, the figures $^{8-7}$ underneath a single bass note designate a root-position triad followed by a root-position seventh chord. An accidental sign below the figures $^{8-7}$ applies to the third above the bass.

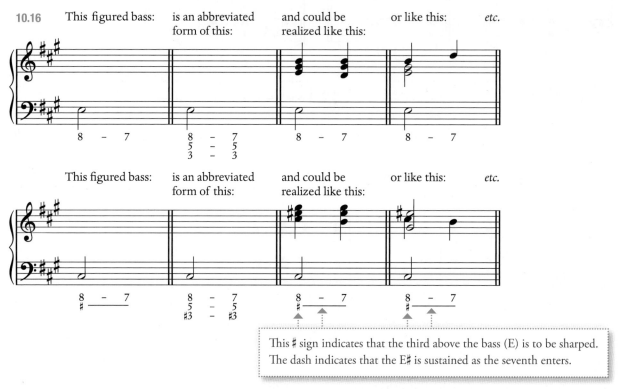

10.16 This figured bass: is an abbreviated form of this: and could be realized like this: or like this: *etc.*

8 – 7
8 5 3 – 7 5 3

This figured bass: is an abbreviated form of this: and could be realized like this: or like this: *etc.*

8 – 7
♯
8 5 ♯3 – 7 5 ♯3

> This ♯ sign indicates that the third above the bass (E) is to be sharped. The dash indicates that the E♯ is sustained as the seventh enters.

V⁷ AT CADENCES

Much like V–I, either V⁷–I or V⁸⁻⁷–I may appear at a perfect authentic cadence (PAC) or an imperfect authentic cadence (IAC). The instability of V⁷ makes it less well suited to serve as a resting point at a *half cadence* (HC), however. Accordingly, in basic four-part harmony a half cadence should arrive on V, *not* on V⁷.

10.17 Gioachino Rossini, *William Tell* Overture

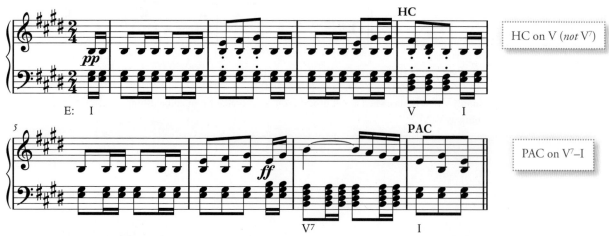

HC on V (*not* V⁷)

E: I   V   I

PAC on V⁷–I

V⁷   I

HARMONIZATION

Certain standard melodic patterns may be harmonized with a I–V⁷–I progression.

10.18

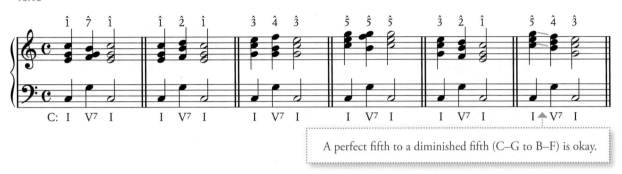

A perfect fifth to a diminished fifth (C–G to B–F) is okay.

For more on chordal sevenths, see A Closer Look.

POINTS FOR REVIEW

- V⁷ functions like V—both chords function as Dominants and lead to I.

- The chordal seventh within V⁷ must resolve down by step when V⁷ moves to I, even if the chordal seventh appears in an inner voice.

- The leading tone tends to resolve up by step, but need not do so if it appears in an inner voice.

- When V⁷ resolves to I, you may omit the fifth and double the root of V⁷, or you may omit the fifth and triple the root of I. Do not omit the third of a chord.

- V may not follow V⁷, but V⁷ may follow V.

- The progression V–V⁷ is labeled V⁸⁻⁷.

- V⁷ often comes before I in an authentic cadence (AC), but avoid V⁷ at a half cadence (HC).

1. Spell V⁷ **a.** in the key of G; **b.** in E; **c.** in E♭; **d.** in D♭.

2. Identify the minor key for each key signature. For each seventh chord, what accidental is needed to make it a V⁷?

3. In the excerpts below, some chords are missing one or two notes. What are the missing notes? Complete excerpts (a) and (b) in different ways, and also complete (c) and (d) in different ways.

4. Identify the chords below with Roman numerals, in two different ways.

5. Some of the following I–V⁷–I progressions contain voice-leading errors. Identify the key of each. Then identify any errors (such as faulty parallel fifths or octaves or incorrectly omitted tones).

I^6 and V^6 can be used in place of root-position chords in the middle of a phrase.

I^6	V^6
Harmonic progression	Harmonic progression
I^6 in four-part harmony	V^6 in four-part harmony

Using I^6 and V^6 in place of root-position I and V chords allows for more variety in the bass line. I^6 and V^6 can appear anywhere except at the very end of a phrase.

I^6

HARMONIC PROGRESSION

The I^6 chord—a first-inversion tonic triad—functions like I in root position. It is somewhat less stable, however, because its bass is $\hat{3}$ rather than $\hat{1}$. I^6 appears toward the beginning or middle of a phrase, rather than at its end; it allows for an active bass line by extending, alternating with, or substituting for I (tonic triad in root position).

11.1

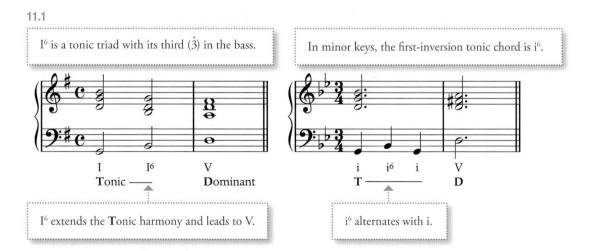

I^6 is a tonic triad with its third ($\hat{3}$) in the bass.

In minor keys, the first-inversion tonic chord is i^6.

I I^6 V
Tonic ——   Dominant

i i^6 i   V
T ——   D

I^6 extends the **T**onic harmony and leads to V.

i^6 alternates with i.

11.2 Lady Sempill, "Capt. Bosvill's March"

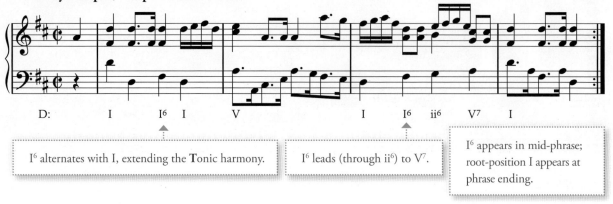

D: I   I⁶ I   V   I   I⁶   ii⁶   V⁷   I

I⁶ alternates with I, extending the **T**onic harmony.

I⁶ leads (through ii⁶) to V⁷.

I⁶ appears in mid-phrase; root-position I appears at phrase ending.

Like I, I⁶ may be followed by any harmony. In particular, I⁶ frequently leads to V (in root position) in a half or an authentic cadence. However, I—*not* I⁶—must serve as the final harmony of an authentic cadence.

11.3 Ludwig van Beethoven, Symphony No. 2, ii

The final chord of the cadence is root-position I, *not* I⁶.

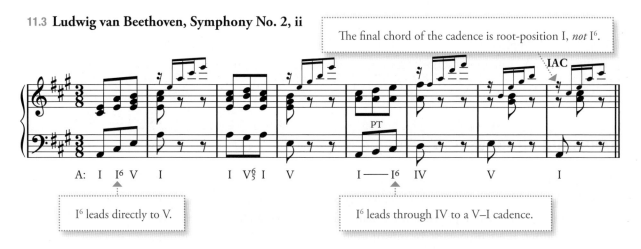

A: I   I⁶ V   I   I   V⁶₅ I   V   I ——— I⁶   IV   V   I

I⁶ leads directly to V.

I⁶ leads through IV to a V–I cadence.

Sometimes a perfect authentic cadence (PAC) is surprisingly averted when the expected appearance of I toward the end of a phrase is replaced with I⁶. This creates what is known as an **evaded cadence**, which often also involves a sudden shift or break in the melody.

11.4 Isabella Colbran, Cavatina

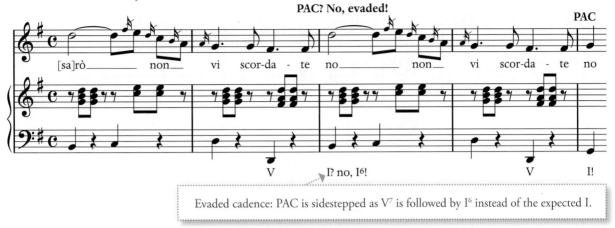

[sa]rò_____ non___ vi scor-da-te no_____ non_____ vi scor-da-te no

Evaded cadence: PAC is sidestepped as V⁷ is followed by I⁶ instead of the expected I.

Translation: I will not forget, no!

I⁶ IN FOUR-PART HARMONY

In four-part harmony, you may double any note of I⁶: root, third, or fifth.

11.5 John Gauntlet, "Ascalon"   **11.6 "The Lord shall come" (hymn)**

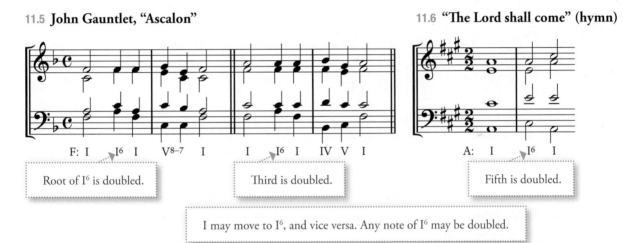

Root of I⁶ is doubled.   Third is doubled.   Fifth is doubled.

I may move to I⁶, and vice versa. Any note of I⁶ may be doubled.

11.7 C. P. E. Bach, "Bald oder spät"   **11.8 J. M. Nunes Garcia, "Regina"**

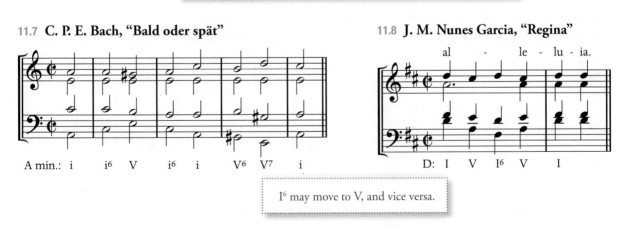

I⁶ may move to V, and vice versa.

When using I⁶ in four-part harmony, be careful to avoid **parallel octaves**, which are far more likely to arise than when dealing with root-position I.

11.9

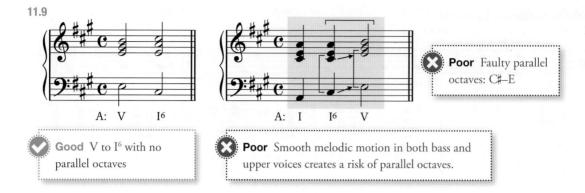

A: V   I⁶

✅ **Good** V to I⁶ with no parallel octaves

❌ **Poor** Smooth melodic motion in both bass and upper voices creates a risk of parallel octaves.

A: I   I⁶   V

❌ **Poor** Faulty parallel octaves: C♯–E

I⁶ may also lead to V⁷. A V⁷–I⁶ progression is problematic, however, since it can create faulty similar octaves. V⁷ more normally leads to I, not to I⁶.

11.10

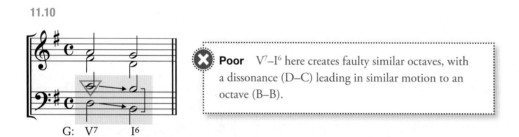

G: V⁷   I⁶

❌ **Poor** V⁷–I⁶ here creates faulty similar octaves, with a dissonance (D–C) leading in similar motion to an octave (B–B).

V⁶

HARMONIC PROGRESSION

V⁶ is a dominant triad in first inversion; the leading tone is in the bass. V⁶ functions as a **D**ominant (like V). In moving to I, there is usually stepwise motion in the bass and smooth motion in the upper voices.

11.11 Samuel Webbe, "Corinth"

11.12 Anna Bon, Trio in D Minor, Op. 3, No. 3, iii

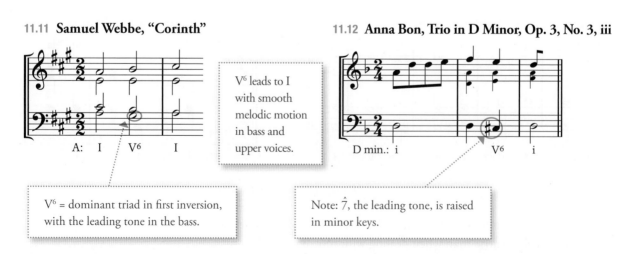

A: I   V⁶   I

V⁶ leads to I with smooth melodic motion in bass and upper voices.

D min.: i   V⁶   i

V⁶ = dominant triad in first inversion, with the leading tone in the bass.

Note: $\hat{7}$, the leading tone, is raised in minor keys.

Since a leading tone in an outer voice should resolve to the tonic, V^6 does not typically progress to I^6. On the other hand, a I^6–V^6 progression is common, providing that the bass leaps *down*.

11.13

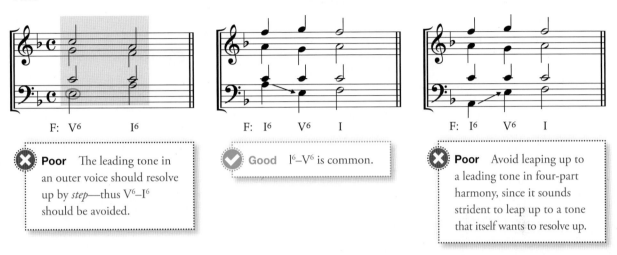

F: V^6 I^6

❌ **Poor** The leading tone in an outer voice should resolve up by *step*—thus V^6–I^6 should be avoided.

F: I^6 V^6 I

✓ **Good** I^6–V^6 is common.

F: I^6 V^6 I

❌ **Poor** Avoid leaping up to a leading tone in four-part harmony, since it sounds strident to leap up to a tone that itself wants to resolve up.

11.14 Hélène de Montgeroult, Piano Sonata, Op. 2, No. 3, iii

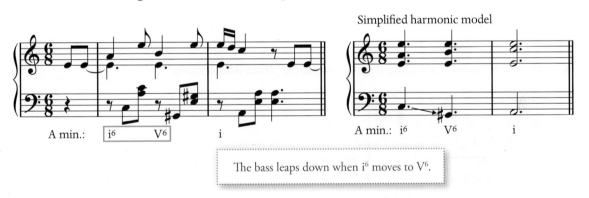

Simplified harmonic model

A min.: i^6 V^6 i A min.: i^6 V^6 i

The bass leaps down when i^6 moves to V^6.

V^6 also frequently alternates with other V chords; it is particularly common for V^6 to be followed by V or V^7, or for V to be followed by V^6. However, V^6 should not follow V^7, since the chordal dissonance within V^7 would not resolve properly.

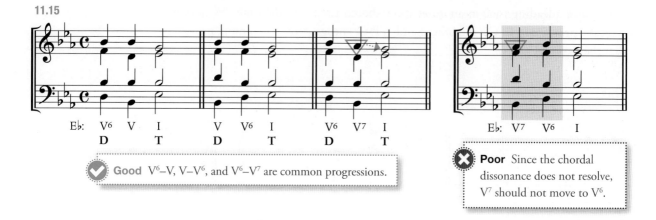

Good V⁶–V, V–V⁶, and V⁶–V⁷ are common progressions.

Poor Since the chordal dissonance does not resolve, V⁷ should not move to V⁶.

11.16 Bianca Maria Meda, "Cari musici"

11.17 Justin Holland, "Bouquet of Melodies"

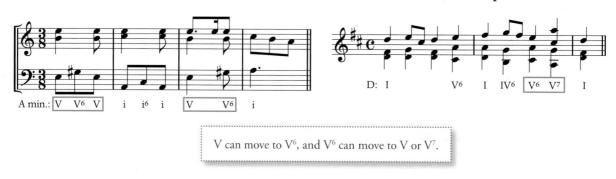

V can move to V⁶, and V⁶ can move to V or V⁷.

11.18 Karl Heinrich Graun, "Somiglia il buon monarca," from *Montezuma*

V⁶ moves to V⁷ (but not vice versa).

Like I⁶, V⁶ typically appears at the beginning or middle of a phrase. V⁶ should not be the final chord of a half cadence (HC) or the dominant chord in a perfect authentic cadence (PAC). At a cadence, the dominant chord must be in root position.

11.19 G. F. Handel, Violin Sonata in E, HWV 373, iii

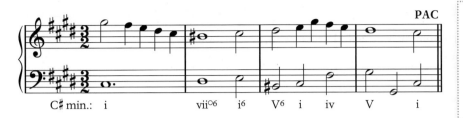

C♯ min.: i   vii°⁶ i⁶ V⁶ i iv V i

> The tonic and dominant chords at the cadence should be in root position, *not* in inversion; i⁶ and V⁶ chords appear in the middle of the phrase.

V⁶ IN FOUR-PART HARMONY

In four-part harmony, you may double any note of V⁶ *except* the bass—the third of the chord, which is the leading tone within the key. When moving between I and V⁶, the upper voices usually stay on the same notes or move smoothly by step or third.

11.20

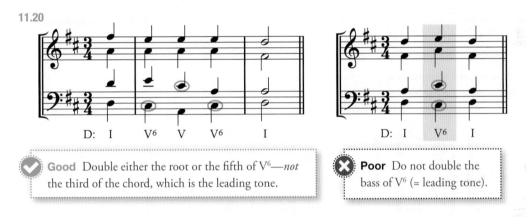

D: I V⁶ V V⁶ I

D: I V⁶ I

> ✓ **Good** Double either the root or the fifth of V⁶—*not* the third of the chord, which is the leading tone.

> ✗ **Poor** Do not double the bass of V⁶ (= leading tone).

Various standard melodic patterns may be harmonized I–V⁶–I.

11.21

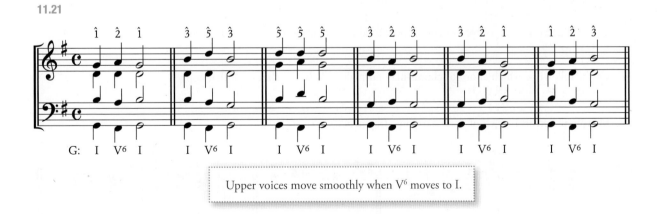

G: I V⁶ I   I V⁶ I   I V⁶ I   I V⁶ I   I V⁶ I   I V⁶ I

> Upper voices move smoothly when V⁶ moves to I.

- **I⁶ (the tonic chord in first inversion) may extend, alternate with, or substitute for I (the root-position tonic chord).**
  - Phrases that end with an authentic cadence should end with I, *not* I⁶.
  - Any tone of I⁶ may be doubled.
- **V⁶ may extend, alternate with, or substitute for V (the root-position dominant chord).**
  - V⁶ often leads directly to I, with smooth motion in all voices.
  - V⁶ may move to V or V⁷, but V⁶ may not follow V⁷.
  - Any tone of V⁶ may be doubled except the bass (the third of the chord, which is the leading tone).
  - Use V—*not* V⁶—in a cadence.

TEST YOURSELF

1. In each of the following, the soprano is missing from the second chord. What note(s) could be used to complete the chord?

G min.: i   i⁶   A: I   V⁶   F: V   V⁶

2. Of the following, which chord or chords may follow I⁶ (choose all that apply): I, V, V⁶, or V⁷?

3. Of the following, which chord or chords may follow V⁶ (choose all that apply): I, I⁶, V, or V⁷?

4. Of the following, which chord or chords may normally follow V⁷ (choose all that apply): I, I⁶, V, or V⁶?

5. Identify the errors in each of these harmonic fragments.

D min.: i V⁶ i   E: I⁶ V⁶ I   F♯ min.: i i⁶ V i   B♭: I V⁷ V⁶ I   G: I V⁶ I⁶

12

$$V^6_5 \text{ and } V^4_2$$

V^6_5 **and** V^4_2 **are inversions of** V^7 **that embellish Tonic harmony:** V^6_5 **leads to I,** V^4_2 **leads to** I^6.

Harmonic Progressions

V^6_5 and V^4_2 as Embellishing Harmonies

Voice Leading in Four-Part Harmony

Figured Bass

Like inversions of I and V triads, inversions of V^7 add variety to the bass line. V^6_5 and V^4_2 are particularly potent inversions of V^7, since they each feature a tendency tone in the bass.

HARMONIC PROGRESSIONS

V^6_5 and V^4_2 are the first and third inversions of V^6_5, respectively.

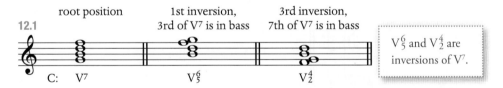

12.1

root position   1st inversion,   3rd inversion,
    3rd of V^7 is in bass   7th of V^7 is in bass

C: V^7 V^6_5 V^4_2

V^6_5 and V^4_2 are inversions of V^7.

Like other **D**ominant harmonies, V^6_5 and V^4_2 lead toward the tonic chord. Since the leading tone is in the bass of V^6_5 and must resolve *up by step*, V^6_5 resolves to I in root position (I), *not* first inversion (I^6). Similarly, since the chordal seventh in the bass of V^4_2 must resolve *down by step*, V^4_2 resolves to I^6, *not* to I in root position.

12.2 Maria Theresia von Paradis, "Die Tanne"

V_5^6 and V_2^4 are **D**ominant harmonies that lead to **T**onic (I or I⁶) with stepwise motion in the bass.

die Tan - ne gläntzt so schön

G: V V₂⁴ I⁶ V₅⁶ I V

V_2^4 leads to I⁶, as the chordal seventh in the bass resolves down.

V_5^6 leads to I, as the leading tone in the bass resolves up by step.

G: V V₂⁴ I⁶ V₅⁶ I V

G: V V₂⁴ I (?!) V₅⁶ I⁶ (?!) V

❌ **Poor** V_2^4 may not move to I.

❌ **Poor** V_5^6 may not move to I⁶.

V_5^6 may follow any of the harmonies discussed in the previous chapters (I, I⁶, V, V⁷, and V⁶).

12.3 Ludwig van Beethoven, Symphony No. 9, iii

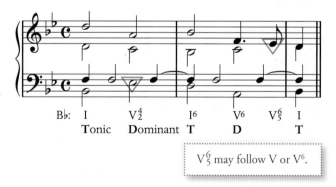

B♭: I V₂⁴ I⁶ V⁶ V₅⁶ I

Tonic Dominant T D T

V_5^6 may follow V or V⁶.

V_5^6 also may lead to V⁷ in root position or in inversion. V_5^6 may not be directly followed by V or V⁶, however, since if it did its chordal seventh would not be able to resolve down by step.

12.4 Lizzie Tourjée, "Wellesley" (hymn)   **12.5**

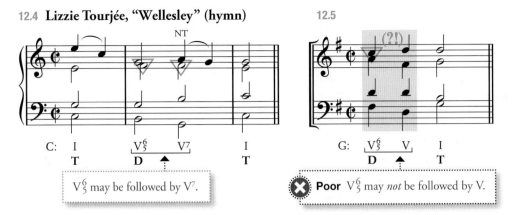

C: I   V⁶₅   V⁷   I
      T   D ▲   T

> V⁶₅ may be followed by V⁷.

> ❌ **Poor** V⁶₅ may *not* be followed by V.

V⁴₂, too, may follow any of the harmonies discussed in the previous chapters. It is especially common for V⁴₂ to follow root-position V. However, V⁴₂ should not *precede* a root-position V. The chordal seventh in the bass is so prominent that V⁴₂ should resolve directly to I⁶.

12.6 Helen Hopekirk, "My Brown-Haired Maiden"   **12.7 Ann S. Mounsey, "Kyrie Eleison"**

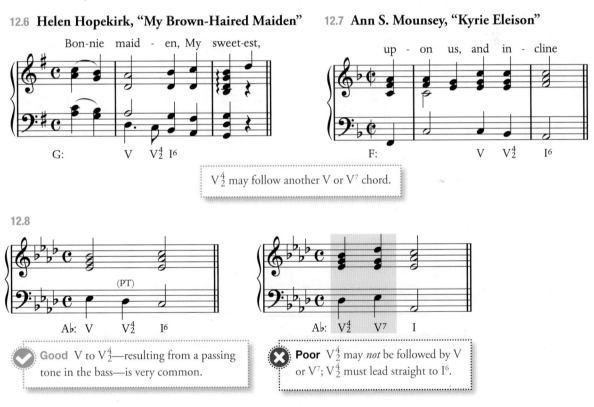

G: V   V⁴₂ I⁶   F: V   V⁴₂ I⁶

> V⁴₂ may follow another V or V⁷ chord.

12.8

A♭:   V   V⁴₂ I⁶   A♭: V⁴₂ V⁷   I

> ✔ **Good** V to V⁴₂—resulting from a passing tone in the bass—is very common.

> ❌ **Poor** V⁴₂ may *not* be followed by V or V⁷; V⁴₂ must lead straight to I⁶.

V⁶₅ AND V⁴₂ AS EMBELLISHING HARMONIES

The bass motions involving V⁶₅–I and V⁴₂–I⁶ often resemble neighbor-tone or incomplete neighbor-tone motions. This is because V⁶₅ and V⁴₂ are relatively unstable tonally and their basses resolve by step to notes of the tonic triad. Thus, much as neighbor or incomplete neighbor tones embellish a given note, so V⁶₅ and V⁴₂ may be regarded as embellishing a **T**onic harmony.

12.9

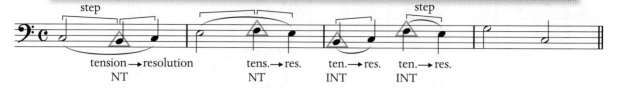

These neighbor and incomplete neighbor tones embellish the notes C and E, to which they resolve by step.

Similarly, these V$^6_5$ and V$^4_2$ chords embellish the I and I^6 chords, to which they resolve by step in the bass.

12.10 Ignatius Sancho, Minuet No. 13   12.11 Marie-Elizabeth Cléry, Harp Sonata Op. 1, No. 1, ii

Often, V$^6_5$–I and V$^4_2$–I^6 progressions appear in direct succession, creating a **voice exchange** in which the bass moves $\hat{1}$–$\hat{2}$–$\hat{3}$ while at the same time an upper voice moves $\hat{3}$–$\hat{2}$–$\hat{1}$.

12.12 Franz Benda, Flute Sonata in A Minor

Voice exchanges between bass and melody (with D–C and G♯–A alternating in outer voices) as V$^6_5$–I and V$^4_2$–I^6 embellish **T**onic harmony.

Like other inversions of V, V$^6_5$ and V$^4_2$ may be used anywhere within the phrase except for the cadence, where V or I is required. Indeed, since a cadence must involve root-position V or V–I, inversions earlier within the phrase are extremely helpful in promoting variety and providing an interesting bass line.

Good Embellishing harmonies appear at the beginning and middle of the phrase; V and I in root position appear at the cadence.

Poor Root-position V–I motions are overused in the first parts of the phrase; inverted chords appear at the cadence.

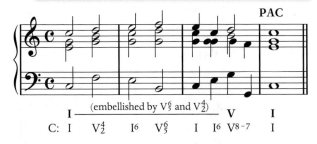

VOICE LEADING IN FOUR-PART HARMONY

In four-part harmony the upper voices typically move smoothly within V^6_5–I and V^4_2–I^6 progressions, with the chordal seventh resolving down by step and the leading tone resolving up by step. Usually none of the notes (not even the chordal fifth) of V^6_5 or V^4_2 is omitted in four-part harmony, and thus usually none of the notes in the chord is doubled.

12.14

Upper voices usually move by step or common tone in V^6_5–I and V^4_2–I^6 progressions.

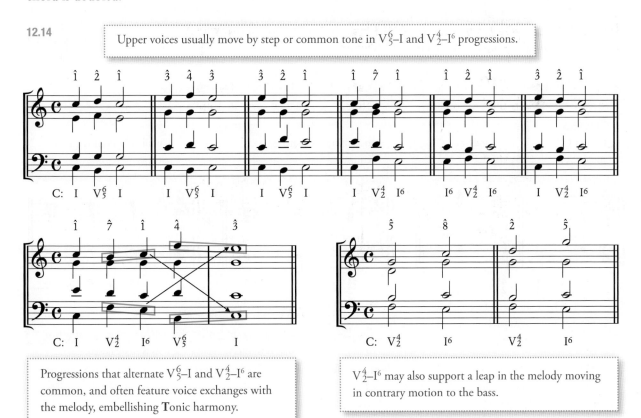

Progressions that alternate V^6_5–I and V^4_2–I^6 are common, and often feature voice exchanges with the melody, embellishing **T**onic harmony.

V^4_2–I^6 may also support a leap in the melody moving in contrary motion to the bass.

FIGURED BASS

In figured bass, V^6_5 is indicated either with the numbers $^6_3$ or (more commonly) $^6_5$ placed below the leading tone in the bass. Note that the fifth above the bass in this case is diminished, not perfect. However, as always, you should assume that a note needs no accidental unless an accidental is expressly indicated by the figures.

12.15

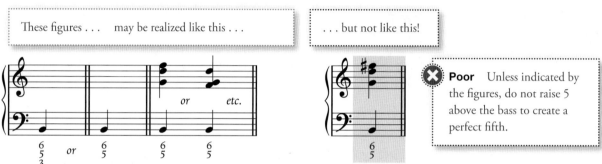

> **Poor** Unless indicated by the figures, do not raise 5 above the bass to create a perfect fifth.

V^4_2 in figured bass is indicated either with the figures $^6_4$ or (more commonly) $^4_2$ placed below $\hat{4}$ in the bass. The fourth above the bass of V^4_2 is a leading tone and thus must be raised in minor keys. In figured bass, this raising of the fourth above the bass is indicated by placing a sharp or natural next to the number 4, or shown with a diagonal slash through or plus sign attached to the number 4.

12.16

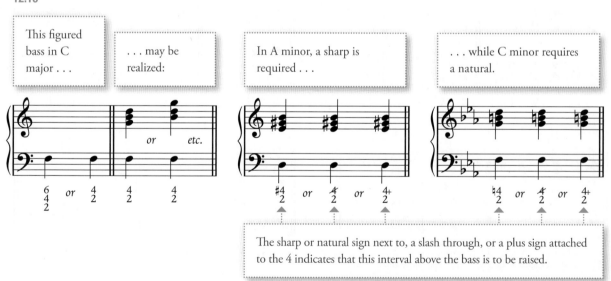

The sharp or natural sign next to, a slash through, or a plus sign attached to the 4 indicates that this interval above the bass is to be raised.

- V^6_5 and V^4_2 are inversions of V^7; they are Dominant harmonies.

- V^6_5 resolves to I; V^4_2 resolves to I^6.

- V^6_5 may follow another Dominant harmony. V^6_5 may also be followed directly by V^7 or an inversion of V^7, but it may *not* be followed by V or V^6.

- V^4_2 may follow another Dominant harmony. V^4_2 may *not* be followed by another V or V^7, however, but rather must resolve directly to I^6.

- Do not use V^6_5 or V^4_2 at cadences.

TEST YOURSELF

1. In the example below:
   a. Label the chord with a Roman numeral in the key indicated.
   b. Which of the following **T**onic harmonies could *follow* this chord: I or I^6? Which of the following **D**ominant harmonies could *follow* this chord (choose all that apply): V, V^6, V^7, or V^4_2?
   c. Which of the following harmonies could *precede* the chord (choose all that apply): I, I^6, V, V^7, or V^4_2?

   E♭:

2. In the example below:
   a. Label the chord with a Roman numeral in the key indicated.
   b. Which of the following harmonies could *follow* this chord (choose all that apply): i, i^6, V, V^6, or V^7?
   c. Which of the following harmonies could *precede* the chord (choose all that apply): i, i^6, V, V^7, or V^6_5?

   E min.:

3. Below is a melodic phrase in D major.

   a. Which of the notes with an asterisk could be harmonized with V$^6_5$? Which of the notes with an asterisk could be harmonized with V$^4_2$? (Hint: the chord chosen should not create a poor doubling.)

   b. What harmonies should you use in measure 4?

   c. In which measure could you place a voice exchange between the bass and melody?

4. What notes are in the following chords, as indicated by the figured basses?

5. Identify the errors in the following.

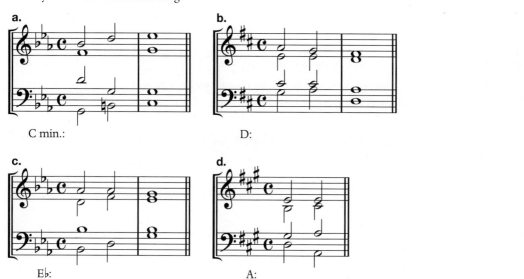

13

V_3^4 and vii$^{\circ 6}$

V_3^4 and vii$^{\circ 6}$ are **Dominant** harmonies that embellish the tonic, usually with passing or neighbor motion in the bass leading to I or I^6.

<table>
<tr><td>

Harmonic Progressions

V_3^4 and vii$^{\circ 6}$ as passing chords between I and I^6

V_3^4 and vii$^{\circ 6}$ as neighbor chords to I

Alternating with Other Dominant-to-Tonic Progressions

Moving from V_3^4 or vii$^{\circ 6}$ to other **Dominant** harmonies

</td><td>

Voice-Leading in Four-Part Harmony

V_3^4 or vii$^{\circ 6}$ to I

Harmonizing $\hat{3}$–$\hat{4}$–$\hat{5}$: special exceptions involving V_3^4 or vii$^{\circ 6}$

Figured Bass

A Closer Look

Tonic as an embellishing chord

Contrapuntal cadences

</td></tr>
</table>

V_3^4 is the second inversion of V^7; vii$^{\circ 6}$ is a first-inversion diminished triad whose root is the leading tone. V_3^4 and vii$^{\circ 6}$ are extremely similar, since they share the same bass ($\hat{2}$) and most of the same tones ($\hat{7}$, $\hat{2}$, and $\hat{4}$ are in both).

13.1

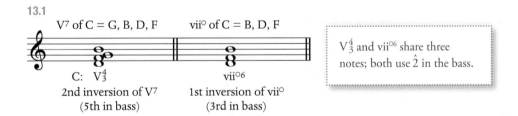

V^7 of C = G, B, D, F vii$^{\circ}$ of C = B, D, F

C: V_3^4 vii$^{\circ 6}$

2nd inversion of V^7 1st inversion of vii$^{\circ}$
(5th in bass) (3rd in bass)

> V_3^4 and vii$^{\circ 6}$ share three notes; both use $\hat{2}$ in the bass.

HARMONIC PROGRESSIONS

In addition to sharing notes, V_3^4 and vii$^{\circ 6}$ function similarly as well. They both are **Dominant** chords, leading to I or I^6 with stepwise motion in the bass. Because they often lead to a tonic chord with smooth motion in all voices, V_3^4 and vii$^{\circ 6}$ tend to embellish the tonic harmony, and thus they usually do not appear at cadences.

V$_3^4$ AND vii^{o6} AS PASSING CHORDS BETWEEN I AND I^6

V$_3^4$ and vii^{o6} often lead between I and I^6 with **passing motion** in the bass.

13.2

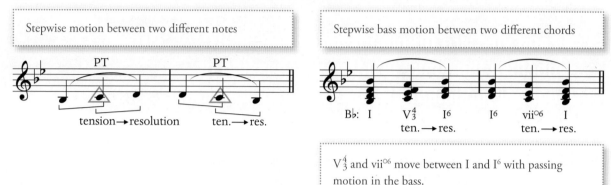

V$_3^4$ and vii^{o6} move between I and I^6 with passing motion in the bass.

13.3 J. S. Bach, Chorale 269

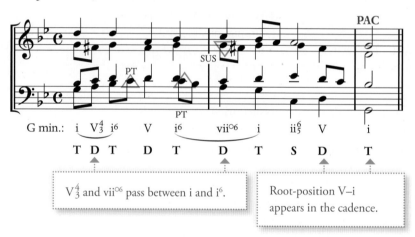

V$_3^4$ and vii^{o6} pass between i and i^6.

Root-position V–i appears in the cadence.

13.4 Joseph Haydn, Menuet, Hob. XI:11/2

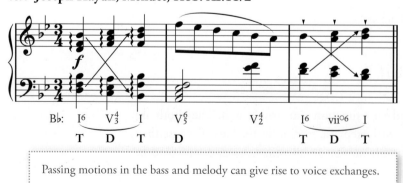

Passing motions in the bass and melody can give rise to voice exchanges.

V$_3^4$ AND vii°⁶ AS NEIGHBOR CHORDS TO I

V$_3^4$ or vii°⁶ may also appear between two I chords with **neighbor motion** in the bass.

13.5

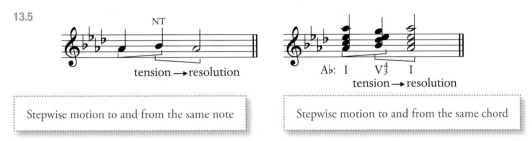

Stepwise motion to and from the same note

Stepwise motion to and from the same chord

13.6 J. M. Nunes Garcia, *Matinas e encomendação de defuntos*

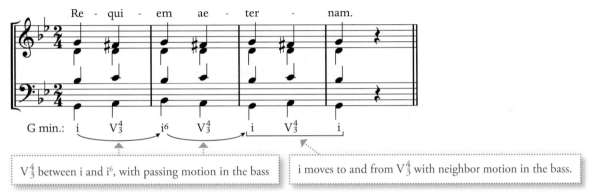

V$_3^4$ between i and i⁶, with passing motion in the bass

i moves to and from V$_3^4$ with neighbor motion in the bass.

Translation: Eternal rest.

ALTERNATING WITH OTHER DOMINANT-TO-TONIC PROGRESSIONS

V$_3^4$ or vii°⁶–I progressions frequently alternate with other progressions that use inverted V chords (such as V$_5^6$–I or V$_2^4$–I⁶). In many cases this gives rise to voice exchanges that involve pairs of notes in the outer voices and that embellish tonic harmony.

13.7 Ludwig van Beethoven, Piano Sonata in G, Op. 14, No. 2, ii

13.8 Theophania Cecil, "St. Katherine's"

Voice exchange between $\hat{7}$–$\hat{1}$ and $\hat{2}$–$\hat{3}$

Voice exchange between $\hat{7}$–$\hat{1}$ and $\hat{2}$–$\hat{3}$

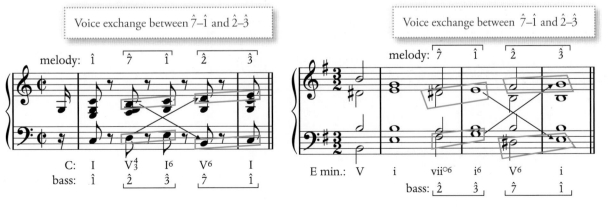

13.9 Louise Reichardt, "Das Veilchen" ("The Violet")

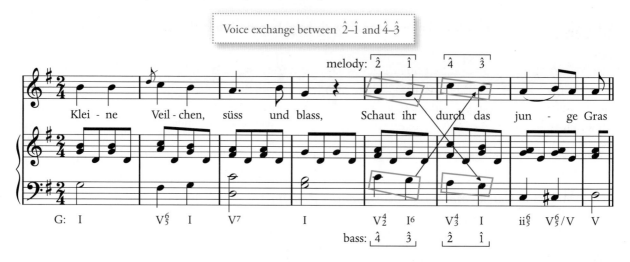

MOVING FROM V$^4_3$ AND vii°⁶ TO OTHER DOMINANT HARMONIES

At times V$^4_3$ moves to V⁷ in root position or to another inversion of V⁷ before resolving to I or I⁶.

13.10 Emilie Zumsteeg, "Der Geburtstag"

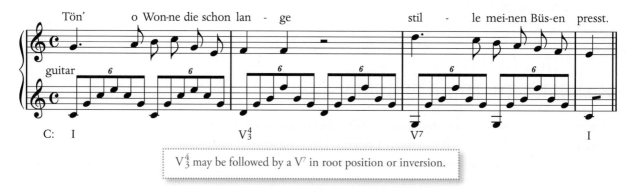

VOICE LEADING IN FOUR-PART HARMONY

V$\frac{4}{3}$ AND vii^{o6} TO I

The root of the vii^{o6} triad is the leading tone and may not be doubled; instead, double the third or fifth. In four-part harmony, V$\frac{4}{3}$ should use four different pitches, with none of its notes doubled. When V$\frac{4}{3}$ or vii^{o6} resolves to I or I^6, all of the notes usually either move by step or repeat from one chord to the next.

13.11

> All notes usually move smoothly when V$\frac{4}{3}$ or vii^{o6} moves to I or I^6. Do not double the root (= leading tone) of vii^{o6}.

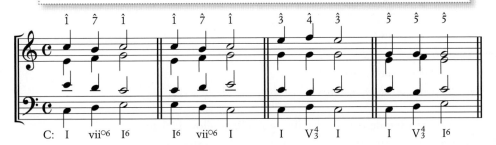

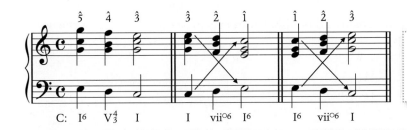

> Augmented fourth to perfect fourth (F–B to G–C) is okay between upper voices when vii^{o6} moves to I or I^6.

> These harmonies can be used with passing motion in the top voice, either with the bass moving in parallel motion with the top voice . . .

> . . . or with the bass moving in contrary motion so as to form a voice exchange with the top voice.

HARMONIZING 3̂–4̂–5̂: SPECIAL EXCEPTIONS INVOLVING V$_3^4$ OR vii$^{\circ6}$

The melodic pattern 3̂–4̂–5̂ can be difficult to harmonize without creating voice-leading problems.

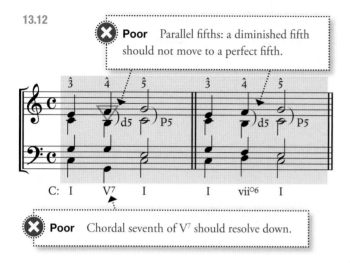

13.12

❌ **Poor** Parallel fifths: a diminished fifth should not move to a perfect fifth.

C: I V^7 I I vii$^{\circ6}$ I

❌ **Poor** Chordal seventh of V^7 should resolve down.

However, special exceptions to standard voice-leading guidelines allow you to harmonize the melodic pattern 3̂–4̂–5̂ with either I–V$_3^4$–I^6 or I–vii$^{\circ6}$–I^6. In these situations, the bass moves in parallel tenths (compound thirds) with the top voice. One of the special exceptions is that in these progressions a diminished fifth may move to a perfect fifth when V$_3^4$ or vii$^{\circ6}$ moves to I^6.

13.13

✅ **Good** Although moving from a perfect to a diminished fifth is always okay (because a perfect interval is not *approached* in parallel motion) . . .

❌ **Poor** . . . moving from a diminished to a perfect fifth is normally *not* okay (because here the P5 *is* approached in parallel motion) . . .

✅ **Good** . . . but d5 to P5 is fine when V$_3^4$ or vii$^{\circ6}$ moves to I^6.

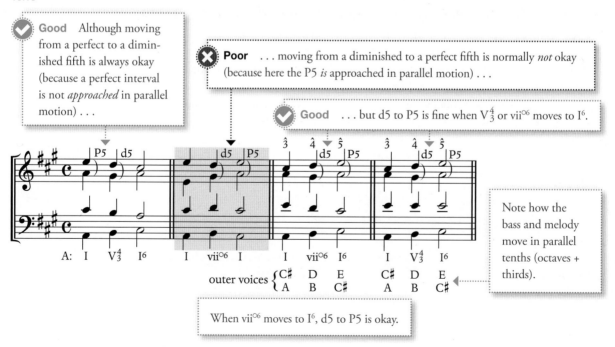

A: I V$_3^4$ I^6 I vii$^{\circ6}$ I   I vii$^{\circ6}$ I^6 I V$_3^4$ I^6

outer voices { C♯ D E   C♯ D E
              A B C♯   A B C♯

Note how the bass and melody move in parallel tenths (octaves + thirds).

When vii$^{\circ6}$ moves to I^6, d5 to P5 is okay.

13.14 **J. S. Bach, Chorale 26**

F: I   I vii°6 I6   I

$\hat{3}$–$\hat{4}$–$\hat{5}$ harmonized with I–vii°6–I6, creating parallel tenths between outer voices.

13.15 **Frederick J. Work, "Plenty Good Room"**

There's plen-ty good room,＿ There's plent-y good room,

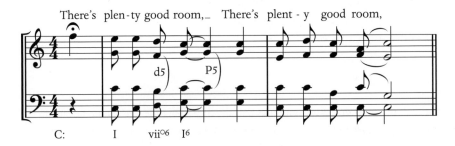

C: I vii°6 I6

Likewise, although normally the chordal seventh of V^7 must resolve down, a special exception arises when V_3^4 moves to I^6. In such a case, the chordal seventh of V_3^4 may move up by step, in parallel motion with the bass.

13.16   **13.17** **R. Nathaniel Dett, "If you love God, serve him"**

Good Chordal seventh of V^7 need not resolve down when V_3^4 moves to I^6.

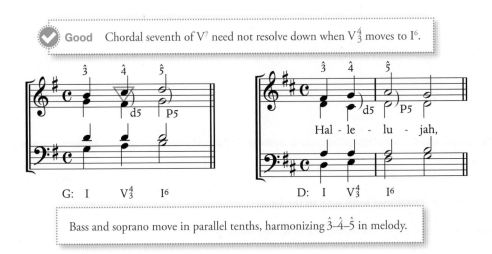

G: I V_3^4 I6   D: I V_3^4 I6

Bass and soprano move in parallel tenths, harmonizing $\hat{3}$–$\hat{4}$–$\hat{5}$ in melody.

13.18 Corona Schröter, "Der Brautschmuck"

Translation: If my beloved would love me, and be faithful and gentle.

FIGURED BASS

In figured bass, V^4_3 is indicated with either $^6_4$ or $^4_3$ below $\hat{2}$; vii°6 is indicated with either $^6_3$ or ^{6}. In minor keys, the sixth above the bass is the leading tone, and thus must be raised. This is indicated either as ♯6 or ♮6, or else by 6̸.

13.19

> The sharp or natural next to (or slash through) the figure ^{6} indicates that the sixth above the bass should be raised.

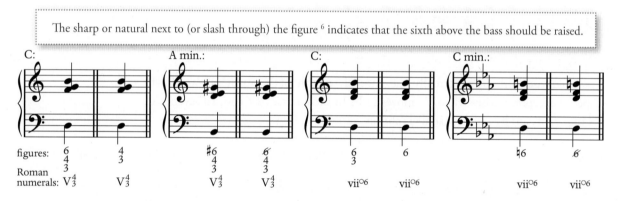

To learn about the tonic as an embellishing chord and about contrapuntal cadences, see A Closer Look.

POINTS FOR REVIEW

- V^4_3 and vii°6 are both Dominant harmonies built on $\hat{2}$ in the bass.

- V^4_3 and vii°6 share most of the same notes, including the bass, and both move with stepwise motion in the bass to I or I⁶.

- V^4_3 and vii°6 are sometimes used between I and I⁶ (passing motion) or between two I chords (neighbor motion).

- The root of the vii°⁶ triad is the leading tone and may not be doubled in four-part harmony; double the third or fifth.

- The progression I–V$^4_3$–I⁶ (or I–vii°⁶–I⁶) frequently is used to harmonize the melodic progression $\hat{3}$–$\hat{4}$–$\hat{5}$ (with parallel tenths in the outer voices), owing to special voice-leading exceptions involving these progressions:
  - When V$^4_3$ or vii°⁶ moves to I⁶, a diminished fifth may move to a perfect fifth.
  - When V$^4_3$ moves to I⁶, the seventh of the chord may move up by step.

TEST YOURSELF

1. Name the notes of both V$^4_3$ and vii°⁶ in the following keys, and identify the bass note for each: **a.** G major **b.** B♭ major **c.** E major **d.** E minor

2. In the example below, determine whether each of the labeled chords (a, b, c, d) is a V$^4_3$, vii°⁶, V$^6_5$, or V$^4_2$.

3. In each of the following, determine if there is a faulty approach to a perfect fifth and/or an improper treatment of a chordal seventh, and explain why or why not.

14 Approaching the Dominant: IV, ii⁶, and ii$_5^6$

IV, ii⁶, and ii$_5^6$ are Subdominant harmonies that lead toward the Dominant.

Moving toward **D**ominant Harmonies	Voice Leading in Four-Part Harmony
Subdominant harmonies	Subdominant to Dominant: IV and ii⁶
Leading to **D**ominant harmonies	Subdominant to Dominant: ii$_5^6$
Subdominant harmonies do not follow **D**ominant harmonies	Subdominant to Dominant: iv, ii°⁶, and ii°$_5^6$ in minor keys
Moving between Subdominant harmonies	

MOVING TOWARD **D**OMINANT HARMONIES

SUBDOMINANT HARMONIES

IV, ii⁶, and ii$_5^6$ all function as **S**ubdominant harmonies. They use $\hat{4}$ in the bass, share most of the same notes, and function similarly.

14.1

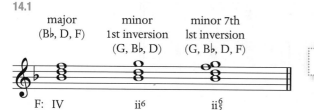

> IV, ii⁶, and ii$_5^6$ are **S**ubdominant harmonies.

Each **S**ubdominant harmony contains $\hat{6}$. In minor keys, $\hat{6}$ is a semitone lower than in major keys. As a result, iv, ii°⁶, and ii°$_5^6$ have different qualities in minor keys than the analogous chords in major keys, though their function is the same:

14.2

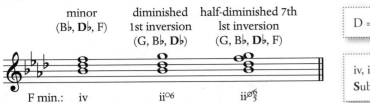

minor
(B♭, D♭, F)

diminished
1st inversion
(G, B♭, D♭)

half-diminished 7th
1st inversion
(G, B♭, D♭, F)

F min.:   iv   ii°⁶   ii⌀⁶₅

D = 6̂ in F major; D♭ = 6̂ in F minor

iv, ii°⁶, and ii⌀⁶₅ likewise function as **S**ubdominant harmonies.

LEADING TO DOMINANT HARMONIES

Most commonly, IV, ii⁶, and ii⁶₅ lead to **D**ominant harmonies, such as V or V⁷ (in root position or inversion) or vii°⁶. The **T**onic–**S**ubdominant–**D**ominant–**T**onic pattern (**T–S–D–T**) includes all of the notes within the key, and thus typically allows for more-secure establishment of the key than the simpler **T**onic–**D**ominant–**T**onic pattern discussed in Chapters 9–13.

14.3

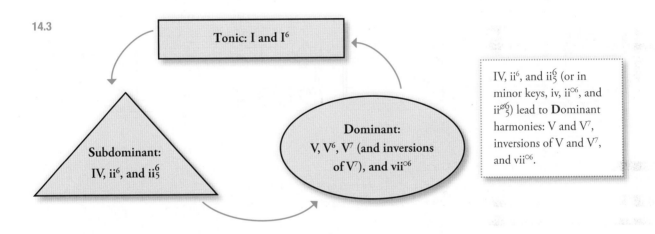

Tonic: I and I⁶

Subdominant:
IV, ii⁶, and ii⁶₅

Dominant:
V, V⁶, V⁷ (and inversions
of V⁷), and vii°⁶

IV, ii⁶, and ii⁶₅ (or in minor keys, iv, ii°⁶, and ii⌀⁶₅) lead to **D**ominant harmonies: V and V⁷, inversions of V and V⁷, and vii°⁶.

14.4 **Emily Swan Perkins, "Burg"**

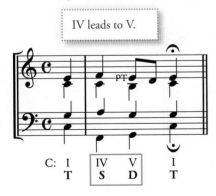

IV leads to V.

C: I   IV   V   I
    T   S   D   T

14.5 **Manuel Dias de Oliveira, "Surrexit Dominus vere"**

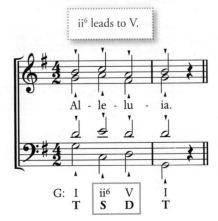

ii⁶ leads to V.

Al - le - lu - ia.

G: I   ii⁶   V   I
    T   S   D   T

14.6 Marcos Coelho Neto, "Maria Mater gratiae"

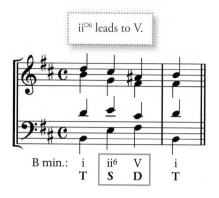

ii°⁶ leads to V.

B min.: i   ii⁶ V   i
        T   S   D   T

14.7 Henry Purcell, "Dido's Lament," from *Dido and Aeneas*

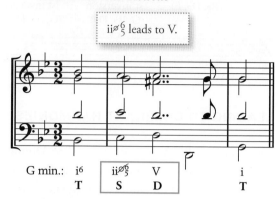

ii∅⁶₅ leads to V.

G min.: i⁶   ii∅⁶₅ V   i
         T   S   D   T

14.8 Johannes Brahms, "Die Wollust in den Maien" ("The Merry Month of May")

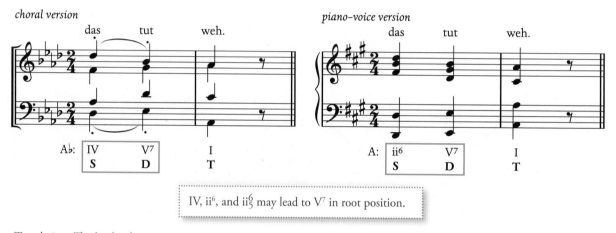

choral version

das   tut   weh.

A♭: IV   V⁷   I
     S   D   T

piano-voice version

das   tut   weh.

A: ii⁶   V⁷   I
    S   D   T

IV, ii⁶, and ii⁶₅ may lead to V⁷ in root position.

Translation: That's what hurts.

14.9 Charles Gounod, "Si le bonheur," from *Faust*

Si le bon-heur__ à sou-ri-re t'in-vi-te

B♭: I   IV   V⁷   I
     T   S   D   T

Translation: If happiness invites you to smile

14.10 **Frédéric Chopin, Prelude in C Minor**   **14.11** **Theophania Cecil, Psalm 26**

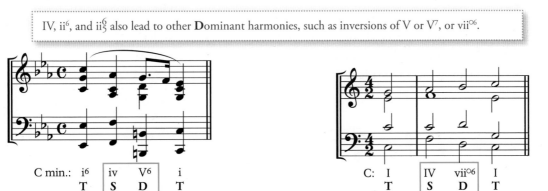

IV, ii⁶, and ii$^6_5$ also lead to other **D**ominant harmonies, such as inversions of V or V⁷, or vii°⁶.

IV, ii⁶, and ii$^6_5$ may not appear as the very last chord of a phrase. However, these chords lead very effectively to a root-position dominant chord in an authentic or half cadence.

14.12 **W. A. Mozart, Violin Sonata in D Minor, K. 377**

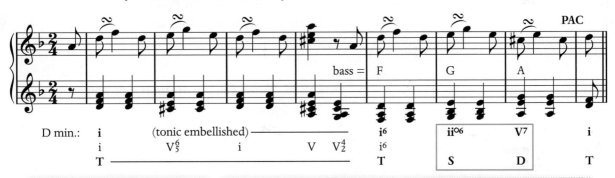

IV, ii⁶, and ii$^6_5$ often precede the V that serves as part of the cadence.

It is especially effective if I⁶ precedes the **S**ubdominant harmony that leads to the cadential V, allowing for stepwise motion up to $\hat{5}$ in the bass.

14.13 **Marie Emmanuelle Bayon, Keyboard Sonata 1, i**

SUBDOMINANT HARMONIES DO NOT FOLLOW DOMINANT HARMONIES

Except in very special situations (to be discussed in later chapters) IV, ii⁶, and ii⁶₅ should not follow a **D**ominant chord in harmony exercises, since the progression of **D**ominant to **S**ubdominant is not idiomatic in this style.

14.14

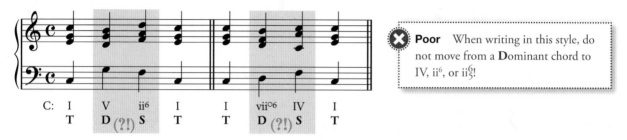

> ⊗ **Poor** When writing in this style, do not move from a **D**ominant chord to IV, ii⁶, or ii⁶₅!

MOVING BETWEEN SUBDOMINANT HARMONIES

Before proceeding to V, IV may be followed by ii⁶ (the reverse—ii⁶ followed by IV—is far less common). Since the two chords function so similarly, the resulting IV–ii⁶ succession essentially represents an elaboration of a single harmony.

14.15

14.16 J. M. Nunes Garcia, *Matinas e encomendação de defuntos*

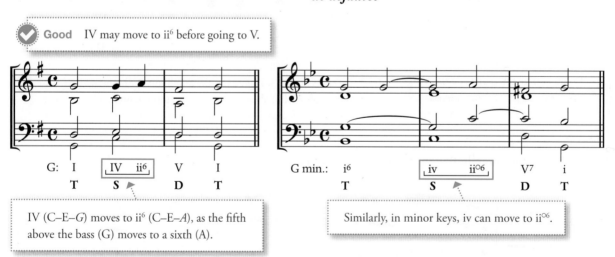

> ✓ **Good** IV may move to ii⁶ before going to V.

> IV (C–E–*G*) moves to ii⁶ (C–E–*A*), as the fifth above the bass (G) moves to a sixth (A).

> Similarly, in minor keys, iv can move to ii°⁶.

VOICE LEADING IN FOUR-PART HARMONY

SUBDOMINANT TO DOMINANT: IV AND ii⁶

In four-part harmony, you should double the bass (that is, the root, $\hat{4}$) of IV, and double either the root ($\hat{2}$) or bass ($\hat{4}$, the chordal third) of ii⁶. Moving from IV or ii⁶ to V creates the risk of parallel octaves and fifths.

14.17

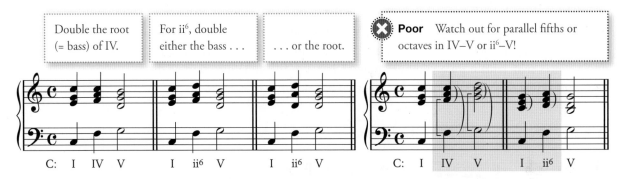

A standard strategy for avoiding faulty parallel motion is to have the upper voices move in contrary motion with the bass when IV or ii⁶ moves to V. Indeed, whenever moving between two root-position triads whose roots are separated by a step—such as IV and V—it is usually best to double the roots of both chords, and for all the upper voices to move to the nearest chord tone in the *opposite* direction from the bass.

14.18

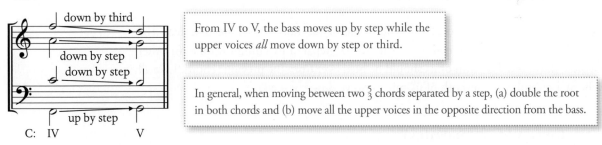

Similarly, when the bass of ii⁶ is doubled (as it often is), all of its voices should move down to the nearest chord tone—in the *opposite* direction from the bass—when ii⁶ progresses to V.

> From ii⁶ to V, if the bass (that is, the third of the chord) of ii⁶ is doubled, *all* of the upper voices should move down by step or third.

Other voice-leading possibilities arise when the root of ii⁶ is doubled, or when ii⁶ or IV progresses to V⁷ (or an inversion of V or V⁷). Although contrary motion between the bass and upper voices remains the norm, in these situations one or more of the upper voices may remain on a common tone or move in the same direction as the bass—providing that special care is taken to avoid parallel fifths or octaves.

14.20

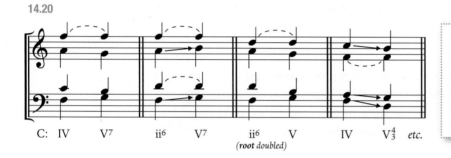

> The upper voices may remain on the same note or move in the same direction as the bass if IV or ii⁶ moves to V⁷ or an inversion of V, or if the root of ii⁶ is doubled.

SUBDOMINANT TO DOMINANT: ii⁶₅

Because it is a seventh chord, normally none of the notes of ii⁶₅ are doubled. The chordal seventh of ii⁶₅—which is $\hat{1}$—should be prepared by common tone: in other words, the chordal seventh of ii⁶₅ should be held over from the previous chord. Like all chordal sevenths, the seventh of ii⁶₅ must resolve down by step.

14.21 **Emma Ashford, "Sutherland"**

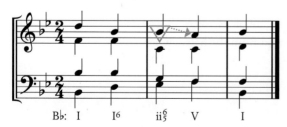

> The chordal seventh of ii⁶₅ (C, $\hat{1}$) is prepared by common tone (notice the soprano B♭ in the previous chord) and resolves down by step.

SUBDOMINANT TO DOMINANT: iv, ii°6, AND ii∅⁶₅ IN MINOR KEYS

In minor keys, the minor form of 6̂ (that is, 6̂ as it appears in the natural minor, harmonic minor, or descending melodic minor scales) is a tendency tone that pulls strongly *down* toward 5̂. The minor form of 6̂ should not move up to the leading tone, since that would create a melodic **augmented second**, which sounds too exotic for basic four-part harmony. As with other tendency tones, avoid doubling the minor form of 6̂.

14.22

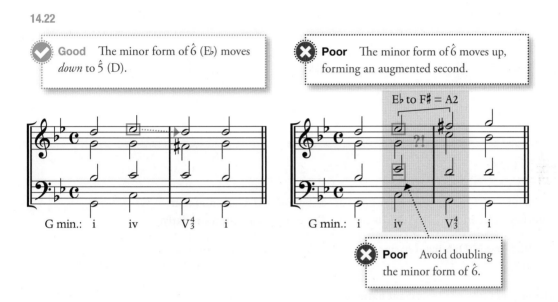

14.23 **Johanna Kinkel, "Vorüberfahrt" ("Passing by")**

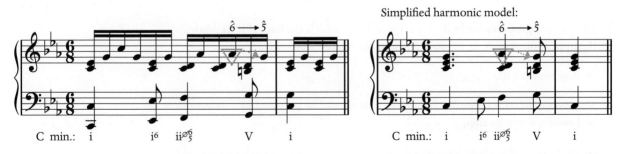

It is also possible to raise 6̂ in minor keys, as in the ascending melodic minor scale, thereby changing the quality of iv, ii°6, or ii∅⁶₅ to IV, ii⁶, or ii⁶₅. Raised 6̂ moves up to the leading tone without creating an augmented second.

14.24 **Christian Gregor, "Rise, Ye Children"**

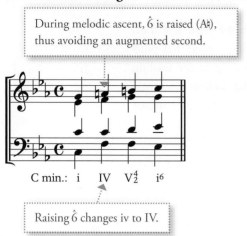

During melodic ascent, $\hat{6}$ is raised (A♮), thus avoiding an augmented second.

C min.:   i   IV   V$\frac{4}{2}$ i^6

Raising $\hat{6}$ changes iv to IV.

POINTS FOR REVIEW

- IV, ii^6, and ii$^6_5$ (and iv, ii$^{\circ 6}$, and ii$^{\varnothing 6}_5$ in minor keys) are Subdominant harmonies that share the same bass tone and most of the same notes. These chords function similarly.

- IV, ii^6, and ii$^6_5$ lead toward Dominant harmonies such as V or V^7 (in root position or inversion) or vii$^{\circ 6}$.

- IV, ii^6, and ii$^6_5$ may not follow a Dominant harmony.

- Double the bass (= root, $\hat{4}$) of IV; double either the bass (= third of chord, $\hat{4}$) or root ($\hat{2}$) of ii^6.

- In IV–V progressions (or in ii^6–V progressions in which the bass of ii^6 is doubled), the upper voices of IV or ii^6 move down to the nearest note of the V triad.

- IV may move to ii^6.

- The seventh of ii$^6_5$ is a chordal dissonance that should be prepared by common tone and resolve down by step.

- In minor keys, the minor form of $\hat{6}$ should move down, not up to the leading tone (which would create an augmented second). If $\hat{6}$ is raised in minor, however, it may move up to the leading tone.

1. Which of the following chord progressions are stylistically correct in standard four-part harmony?

   a. I–V–I

   b. I–IV–V–I⁶

   c. I–ii⁶–vii°⁶–I

   d. I–V⁶–ii₅⁶–I

   e. I–IV–V–ii⁶–I

   f. I⁶–ii₅⁶–V₂⁴–I⁶

   g. I–vii°⁶–IV–I

   h. I–IV–ii⁶–V⁷–I

   i. I–IV–ii⁶–V–V⁶–I–V–I

2. Below are the Roman numerals of chords and their qualities in major keys. What are the analogous chords and qualities in minor keys (using the notes in the natural minor scale)?

major key	minor key
I, quality = major	i, quality = minor
a. IV, quality = major	_____, quality = _____
b. ii⁶, quality = minor	_____, quality = _____
c. ii₅⁶, quality = minor 7th	_____, quality = _____

3. What notes of the chord (root, third, or fifth) and scale degrees are best to double in the following triads? For some of these there is more than one answer.

   a. I   b. I⁶   c. V   d. V⁶   e. IV   f. ii⁶

4. Below are a series of ii₅⁶ chords and V⁷ chords in various keys. Identify the note and scale degree of the chordal seventh in each:

   a. D: ii₅⁶   b. E♭: V⁷   c. B♭: ii₅⁶   d. A: V₂⁴   e. C♯ min.: ii°₅⁶   f. D min.: V₅⁶

5. Which of the following statements are true in standard four-part harmony?

   a. A chordal seventh must resolve down by step.

   b. 4̂ must resolve down by step.

   c. 4̂ must resolve down by step if it is the seventh of V⁷.

   d. 1̂ must resolve down by step if it is the seventh of ii₅⁶.

6. Identify the errors in the following fragments:

   a. C: IV   V⁷   b. D: ii₅⁶   V₂⁴   c. C min.: iv   V₂⁴   d. G: ii⁶   V   e. G min.: iv   V₃⁴

The cadential $\begin{smallmatrix}6\\4\end{smallmatrix}$ consists of accented embellishing tones that resolve down by step to the upper notes of a root-position V chord.

Embellishing V

Harmonic Progression and Voice Leading

    Doubling

    Resolving the cadential $\begin{smallmatrix}6\\4\end{smallmatrix}$

    Rhythmic position

Labeling the Cadential $\begin{smallmatrix}6\\4\end{smallmatrix}$

    Figured bass

    Roman numerals

    I$\begin{smallmatrix}6\\4\end{smallmatrix}$

The Cadential $\begin{smallmatrix}6\\4\end{smallmatrix}$ within Phrases

A Closer Look

    Cadential $\begin{smallmatrix}6\\4\end{smallmatrix}$ moving to V$\begin{smallmatrix}4\\2\end{smallmatrix}$

    Implied resolution of dissonant fourth

EMBELLISHING V

Root-position dominant chords frequently are embellished by the intervals of a sixth and fourth above $\hat{5}$ in the bass. These embellishing tones are metrically accented and they delay the arrival of the dominant chord's third and fifth. The sonority that embellishes V is known as a **cadential $\begin{smallmatrix}6\\4\end{smallmatrix}$**. Notice that the scale degrees of the cadential $\begin{smallmatrix}6\\4\end{smallmatrix}$ ($\hat{5}$, $\hat{1}$, and $\hat{3}$) are the same as those of the tonic triad, but here are used to embellish V: this is an embellishment of a **D**ominant harmony, not a **T**onic harmony.

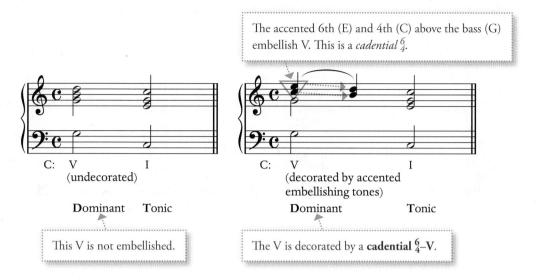

The accented 6th (E) and 4th (C) above the bass (G) embellish V. This is a *cadential* $^6_4$.

C: V   I
(undecorated)

Dominant   Tonic

This V is not embellished.

C: V   I
(decorated by accented
embellishing tones)

Dominant   Tonic

The V is decorated by a **cadential $^6_4$–V.**

15.2

Cadential $^6_4$ chords are usually formed by suspensions or accented passing tones that embellish V.

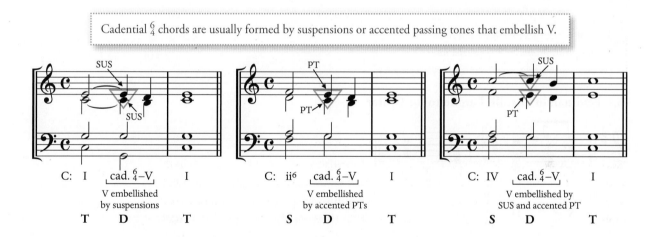

C: I   cad. $^6_4$–V   I
V embellished
by suspensions

T   D   T

C: ii⁶   cad. $^6_4$–V   I
V embellished
by accented PTs

S   D   T

C: IV   cad. $^6_4$–V   I
V embellished by
SUS and accented PT

S   D   T

The cadential $^6_4$ should be directly followed by *root-position* V or V⁷ (not by an inversion of V or V⁷).

15.3

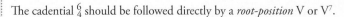

The cadential $^6_4$ should be followed directly by a *root-position* V or V⁷.

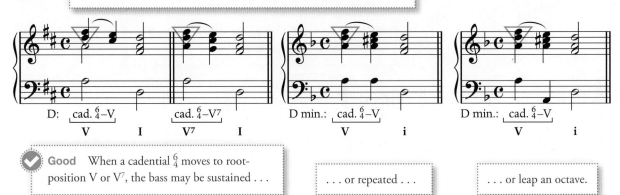

D: cad. $^6_4$–V
V   I

cad. $^6_4$–V⁷
V⁷   I

D min.: cad. $^6_4$–V
V   i

D min.: cad. $^6_4$–V
V   i

✓ **Good**   When a cadential $^6_4$ moves to root-position V or V⁷, the bass may be sustained . . .

. . . or repeated . . .

. . . or leap an octave.

D min.: cad. $^6_4$–V$^6_5$

(?!)

✗ **Poor**   The cadential $^6_4$ should move to V in root position, *not* in first inversion.

15.4 Ferdinando Carulli, Larghetto for Guitar

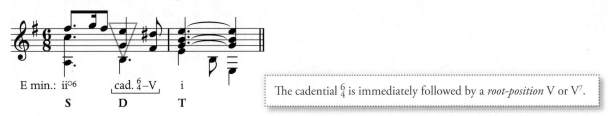

E min.: ii°⁶
S

cad. $^6_4$–V
D

i
T

The cadential $^6_4$ is immediately followed by a *root-position* V or V⁷.

15.5 Annette von Droste-Hülshoff, "Trinklied"   **15.6 James Bland, "In the Morning by the Bright Light"**

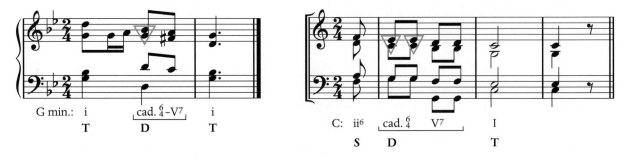

G min.: i
T

cad. $^6_4$–V⁷
D

i
T

C: ii⁶
S

cad. $^6_4$
D

V⁷

I
T

HARMONIC PROGRESSION AND VOICE LEADING

A cadential $^6_4$ may be preceded by any **T**onic or **S**ubdominant chord. Since a cadential $^6_4$ delays the arrival of V, however, it may *not* follow a **D**ominant harmony, such as V, V^7, or vii^{o6}.

15.7

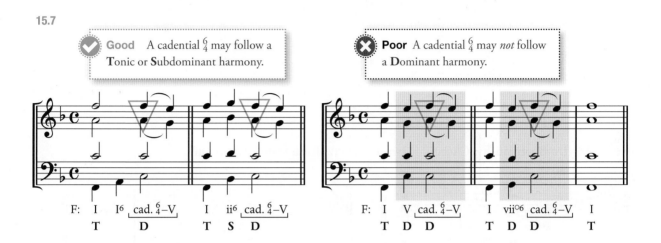

DOUBLING

In four-part harmony, you should double the bass of the cadential $^6_4$. The fourth above the bass is dissonant with the bass and should never be doubled.

15.10

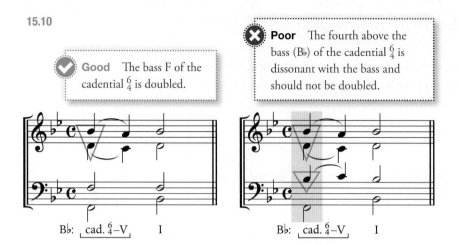

Good The bass F of the cadential $^6_4$ is doubled.

Poor The fourth above the bass (B♭) of the cadential $^6_4$ is dissonant with the bass and should not be doubled.

B♭: cad. $^6_4$–V I

B♭: cad. $^6_4$–V I

15.11 Dmytro Bortniansky, Cherubic Hymn

15.12 Rose Dale, "Barnham"

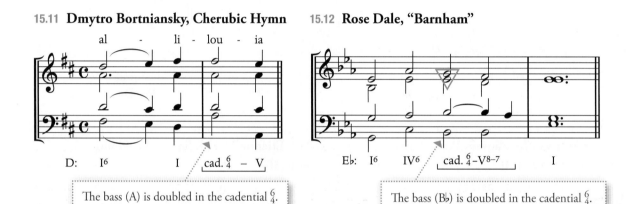

al - li - lou - ia

D: I⁶ I cad. $^6_4$ – V

E♭: I⁶ IV⁶ cad. $^6_4$–V⁸⁻⁷ I

The bass (A) is doubled in the cadential $^6_4$.

The bass (B♭) is doubled in the cadential $^6_4$.

RESOLVING THE CADENTIAL $^6_4$

The fourth of the cadential $^6_4$ is a dissonance and should resolve down by step. The sixth, though also an embellishment, does not form a dissonance, and thus may move in either direction—though it, too, usually moves downward.

15.13

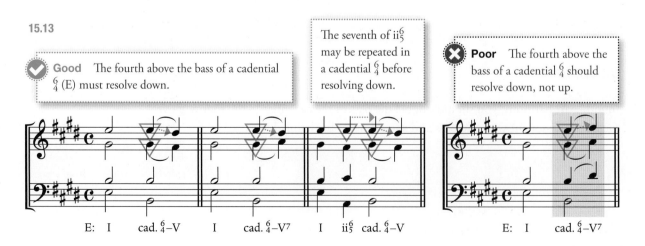

Good The fourth above the bass of a cadential $^6_4$ (E) must resolve down.

The seventh of ii$^6_5$ may be repeated in a cadential $^6_4$ before resolving down.

Poor The fourth above the bass of a cadential $^6_4$ should resolve down, not up.

E: I cad. $^6_4$–V I cad. $^6_4$–V⁷ I ii$^6_5$ cad. $^6_4$–V

E: I cad. $^6_4$–V⁷

15.14 Maria Teresa Agnesi, Overture to *L'Insubria consolata*

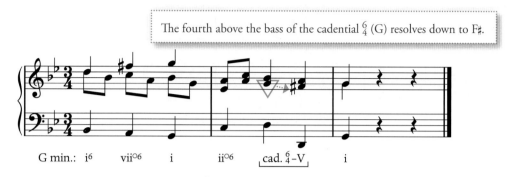

The fourth above the bass of the cadential $^6_4$ (G) resolves down to F♯.

G min.: i⁶   vii°⁶   i   ii°⁶   cad. $^6_4$–V   i

RHYTHMIC POSITION

Since it derives from suspensions or other accented embellishing tones that decorate a **D**ominant harmony, a cadential $^6_4$ must appear on a *stronger* beat (or stronger part of the beat) than the V or V⁷ to which it resolves.

15.15

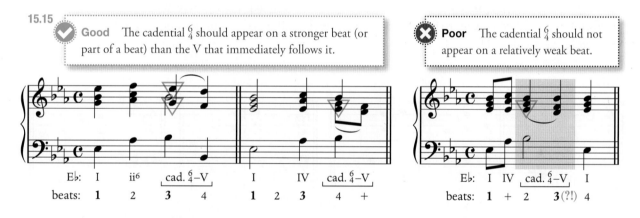

Good The cadential $^6_4$ should appear on a stronger beat (or part of a beat) than the V that immediately follows it.

Poor The cadential $^6_4$ should not appear on a relatively weak beat.

E♭: I   ii⁶   cad. $^6_4$–V   I   IV   cad. $^6_4$–V
beats: 1   2   3   4   1   2   3   4   +

E♭: I   IV   cad. $^6_4$–V   I
beats: 1   +   2   3(?!)   4

15.16 Edward Barnes, "Gloria"

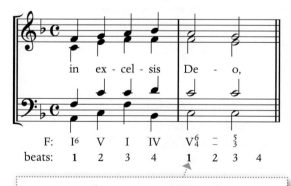

in ex- cel- sis De - o,

F: I⁶   V   I   IV   V$^6_4$ – $^5_3$
beats: 1   2   3   4   1   2   3   4

The cadential $^6_4$ appears on a stronger beat (beat 1) than the V that follows it (beat 3).

15.17 Luigi Boccherini, String Quintet in E, Trio

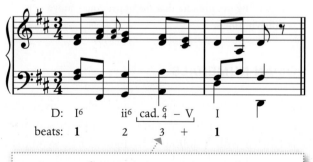

D: I⁶   ii⁶ cad. $^6_4$ – V   I
beats: 1   2   3   +   1

The cadential $^6_4$ appears on a stronger part of the beat (the first half) than the V that follows it.

15.18 John Bull (attrib.), "God Save the Queen"

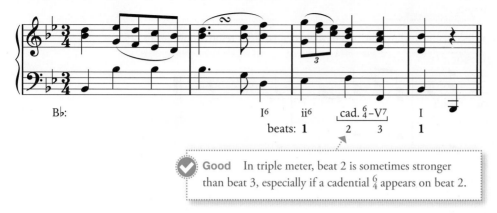

B♭:   I⁶   ii⁶   cad. $^6_4$–V⁷   I

beats: 1   2   3   1

> ✓ **Good** In triple meter, beat 2 is sometimes stronger than beat 3, especially if a cadential $^6_4$ appears on beat 2.

LABELING THE CADENTIAL $^6_4$

FIGURED BASS

In figured bass, a dominant harmony embellished by a cadential $^6_4$ is indicated with two sets of figures ($^{6-5}_{4-3}$) below a single bass tone (or one that repeats or leaps an octave). If the third of V needs to be raised by a half step (as is the case in minor keys), then write the accidental by itself.

15.19

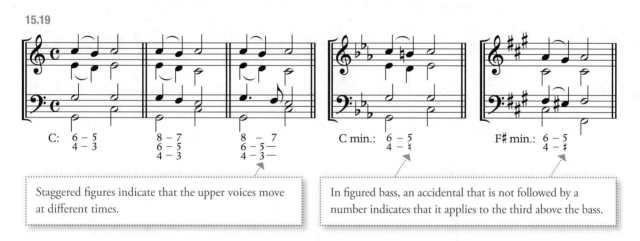

C: 6 − 5   8 − 7   8 − 7   C min.: 6 − 5   F♯ min.: 6 − 5
    4 − 3   6 − 5   6 − 5—   4 − ♮   4 − ♯
               4 − 3   4 − 3—

> Staggered figures indicate that the upper voices move at different times.

> In figured bass, an accidental that is not followed by a number indicates that it applies to the third above the bass.

ROMAN NUMERALS

Since it embellishes an underlying V chord, the cadential $^6_4$ generally is not labeled with its own Roman numeral. Rather, a **D**ominant harmony decorated by a cadential $^6_4$ is labeled with V followed by figured bass symbols indicating the intervals above the bass. Thus cadential $^6_4$–V is labeled as V$^{6-5}_{4-3}$, and cadential $^6_4$–V⁷ is labeled as V$^{8-7}_{6-5}$. The "$^6_4$" within the label V$^{6-5}_{4-3}$ does *not* refer to a second inversion of a V triad (an uncommon chord with $\hat{2}$ in the bass). Instead, these figures indicate that a sixth and fourth move to a fifth and third above $\hat{5}$ in the bass.

15.20

Task: Write V^{6-5}_{4-3} in **F major.**

1. Find $\hat{5}$; this note should be in the bass and be doubled: *in the key of F, $\hat{5}$ = C.*

2. Then find the intervals of a sixth and a fourth above $\hat{5}$: *6th above $\hat{5}$ = A; 4th above $\hat{5}$ = F.*

3. 6 and 4 above the bass should move down to 5 and 3 above the bass, while the bass remains on $\hat{5}$: *A and F should move to G and E, respectively, while the bass remains on C.*

Some possible solutions:

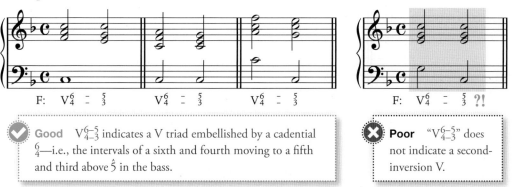

✓ **Good** V^{6-5}_{4-3} indicates a V triad embellished by a cadential $^6_4$—i.e., the intervals of a sixth and fourth moving to a fifth and third above $\hat{5}$ in the bass.

✗ **Poor** "V^{6-5}_{4-3}" does not indicate a second-inversion V.

15.21 Franziska Lebrun, Sonata Op. 1, No. 4, ii   **15.22 Maria Szymanowska, March No. 3**

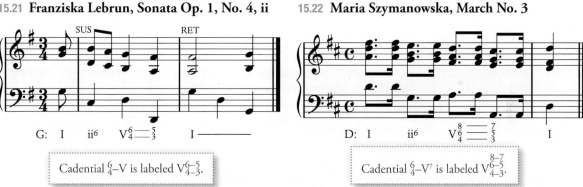

Cadential $^6_4$–V is labeled V^{6-5}_{4-3}.   Cadential $^6_4$–V^7 is labeled $V^{8-7}_{6-5}_{4-3}$.

I^6_4

Notice that the cadential $^6_4$ uses the notes of a tonic triad in second inversion—that is, I^6_4. Thus you can also spell a cadential $^6_4$ by thinking of a tonic triad in second inversion.

15.23

Task: Determine the notes in V_{4-3}^{6-5} in F major, thinking of it as a tonic triad in second inversion.

1. Find the notes of I_4^6, and double the bass: *in the key of F, I_4^6 = C–F–A, and the bass note C should be doubled.*

2. The notes of I_4^6 should move to the notes of V: *C–F–A (I_4^6) should move to C–E–G (V).*

Some possible solutions:

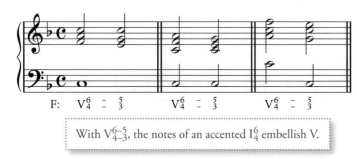

F: V_4^6 – $_3^5$ V_4^6 – $_3^5$ V_4^6 – $_3^5$

> This method of determining the notes of V_{4-3}^{6-5} in F major yields the same results as the method shown in 15.20.

> With V_{4-3}^{6-5}, the notes of an accented I_4^6 embellish V.

Indeed, some musicians refer to the cadential $\frac{6}{4}$ as "I_4^6." Regardless of how you label it, however, the cadential $\frac{6}{4}$ embellishes V. It is therefore part of an embellished **D**ominant harmony, unlike I and I^6, which are always **T**onic harmonies.

15.24

TONIC CHORD (I OR I^6)	CADENTIAL $\frac{6}{4}$ (SAME NOTES AS I OR I^6, BUT WITH THE FIFTH IN THE BASS)
Very stable chord.	Very *unstable*, dissonant chord.
Usually follows dominant chord.	*Never* follows a dominant chord.
May be followed by any chord.	Must be followed by V or V^7.
Usually its root is doubled (in I^6, any note may be doubled).	Its "root" (the note that lies a fourth above the bass) is a dissonance that must *never* be doubled.
May appear on any beat of a measure.	Must appear on a stronger beat than the V or V^7 that follows it.

THE CADENTIAL $\frac{6}{4}$ WITHIN PHRASES

The cadential $\frac{6}{4}$ often embellishes a V or V^7 that appears as part of a half cadence or authentic cadence.

15.25 W. A. Mozart, Piano Sonata in A, K. 331, i

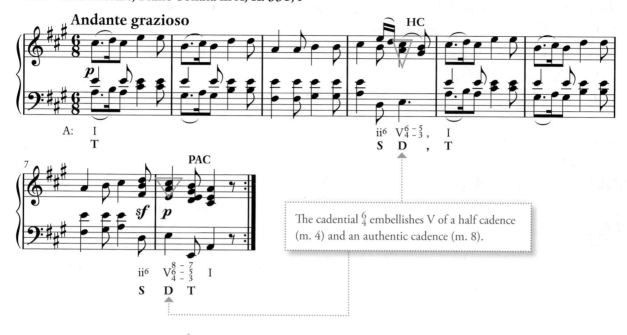

The cadential $^6_4$ embellishes V of a half cadence (m. 4) and an authentic cadence (m. 8).

However, the cadential $^6_4$ is not restricted to appearing at cadences: despite its name, a cadential $^6_4$ may appear anywhere within a phrase.

15.26 John W. Work Jr., "O Mary, Don't You Weep" (spiritual)

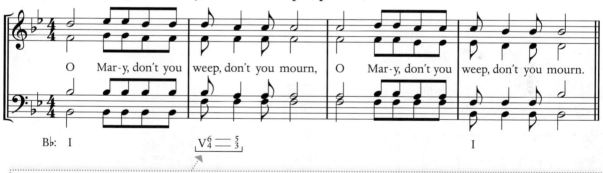

A cadential $^6_4$ may decorate a non-cadential dominant harmony that appears in the beginning or the middle of a phrase.

🔍 For more on the resolution of the cadential $^6_4$, see A Closer Look.

POINTS FOR REVIEW

- A cadential $^6_4$ embellishes upper notes of a V or V^7 chord, with an accented sixth and fourth above $\hat{5}$ in the bass.

- Cadential $^6_4$–V is conventionally labeled as "V^{6-5}_{4-3}."

- A cadential $^6_4$ has the same notes as a tonic chord in second inversion.

- A cadential $^6_4$ may appear anywhere in a phrase, not only at the cadence.

- **Checklist for using cadential $^6_4$ in four-part harmony:**
  - A cadential $^6_4$ should be followed directly by either V or V^7 in *root position*.
  - A cadential $^6_4$ can follow any chord *except* for a **D**ominant harmony.
  - The bass of a cadential $^6_4$ should be doubled.
  - The fourth above the bass of a cadential $^6_4$ should resolve down by step.
  - A cadential $^6_4$ should appear on a stronger beat or part of the beat than the V or V^7 that immediately follows it.

TEST YOURSELF

1. Identify the following scale degrees and intervals above the bass.
   a. In G major, $\hat{5}$ is D. What notes are a sixth and fourth above? _____ and _____.
   b. In E♭ major, $\hat{5}$ is _____. A sixth and fourth above this are _____ and _____.
   c. In D minor, $\hat{5}$ is _____. A sixth and fourth above this are _____ and _____.
   d. In E minor, $\hat{5}$ is _____. A sixth and fourth above this are _____ and _____.

2. Spell a cadential $^6_4$, starting with the bass, in the following keys.
   a. F major
   c. G minor
   b. B major
   d. A minor

3. Complete the progressions by filling in the missing note(s).

   a.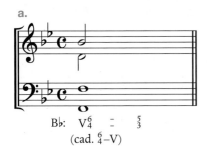
   b.
   c.

   B♭: V^6_4 – $^5_3$
   (cad. $^6_4$–V)

   F♯ min.: V^6_4 – $^5_3$

   G: V^6_4 – $^5_3$

4. Which of the excerpts use cadential $^6_4$–V (i.e., V^{6-5}_{4-3}) incorrectly? Identify the errors.

   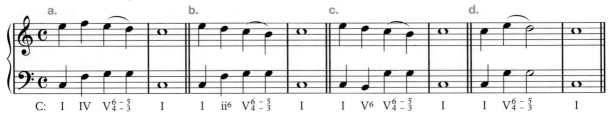

   C: a. I IV V^{6-5}_{4-3} I   b. I ii^6 V^{6-5}_{4-3} I   c. I V^6 V^{6-5}_{4-3} I   d. I V^{6-5}_{4-3} I

16

Leading to the Tonic: IV

IV may embellish the tonic harmony by appearing between two I chords.

Harmonic Progression
IV as an Embellishment
Plagal Cadence

A Closer Look
Embellishing tonic with IV⁶
Embellishing IV with I or I⁶
Embellishing tonic with ii⁶ and ii⁶₅
Structurally important subdominant–tonic progressions

HARMONIC PROGRESSION

IV typically progresses to V or a similar **D**ominant harmony (see Chapter 13). However, IV can also be followed directly by I or I⁶. When IV is sandwiched between two tonic chords, it forms a **T**onic–**S**ubdominant–**T**onic pattern. Since IV lacks a leading tone, IV–I motion tends to confirm the tonic less strongly than V–I.

16.1

I–IV–I progressions are common.

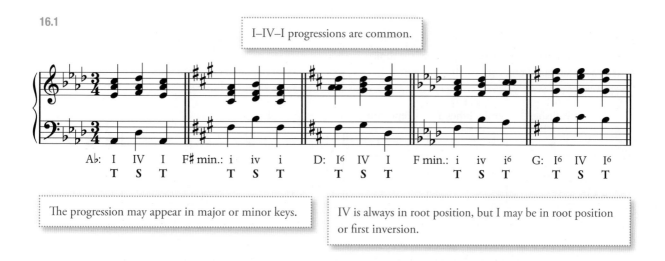

The progression may appear in major or minor keys.

IV is always in root position, but I may be in root position or first inversion.

16.2 Phoebe Knapp, "Blessed Assurance"

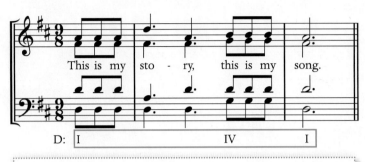

This is my sto - ry, this is my song.

D: I   IV   I

16.3 Charles Albert Tindley, "I'll Overcome Some Day"

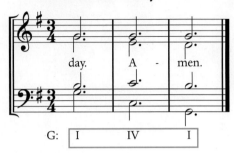

day.   A -   men.

G: I   IV   I

In each example, root-position IV comes from and returns to I or I⁶.

16.4 Elizabeth Cuthbert, "Howard"

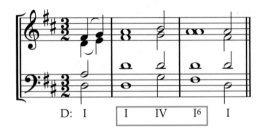

D: I   I   IV   I⁶   I

16.5 Pyotr Tchaikovsky, "The Witch"

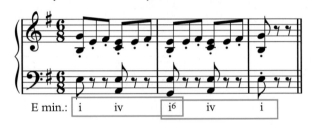

E min.: i   iv   i⁶   iv   i

IV AS AN EMBELLISHMENT

Typically, in the progression I–IV–I, one upper voice sustains $\hat{1}$, while the others employ neighboring motion, as the I–IV–I progression embellishes tonic harmony.

16.6

Much as its upper voices embellish notes of the tonic triad with sustained tones or neighbor motions . . .

. . . so I–IV–I often embellishes the tonic harmony.

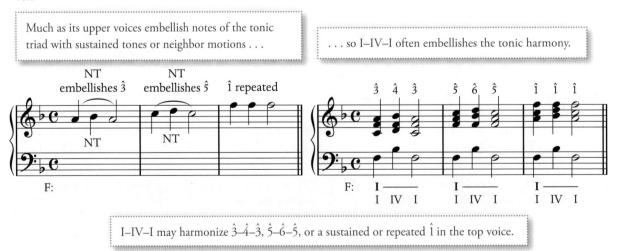

I–IV–I may harmonize $\hat{3}$–$\hat{4}$–$\hat{3}$, $\hat{5}$–$\hat{6}$–$\hat{5}$, or a sustained or repeated $\hat{1}$ in the top voice.

16.7 **Johannes Brahms,** *Variations on a Theme by Haydn*

16.8 **G. F. Handel, "Hallelujah" Chorus, from** *Messiah*

opening passage:

closing passage:

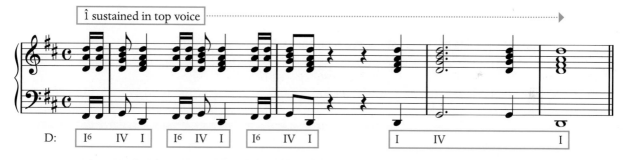

When IV progresses to I, the melody usually moves *down* by step or else stays on the tonic; it is less common for the melody to ascend when IV moves to I. Furthermore, although either of the tonic chords within the I–IV–I progression may appear in first inversion, IV must be in root position: do not use a I–IV⁶–I progression.

16.9

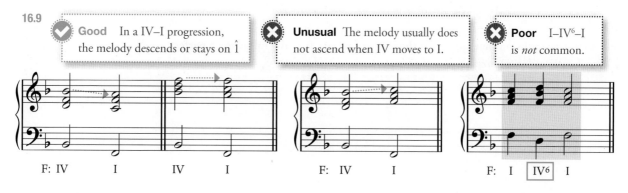

PLAGAL CADENCE

IV–I motion typically appears toward the beginning of a phrase as it embellishes the tonic harmony. However, IV–I sometimes appears immediately after a strong perfect authentic cadence, as though to provide added confirmation of the phrase's ending. IV–I at the end of a phrase forms a **plagal cadence**.

16.10 Johann Nepomuk Hummel (attrib.), "Hark! What mean those holy voices"

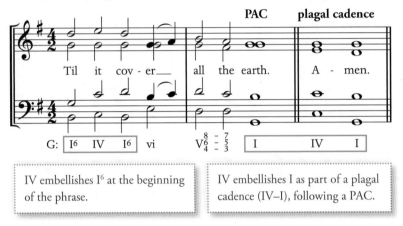

IV embellishes I⁶ at the beginning of the phrase.

IV embellishes I as part of a plagal cadence (IV–I), following a PAC.

🔍 For more on embellishing the tonic with IV, see A Closer Look.

POINTS FOR REVIEW

- **IV may appear between two tonic chords (I or I⁶).**

- **I–IV–I often supports 3̂–4̂–3̂, 5̂–6̂–5̂, or 1̂–1̂–1̂ in the upper voice, embellishing the tonic harmony. When IV moves to I, the upper voices should descend.**

- **Avoid the progression I–IV⁶–I.**

- **A IV–I progression that appears at the end of a phrase (usually following a perfect authentic cadence) forms a *plagal cadence*.**

1. Which of these progressions commonly occur?

    a. I–IV–I b. I–IV–I⁶ c. I⁶–IV–I d. I–IV⁶–I e. I⁶–IV–I⁶

2. What are the scale degrees of the three-note melodic patterns that often are harmonized with I–IV–I?

3. Which of these melodies (all in major keys) could be harmonized with I–IV–I?

    a. b. c. d. e.

4. What are the Roman numerals of the following chord progressions? If they appeared at the very end of a phrase, what type of cadence would be formed by each: a perfect authentic cadence, imperfect authentic cadence, half cadence, or plagal cadence?

    a. b. c. d.

A: B min.: C♯ min.: B♭:

chapter 17

The Leading-Tone Seventh Chord: vii°⁷ and vii⌀⁷

Leading-tone seventh chords (vii°⁷, vii⌀⁷, and their inversions) function as Dominants, leading to Tonic (I and I⁶).

vii°⁷   vii⌀⁷

    Harmonic progressions
    Moving between vii°⁷ and V⁷
    Voice leading

The vii°⁷ and vii⌀⁷ chords are both built on the leading tone. Both share three notes (7̂, 2̂, 4̂), as well as **D**ominant function, with V⁷.

vii°⁷

The vii°⁷ chord is found mostly in minor keys, though it sometimes appears in major keys. Since it contains two tritones (augmented fourths or diminished fifths), vii°⁷ sounds somewhat more dissonant than V⁷, and it always requires an accidental.

17.1

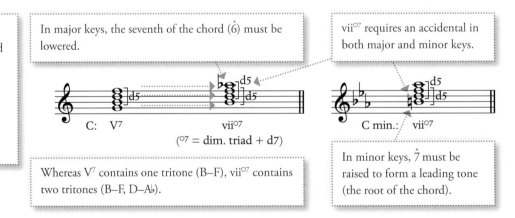

°⁷ = diminished triad + diminished seventh. vii°⁷ and V⁷ share three of the same notes; these chords function as **D**ominants.

In major keys, the seventh of the chord (6̂) must be lowered.

vii°⁷ requires an accidental in both major and minor keys.

C: V⁷   vii°⁷
(°⁷ = dim. triad + d7)

Whereas V⁷ contains one tritone (B–F), vii°⁷ contains two tritones (B–F, D–A♭).

In minor keys, 7̂ must be raised to form a leading tone (the root of the chord).

HARMONIC PROGRESSIONS

Unlike the vii° triad, which is *not* normally used in root position, vii°7 may appear in root position or inversion. In each case, it is treated like the inversion of V7 that has the same bass tone, leading to either I or I6.

17.2

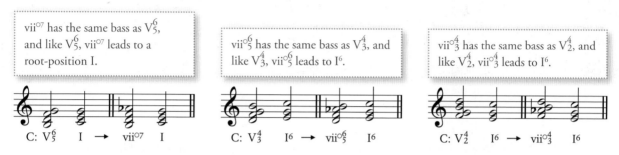

17.3 Christoph Willibald Gluck, *Orfeo ed Euridice,* **Act I**

Translation: [You hover around] this funeral urn, Eurydice, sweet spirit.

MOVING BETWEEN vii°7 AND V7

The vii°7 and all of its inversions—including vii°$_2^4$—may follow or be followed by an inversion of V7 before resolving to I. Since vii°7 and V7 share three notes, only one note of the chord needs to change when moving between them. Consequently, motions between vii°7 and V7 usually result from neighbor motion in one of the voices.

17.4

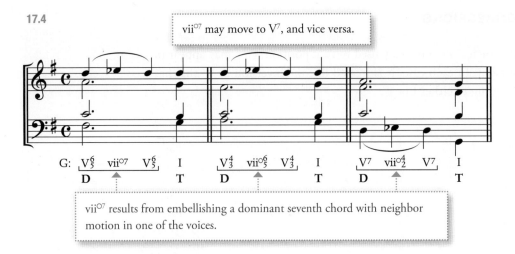

vii°⁷ may move to V⁷, and vice versa.

G: V^6_5 vii°⁷ V^6_5 I | V^4_3 vii°⁶₅ V^4_3 I | V^7 vii°⁴₂ V^7 I
D ▲ T | D ▲ T | D ▲ T

vii°⁷ results from embellishing a dominant seventh chord with neighbor motion in one of the voices.

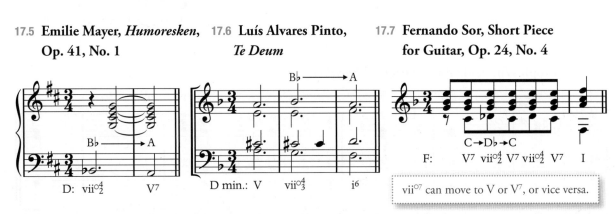

17.5 Emilie Mayer, *Humoresken,* **Op. 41, No. 1**

D: vii°⁴₂   V⁷

17.6 Luís Alvares Pinto, *Te Deum*

D min.: V vii°⁴₃ i⁶

17.7 Fernando Sor, Short Piece for Guitar, Op. 24, No. 4

F: V^7 vii°⁴₂ V^7 vii°⁴₂ V^7 I

vii°⁷ can move to V or V⁷, or vice versa.

VOICE LEADING

When vii°⁷ or one of its inversions resolves to I or I⁶, the chordal seventh of vii°⁷ must resolve down by step, and the root of vii°⁷—the leading tone—must resolve up by step. When resolving vii°⁷, be careful to avoid having a diminished fifth move to a perfect fifth. To avoid this parallel motion to a perfect fifth, you may need to double the third of the tonic chord, rather than its root.

17.8

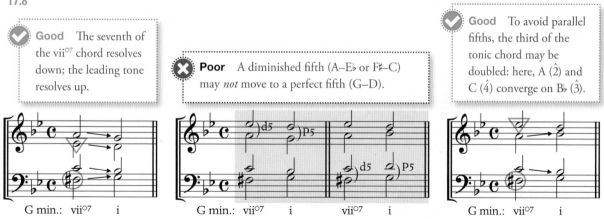

Good The seventh of the vii°7 chord resolves down; the leading tone resolves up.

Poor A diminished fifth (A–E♭ or F♯–C) may *not* move to a perfect fifth (G–D).

Good To avoid parallel fifths, the third of the tonic chord may be doubled: here, A ($\hat{2}$) and C ($\hat{4}$) converge on B♭ ($\hat{3}$).

G min.: vii°7   i

G min.: vii°7   i   vii°7   i

G min.: vii°7   i

17.9 J. F. Schwencke, "Ich ruf' zu dir"

17.10 W. A. Mozart, "Schon weicht dir, Sonne" ("Already you depart, sun"), from *King Thamos*

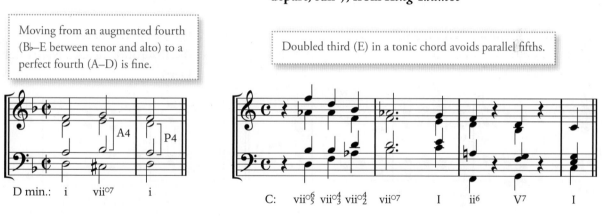

Moving from an augmented fourth (B♭–E between tenor and alto) to a perfect fourth (A–D) is fine.

Doubled third (E) in a tonic chord avoids parallel fifths.

D min.:   i   vii°7   i

C: vii°$^6_5$ vii°$^4_3$ vii°$^4_2$ vii°7   I   ii6   V7   I

vii^{ø7}

vii^{ø7} is a half-diminished seventh chord (diminished triad plus minor seventh) whose root is the leading tone. It is treated much like vii°7, except that vii^{ø7} is found only in major keys and does not require an accidental. Both vii°7 and vii^{ø7} and their inversions function as **D**ominants: they lead to I or I6.

17.11

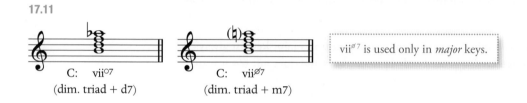

C: vii°7
(dim. triad + d7)

C: vii^{ø7}
(dim. triad + m7)

vii^{ø7} is used only in *major* keys.

As with vii°7, in progressing from viiø7 to I the chordal seventh resolves down by step, and the leading tone resolves up by step. Often special care must be taken in order to avoid parallel fifths in moving from viiø7 to I.

17.12

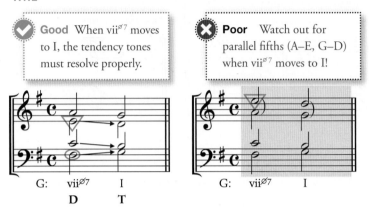

Good When viiø7 moves to I, the tendency tones must resolve properly.

Poor Watch out for parallel fifths (A–E, G–D) when viiø7 moves to I!

17.13 Ann S. Mounsey, "Greenland"

17.14 Katharine Lee Bates, "America the Beautiful" (arr. R. Nathaniel Dett)

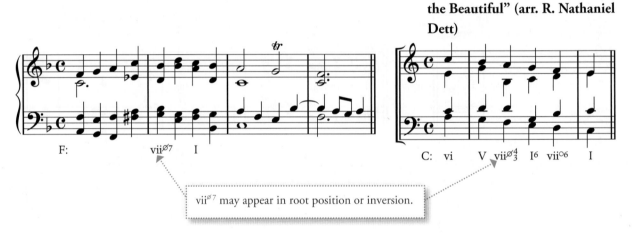

viiø7 may appear in root position or inversion.

POINTS FOR REVIEW

- vii°7 and viiø7 function as Dominants that lead to Tonic; they may appear in root position or inversion.

- vii°7 is used mostly in minor keys, but may also appear in major keys; it always requires an accidental. viiø7 is used only in major keys and does not require an accidental.

- When a vii°7 or viiø7 leads to I, its chordal seventh must resolve down by step and the leading tone must resolve up by step.

- Before moving to Tonic, vii°7 or viiø7 may move to or from an inversion of V7.

- With the vii°7–I and viiø7–I progressions, be careful to avoid approaching a perfect fifth in parallel motion.

TEST YOURSELF

1. Add accidentals to the chords below (as needed) to create the specified harmonies. Some chords may not require an accidental.

a. D: vii°7   b. D min.: vii°7   c. E: vii°7   d. E min.: vii°7   e. B♭: viiø7

2. Label the chords below with Roman numerals and figures in the keys indicated. Then indicate the chordal seventh and the leading tone in each.

a. A: b. F min.:   c. D: d. G min.:   e. E:

3. Label the chords below with Roman numerals and figures in the keys indicated. Then indicate which chord best follows each: I, I6, or V7.

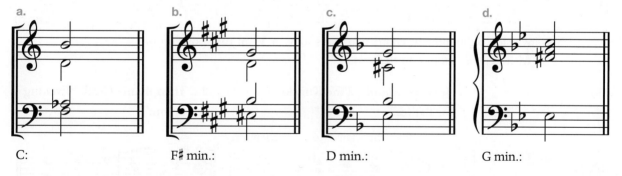

a. C: b. F♯ min.:   c. D min.:   d. G min.:

4. Fill in the missing note in the following chord progressions; explain your choice.

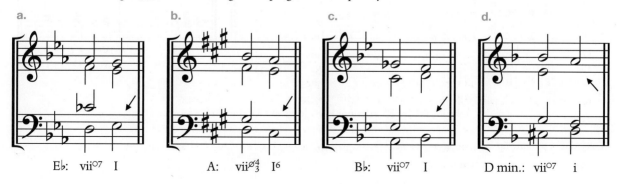

a. E♭: vii°7 I   b. A: viiø4/3 I6   c. B♭: vii°7 I   d. D min.: vii°7 i

IV⁶, ii, ii⁷, and IV⁷ appear in a variety of positions as Subdominant harmonies that lead to V.

IV⁶	**ii⁷ and IV⁷**
Doubling and voice leading	**ii⁷**
Root-Position ii	**IV⁷**
Doubling and voice leading	Four-part harmony and voice leading
	Alternating between Subdominant Harmonies

Like IV, ii⁶, and ii$^6_5$, other inversions of IV and ii triads and seventh chords are **S**ubdominants that lead to **D**ominant harmonies.

IV⁶

IV⁶ is a first-inversion **S**ubdominant chord that leads to V or V⁷ in root position or first inversion with stepwise motion in the bass.

18.1

18.2 John Dowland, "Fine Knacks for Ladies"

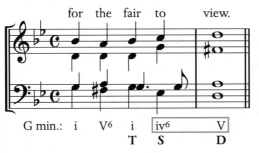

18.3 Theophania Cecil, "Evening Hymn"

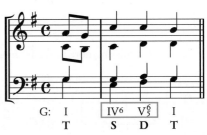

Like IV, IV⁶ (or iv⁶ in minor keys) leads to a **D**ominant harmony.

Translation: From my lips hear me say my name.

In minor keys, iv⁶ often precedes the V of a half cadence. A half cadence that concludes with a iv⁶–V progression is called a **Phrygian cadence**.

18.4 **18.5 Gioachino Rossini,** *Barber of Seville*

dal mio lab-bro il mio no-me as-col-ta   -   te.

C min.: iv⁶   V   A min.: i   iv⁶   V

> A Phrygian cadence ends iv⁶–V.

DOUBLING AND VOICE LEADING

You can double any note of IV⁶.

18.6 Robert Schumann,
"Ein Choral"

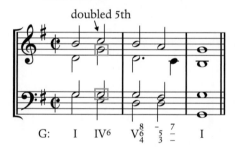

doubled 5th

G: I   IV⁶   V$_4^8$ $_3^-$ $_-^7$ I

18.7 Rose Dale, "Barnham"

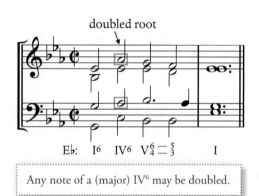

doubled root

E♭:   I⁶   IV⁶   V$_4^6$—$_3^5$ I

> Any note of a (major) IV⁶ may be doubled.

18.8 Frei Jesuíno do Monte Carmelo, "Pange Lingua"

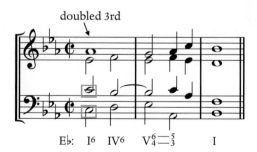

doubled 3rd

E♭:   I⁶   IV⁶   V$_4^6$—$_3^5$ I

In minor keys, however, you usually should not double the third (the bass) of iv⁶. This is because the third of iv⁶ is the minor form of $\hat{6}$, a tendency tone that pulls down to $\hat{5}$ (as in the descending melodic minor scale).

18.9

18.10 **Emma Ashford, "Sutherland"**

✓ **Good** It is often helpful to double the fifth of iv⁶ (=$\hat{1}$).

✗ **Poor** The third of (minor) iv⁶ should not be doubled, as it creates voice-leading problems.

The fifth of iv⁶ (=$\hat{1}$) is doubled.

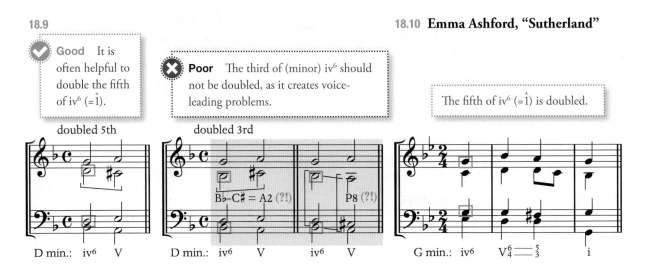

doubled 5th

doubled 3rd

Bb–C♯ = A2 (?!)   P8 (?!)

D min.: iv⁶   V   D min.: iv⁶   V   iv⁶   V   G min.: iv⁶   V⁶₄ — ⁵₃   i

If the bass in a minor key ascends from $\hat{6}$ to $\hat{7}$, you should use the raised form of $\hat{6}$ (as in the ascending melodic minor scale), turning iv⁶ into IV⁶.

18.11

✓ **Good** In minor keys, IV⁶ (with raised $\hat{6}$)—*not* iv⁶—goes to V⁶ (or V⁶₅).

✗ **Poor** In minor keys, moving from iv⁶ to V⁶ gives rise to a melodic augmented 2nd in the bass.

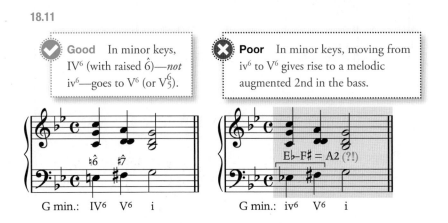

♮$\hat{6}$ ♯$\hat{7}$ Eb–F♯ = A2 (?!)

G min.: IV⁶   V⁶   i   G min.: iv⁶   V⁶   i

ROOT-POSITION ii

Much like IV, IV⁶, and ii⁶, ii⁵₃ functions as a **S**ubdominant that leads to V or V⁷.

18.12

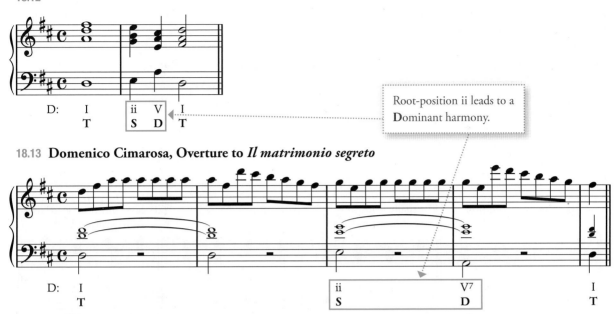

D: I   ii   V   I
    T   S   D   T

Root-position ii leads to a **D**ominant harmony.

18.13 **Domenico Cimarosa, Overture to *Il matrimonio segreto***

D: I   ii   V⁷   I
    T   S   D   T

Whereas in major keys the quality of the ii triad is minor, in minor keys its quality is diminished (ii°). Although first-inversion ii°⁶ is quite common in minor keys (see Chapter 13), a *root-position* ii°⁵₃—like all root-position diminished triads—sounds too harsh to be used in four-part harmony.

18.14

Good In minor keys, ii°⁶ is common . . .

G min.: i   ii°⁶   V   i

Poor . . . but a *root-position* ii° triad should be avoided.

G min.: i   ii°(?!) V   i

DOUBLING AND VOICE LEADING

In four-part harmony you normally should double the root of a ii⁵₃ triad. To avoid parallel fifths and octaves, usually all of the upper voices move in contrary motion with the bass when I progresses to ii.

18.15

Poor Parallel fifths and octaves can result when I progresses to ii.

E: I   ii   V

Good Parallel fifths and octaves are avoided by having all of the upper voices move in contrary motion to the bass.

E: I   ii   V

ii⁷ AND IV⁷

ii⁷

The ii^7 (in minor keys, ii$^{\varnothing7}$) also functions as a **S**ubdominant that leads to the **D**ominant. ii^7 usually appears in first inversion, as ii$^6_5$ (see Chapter 13). However, ii^7 also may appear in root position or in second or third inversion. When it progresses to V, the chordal seventh of ii^7 must resolve down by step.

18.16

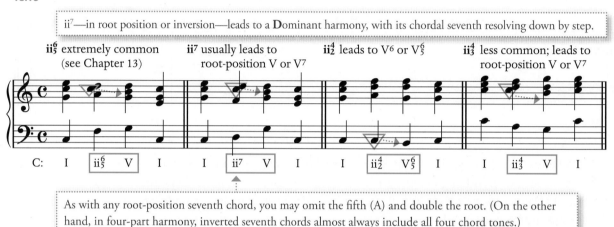

ii^7—in root position or inversion—leads to a **D**ominant harmony, with its chordal seventh resolving down by step.

ii$^6_5$ extremely common (see Chapter 13) **ii^7** usually leads to root-position V or V^7 **ii$^4_2$** leads to V^6 or V$^6_5$ **ii$^4_3$** less common; leads to root-position V or V^7

C: I | ii$^6_5$ V | I   I | ii^7 V | I   I | ii$^4_2$ V$^6_5$ | I   I | ii$^4_3$ V | I

As with any root-position seventh chord, you may omit the fifth (A) and double the root. (On the other hand, in four-part harmony, inverted seventh chords almost always include all four chord tones.)

18.17 Edvard Grieg, *Holberg Suite*, Gavotte

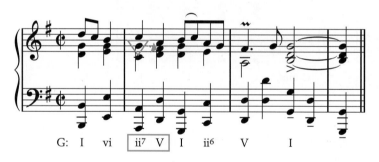

G: I vi | ii^7 V | I ii^6 V I

18.18 Hélène de Montgeroult, Étude No. 15

G min.: i | ii$^{\varnothing4}_2$ V$^6_5$ | i

IV⁷

IV^7 likewise leads to a **D**ominant harmony. Although it may appear in any inversion, IV^7 usually is used in either root position or first inversion. In each case, the chordal seventh of IV^7 must resolve down by step.

18.20 Arcangelo Corelli, Concerto Grosso No. 10, iv

18.21 A. W. Bach, "Ach! Schönster Jesu"

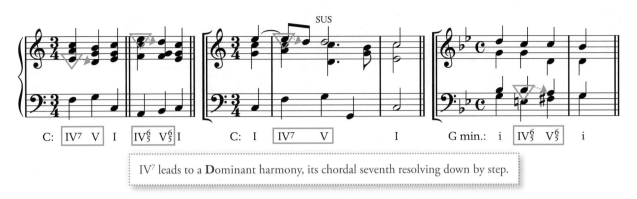

C: IV⁷ V I IV⁶₅ V⁶₅ I   C: I IV⁷ V I   G min.: i IV⁶₅ V⁶₅ i

IV⁷ leads to a **D**ominant harmony, its chordal seventh resolving down by step.

FOUR-PART HARMONY AND VOICE LEADING

Special care must be taken to avoid parallel fifths when using ii⁷ or IV⁷ in four-part harmony. Voice-leading problems that may arise in progressing from I to ii⁷ sometimes can be averted by omitting the fifth and doubling the root of ii⁷. Likewise, voice-leading problems in IV⁷–V progressions often can be avoided by a large leap in an inner voice, or by delaying the resolution of the chordal seventh by embellishing V with a cadential $^6_4$.

18.22

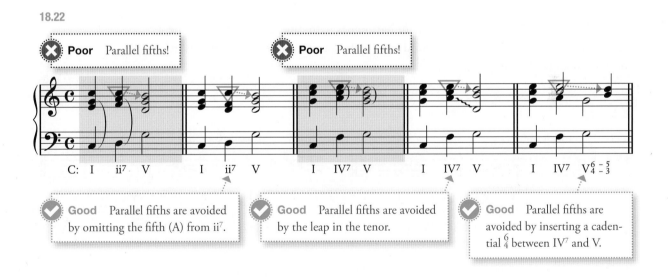

Poor Parallel fifths!   **Poor** Parallel fifths!

C: I ii⁷ V   I ii⁷ V   I IV⁷ V   I IV⁷ V   I IV⁷ V⁶₄ ⁻ ⁵₃

Good Parallel fifths are avoided by omitting the fifth (A) from ii⁷.

Good Parallel fifths are avoided by the leap in the tenor.

Good Parallel fifths are avoided by inserting a cadential $^6_4$ between IV⁷ and V.

ALTERNATING BETWEEN **S**UBDOMINANT HARMONIES

Subdominant chords may alternate with one another before progressing to V. For instance, a ii or IV triad may move between root position and first inversion.

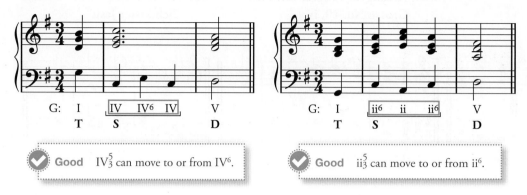

Good IV$_3^5$ can move to or from IV^6.

Good ii$_3^5$ can move to or from ii^6.

18.24 Jacob Sawyer, "All the Rage"

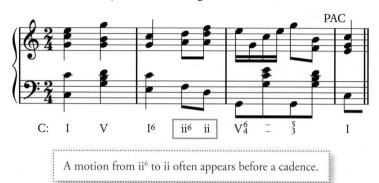

A motion from ii^6 to ii often appears before a cadence.

When moving between **S**ubdominant harmonies with different roots, it is more typical for the root to move down by third than up by a third. Thus, IV–ii is far more common than ii–IV.

18.25

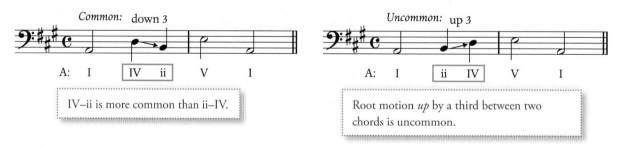

IV–ii is more common than ii–IV.

Root motion *up* by a third between two chords is uncommon.

18.26 Hector Berlioz, *Symphonie fantastique* (arr. Liszt), ii

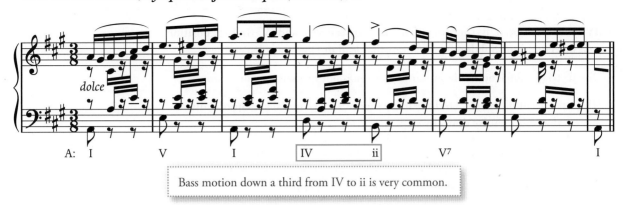

Bass motion down a third from IV to ii is very common.

Just as V may lead to but not follow V⁷, ii or IV may lead to—but *not* follow—ii⁷ or IV⁷. If ii⁷ or IV⁷ did move to a ii or IV triad, the chordal seventh in these harmonies would not be able to resolve properly.

18.27

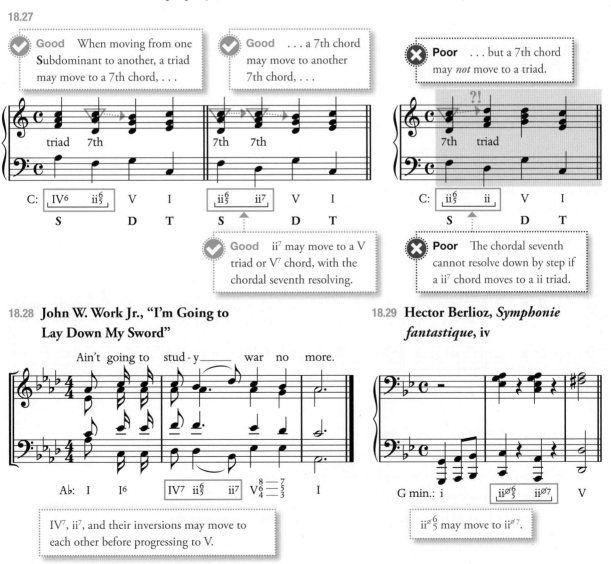

Good When moving from one **S**ubdominant to another, a triad may move to a 7th chord, . . .

Good . . . a 7th chord may move to another 7th chord, . . .

Poor . . . but a 7th chord may *not* move to a triad.

Good ii⁷ may move to a V triad or V⁷ chord, with the chordal seventh resolving.

Poor The chordal seventh cannot resolve down by step if a ii⁷ chord moves to a ii triad.

18.28 John W. Work Jr., "I'm Going to Lay Down My Sword"

IV⁷, ii⁷, and their inversions may move to each other before progressing to V.

18.29 Hector Berlioz, *Symphonie fantastique*, iv

ii⁷⁶₅ may move to ii⁷⁷.

POINTS FOR REVIEW

- IV^6, root-position ii, ii^7 (in root position and inversions), and IV^7 (in root position and inversions) are Subdominant chords that lead to Dominant harmonies.

- The ii$^\circ$ triad, which occurs in minor keys, should not be used in root position.

- The sevenths of ii^7 and IV^7 (and the inversions of these chords) are chordal dissonances that must resolve down by step.

- Subdominant harmonies may move to or from one another before progressing to a Dominant harmony. In moving between Subdominant harmonies, root motion by descending thirds is more common than by ascending thirds.

- The ii^7 and IV^7 chords may not move to IV or ii triads.

- A Phrygian cadence ends with the progression iv^6–V in a minor key.

TEST YOURSELF

1. Compare the progressions in each of the following pairs. Which (if either) contains errors, and what are the errors? (Note that both progressions may be good.)

   a. I –ii–V–I; I–V–ii–I

   b. I–IV–ii–V; I–ii–IV–V

   c. I–ii^7–V$^{6-5}_{4-3}$–I; I–IV^7–V$^{6-5}_{4-3}$–I

   d. I–ii–ii^7–V–I; I–ii^7–ii–V–I

2. Which of each of the following pairs of progressions has voice-leading problems? What is the error?

G min.:   i iv^6 V   i iv^6 V   D: ii^7 V^7 I   ii^7 V^7 I   E$\flat$:   IV^7 V$^{6-5}_{4-3}$ IV^7 V^7 I

3. Which of the following statements is true?

   a. In a iv^6 chord, you should always double the bass.

   b. A Phrygian cadence consists of the progression iv^6–V in a minor key.

   c. It is typical for a root-position ii$^\circ$ triad to appear in minor keys.

   d. The chordal seventh of both ii^7 and IV^7 must resolve down by step, whether the chord appears in root position or in inversion.

19

Multiple Functions: VI

VI has several different functions: it may follow either I or V and lead to a variety of harmonies.

Harmonies That Follow VI	**Voice Leading**
Leading to **S**ubdominant harmonies	I to vi
Leading to I⁶	V–vi (or V⁷–vi)
Leading to **D**ominant chords	"VI⁶"
Harmonies That Lead to VI	
Deceptive cadence	

Like I⁶, vi (or in minor keys, VI) usually functions as an intermediary chord leading from I to a **S**ubdominant harmony. The vi chord can also substitute for I following root-position V or V⁷.

HARMONIES THAT FOLLOW VI

LEADING TO SUBDOMINANT HARMONIES

The vi chord may lead from I to IV, ii⁶, or ii⁶₅, often with descending third motion in the bass.

19.1

Instead of moving directly from I to IV . . .	. . . I can move through vi to IV.

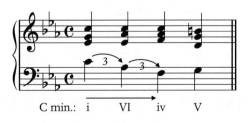

In minor keys, i can move through VI to iv.

19.2 Clara Schumann, Prelude in A♭

19.3 Theophania Cecil, "St. Jerome's" (hymn)

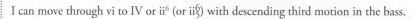

I can move through vi to IV or ii⁶ (or ii⁶₅) with descending third motion in the bass.

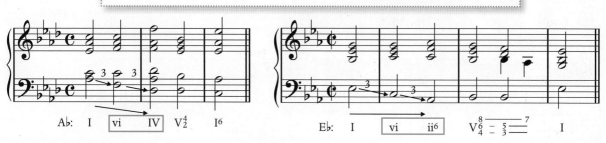

A♭: I | vi IV | V$^4_2$ I⁶

E♭: I | vi ii⁶ | V$^8_6{}^{\,4}$ – $^5_3$ —— ^{7} I

19.4 Franz Schubert, "Ständchen" ("Serenade")

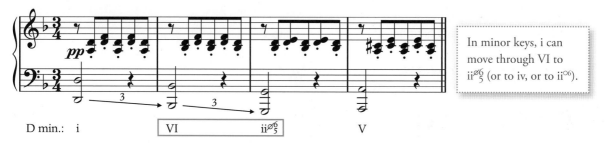

In minor keys, i can move through VI to ii$^{\varnothing6}_5$ (or to iv, or to ii°⁶).

D min.: i | VI ii$^{\varnothing6}_5$ | V

A vi may also lead from I to other **S**ubdominant chords, like ii or to IV⁶.

19.5 "Let us all with gladsome voice" (hymn)

19.6 Edvard Grieg, *Holberg Suite*, Sarabande

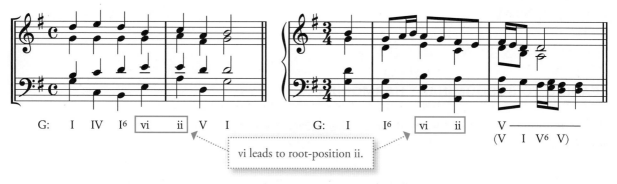

G: I IV I⁶ | vi ii | V I

G: I I⁶ | vi ii | V ———
(V I V⁶ V)

vi leads to root-position ii.

19.7 "Suabia" (hymn)

19.8 Bert Williams, "Dora Dean"

bakes the crack-lin' bread up-on   the coals!

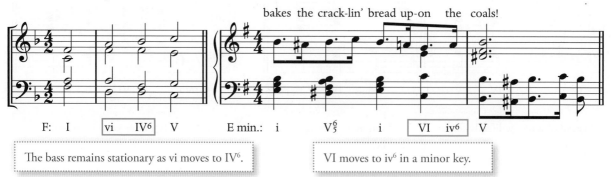

F: I | vi IV⁶ | V

E min.: i V$^6_5$ i | VI iv⁶ | V

The bass remains stationary as vi moves to IV⁶.

VI moves to iv⁶ in a minor key.

LEADING TO I⁶

A vi chord may be followed by I^6, usually with the bass moving down by a fourth.

19.9 Louise Farrenc, Nonet, Op. 38, i

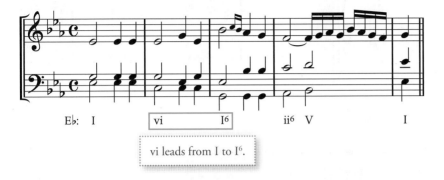

E♭: I   vi   I^6 ii^6 V   I

vi leads from I to I^6.

19.10 Franz Schubert, "Auf dem Flusse" ("On the River")

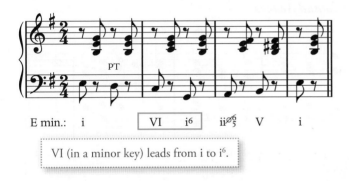

E min.: i   VI   i^6 ii$^{ø6}_5$ V   i

VI (in a minor key) leads from i to i^6.

LEADING TO DOMINANT CHORDS

A V triad or seventh chord in root position or first inversion may sometimes directly follow vi. This is a less common option, however: it is much more normal for vi to lead to a **S**ubdominant harmony than to a **D**ominant harmony.

19.11 Jules Massenet, Gavotte, from *Manon*   **19.12 R. Nathaniel Dett, "Ave Maria"**

G: I   I^6 vi   V^7 I

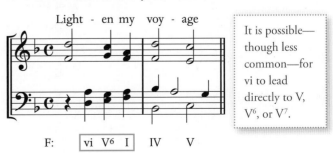

Light - en my voy - age

F: vi V^6 I   IV   V

It is possible—though less common—for vi to lead directly to V, V^6, or V^7.

HARMONIES THAT LEAD TO VI

As with all other harmonies, vi may directly follow I or I⁶.

19.13 Dmytro Bortniansky, Hymn

vi may follow I.

A vi chord may also follow root-position V or V⁷. In such a case the resulting V–vi substitutes for the more typical V–I progression.

19.14   **19.15 Henry Purcell, "To the hills and the vale,"**
                             from *Dido and Aeneas*

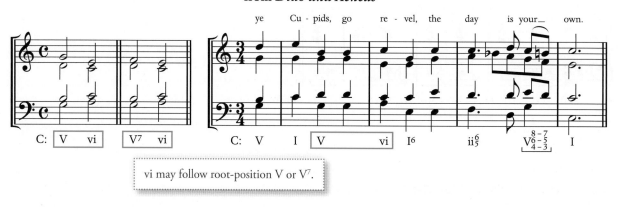

vi may follow root-position V or V⁷.

DECEPTIVE CADENCE

At times an expected authentic cadence is thwarted when a root-position V or V⁷ moves to vi instead of to I. This is known as a **deceptive cadence (DC)**. A deceptive cadence must involve a *root-position* V or V⁷ (*not* an inverted V).

19.16 Frédéric Chopin, Prelude in B Minor, Op. 28

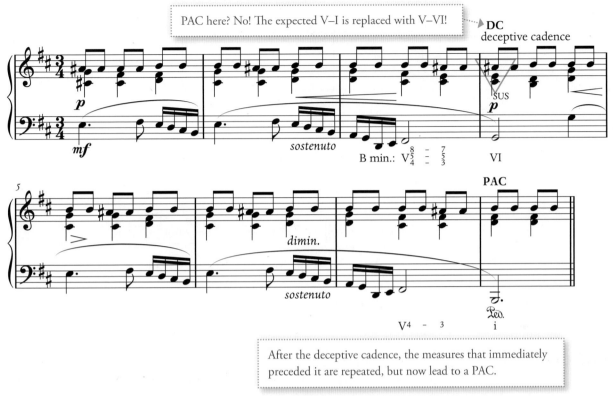

PAC here? No! The expected V–I is replaced with V–VI!

DC
deceptive cadence

B min.: V^{8-7}_{4-3} VI

PAC

V^{4-3} i

After the deceptive cadence, the measures that immediately preceded it are repeated, but now lead to a PAC.

The following chart summarizes chords that lead to and from vi:

19.17

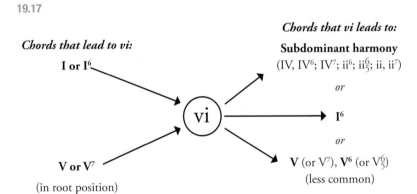

Chords that lead to vi:

I or I⁶

vi

V or V⁷
(in root position)

Chords that vi leads to:

Subdominant harmony
(IV, IV⁶; IV⁷; ii⁶; ii$^6_5$; ii, ii⁷)

or

I⁶

or

V (or V⁷), **V⁶** (or V$^6_5$)
(less common)

VOICE LEADING

I TO vi

When I moves to vi in four-part harmony, usually the root of vi is doubled. Like other chords whose roots are a third apart, I and vi share two tones in common. Accordingly, when moving between root-position triads whose roots are separated by a third, usually the two common tones repeat in the upper voices, and a third upper voice moves by step in contrary motion to the bass.

19.18

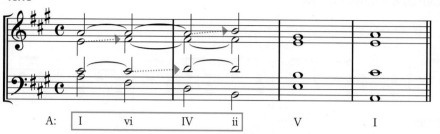

A: I   vi   IV   ii   V   I

When root-position chords progress down by thirds, the two shared tones in the upper voices repeat (see tied notes) while the other upper voice moves in contrary motion to the bass.

Incidentally, although descending root motion by third occurs frequently, ascending root motion by third is far less common.

19.19

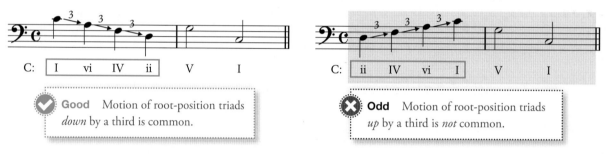

C: I   vi   IV   ii   V   I

C: ii   IV   vi   I   V   I

Good Motion of root-position triads *down* by a third is common.

Odd Motion of root-position triads *up* by a third is *not* common.

V–vi (OR V⁷–vi)

When one root-position chord moves up by step to another, the upper voices usually all move down, in contrary motion with the bass, and the root is doubled in both chords. With V–vi (or V^7–vi), however, matters are complicated by the leading tone within V, which leads up to the tonic. Accordingly, when V or V^7 moves to vi, the leading tone moves up by step, and the third of vi (i.e., $\hat{1}$) is doubled, rather than its root.

19.20

Typically, all upper voices move *down* when the bass moves up by step from one root-position chord to another . . .

. . . but with V–vi (or V^7–vi), usually the bass and $\hat{7}$ move up by step, and the other two upper voices move down to the nearest chord tone.

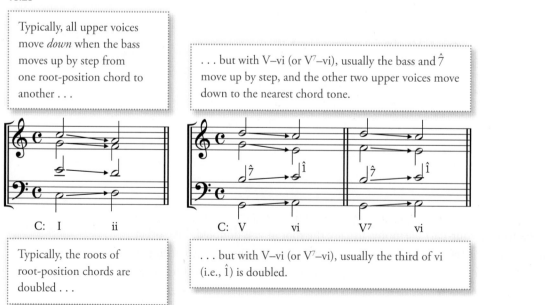

C: I   ii

C: V   vi V^7 vi

Typically, the roots of root-position chords are doubled . . .

. . . but with V–vi (or V^7–vi), usually the third of vi (i.e., $\hat{1}$) is doubled.

19.21 **W. A. Mozart, Clarinet Quintet in A, K. 581, i**

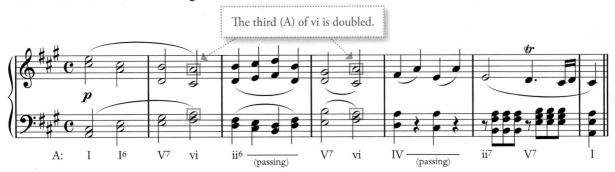

The third (A) of vi is doubled.

A: I   I⁶   V⁷   vi   ii⁶ (passing)   V⁷   vi   IV (passing)   ii⁷   V⁷   I

In major keys, it is also possible in a V–vi progression for all the upper voices to move in contrary motion to the bass, so that the root of vi is doubled. This alternate voice-leading pattern should not be used in minor keys, however, since it would give rise to a melodic augmented second between $\hat{7}$ and $\hat{6}$.

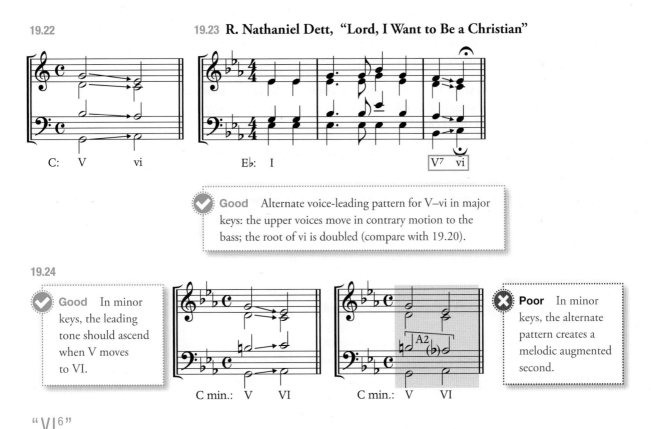

19.22

C: V   vi

19.23 **R. Nathaniel Dett, "Lord, I Want to Be a Christian"**

E♭:   I   V⁷   vi

✓ **Good**   Alternate voice-leading pattern for V–vi in major keys: the upper voices move in contrary motion to the bass; the root of vi is doubled (compare with 19.20).

19.24

✓ **Good**   In minor keys, the leading tone should ascend when V moves to VI.

C min.:   V   VI

C min.:   V   VI

✗ **Poor**   In minor keys, the alternate pattern creates a melodic augmented second.

"VI⁶"

Sometimes neighbor tones, passing tones, or other embellishments in an upper voice give rise to what is literally vi⁶. In identifying harmonies, this chord is usually understood as a **T**onic chord decorated with an embellishing tone. Except when used as part of a modulation (see Chapters 27 and 28), a "vi⁶" should *not* be used in basic four-part harmony exercises.

19.25 **Maria Xaveria Peruchona, "Solvite," from** *Sacri Concerti de Mottetti,* **Op. 1**

G: I ——————————— ii$^4_2$ V$^6_5$ I
(= I ——————— "vi^6")

> Although the incomplete neighbor tone E in the melody creates what is literally a vi^6 (G–B–E), the chord here essentially is a decorated **I**.

POINTS FOR REVIEW

- vi (or VI in minor) often leads to a Subdominant harmony, such as IV, IV^6, IV^7, ii^6, ii$^6_5$, ii, or ii^7. It also often leads to I^6. Less commonly, it may lead directly to V or V^6.

- vi (or VI in minor) may follow Tonic harmony; it may also follow V or V^7 in root position.

- Sometimes an expected authentic cadence is thwarted when a root-position V (or V^7) moves to vi (or VI in minor) instead of I. This creates a *deceptive cadence.*

- When V (or V^7) moves to vi (or VI) in four-part harmony, usually (a) the bass and leading tone move up by step, (b) the other two voices move down by step or by third, and (c) the third of the vi chord is doubled.

- In most cases "vi^6" is best understood as a Tonic decorated with an embellishing tone; vi^6 should *not* be used in basic harmony exercises.

TEST YOURSELF

1. In standard harmonic practice, which of the following chords may follow vi?
   a. IV, ii^6, ii$^6_5$, iv^6, ii, or ii^7 **b.** I or I^6 **c.** V or V^6

2. Which of the following chords do not commonly precede vi?
   I; I^6; V; V^7; IV; ii

3. Which of the following chord progressions may be found at a deceptive cadence?
   a. V–vi   **b.** V^7–vi   **c.** V$^6_5$–vi   **d.** V–vi^6 **e.** I–vi

4. Which (if any) of the following chord progressions contain a voice-leading error? What is the error, and how should it be fixed?

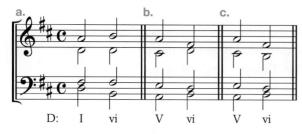

D: I vi   V vi   V vi

D min.: i VI   V VI   V VI

20

Voice Leading with Embellishing Tones

Embellishing tones elaborate harmonies, but can also create or solve voice-leading problems.

Voice Leading (Creating and Removing Parallels)	Pedal Point
	Figured Bass for Embellishing Tones
Accented Dissonances in Four-Part Harmony	9 as Suspension and V⁹

As we've already seen, chords in four-part harmony are frequently embellished, intensifying the harmonic framework. These embellishing tones can sometimes create or solve voice-leading problems.

VOICE LEADING (CREATING AND REMOVING PARALLELS)

When using embellishing tones (such as passing tones) you must be careful that they do not result in parallel fifths and octaves. Such faulty parallels might arise when using two embellishing tones at the same time.

20.1   **20.2 Johann Friedrich Doles, "Ein feste Burg" (chorale)**

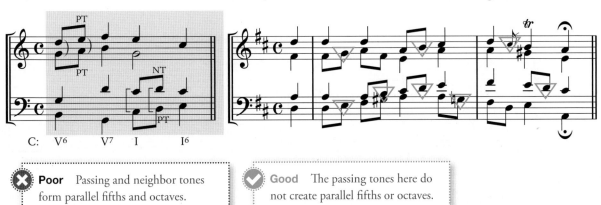

❌ **Poor** Passing and neighbor tones form parallel fifths and octaves.

✅ **Good** The passing tones here do not create parallel fifths or octaves.

Parallel octaves and fifths may also arise between a single embellishing tone and a chord tone. As a result, adding embellishing tones to a passage with good voice leading might give rise to faulty parallels.

20.3

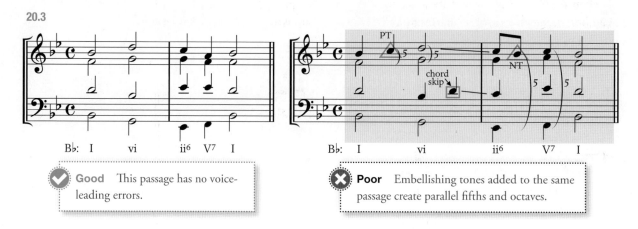

> ✓ **Good** This passage has no voice-leading errors.

> ✗ **Poor** Embellishing tones added to the same passage create parallel fifths and octaves.

While added dissonant embellishing tones can create faulty parallels, they are less effective in removing them. In particular, dissonant embellishing tones cannot be added to correct parallel octaves.

20.4

> ✗ **Poor** Parallel octaves between bass and soprano.

> ✗ **Poor** Adding a passing tone doesn't fix the parallel octaves.

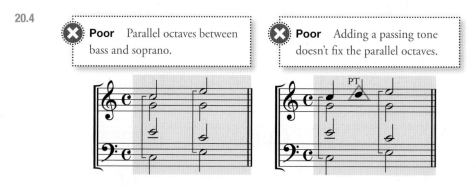

A chord skip (leaping from one chord tone to another), however, can be used to avoid parallel fifths or octaves.

20.5

20.6 J. S. Bach, Chorale 51

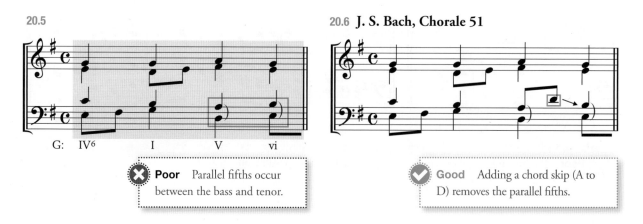

> ✗ **Poor** Parallel fifths occur between the bass and tenor.

> ✓ **Good** Adding a chord skip (A to D) removes the parallel fifths.

ACCENTED DISSONANCES IN FOUR-PART HARMONY

At times an accented embellishing tone may delay the full arrival of a harmony. That is, when a chord is decorated by a suspension, accented passing tone, or accented neighbor tone, the complete harmony might appear only when the embellishment resolves to the chord tone.

20.7

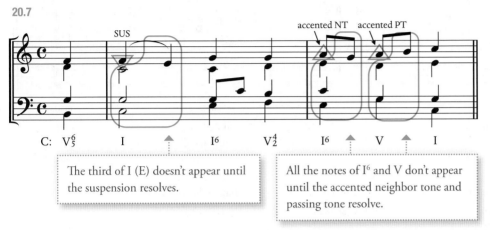

The third of I (E) doesn't appear until the suspension resolves.

All the notes of I^6 and V don't appear until the accented neighbor tone and passing tone resolve.

Indeed, when it is decorated by an accented dissonance, the third of a chord should not appear in any other voice until the dissonance resolves.

20.8

The thirds of both I and V are decorated by accented, dissonant embellishing tones.

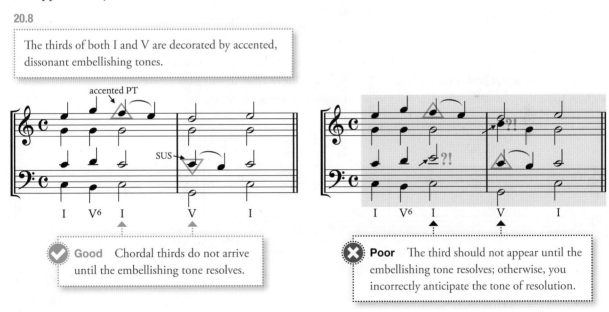

Good Chordal thirds do not arrive until the embellishing tone resolves.

Poor The third should not appear until the embellishing tone resolves; otherwise, you incorrectly anticipate the tone of resolution.

PEDAL POINT

A **pedal point** arises when a single tone is sustained—usually in the bass—as the chords around it change. Whereas most embellishing tones decorate the underlying chord, a pedal point is itself decorated by chords that sound above it. Pedal points usually appear toward the start or conclusion of a piece or large section of a piece. They often are used to embellish either a tonic or dominant chord that appears at both the start and end of the pedal point.

20.9 J. M. Nunes Garcia, "O Triunfo da América"

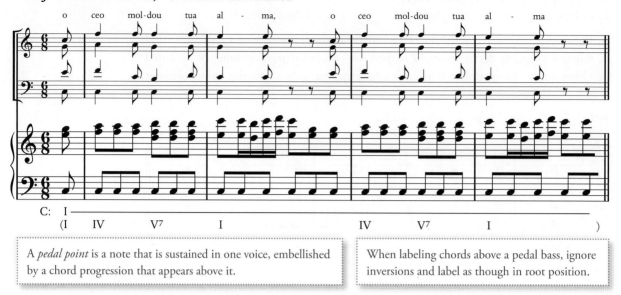

> A *pedal point* is a note that is sustained in one voice, embellished by a chord progression that appears above it.

> When labeling chords above a pedal bass, ignore inversions and label as though in root position.

Translation: The sky has molded your soul.

FIGURED BASS FOR EMBELLISHING TONES

In figured bass, a succession of figures under a single bass note often indicates embellishing tones. In such a case, the upper voice moves from one note to another as indicated by intervals above the bass. If a long dash follows a number, then that note should be sustained while other voices move. Remember that the figures refer to intervals above a given bass: they do *not* necessarily refer to an inversion of a triad or seventh chord.

20.10

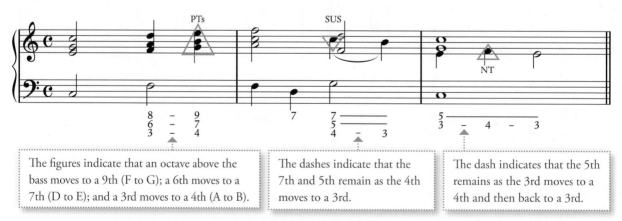

> The figures indicate that an octave above the bass moves to a 9th (F to G); a 6th moves to a 7th (D to E); and a 3rd moves to a 4th (A to B).

> The dashes indicate that the 7th and 5th remain as the 4th moves to a 3rd.

> The dash indicates that the 5th remains as the 3rd moves to a 4th and then back to a 3rd.

A particularly common figured bass that involves an embellishing tone occurs when the third of a root-position triad is decorated by an accented dissonant fourth above $\hat{5}$ in the bass. The figured bass for this is "$^5_{4-3}$," which may be abbreviated as either "4–3" or—if the third above the bass is raised by means of an accidental—as "4–#"

or "4–♮." In such cases, the bass should be doubled, not the fourth above the bass (which is a dissonance). The resulting harmony is labeled with Roman numerals as "V⁴⁻³."

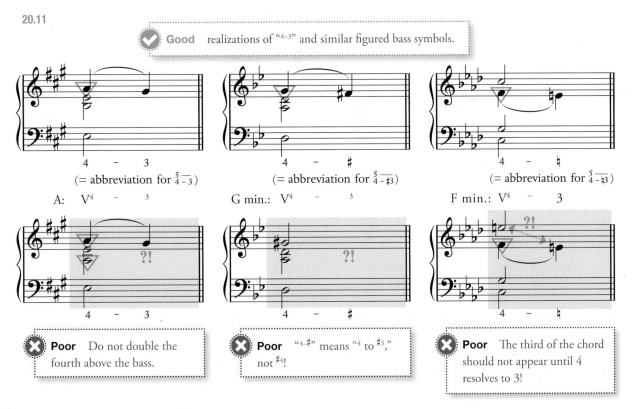

20.11

Good   realizations of "4–3" and similar figured bass symbols.

4   –   3
(= abbreviation for ⁵₄ – 3)
A: V⁴   –   3

4   –   ♯
(= abbreviation for ⁵₄ – ♯3)
G min.:   V⁴   –   3

4   –   ♮
(= abbreviation for ⁵₄ – ♮3)
F min.:   V⁴   –   3

4   –   3

4   –   ♯

4   –   ♮

Poor   Do not double the fourth above the bass.

Poor   "4–♯" means "4 to ♯3," not ♯4!

Poor   The third of the chord should not appear until 4 resolves to 3!

Sometimes an embellishing tone is found in the bass while the upper voices remain stationary. This often is indicated in the figured bass with a dash below the embellishing bass note. When the only symbol below a bass note is a dash, the upper voices should stay on the same notes while only the bass voice moves.

20.12

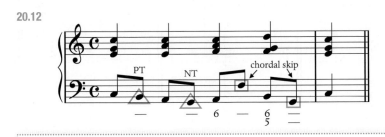

PT   NT   chordal skip

—   — 6   — 6   —
              5

If the only figured bass symbol below a bass note is a dash, only the bass moves.

While most dissonances indicated by figures (such as sevenths) relate to an upper voice that then must resolve, the figure "2" indicates that the bass is dissonant. In such a case the bass should not be doubled.

20.13

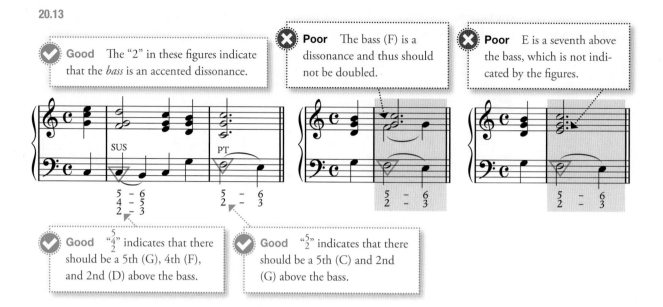

✓ Good The "2" in these figures indicate that the *bass* is an accented dissonance.

✗ Poor The bass (F) is a dissonance and thus should not be doubled.

✗ Poor E is a seventh above the bass, which is not indicated by the figures.

✓ Good "$\frac{5}{4}$" indicates that there should be a 5th (G), 4th (F), and 2nd (D) above the bass.

✓ Good "$\frac{5}{2}$" indicates that there should be a 5th (C) and 2nd (G) above the bass.

9 AS SUSPENSION AND V⁹

The suspension of a ninth above the bass of a root-position chord is an especially powerful embellishment. The suspended ninth, which resolves down by step, must appear at least an octave above the chord root; if the chord root is doubled, the ninth must appear at least an octave above the highest chord root.

20.14

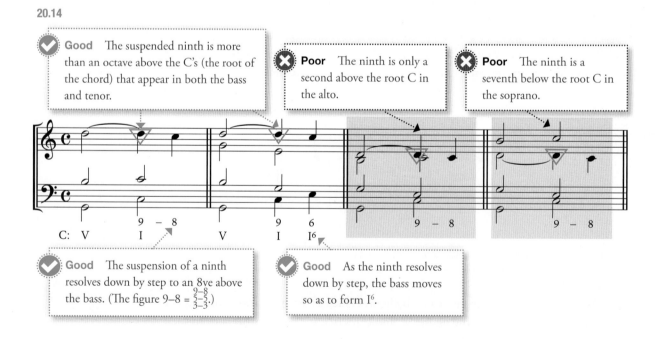

✓ Good The suspended ninth is more than an octave above the C's (the root of the chord) that appear in both the bass and tenor.

✗ Poor The ninth is only a second above the root C in the alto.

✗ Poor The ninth is a seventh below the root C in the soprano.

✓ Good The suspension of a ninth resolves down by step to an 8ve above the bass. (The figure 9–8 = $\frac{9-8}{5-5}$.)

✓ Good As the ninth resolves down by step, the bass moves so as to form I⁶.

A ninth is treated with particular freedom when used in conjunction with the notes of V^7. V^9_7 (abbreviated V^9) is a **D**ominant harmony that uses the notes of V^7 plus a ninth above the bass. V^9 may appear in root position or (more rarely) in inversion, often in thick textures of more than four voices. Although the dissonant chordal ninth of V^9 tends to resolve down by step, in practice this resolution often is treated quite freely.

20.15

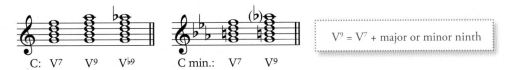

> $V^9 = V^7$ + major or minor ninth

20.16 Harriett Abrams, "A Smile and a Tear"

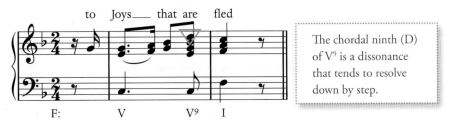

> The chordal ninth (D) of V^9 is a dissonance that tends to resolve down by step.

Translation: Oh sunshine, do you believe . . .?

20.17 Charles Gounod, "Romance de Siébel," from *Faust*

> The resolution of the chordal ninth (F♯–E) is merely implied here.

20.18 Eva Jessye, "So I can write my name"

> The chordal ninth of V^9 (C) resolves up to tonic here.

- The addition of embellishing tones might create parallel fifths or octaves, either between the embellishing tones themselves or between the embellishing tones and the chord tones.

- Adding an embellishing tone to a passage cannot fix parallel octaves.

- Suspensions, accented passing tones, and accented neighbor tones can delay the appearance of chord tones.

- A *pedal point* occurs when a note is sustained in one voice (usually the bass) while there is a chord progression in the other voices.

- Figured bass symbols may indicate the presence of embellishing tones in the upper voices by using successive sets of numerals under a single bass tone.

- The figured bass symbol "4–3" is an abbreviation for "$\frac{5}{4-3}$."

- A dash under a bass tone in the figured bass indicates that the bass moves while the upper voices remain on the same notes.

- A suspended ninth should appear an octave or more above the chord root and resolve down by step.

- V^9 is a Dominant harmony consisting of a V^7 with an added ninth.

TEST YOURSELF

1. Which of the following include parallel fifths or octaves?

2. In four-part harmony, what are the notes in the upper voices of the following chords? If the chords use only three different pitches, make sure to indicate which tone(s) can be doubled in four-part harmony.

21

III and VII

The III and VII chords occasionally substitute for more-common harmonies.

Root-Position III	Subtonic VII
"III^6"	A Closer Look
vii$^{\circ 5}_{3}$	"vii$^{\circ 6}_{4}$"
	"V$^{7}_{6}$"

The iii and vii$^{\circ 5}_{3}$ triads—III and VII in minor keys—are not often used in **diatonic** contexts (that is, where the music stays within a single key). In the relatively infrequent instances they do appear, these triads usually substitute for more-common harmonies.

ROOT-POSITION III

A root-position mediant chord—iii in major keys or III in minor keys—shares the same bass and two of the same notes as I^6. Occasionally, iii substitutes for I^6—that is, it is found in situations similar to those in which I^6 appears.

21.1

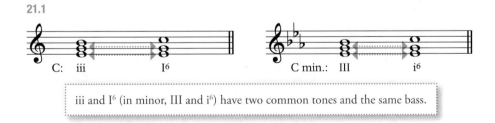

C: iii   I^6 C min.:   III   i^6

iii and I^6 (in minor, III and i^6) have two common tones and the same bass.

21.2 J. S. Bach, Chorale 14

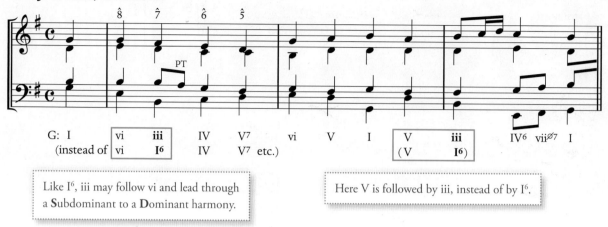

G: I | vi iii | IV V⁷ vi V I | V iii | IV⁶ vii°⁷ I
(instead of | vi I⁶ | IV V⁷ etc.) | (V I⁶)

> Like I⁶, iii may follow vi and lead through a **S**ubdominant to a **D**ominant harmony.

> Here V is followed by iii, instead of by I⁶.

The $\hat{7}$ within the iii chord does not need to ascend to the tonic. Accordingly, iii is sometimes used to harmonize melodies in which $\hat{7}$ descends to $\hat{6}$. And since it does not lead up to the tonic, $\hat{7}$ within III is not raised in minor keys.

21.3 "Ach Gott und Herr" (hymn)

21.4 Ludwig van Beethoven, Piano Sonata in C♯ Minor, Op. 27, No. 1, i ("Moonlight")

> $\hat{7}$ within iii (A) does not need to resolve to the tonic; it may descend to $\hat{6}$.

> $\hat{7}$ (B) within III in minor keys is *not* raised.

B♭: I iii IV I
(instead of I I⁶ IV I)

C♯ min.: III V⁴₃ i

> Like i⁶, iii may lead to a **S**ubdominant harmony.

> Like i⁶, III may lead directly to a **D**ominant.

21.5

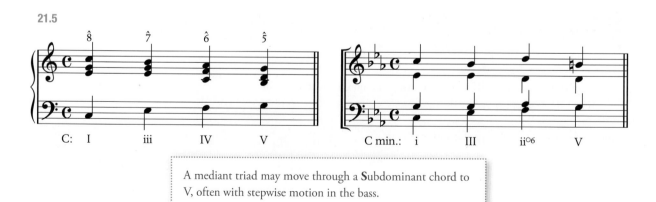

C: I iii IV V

C min.: i III ii°⁶ V

> A mediant triad may move through a **S**ubdominant chord to V, often with stepwise motion in the bass.

The mediant chord is most often found in passages where there are **modulations**, or **tonicizations** (that is, changes of key), and chromatic alterations (see Part 4). The diatonic situations where the mediant triad is most normally found are those that involve repeated harmonic patterns known as **sequences** (as will be discussed in Chapter 22, any chord may be used in a sequence). Except for passages containing sequences, modulations, or tonicizations, iii should be used only sparingly—if at all—in harmonizing diatonic chorale melodies.

21.6

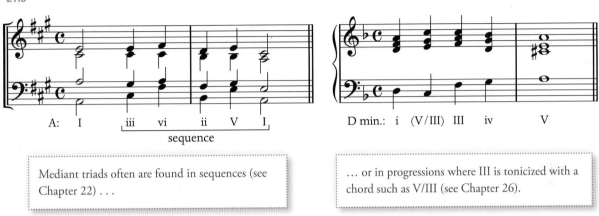

A: I   iii   vi   ii   V   I

sequence

Mediant triads often are found in sequences (see Chapter 22) . . .

D min.: i   (V/III) III   iv   V

. . . or in progressions where III is tonicized with a chord such as V/III (see Chapter 26).

"III⁶"

The "iii⁶" in major keys and "III+⁶" in minor keys each function like a root-position V in which the fifth of the chord is replaced with a sixth above the bass. Indeed, a chord that literally forms "iii⁶" is usually simply labeled as a V that is decorated with an embellishing tone.

21.7

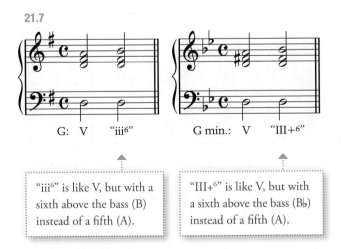

G: V   "iii⁶"   G min.: V   "III+⁶"

"iii⁶" is like V, but with a sixth above the bass (B) instead of a fifth (A).

"III+⁶" is like V, but with a sixth above the bass (B♭) instead of a fifth (A).

21.8 Harry T. Burleigh, "Let Us Cheer the Weary Traveler"

Especially in later nineteenth-century music, "iii⁶" often substitutes for V. However, this chord is not suited for simple chorale contexts. Accordingly, you should *not* use "iii⁶" in four-part harmony exercises.

vii°$^5_3$

Whereas vii°⁶ is extremely common in four-part harmony, the root-position vii° triad is *not*. Indeed, even when it appears in textures with three voices, what appears to be a vii°$^5_3$ triad is to be understood as a V$^6_5$ in which the root is omitted. Except within sequences (see Chapter 22), do *not* use a root-position vii° triad in four-part harmony exercises.

21.9 Manuel Dias de Oliveira, *Magnificat*

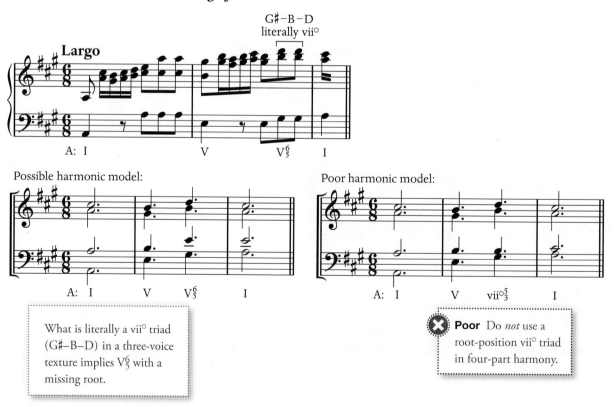

Possible harmonic model:

Poor harmonic model:

What is literally a vii° triad (G♯–B–D) in a three-voice texture implies V$^6_5$ with a missing root.

Poor Do *not* use a root-position vii° triad in four-part harmony.

SUBTONIC VII

While $\hat{7}$ is regularly raised in minor keys to form the leading tone, the **subtonic** or unaltered form of $\hat{7}$ can also be used harmonically as the root of **subtonic VII**. Since raised $\hat{7}$ is so important in establishing a minor key, a strongly emphasized subtonic VII can undermine a minor-key tonality. Accordingly, subtonic VII is most often used to move to the relative major, either briefly or in a more extended way (see Chapters 26 and 28). It is also possible for the subtonic VII to lead directly to V^6 or V_5^6, though even in such cases the subtonic VII usually hints at a change of key.

21.10 Theophania Cecil, "St. Katherine's" (hymn)

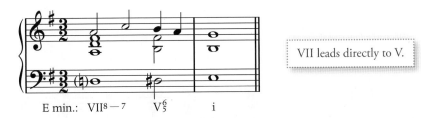

E min.:   VII$^{8-7}$ V$_5^6$ i

> VII leads directly to V.

As a result of these complications, except within sequences (see Chapter 22) you should *not* use the subtonic VII in diatonic four-part harmony exercises.

🔍 To learn about "vii$^{\circ 6}_4$" and "V$_6^7$", see A Closer Look.

POINTS FOR REVIEW

- The root-position mediant (iii in major keys and III in minor keys) occasionally substitutes for I^6.

- $\hat{7}$ within the root-position mediant triad does not need to resolve up to the tonic, and thus iii is sometimes used to harmonize melodic motions from $\hat{7}$ to $\hat{6}$.

- In minor keys, do not raise $\hat{7}$ within III$_3^5$.

- "iii^6" (in minor keys, "III+^{6}") is essentially a V triad with a sixth above the bass replacing the fifth of the chord; "iii^6" should *not* be used in basic harmony exercises.

- When they appear in three-voice textures, root-position vii$^{\circ}$ triads suggest V$_5^6$ with an implied root; they should *not* be used in four-part harmony.

- The subtonic VII is a chord whose root is natural-minor $\hat{7}$. Occasionally, the subtonic VII may lead to V^6 or V$_5^6$.

1. Are the following statements true or false?

   a. The use of iii is often similar to the use of I⁶.

   b. The leading tone within the iii triad must ascend to the tonic when it appears in the top voice.

   c. $\hat{7}$ within the III chord in minor keys normally should not be raised.

   d. The iii⁶ chord essentially functions as a **D**ominant.

   e. iii and iii⁶ are often used within basic melody harmonization exercises.

   f. You should not use a vii°⁶ chord in four-part harmony exercises.

   g. A subtonic VII chord (whose root is a whole step below $\hat{1}$) may lead to V⁶.

2. Label the Roman numerals in the blank lines provided:

   a. Franz Schubert, "Im Frühling"

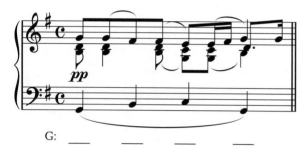

   G: ___ ___ ___ ___

   b. Johannes Brahms, Symphony No. 4, iii

   C: ___ ___ ___ IV⁶ V

   c. Robert Schumann, *Symphonic Etudes*

   C♯ min.: ___ ___ ___

   d. Edward Barnes, "Gloria"

   F: ___ ___ ___ ii ___ ___

   e. Elizabeth Mounsey, "Charity Hymn"

   C: ___ ___ ___ ___ ___ ___

22

Sequences

Sequences are repeated musical segments that are transposed in a regular pattern.

Repeated Patterns	Ascending Sequences
Descending Sequences	Roots alternate down 3, up 4
Descending fifths (roots alternate up 4, down 5)	Ascending fifths (roots alternate up 5, down 4)
Roots alternate down 4, up 2	Voice Leading in Sequences
Descending parallel $^6_3$ chords	

REPEATED PATTERNS

A **sequence** occurs when a segment of music repeats one or more times in succession, transposed in a regular pattern. The segment that forms the basis of a sequence can last as briefly as a single beat and consist of only a single harmony, or as long as several measures and involve a melody (**melodic sequence**), a progression of several harmonies (**harmonic sequence**), or both.

22.1 **José Silvestre White, Etude for Violin, Op. 13, No. 1**

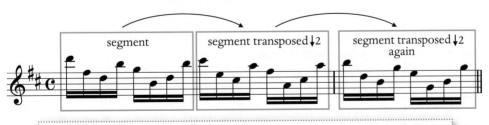

In this melodic sequence, the melody repeats, transposed down a second each time.

22.2 J. S. Bach, C Major Invention

> In this sequence involving two contrapuntal lines, a segment is repeated twice, transposed down a third each time.

Typically, a harmonic sequence involves a repeated two-chord pattern in which every pair of chords is transposed up or down in a systematic fashion.

22.3

> As a result of the sequential pattern, every pair of chords here (indicated by the brackets above the staff) is systematically transposed up by step.

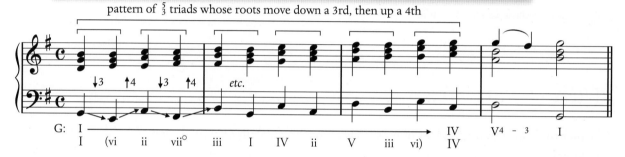

The harmonies of a sequence lead from the sequence's first chord to its last. Once a sequence starts, there is an expectation that the pattern of transposition will continue. As a result, the logic of chord successions within the middle of a sequence derives from the harmonic pattern, not from the functions (**T**onic, **D**ominant, or **S**ubdominant) of the individual chords. Accordingly, in the middle of a sequence you may find chords or harmonic successions that in other contexts would be unusual.

22.4

> **Good** Although in a standard functional progression, you avoid chords such as iii⁶, vi⁶, and vii°⁵₃, or chord progressions such a V (**D**ominant) moving to ii (**S**ubdominant), in the middle of a sequence they are fine!

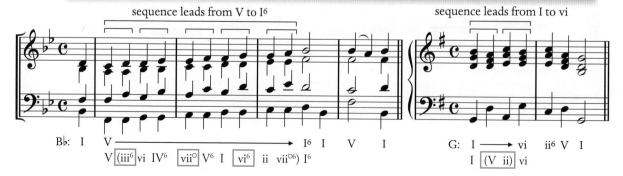

DESCENDING SEQUENCES

DESCENDING FIFTHS (ROOTS ALTERNATE UP 4, DOWN 5)

The chord progressions that make up sequences often are labeled by the pattern formed by their roots. Of the numerous possible harmonic patterns that may govern a sequence, some are particularly common. The one used most often is the **descending fifth sequence**, also known as the **circle of fifths progression**. This sequence involves chords whose roots alternately move up by a fourth and down by a fifth, so that every other chord is transposed down a scale step.

22.5

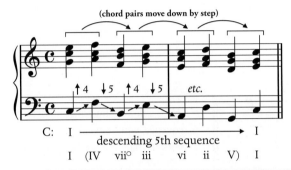

In a descending fifth sequence, chord roots alternately move up a fourth and down a fifth, so that every pair of chords moves down by step.

22.6 **Anna Bon, Flute Sonata, Op. 1, No. 1, iii**

Descending fifth sequences can be varied by replacing some or all of the root-position triads with seventh chords, inverted chords, or both.

> Within the descending fifth sequence every chord (or every other chord) may be a seventh chord, inverted, or both.

Descending fifth sequence in which:

a. every chord is a seventh chord   **b.** every other chord is in first inversion   **c.** every other chord is a seventh chord in first inversion

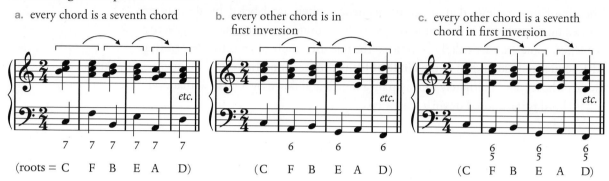

(roots = C F B E A D)   (C F B E A D)   (C F B E A D)

22.8 G. F. Handel, Violin Sonata in E, HWV 373, iii

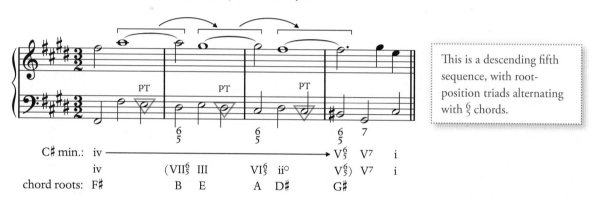

> This is a descending fifth sequence, with root-position triads alternating with $\frac{6}{5}$ chords.

ROOTS ALTERNATE DOWN 4, UP 2

In another common descending sequence, the roots of the chords move alternately down by a fourth, then up by step.

22.9   **22.10 Johann Pachelbel, Canon in D**

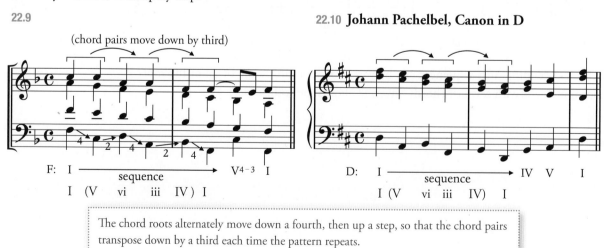

> The chord roots alternately move down a fourth, then up a step, so that the chord pairs transpose down by a third each time the pattern repeats.

A variant of this sequence arises when every other chord is in first inversion, so that the bass moves stepwise down the scale.

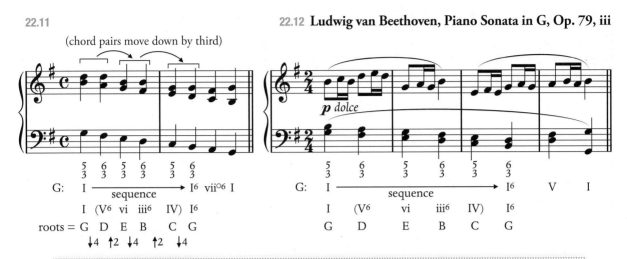

22.11

22.12 **Ludwig van Beethoven, Piano Sonata in G, Op. 79, iii**

In a variant of the "down 4, up 2" sequence, the bass descends by step, alternately supporting $\frac{5}{3}$ and $\frac{6}{3}$ chords.

DESCENDING PARALLEL $\frac{6}{3}$ CHORDS

Another common descending sequence involves **descending parallel $\frac{6}{3}$ chords**, in which a first-inversion chord is repeatedly transposed down by step. Only first-inversion triads can move in parallel motion without producing voice-leading errors: parallel $\frac{5}{3}$ chords result in parallel fifths, and parallel $\frac{6}{4}$ chords involve dissonances that do not resolve. In order to avoid voice-leading errors, however, the two upper voices of parallel $\frac{6}{3}$ chords must move in parallel fourths, not fifths. Parallel $\frac{6}{3}$ chords most often appear in three-part rather than four-part textures.

22.13

Good Descending parallel $\frac{6}{3}$ chords. Parallel perfect fourths between the two top voices (unlike perfect fifths) are fine.

Poor Parallel $\frac{5}{3}$ or parallel $\frac{6}{4}$ chords would create parallel fifths or unresolved dissonances.

Poor Parallel $\frac{6}{3}$ chords can use perfect fourths in the top voices, but not perfect fifths.

22.14 Maria Cosway, "Mormora il fiumicello" ("The Stream Murmurs")

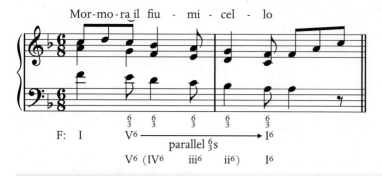

All the notes of each chord move down by step within each stage of this parallel ⁶₃ sequence.

Sequences of descending parallel ⁶₃ chords often are decorated by suspensions.

22.15

22.16 W. A. Mozart, Piano Sonata in G, K. 283, i

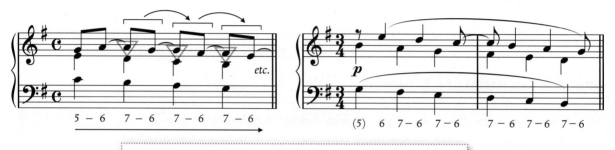

Descending parallel ⁶₃ chords decorated by a series of 7–6 suspensions

ASCENDING SEQUENCES

ROOTS ALTERNATE DOWN 3, UP 4

The most common ascending sequence is one in which the roots alternately move down by a third, then up by a fourth.

22.17

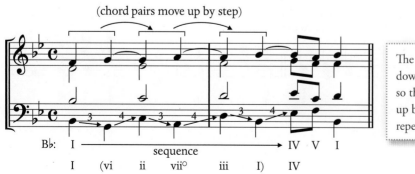

The chord roots alternate moving down a third and up a fourth, so that the chord pairs transpose up by step each time the pattern repeats.

22.18 **François Couperin, "Les brinborions"**

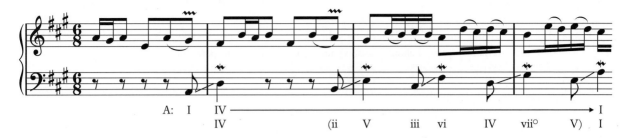

In a common variant of this sequence, every other chord appears in first inversion. In this variant, the bass line ascends by step, with each bass note of the sequence supporting a $\frac{5}{3}$ triad followed by a $\frac{6}{3}$ triad. This variant of the "down 3, up 4" sequence is called an **ascending 5–6 sequence**. This sequence most often appears in three-voice texture, rather than in four voices.

22.19

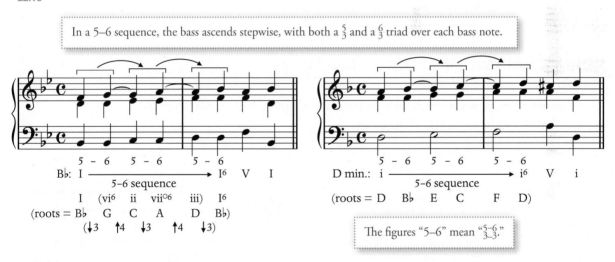

In a 5–6 sequence, the bass ascends stepwise, with both a $\frac{5}{3}$ and a $\frac{6}{3}$ triad over each bass note.

The figures "5–6" mean "$\frac{5\text{–}6}{3\text{–}3}$."

ASCENDING FIFTHS (ROOTS ALTERNATE UP 5, DOWN 4)

Another somewhat common pattern is the **ascending fifth sequence**, involving chords whose roots alternately move up by a fifth and down by a fourth. All the triads used within an ascending fifth sequence must be either major or minor; diminished triads sound too harsh within this sequence.

22.21 Ludwig van Beethoven, Piano Sonata in C, Op. 53, iii

In an ascending fifth sequence, chord roots alternately move up a fifth and down a fourth, so that the pairs of chords transpose up by step each time the pattern repeats.

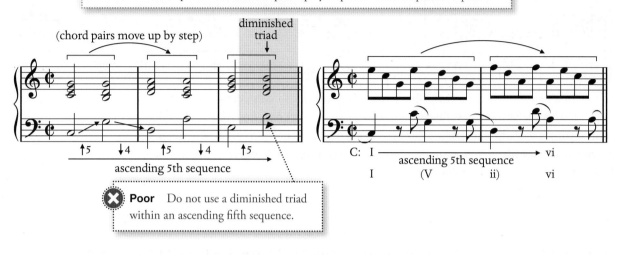

(chord pairs move up by step)

diminished triad

↑5 ↓4 ↑5 ↓4 ↑5

ascending 5th sequence

❌ **Poor** Do not use a diminished triad within an ascending fifth sequence.

C: I ——— ascending 5th sequence ——→ vi
I (V ii) vi

VOICE LEADING IN SEQUENCES

As in functional progressions, parallel perfect intervals and unresolved chordal sevenths are *not* allowed within sequential progressions.

22.22

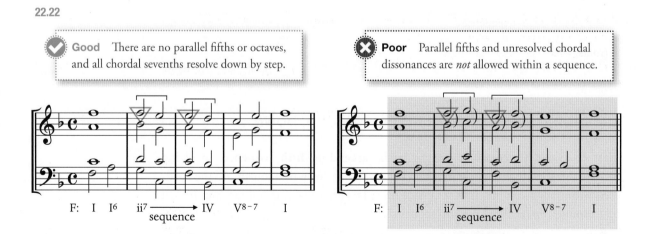

✅ **Good** There are no parallel fifths or octaves, and all chordal sevenths resolve down by step.

❌ **Poor** Parallel fifths and unresolved chordal dissonances are *not* allowed within a sequence.

F: I I⁶ ii⁷ ——→ IV V⁸⁻⁷ I
sequence

F: I I⁶ ii⁷ ——→ IV V⁸⁻⁷ I
sequence

On the other hand, the leading tone may be doubled in the middle of a sequence, since the momentum created by the repetition of the sequential pattern overrides the tendency of the leading tone to ascend. Likewise, in the middle of a minor-key sequence, $\hat{7}$ need not be raised.

22.23

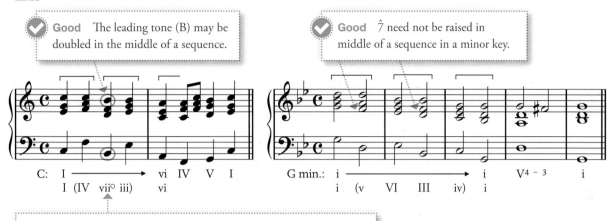

✓ Good The leading tone (B) may be doubled in the middle of a sequence.

✓ Good $\hat{7}$ need not be raised in middle of a sequence in a minor key.

Whereas under normal circumstances a leading tone is expected to lead up to tonic, in mid-sequence one expects the pattern to continue.

POINTS FOR REVIEW

- In a sequence, a music segment or harmonic progression is transposed following a recurring pattern.

- The harmonic function of the chords in the middle of a sequence is determined by the sequential pattern, rather than by the functional categories of the chords.

- Within a sequence, parallel fifths and octaves are not allowed, and chordal sevenths must resolve down by step.

- The leading tone may be doubled in the middle of a sequence; in minor keys, $\hat{7}$ need not be raised in the middle of a sequence.

- In parallel $\substack{6\\3}$ sequences, parallel fourths between the upper voices are fine, but parallel fifths are not.

- Common sequential patterns include the following:

Common descending sequential patterns:

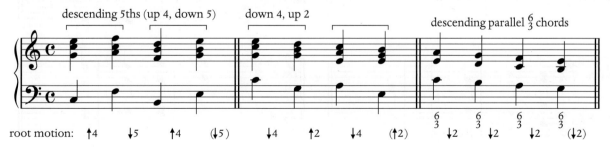

Common ascending sequential patterns:

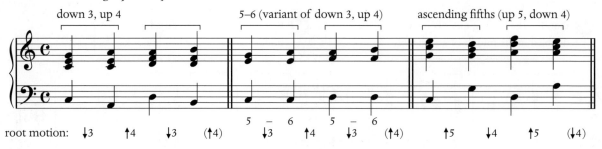

root motion: ↓3 ↑4 ↓3 (↑4)   ↓3 ↑4 ↓3 (↑4)   ↑5 ↓4 ↑5 (↓4)

TEST YOURSELF

1. Which of the following statements are true?

   a. In the middle of a sequence, doubled leading tones are permissible.

   b. In a sequence, parallel fifths and octaves are permissible.

   c. In a sequence, you might find chord successions that are normally forbidden in standard functional harmonic progressions.

   d. In the middle of a minor-key sequence, $\hat{7}$ must be raised to become a leading tone.

   e. In a sequence, chordal sevenths need not resolve down by step.

2. Excerpts (a)–(f) show the first five chords of various sequential patterns (two full units of the pattern and half of the third). If the sequences continued in the same fashion, what would the next chord be?

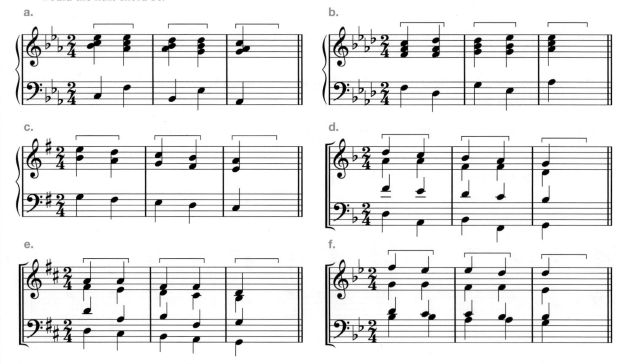

Other $_4^6$ Chords

Because they include a dissonant fourth between the bass and an upper voice, $_4^6$ chords embellish other more-stable harmonies in a variety of contexts.

$_4^6$ chords usually embellish other harmonies. In Chapter 15, we discussed the most important type of $_4^6$ chord, the cadential $_4^6$. Other $_4^6$ chords include the pedal $_4^6$, passing $_4^6$, and arpeggiated $_4^6$, each of which is defined by the harmonies that surround it.

$_4^6$ CHORDS AS EMBELLISHING HARMONIES

Because $_4^6$ chords contain a dissonant fourth above the bass, they generally do not function like the $_3^5$ or $_3^6$ chords with the same root. For instance, I and I[6] function similarly, as do ii and ii[6]. In contrast, I$_4^6$ does *not* function like I or I[6], and ii$_4^6$ is *not* interchangeable with ii or ii[6].

23.1

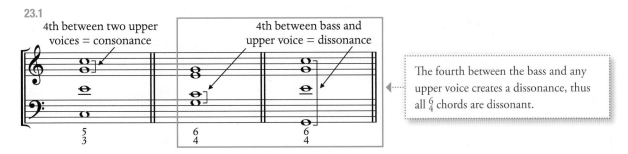

4th between two upper voices = consonance

4th between bass and upper voice = dissonance

The fourth between the bass and any upper voice creates a dissonance, thus all $_4^6$ chords are dissonant.

23.2

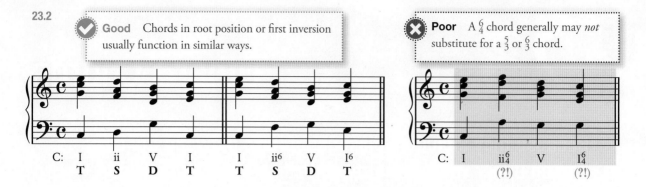

Good Chords in root position or first inversion usually function in similar ways.

Poor A $\frac{6}{4}$ chord generally may *not* substitute for a $\frac{5}{3}$ or $\frac{6}{3}$ chord.

C: I — ii — V — I | I — ii⁶ — V — I⁶
T — S — D — T | T — S — D — T

C: I — ii$^6_4$ — V — I$^6_4$
(?!) — (?!)

Unlike the cadential $\frac{6}{4}$, other types of $\frac{6}{4}$ chords often appear in metrically weak positions. Because $\frac{6}{4}$ chords act as embellishments, the specific function of each is determined by how it is approached and left, rather than by its root. Accordingly, they are usually labeled by their specific function (such as passing or pedal) in addition to their Roman numeral. Unlike the cadential $\frac{6}{4}$, the Roman numerals of the other $\frac{6}{4}$ chords refer to the root of the chord, not the bass.

23.3

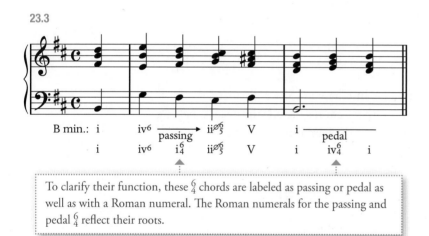

B min.: i — iv⁶ — passing — ii$^{ø6}_5$ — V | i — pedal ——————
i — iv⁶ — i$^6_4$ — ii$^{ø6}_5$ — V | i — iv$^6_4$ — i

To clarify their function, these $\frac{6}{4}$ chords are labeled as passing or pedal as well as with a Roman numeral. The Roman numerals for the passing and pedal $\frac{6}{4}$ reflect their roots.

PEDAL $\frac{6}{4}$

A **pedal** $\frac{6}{4}$ chord results when the bass of a root-position chord is sustained while the upper voices are decorated with embellishing tones that form a $\frac{6}{4}$ chord. A pedal $\frac{6}{4}$ is both preceded and followed by a root-position chord that uses the same bass note. In four-part harmony, usually the bass of a pedal $\frac{6}{4}$ is doubled.

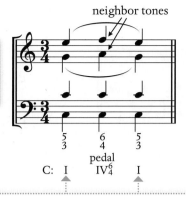

neighbor tones

Neighbor tones in the upper voices give rise to a pedal $^6_4$ over a stationary bass.

$$\begin{array}{ccc} 5 & 6 & 5 \\ 3 & 4 & 3 \end{array}$$

pedal

C: I IV$^6_4$ I

A root-position chord with the same bass note comes before and after a pedal $^6_4$.

23.5 G. F. Handel, "La Paix," from *Royal Fireworks Music*

Each pedal $^6_4$ chord in this passage (an ascending fifth sequence) embellishes (with neighbor tones) the $^5_3$ chord that comes before and after it.

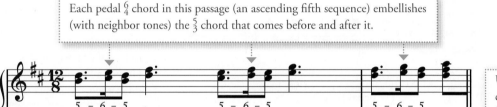

$$\begin{array}{ccccc} 5 & - & 6 & - & 5 \\ 3 & - & 4 & - & 3 \end{array} \qquad \begin{array}{ccccc} 5 & - & 6 & - & 5 \\ 3 & - & 4 & - & 3 \end{array} \qquad \begin{array}{ccccc} 5 & - & 6 & - & 5 \\ 3 & - & 4 & - & 3 \end{array}$$

Unlike the cadential $^6_4$, pedal $^6_4$s usually appear in a metrically weak position.

D: IV ——— pedal ——— I   V ——— pedal ——— ii   vi ——— pedal ——— I^6

(IV vii°$^6_4$ IV I I^6 I V   I$^6_4$ V ii ii^6 i   vi ii$^6_4$ vi I^6)

23.6 Joseph Haydn, Piano Sonata in C, Hob. XVI:35, i

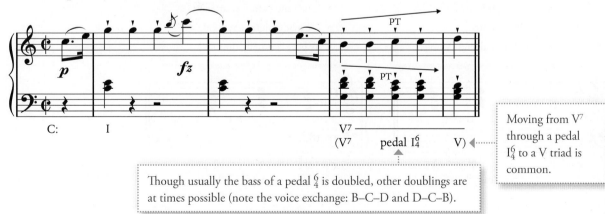

p   *fz*   PT   PT

C: I   V^7 ———————————

(V^7 pedal I$^6_4$ V)

Moving from V^7 through a pedal I$^6_4$ to a V triad is common.

Though usually the bass of a pedal $^6_4$ is doubled, other doublings are at times possible (note the voice exchange: B–C–D and D–C–B).

Although they may decorate any root-position chord, pedal $^6_4$ chords most often embellish either I or V.

23.7 Margaret Casson, "The Cuckoo"

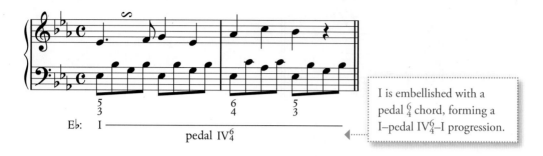

> I is embellished with a pedal $^6_4$ chord, forming a I–pedal IV$^6_4$–I progression.

23.8 Emily Wilson, "The Story of Grace" (hymn)

I am trust-ing in his grace div - ine; Hal - le - lu - ja!

> V is embellished with a pedal $^6_4$ (derived from a passing tone and neighbor tone in the upper voices), forming a V–pedal I$^6_4$–V^7 progression.

Note that both the cadential $^6_4$ and the pedal $^6_4$ are followed immediately by a root-position chord over the same note in the bass. A cadential $^6_4$, however, cannot be *preceded* by V, and it has other restrictions as well that differentiate it from the pedal $^6_4$.

23.9

Cadential $^6_4$	**Pedal $^6_4$**
• comes before—but *not* after—V;	• can come before *or* after V;
• is metrically accented;	• is usually metrically weak;
• its bass is almost always doubled.	• its bass is usually doubled.

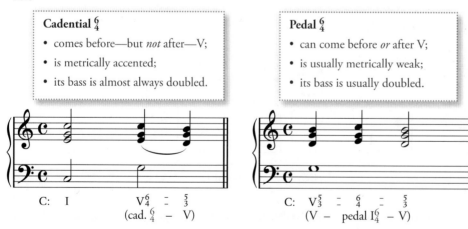

PASSING $\frac{6}{4}$

A **passing** $\frac{6}{4}$ chord is a second-inversion triad whose bass is a passing tone. In four-part harmony the bass of a passing $\frac{6}{4}$ is usually doubled.

23.10

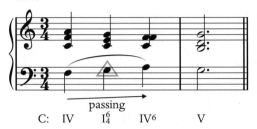

> **Passing $\frac{6}{4}$:** The passing tone G in the *bass* (part of the F–G–A passing motion) supports a $\frac{6}{4}$ chord (G–C–E), with the bass doubled.

C: IV   I$^6_4$ IV^6 V

passing

23.11 José Silvestre White, "Zamacueca"

G: V^7 ii$^6_4$ V$^6_5$ I

passing

> **Passing $\frac{6}{4}$:** The passing tone E in the bass (part of D–E–F♯ passing motion) supports a $\frac{6}{4}$ chord (E–A–C♯).

Although a passing $\frac{6}{4}$ may appear over any scale degree in the bass, it most commonly appears over $\hat{5}$.

23.12 Mikhail Glinka, *Ruslan and Lyudmila*, Act I, Introduction

B♭:   I   vi   I$^6_4$ IV   V$^4_2$ I^6 V$^4_3$ I

passing

> A passing I$^6_4$ chord (i.e., one whose bass is $\hat{5}$) is particularly common.

ARPEGGIATED $^6_4$

An **arpeggiated** $^6_4$ arises when a chord is sustained in the upper voices as the bass voice either arpeggiates the entire triad or oscillates between the root and fifth of the chord. Arpeggiated $^6_4$ chords are found mostly in instrumental genres rather than in four-part chorale settings.

23.13 Fromental Halévy, Overture to *La Juive*

The fifth appears in the bass during an arpeggio, resulting in an *arpeggiated* $^6_4$ chord.

23.14 Scott Joplin, "The Easy Winners"

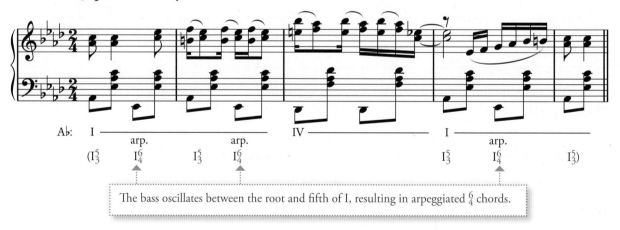

The bass oscillates between the root and fifth of I, resulting in arpeggiated $^6_4$ chords.

COMPARISON OF $^6_4$ CHORD TYPES

Since their function is determined by their context, $^6_4$ chords with the same Roman numeral may have different functions.

23.15

Cadential $\frac{6}{4}$	**Pedal** $\frac{6}{4}$	**Passing** $\frac{6}{4}$	**Arpeggiated** $\frac{6}{4}$
• metrically accented; • leads directly to V^5_3; • doesn't follow V.	• is formed by PT and/or NT above a stationary bass.	• is formed by $\frac{6}{4}$ chord above PT in the bass.	• is formed by a chordal skip in the bass.

passing

C: V^{6-5}_{4-3} I

(= "I^6_4" – V)

C: V————
 pedal

(V I^6_4 V)

C: IV^6 I^6_4 IV

C: I ————
 arp.

(I I^6_4 I^6 I)

 For more on $\frac{6}{4}$ chords, see A Closer Look.

POINTS FOR REVIEW

- The function of a $\frac{6}{4}$ chord differs from that of the $\frac{6}{3}$ and $\frac{5}{3}$ chords with the same root.

- The most important type of $\frac{6}{4}$ chord is the cadential $\frac{6}{4}$ (discussed in Chapter 15).

- A pedal $\frac{6}{4}$ chord results when a root-position chord is decorated with embellishing tones in the *upper* voices so as to form a second-inversion triad, while the bass remains stationary.

- A passing $\frac{6}{4}$ chord results when a passing tone in the *bass* voice supports a second-inversion triad.

- An arpeggiated $\frac{6}{4}$ results when an arpeggio or partial arpeggio in the bass gives rise to a second-inversion triad.

- While a cadential $\frac{6}{4}$ is metrically accented, occurring on a relatively strong beat or part of a beat, other $\frac{6}{4}$ chords usually appear in metrically unaccented positions.

- In four-part harmony, the bass is usually doubled in all types of $\frac{6}{4}$ chords.

TEST YOURSELF

1. Which of the following statements are true?

   a. The interval of a fourth between the bass and an upper voice creates a dissonance.

   b. I_4^6 may be used in situations that are similar to those in which one may find I or I^6.

   c. I_4^6 must be followed by V or V^7.

   d. I_4^6 must appear on a relatively strong beat.

   e. I_4^6 may not follow V or V^7.

   f. The bass of I_4^6 should be doubled.

2. Indicate whether the $_4^6$ chords in the following fragments are pedal $_4^6$s, passing $_4^6$s, arpeggiated $_4^6$s, or cadential $_4^6$s.

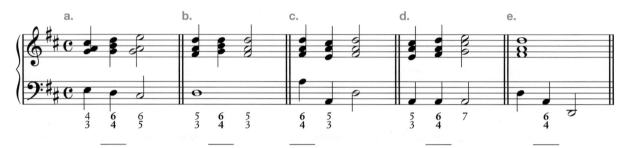

   f. Tom Turpin, "Harlem Rag"

   g. Joseph Haydn, Symphony No. 59, i

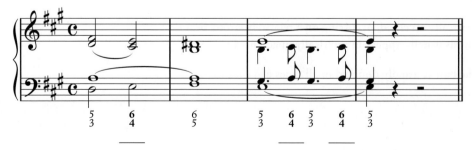

24 Other Embellishing Chords

chapter

Combinations of neighboring or passing tones can create a nonfunctional embellishing chord.

Passing and Neighbor Chords
- Embellishing harmonies within functional harmonic progressions
- Embellishing harmonies within nonfunctional harmonic successions

Passing IV⁶
Passing V⁶
I–IV⁶–I⁶
Harmonizing a Scale in the Bass

PASSING AND NEIGHBOR CHORDS

Embellishing sonorities formed by a passing or neighbor tone in the bass (perhaps along with other embellishing tones in the upper voices) create what are known as **passing chords** or **neighbor chords**.

24.1 **Felix Mendelssohn,** *Songs without Words,* **Op. 102, No. 6**

Passing tones in the bass and melody form a *passing chord* (E–G–C, I⁶) that embellishes the motion between ii⁶₅ and ii⁷.

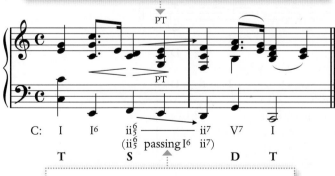

Passing I⁶: the notes of I⁶ appear as a by-product of passing tones.

24.2 Isabella Leonarda, *Salmi Concertati*, Op. 19

A neighbor tone in the bass and embellishing tones in the upper voices form a
neighbor chord that embellishes V.

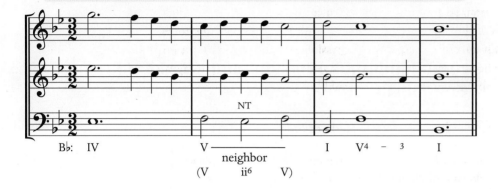

EMBELLISHING HARMONIES WITHIN FUNCTIONAL HARMONIC PROGRESSIONS

Passing and neighbor chords often form part of standard functional harmonic
progressions, such as **T**onic–**D**ominant–**T**onic or **T**onic–**S**ubdominant–**D**ominant–
Tonic. In analyzing passages that include such harmonies, one may choose to label the
Roman numerals of all the chords—including the passing and neighbor chords—or
to label just the underlying harmonies, depending on the level of detail desired.

24.3 J. S. Bach, Chorale 3

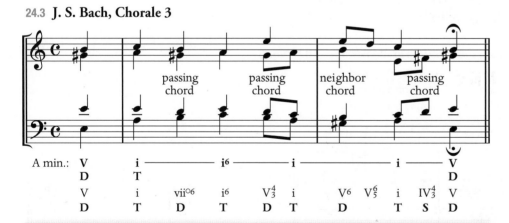

The Roman numerals shown on the top line refer only to the underlying harmonies. A detailed
analysis (the bottom line of Roman numerals) indicates how the passing and neighbor chords
form parts of standard harmonic progressions.

EMBELLISHING HARMONIES WITHIN NONFUNCTIONAL HARMONIC SUCCESSIONS

Passing and neighbor chords do not always form parts of functional harmonic progressions, however. For instance, in the following two excerpts, notice how passing tones along with the sustained tonic in an inner voice combine to spell ii^7. Unlike the IV and vii^{o6} chords of these passages (which also result from embellishing tones), however, this "ii^7" is not part of a functional progression: unlike a typical ii^7, it does not lead to V, and its chordal seventh does not resolve down by step. Accordingly, if this chord is labeled at all, its passing function should be explicitly noted.

24.4 Robert Schumann, "Soldatenmarsch" ("Soldier's March")

Passing tones produce what looks like ii^7: A–C–(E)–G. But this is part of a *non*functional progression: I–"ii^7"–I^6. If labeled at all, the resulting sonority should be called a *passing ii^7*.

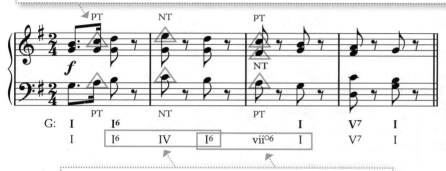

IV and vii^{o6} result from neighbor and passing tones, and they also form part of the standard progressions I^6–IV–I^6 and I^6–vii^{o6}–I.

24.5 J. S. Bach, Prelude in C♯ Major, WTC I

Though D♯–F♯–C♯ lasts for an entire measure and literally produces ii^7, it nonetheless serves as a passing chord between I and I^6.

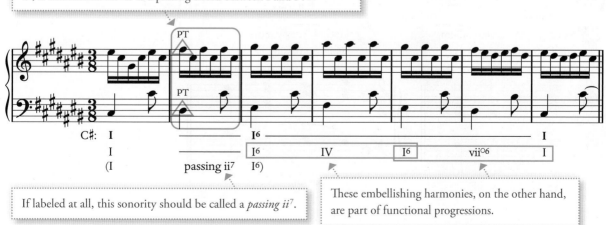

If labeled at all, this sonority should be called a *passing ii^7*.

These embellishing harmonies, on the other hand, are part of functional progressions.

PASSING IV^6

An embellishing chord that is particularly common is the **passing IV^6**, which appears in the middle of a stepwise ascent in the bass leading between V (or V^7) and V^6 (or V$^6_5$).

24.6

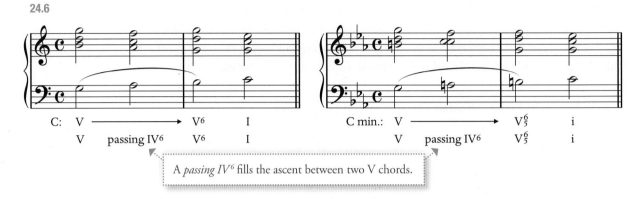

A *passing IV^6* fills the ascent between two V chords.

24.7 **George M. Cohan, "The Yankee Doodle Boy," from** *Little Johnny Jones*

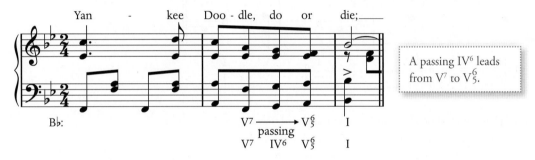

A passing IV^6 leads from V^7 to V$^6_5$.

Note that under most circumstances, a V–IV^6 progression would be considered poor, since it creates a **D**ominant–**S**ubdominant progression. With a passing IV^6, however, V does not move to IV^6, but rather V moves through IV^6 to V^6 or V$^6_5$.

24.8

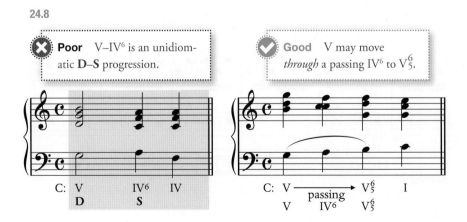

Poor V–IV^6 is an unidiomatic **D**–**S** progression.

Good V may move *through* a passing IV^6 to V$^6_5$.

PASSING V⁶

Another common passing chord is the **passing V⁶**, which arises when the bass moves down in stepwise motion from I to vi or IV⁶.

24.9

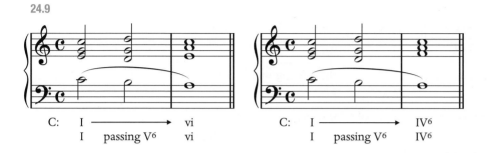

24.10 R. Nathaniel Dett, "Grace Before Meal at Hampton"

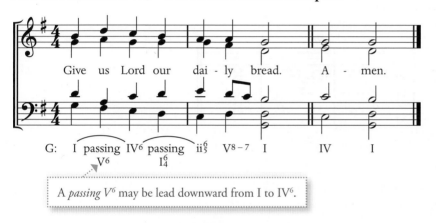

A *passing V⁶* may be lead downward from I to IV⁶.

24.11 Anna Bon, Flute Sonata in F, Op. 1, No. 2, ii

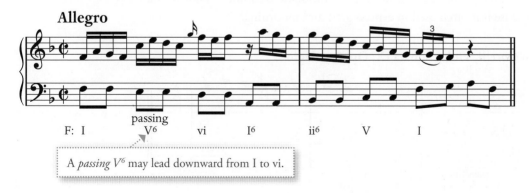

A *passing V⁶* may lead downward from I to vi.

Under most circumstances, a V⁶–IV⁶ or V⁶–vi progression would be considered an improper **D–S** progression. A passing V⁶, however, does not function as a **D**ominant harmony that leads to I, but rather as part of a passing motion in the bass.

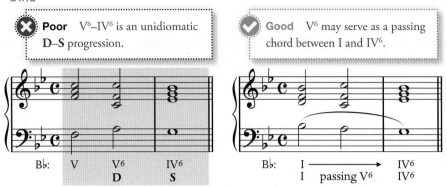

❌ Poor V⁶–IV⁶ is an unidiomatic **D–S** progression.

✓ Good V⁶ may serve as a passing chord between I and IV⁶.

Since it does not function in the manner of a **D**ominant, in minor keys the $\hat{7}$ in the bass of this passing chord need not be raised. As a result, in minor keys this passing chord usually appears as a minor v⁶ triad.

24.13 Theophania Cecil, "St. Katherine's"

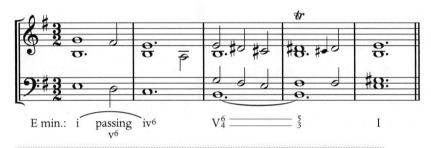

Since it does not lead up to the tonic, $\hat{7}$ need not be raised in a passing v⁶.

Sometimes in minor keys, a passing V⁶ appears as a result of a bass line that uses only half steps in moving from i down to V. This chromatic bass line is known as a **lament bass** (because it is often used to express grief and mourning).

24.14 Arcangelo Corelli, Violin Sonata IX, Op. 5, Adagio

A passing V⁶ may be part of a *lament bass*, in which the bass line moves in half steps from i to V.

I–IV⁶–I⁶

A harmony also may function as an embellishment if it supports a passing or neighbor motion in the melody. A noteworthy instance of this arises when the melodic passing motion $\hat{3}$–$\hat{4}$–$\hat{5}$ is harmonized by the progression I–IV⁶–I⁶. As noted in Chapter 19, IV⁶ rarely moves directly to I; thus a I–IV⁶–I⁶ progression presents an important exception in which IV⁶ does embellish **T**onic harmony.

24.15

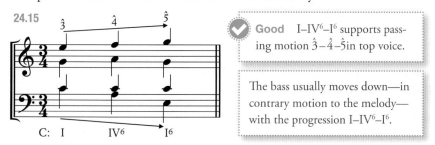

> ✓ **Good**   I–IV⁶–I⁶ supports passing motion $\hat{3}$–$\hat{4}$–$\hat{5}$ in top voice.

> The bass usually moves down—in contrary motion to the melody—with the progression I–IV⁶–I⁶.

24.16 Emily Swan Perkins, "Laufer" (hymn)

The light of God is fall - ing up - on life's com-mon way.

> IV⁶ leads from I to I⁶, supporting $\hat{3}$–$\hat{4}$–$\hat{5}$ in the melody.

HARMONIZING A SCALE IN THE BASS

By using the passing IV⁶ and passing V⁶, along with progressions discussed in previous chapters, you can harmonize ascending and descending major and minor scales that appear in the bass voice.

24.17

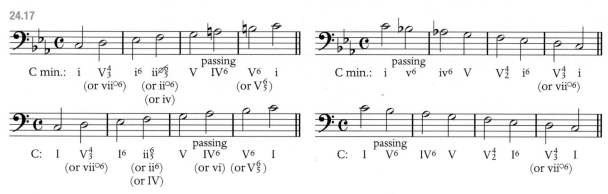

- **Passing and neighbor chords result when a chord is created by tones that embellish an underlying harmony.**

- **Sometimes, passing and neighbor chords form parts of standard harmonic progressions. Where they do not, however, their embellishing function should be noted in labeling these embellishing harmonies.**

- **An important passing chord is the passing IV⁶, which embellishes a stepwise _ascending_ motion in the bass between two Dominant harmonies.**

- **Another common passing chord is the passing V⁶, which embellishes a stepwise _descending_ motion in the bass leading from I to vi or IV⁶.**

- **I–IV⁶–I⁶ often supports the melodic line $\hat{3}-\hat{4}-\hat{5}$.**

- **Both the passing IV⁶ and passing V⁶ may be used in harmonizing a scale in the bass.**

TEST YOURSELF

1. What are the Roman numerals for the sonorities in the following?

   Maria Tiddeman, "Ibstone"

   D: __ __ __ __ __ __

2. What chord succession in the example above is less standard? What is the rationale for this odd chord succession?

3. What chords could be used to harmonize the bass line $\hat{8}-\hat{7}-\hat{6}-\hat{5}$?

4. What chords could be used to harmonize the bass line $\hat{5}-\hat{6}-\hat{7}-\hat{8}$?

5. What chords can be used to harmonize the melody $\hat{3}-\hat{4}-\hat{5}$?

Chromatic Harmony

chapter 25 — Applied Dominants of V

V of V, or V/V, is an applied dominant chord—the dominant of the dominant—that leads to V.

TONICIZATION AND APPLIED DOMINANTS

In the middle of a composition it is possible to momentarily treat a note other than $\hat{1}$ as though it were the tonic. Such a momentary change of key, known as a **tonicization**, almost always requires the use of an accidental.

25.1 Eliza Flower, "Patmos" (hymn)

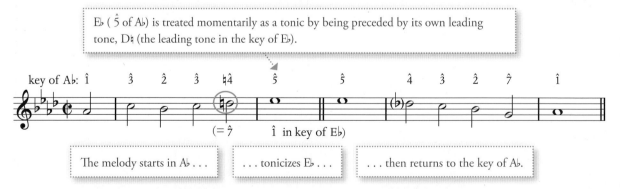

E♭ ($\hat{5}$ of A♭) is treated momentarily as a tonic by being preceded by its own leading tone, D♮ (the leading tone in the key of E♭).

key of A♭: $\hat{1}$ $\hat{3}$ $\hat{2}$ $\hat{3}$ ♮$\hat{4}$ $\hat{5}$ $\hat{5}$ $\hat{4}$ $\hat{3}$ $\hat{2}$ $\hat{7}$ $\hat{1}$

(= $\hat{7}$) $\hat{1}$ in key of E♭

The melody starts in A♭ . . . . . . tonicizes E♭ . . . . . . then returns to the key of A♭.

Just as a *note* can be tonicized, any major or minor *triad* can be tonicized if it is preceded by an **applied dominant** (also known as a **secondary dominant**). An applied dominant contains a chromatic note and functions as a **D**ominant of a harmony other than I.

V/V

The most common applied dominant is **V of V**, notated as **V/V**. Just as V is a major triad whose root is a perfect fifth above I, V/V is a major triad whose root is a perfect fifth above V.

25.2

Task: **Find V/V in the key of D.**

1. The root of V in the key of D = A.
2. V in the key of A = E–G♯–B.
3. Thus V/V in the key of D = E–G♯–B.

D: V   V/V

> The root of V/V (E) is a perfect fifth above the root of V (A).

> V/V must be a major triad; its third must be raised with an accidental (G♯ = leading tone of A).

Just as V leads to I, V/V leads to V.

25.3

> The progression V/V–V in D major has the same notes as V–I in A.

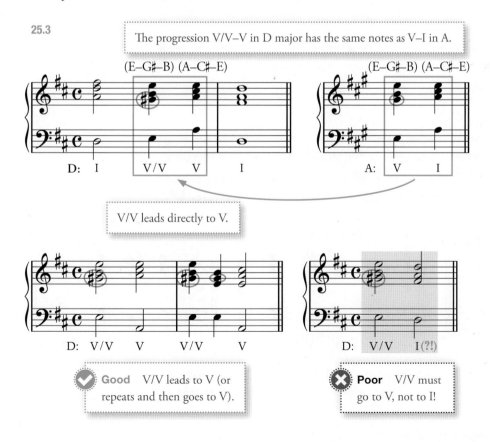

> V/V leads directly to V.

✔ **Good**   V/V leads to V (or repeats and then goes to V).

✘ **Poor**   V/V must go to V, not to I!

25.4 "Vom Himmel Hoch" (hymn)

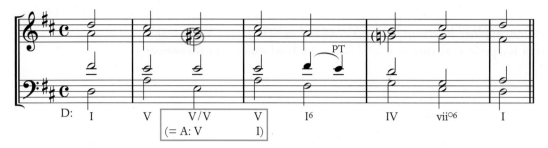

Notice that the root of V/V is $\hat{2}$. It thus has the same notes as a ii chord with the third raised by a half step.

25.5

Task: **Find V/V in D (alternative method).**

1. ii in D = E–G–B.

2. Thus V/V in D = E–G♯–B.

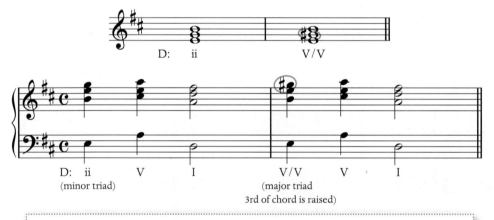

To find the notes of V/V you may first find the notes of ii, then raise the third of the chord.

Since V/V points directly to the V that follows it, any chord that can precede V—such as a **T**onic or **S**ubdominant triad, or another V triad—may also precede V/V.

25.6

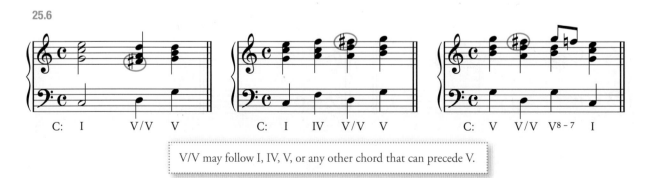

V/V may follow I, IV, V, or any other chord that can precede V.

THE SECONDARY LEADING TONE

Notice that the third of V/V is raised $\hat{4}$, which is the leading tone in the key of V (the key in which the V chord would be the tonic). This raised tone requires an accidental.

25.7

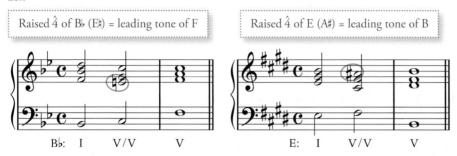

The raised tone in V/V should be treated as a leading tone: it may not be doubled, and if it appears in an outer voice it resolves up by step when V/V moves to V.

25.8

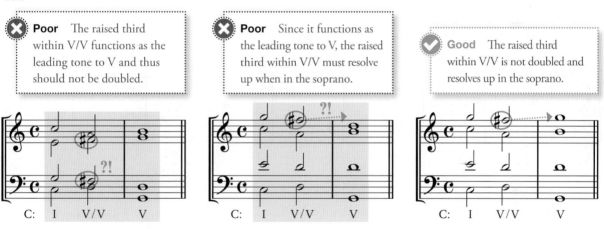

❌ **Poor** The raised third within V/V functions as the leading tone to V and thus should not be doubled.

❌ **Poor** Since it functions as the leading tone to V, the raised third within V/V must resolve up when in the soprano.

✅ **Good** The raised third within V/V is not doubled and resolves up in the soprano.

V⁶/V

V/V may also appear in first inversion—notated as V⁶/V. Just as V⁶ leads to a root-position I, V⁶/V leads to a root-position V.

25.9

25.10 **Isabella Leonarda,** *Magnificat*

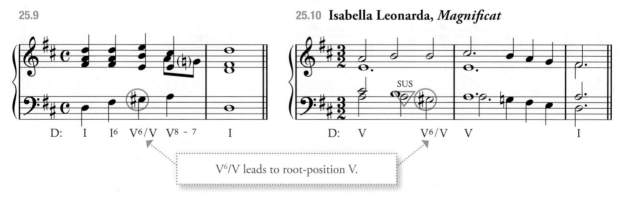

V⁶/V leads to root-position V.

V⁷/V IN ROOT POSITION AND INVERSIONS

A dominant seventh chord (a major triad plus a minor seventh) may also be used as an applied dominant of V (as V⁷/V). Just as with a V⁷, you may use all four notes of V⁷/V in four-part harmony, or you may omit the fifth and double the root.

25.11

V⁷/V is a dominant seventh chord; it has the same notes as V/V, plus a minor seventh above its root.

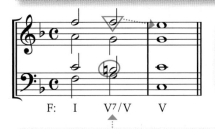

The third of V⁷/V (B♭) must be raised by a half step with an accidental (to B♮). The chordal seventh of V⁷/V (F, Î) resolves down by step.

V⁷/V—G–B♯–F, with the fifth (D) omitted—leads to V.

25.12 Gioachino Rossini, *Il Turco in Italia*, Act I, scene viii

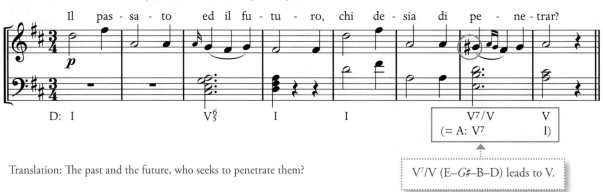

Translation: The past and the future, who seeks to penetrate them?

V⁷/V (E–G♯–B–D) leads to V.

25.13 Clara Scott, "Follow Me"

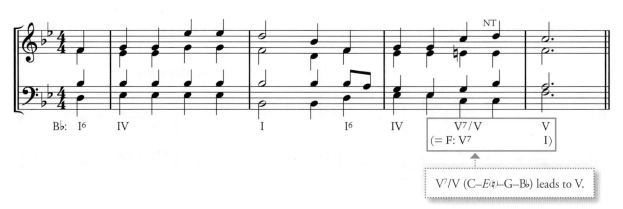

V⁷/V (C–E♮–G–B♭) leads to V.

V^7/V may appear either in root position or in any inversion. In each case, the inversion of V^7/V functions like the analogous inverted V^7 chord, except that it leads to a **D**ominant instead of a **T**onic. For instance, just as V^4_2 leads to I^6 (not to I), V^4_2/V leads to V^6 (not V).

25.14

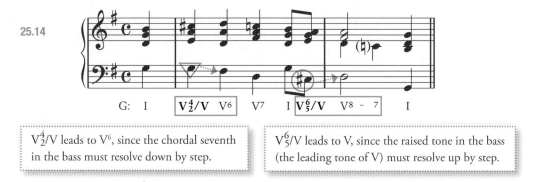

G: I V^4_2/V V^6 V^7 I V^6_5/V $V^{8\text{ }-\text{ }7}$ I

V^4_2/V leads to V^6, since the chordal seventh in the bass must resolve down by step.

V^6_5/V leads to V, since the raised tone in the bass (the leading tone of V) must resolve up by step.

25.15 Felix Mendelssohn, *Songs without Words*, Op. 19, No. 1

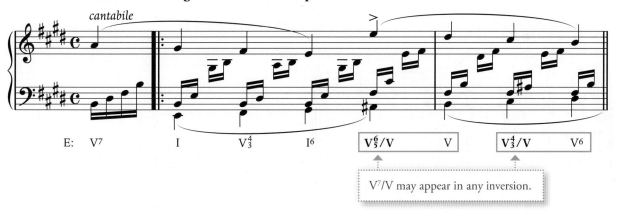

E: V^7 I V^4_3 I^6 V^6_5/V V V^4_3/V V^6

V^7/V may appear in any inversion.

V/V IN MINOR KEYS

Applied dominants of V also may be found in minor keys. In minor keys V/V requires both raised $\hat{4}$ and raised $\hat{6}$.

25.16

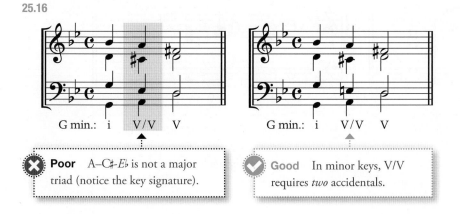

G min.: i   V/V   V   G min.: i   V/V   V

Poor   A–C♯-E♭ is not a major triad (notice the key signature).

Good   In minor keys, V/V requires *two* accidentals.

25.17 Frédéric Chopin, Ballade No. 1 in G Minor, Op. 23

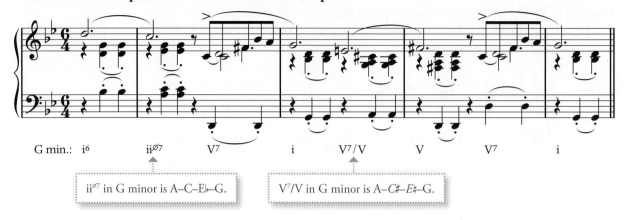

G min.: i⁶   ii⁰⁷   V⁷   i   V⁷/V   V   V⁷   i

ii⁰⁷ in G minor is A–C–E♭–G.

V⁷/V in G minor is A–C♯–E♮–G.

OTHER RESOLUTIONS OF V/V AND V⁷/V

An applied dominant may lead to a V chord that is decorated by a cadential $\frac{6}{4}$.

25.18

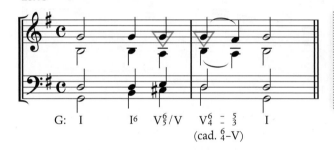

G: I   I⁶   V$\frac{6}{5}$/V   V$\frac{6}{4}$ − $\frac{5}{3}$ I
(cad. $\frac{6}{4}$–V)

The applied dominant of V leads through a cadential $\frac{6}{4}$ to V, delaying the resolution of G (the chordal seventh within V$\frac{6}{4}$/V) down to F♯.

An applied dominant at times may also lead to a V⁷ chord, instead of leading to a V triad. In such a case, a particularly beautiful voice leading can sometimes be used. Usually, raised $\hat{4}$ (a leading tone directed up to $\hat{5}$) ascends to $\hat{5}$. When V⁷/V moves to V⁷, however, raised $\hat{4}$ may instead slide down by a half step, canceling the chromatic alteration to $\hat{4}$. This is possible even if the raised $\hat{4}$ appears in the top voice.

25.19

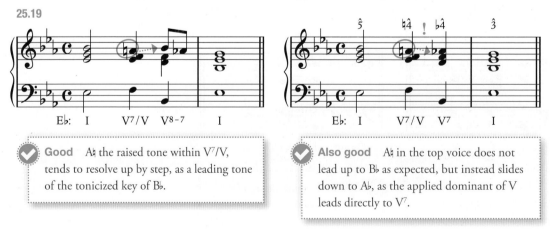

E♭: I   V⁷/V   V⁸⁻⁷   I

E♭: I   V⁷/V   V⁷   I

✓ **Good**   A♮ the raised tone within V⁷/V, tends to resolve up by step, as a leading tone of the tonicized key of B♭.

✓ **Also good**   A♮ in the top voice does not lead up to B♭ as expected, but instead slides down to A♭, as the applied dominant of V leads directly to V⁷.

25.20 **Chris Smith, "My Sweet Savannah Lize"**

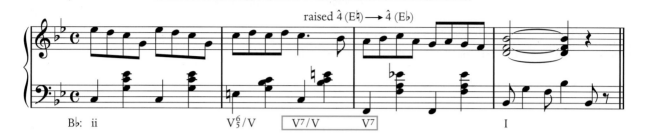

> Raised $\hat{4}$ slides down by semitone to $\hat{4}$ when V/V moves to V^7.

raised $\hat{4}$ (E♮) → $\hat{4}$ (E♭)

B♭:   ii V^6_5/V V^7/V V^7 I

To learn about cross relations, see A Closer Look.

POINTS FOR REVIEW

- An applied dominant is a chord that functions as a dominant of a harmony other than the tonic.

- The most common applied dominants are V/V and V^7/V (read "V of V" and "V^7 of V"), which may appear in root position or inversion.

- V/V leads to a Dominant (V, V^7, inversions of V or V^7, or a cadential $^6_4$ followed by V); it may follow any chord that can precede V (any Tonic or Subdominant chord).

- The root of V/V is $\hat{2}$ (a perfect fifth above $\hat{5}$).

- V/V must be a major triad; V^7/V is a dominant-seventh-type chord (a major triad with a minor seventh). The third of both V/V and V^7/V must be raised by a half step with an accidental.

- The raised tone in V/V is raised $\hat{4}$, which is the same as the leading tone in the key of V.

- The raised tone within V/V must be treated like a leading tone: it may not be doubled, and it normally resolves up by step if it appears in an outer voice.

- If V/V resolves to V^7, the raised $\hat{4}$ may slide down by chromatic semitone to $\hat{4}$, even if it appears in the top voice.

- In minor keys, two notes within V/V must be raised with accidentals, $\hat{4}$ and $\hat{6}$.

1. Which of the following chords may follow V/V?

    a. V or V⁶   **b.** I   **c.** IV or ii⁶   **d.** V⁷   **e.** cadential $^6_4$–V   **f.** another V/V

2. Which of the following chords may precede V/V?

    a. V or V⁶   **b.** I   **c.** IV or ii⁶   **d.** cadential $^6_4$–V   **e.** another V/V

3. What accidentals are missing in the following V/V and V⁷/V chords? (Each one is missing one or two accidentals.)

    a. G: V/V   **b.** E♭: V/V   **c.** B♭: V/V   **d.** B♭ min.: V/V   **e.** E: V⁷/V   **f.** E min.: V⁷/V

4. What is the root of V/V in these keys?

    a. F major   **b.** D major   **c.** E major   **d.** E minor   **e.** A♭ major   **f.** A♭ minor

5. What are the notes in V/V in these keys? Specify which notes need accidentals.

    a. F major   **b.** D major   **c.** E major   **d.** C♯ major

6. What are the notes in V⁷/V in these keys? Specify which notes need accidentals.

    a. F minor   **b.** D minor   **c.** E minor   **d.** C♯ minor

7. Label the Roman numerals of this excerpt.

    Hortense de Beauharnais, "Reine Berthe"

    E♭:   ___   ___   ___   ___   ___   ___   ___

8. Answer the following questions regarding the excerpt above:

    a. Which chord is the applied dominant?

    b. What note is the raised $\hat{4}$ (= leading tone in key of V) within the applied dominant?

    c. Does the raised $\hat{4}$ resolve up by step as expected, or does it slide down by semitone to $\hat{4}$?

26   Other Applied Chords

An applied chord functions like a Dominant, but leads to a harmony other than I.

Applied V and V⁷
> In major keys
> In minor keys

Applied vii°⁶ and vii°⁷
Applied Chords Followed by Other Applied Chords
Using Applied Chords in Harmonizing Melodies

APPLIED V AND V⁷

As discussed in the previous chapter, an *applied dominant* chord functions as a **Dominant**, but leads to a harmony other than I. An applied dominant can lead (or be applied) not only to V, but also to any major or minor triad. Thus V/ii leads to ii, V/vi leads to vi, and so on. In each case, the applied dominant may be a triad or seventh chord in root position or inversion. All applied chords *tonicize* the chord to which they are applied, momentarily treating the goal chord as tonic. The resolution of an applied dominant creates a **Dominant-to-Tonic** progression within the key of the tonicized chord.

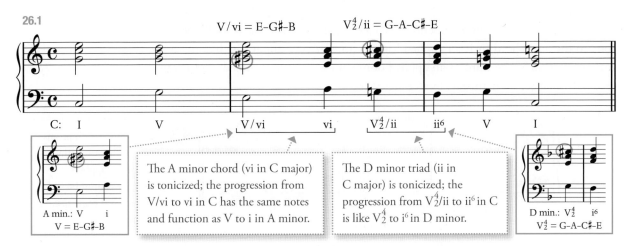

26.1

$V/vi = E-G\sharp-B$ $V_2^4/ii = G-A-C\sharp-E$

C: I   V   V/vi   vi V_2^4/ii   ii⁶   V   I

A min.: V   i
V = E–G♯–B

The A minor chord (vi in C major) is tonicized; the progression from V/vi to vi in C has the same notes and function as V to i in A minor.

The D minor triad (ii in C major) is tonicized; the progression from V_2^4/ii to ii⁶ in C is like V_2^4 to i⁶ in D minor.

D min.: V_2^4 i⁶
V_2^4 = G–A–C♯–E

Since they lead to harmonies other than the tonic, applied dominant chords momentarily depart from the main key. As a result, almost all applied chords use at least one accidental. To spell an applied V triad, build a major triad whose root is a perfect fifth above the root of the goal chord (the tonicized harmony), making sure to use accidentals where needed. Thus V/vi is a major triad whose root is a perfect fifth above $\hat{6}$, V/ii is major triad whose root is a perfect fifth above $\hat{2}$, and so on. The procedure for spelling an applied V^7 is similar: build a dominant seventh chord (a major triad plus a minor seventh) on the note a perfect fifth above the root of the goal chord, using the correct accidentals.

26.2

Task: **Spell V/vi in the key of F.**

1. In the key of F, the root of vi (the goal chord), $\hat{6}$, is D.

2. A perfect 5th above D = A.

3. A major triad = A–C♯–E.

F: V / vi
(accidental is needed for C♯)

26.3

Task: **Spell V⁷/ii in the key of A.**

1. In the key of A, the root of ii, $\hat{2}$, is B.

2. A perfect 5th above B = F♯.

3. F♯ dominant seventh chord = F♯–A♯–C♯–E.

A: V⁷ / ii
(accidental is needed for A♯)

Since an applied chord functions as a **D**ominant, its third acts as the leading tone to the goal chord (it is an applied leading tone). Accordingly, just like the leading tone within V, the third of an applied dominant cannot be doubled, and it must ascend by half step if it appears in an outer voice.

26.4

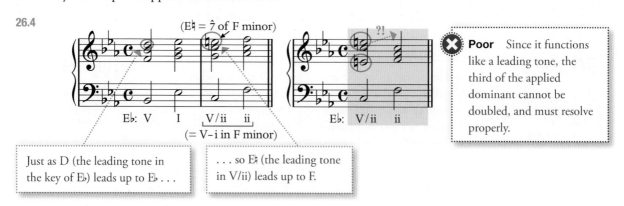

(E♮ = $\hat{7}$ of F minor)

E♭: V   I   V/ii   ii
(= V–i in F minor)

E♭: V/ii   ii

⊗ Poor Since it functions like a leading tone, the third of the applied dominant cannot be doubled, and must resolve properly.

Just as D (the leading tone in the key of E♭) leads up to E♭ . . .

. . . so E♮ (the leading tone in V/ii) leads up to F.

IN MAJOR KEYS

In major keys, ii, iii, IV, V, or vi may be preceded by an applied dominant. Because a diminished triad cannot be the tonic of a key, vii° cannot be tonicized by an applied dominant. Like V/V, all applied dominant triads may appear in root position or first inversion, and applied dominant seventh chords may appear in any inversion.

26.5

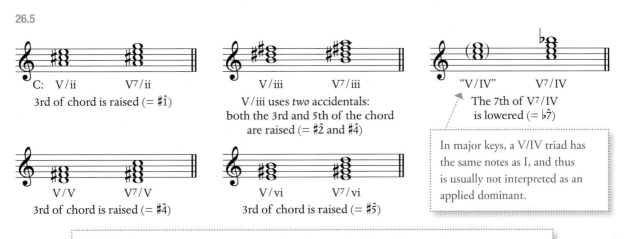

C: V/ii   V7/ii
3rd of chord is raised (= #$\hat{1}$)

V/iii   V7/iii
V/iii uses *two* accidentals:
both the 3rd and 5th of the chord
are raised (= #$\hat{2}$ and #$\hat{4}$)

"V/IV"   V7/IV
The 7th of V7/IV
is lowered (= ♭$\hat{7}$)

V/V   V7/V
3rd of chord is raised (= #$\hat{4}$)

V/vi   V7/vi
3rd of chord is raised (= #$\hat{5}$)

> In major keys, a V/IV triad has the same notes as I, and thus is usually not interpreted as an applied dominant.

> Any major or minor triad may be tonicized with an applied V or V7 in root position or inversion.

26.6 **Joseph Haydn, German Dance, Hob. IX:12/4**

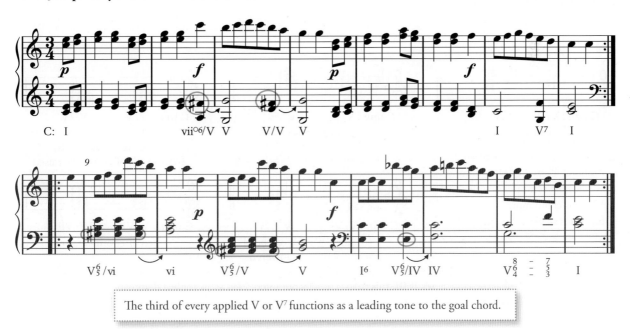

> The third of every applied V or V7 functions as a leading tone to the goal chord.

26.7 Ludwig van Beethoven, Piano Sonata in G, Op. 14, No. 2, ii, excerpts

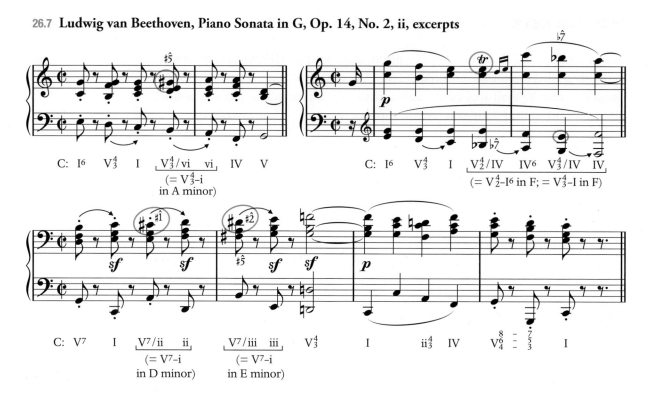

IN MINOR KEYS

In minor keys, too, five different triads can be preceded by an applied dominant: III, iv, V, VI, and VII; ii° cannot, since it is diminished.

26.8

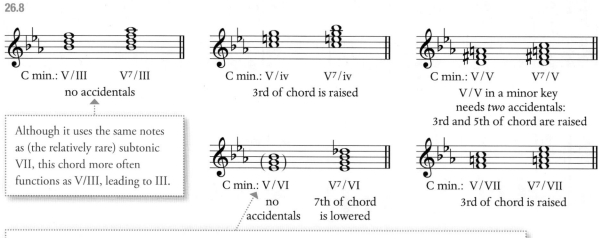

Although it uses the same notes as (the relatively rare) subtonic VII, this chord more often functions as V/III, leading to III.

Since the V/VI triad has the same notes as III, this triad is usually not interpreted as an applied dominant.

26.9 Teresa Milanollo, Grande fantaisie élégiaque for Violin and Piano, Op. 1

26.10 Bianca Maria Meda, "Cari musici"

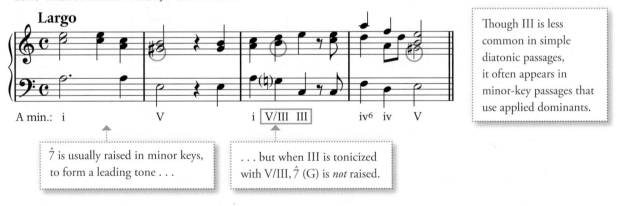

Though III is less common in simple diatonic passages, it often appears in minor-key passages that use applied dominants.

$\hat{7}$ is usually raised in minor keys, to form a leading tone . . .

. . . but when III is tonicized with V/III, $\hat{7}$ (G) is *not* raised.

APPLIED vii^{o6} AND vii^{o7}

Since vii^{o6} and vii^{o7} are **D**ominant harmonies, they too may serve as applied chords to any major or minor triad. The roots of applied vii^{o6} and applied vii^{o7} chords are the leading tones of the harmonies they tonicize. Accordingly, the root of an applied diminished chord must be a minor second (*not* a major second!) below the root of the goal chord. Furthermore, the root of an applied vii^o triad or seventh chord must be treated as a leading tone: it cannot be doubled, and it must resolve up by step when in an outer voice.

26.11

Task: **Spell vii^{o7}/V in D.**

1. In the key of D, the root of V (the goal chord), $\hat{5}$ is A.

2. The leading tone of A is *G♯* (not G♮).

3. G♯ diminished seventh chord (diminished triad plus d7) = G♯–B–D–*F♮*.

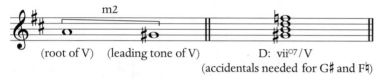

26.12 **Ann and Elizabeth Mounsey, Interlude**

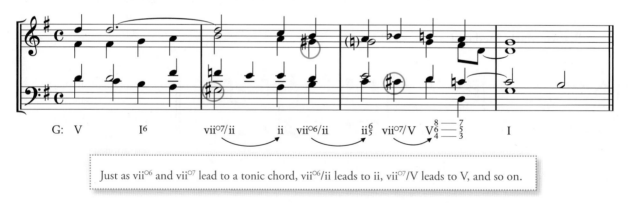

> Just as vii^{o6} and vii^{o7} lead to a tonic chord, vii^{o6}/ii leads to ii, vii^{o7}/V leads to V, and so on.

The vii^{ø7} (a half-diminished seventh chord) may also serve as an applied dominant. However, just as vii^{ø7} occurs only in major keys (not in minor keys), so an applied vii^{ø7} should lead to a major chord (not a minor chord).

26.13

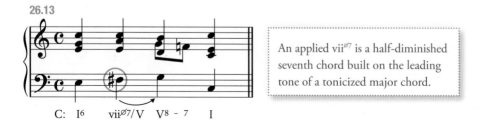

> An applied vii^{ø7} is a half-diminished seventh chord built on the leading tone of a tonicized major chord.

26.14 Frances Havergal, "Golden harps are sounding" (hymn)

Gold - en harps are sound - ing, An - gel voic - es ring,

Ab: ii6   viiø7/V   V

APPLIED CHORDS FOLLOWED BY OTHER APPLIED CHORDS

Any applied chord may be followed by another applied chord that is built on the same
root as the chord to which it leads. For instance, since ii and V/V are both built on $\hat{2}$
as the root, a V/ii may lead either to ii or to V/V.

26.15

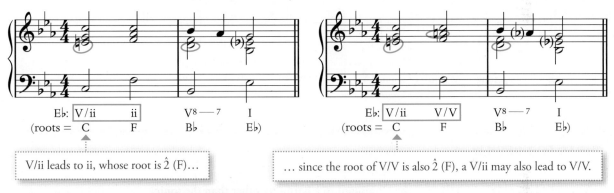

Eb: V/ii   ii   V8 —— 7   I   Eb: V/ii   V/V   V8 —— 7   I
(roots = C   F   Bb   Eb)   (roots = C   F   Bb   Eb)

V/ii leads to ii, whose root is $\hat{2}$ (F)…   … since the root of V/V is also $\hat{2}$ (F), a V/ii may also lead to V/V.

26.16 Eubie Blake, "Gee! I Wish I Had Someone to Rock Me"

Take   me on   their knee and talk some "ba - by talk" to   me.

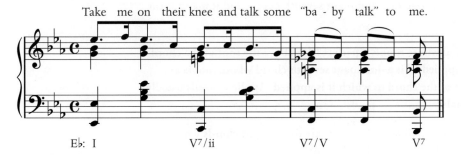

Eb: I   V7/ii   V7/V   V7

Simplified harmonic model:

Eb: I   V7/ii   V7/V   V7

USING APPLIED CHORDS IN HARMONIZING MELODIES

Chromatic tones in melodies can often be harmonized with applied chords. For instance, a raised tone that moves up by step might be harmonized as the third of an applied V (the leading tone to the tonicized chord). Likewise, a lowered $\hat{7}$ that moves down by step can often be harmonized as the seventh of V^7/IV.

26.17

Task: Harmonize the following melodic fragments using applied dominants.

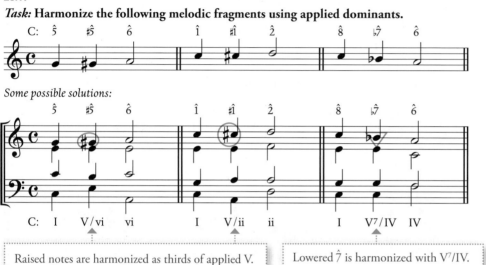

Some possible solutions:

Raised notes are harmonized as thirds of applied V.

Lowered $\hat{7}$ is harmonized with V^7/IV.

POINTS FOR REVIEW

- An applied dominant functions as the Dominant to a harmony other than the tonic.

- An applied dominant may be a triad or a dominant seventh chord, and it may appear in root position or inversion.

- An applied V is a major triad whose root is a perfect fifth above the root of the chord to which it is applied; an applied V^7 is a dominant seventh chord whose root is a perfect fifth above the root of the chord to which it is applied. Applied chords usually require the use of accidentals.

- Applied $vii^{\circ 6}$, applied $vii^{\circ 7}$, and applied $vii^{\varnothing 7}$ chords are diminished chords whose roots are the leading tone of the harmony that they tonicize.

- The third of an applied V chord—and the root of an applied vii° triad or seventh chord—is a leading tone: it may not be doubled, and it should resolve up by step if it appears in an outer voice.

- Only major and minor triads (not diminished triads) may be preceded by applied dominants, because only major and minor triads may be tonicized (treated like a tonic).

- An applied chord can lead directly to another applied chord.

1. Which of these chords typically follow a V/ii?

   a. ii **b.** ii⁶ **c.** I **d.** another V/ii

2. Which accidentals (if any) are missing in these chords (in major keys)?

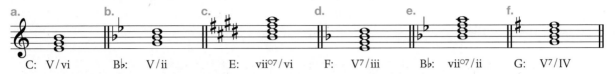

   C: V/vi   B♭: V/ii   E: vii°⁷/vi   F: V⁷/iii   B♭: vii°⁷/ii   G: V⁷/IV

3. Which accidentals (if any) are missing in these chords (in minor keys)?

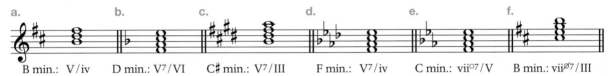

   B min.: V/iv   D min.: V⁷/VI   C♯ min.: V⁷/III   F min.: V⁷/iv   C min.: vii°⁷/V   B min.: viiø⁷/III

4. Which notes of the following triads may not be doubled?

   F: V⁶/vi   A: V/ii   D: vii°⁶/V   B♭: vii°⁶/IV   C♯ min.: V/III   E min.: vii°⁶/VI

5. Below are melodic fragments within major keys. In each, what applied chord(s) could be used to harmonize the note marked by an asterisk?

27

Modulation to the Dominant Key

A modulation occurs when the key changes temporarily; the most common modulation is to the dominant key.

Modulation
   Modulation to the dominant key (key of V)

Pivot Chords

Distinguishing Tonicizations from Modulations

Harmonizing Melodies

A Closer Look
   Reinterpreted half cadence

MODULATION

Pieces usually begin and end in the same key, known as the **main key** (or **home key** or **tonic key**). Within the course of the composition, however, the key may change, so that a harmony other than the original I chord is temporarily treated as though it were the tonic. Chapters 25 and 26 discussed how applied chords can create brief changes of key, known as *tonicizations*. A change of key that is lengthier and more substantial, and whose tonic is confirmed by a cadence, is known as a **modulation**. In the vast majority of cases, a modulation is not notated with a new key signature; rather, the modulation is indicated by the use of accidentals.

27.1 Fernando Sor, *Leçons progressives* for Guitar, No. 5

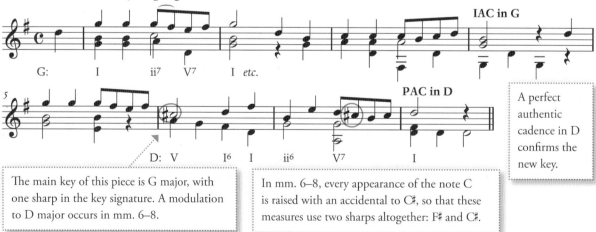

The main key of this piece is G major, with one sharp in the key signature. A modulation to D major occurs in mm. 6–8.

In mm. 6–8, every appearance of the note C is raised with an accidental to C♯, so that these measures use two sharps altogether: F♯ and C♯.

A perfect authentic cadence in D confirms the new key.

Once a modulation has begun, all the harmonies, scale degrees, and cadences are to be understood to function in the new key, and they should be labeled within the new key as well.

27.2 Friedrich Filitz, "Blessed Night" (hymn)

The music starts in D (2♯s), modulates in mm. 3–4 to A (3♯s), and ends by returning to the main key of D (2♯s).

After the modulation has begun, the cadence, scale degrees, and chords all function within the key of A (G♯, for example, is the leading tone of A).

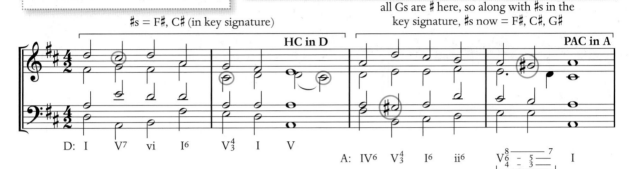

MODULATION TO THE DOMINANT KEY (KEY OF V)

A new key that is established by a modulation is identified by its relationship with the main key—that is, by the position of its tonic within the scale of the main key. The most common modulation, particularly in major keys, is to the **dominant key** (or **key of V**). For instance, D-major compositions generally modulate to A major, A major being the dominant (V) in the key of D. Moving to the dominant key involves raising $\hat{4}$ of the main key, which becomes the leading tone $\hat{7}$ in the key of V.

27.3 Elizabeth Turner, Lesson 6, Giga

The main key of this movement is F major.

In mm. 5–8 there is a modulation to C, the dominant key (key of V): all of the B♭s ($\hat{4}$ in the main key of F) are raised to B♮s ($\hat{7}$ in the new key of C).

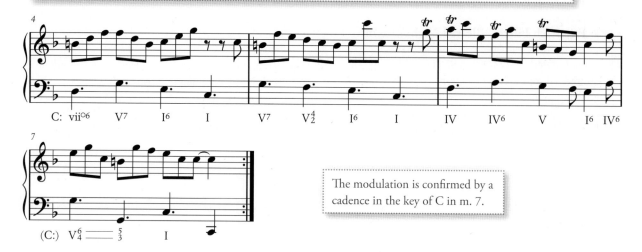

The modulation is confirmed by a cadence in the key of C in m. 7.

PIVOT CHORDS

In a modulation from one key to another, in many cases the first chord in the new key is also a chord in the main key. Thus a harmony originally heard within the first key is subsequently reinterpreted in the new key, allowing for smooth motion from one key to the other. The shared harmony is known as a **pivot chord**. Pivot chords must be diatonic in both keys—that is, they should not require any accidentals in either key.

27.4

Modulation from C to G using pivot chord: Progression that does not use pivot chord:

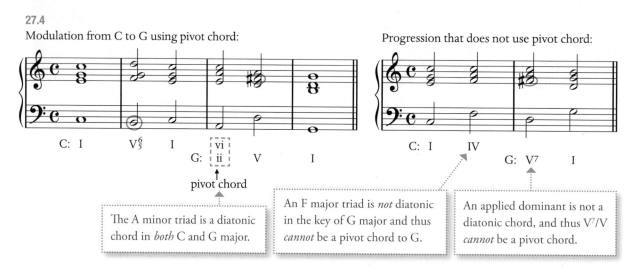

pivot chord

The A minor triad is a diatonic chord in *both* C and G major.

An F major triad is *not* diatonic in the key of G major and thus *cannot* be a pivot chord to G.

An applied dominant is not a diatonic chord, and thus V⁷/V *cannot* be a pivot chord.

27.5 Franz Schubert, "Heidenröslein" ("Wild Rose")

The pivot chord (I in G = IV in D) introduces the modulation to the dominant key.

The pivot chord (I in D = V in G) ushers in the return to the main key of G.

Translation: A boy saw a wild rose amid the heather, as fresh and beautiful as the morning. He ran to it quickly and gazed on it with great joy. Little rose amid the heather.

To determine what harmonies may be used as pivot chords in modulating from one key to another, find the chords that are in both keys. In modulating from I to V, here are the possibilities:

Key of I		Key of V		Key of I		Key of V
I	*becomes*	IV		V	*becomes*	I
iii	*becomes*	vi		vi	*becomes*	ii

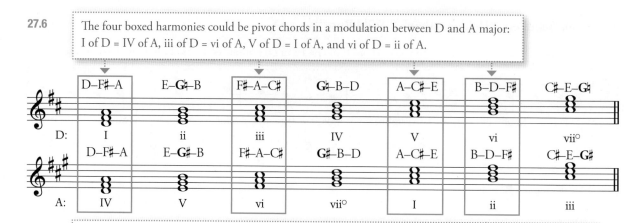

The four boxed harmonies could be pivot chords in a modulation between D and A major: I of D = IV of A, iii of D = vi of A, V of D = I of A, and vi of D = ii of A.

The other harmonies cannot be used as pivot chords: E minor, G major, and C♯ diminished are *not* diatonic chords in the key of A; E major, G♯ diminished, and C♯ minor are *not* diatonic chords in the key of D.

DISTINGUISHING TONICIZATIONS FROM MODULATIONS

As noted at the top of this chapter and in Chapter 25, a tonicization occurs when a harmony other than I is briefly treated as a tonic. The appearance of a few chords in a new key in mid-phrase is usually interpreted as a tonicization, rather than a modulation. To be sure, there is no strict dividing line between these two categories, and in some cases a harmonic progression might be characterized either way, as involving a tonicization or a modulation. In general, however, a modulation tends to be a key change that is long and substantial, involves a pivot chord, and—most importantly—is confirmed with a cadence.

27.7 W. A. Mozart, "March of the Priests," from *The Magic Flute*

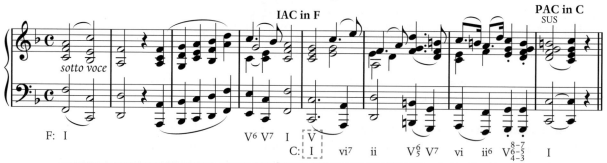

Modulation: The key of C (i.e., the key of V) is introduced with a pivot chord, in mm. 5–8 all the chords and scale degrees function within the key of C, and there is a PAC in C at the end of the phrase.

In contrast, a change of key is regarded as a tonicization if it is brief, not introduced with a pivot chord, and not confirmed with a cadence.

27.8 Felix Mendelssohn, *Kinderstücke* (*Children's Pieces*), Op. 72, No. 6

F: V⁷ I (bass implied) V⁶₅/V V V⁴₂/V V⁶ V⁷ vi IV ii⁶ V⁶⁻⁵₄⁻³ **HC in F**

> *Tonicization* (not modulation): A series of applied chords tonicize C in mid-phrase, but the music does not stay in the key of C for long (note B♭ in the melody in m. 4), and there is no cadence in C.

27.9 Francis Johnson, "Le Pre aux Clercs," from *The Citizen's Quadrilles*, No. 5

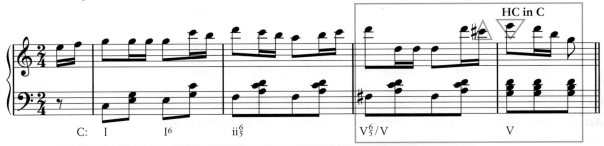

C: I I⁶ ii⁶₅ V⁶₅/V V **HC in C**

> *Tonicization* (not modulation): Although G (the goal V within the half cadence in the main key) is tonicized at the end of the phrase, there is no pivot chord, nor is there a cadence in G.

HARMONIZING MELODIES

To identify a melody that might be harmonized with a modulation, look for an appearance (or repeated appearance) of an accidental shortly before the end of a phrase, or for a succession of scale degrees that seems more compatible with a progression in a new key.

27.10

Task: **Harmonize the melody.**

> As the leading tone if C major, B normally leads up to C. The downward motion here could be harmonized with a modulation to G, in which the melodic succession B–A is more normal.

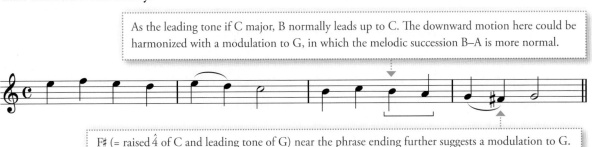

> F♯ (= raised 4̂ of C and leading tone of G) near the phrase ending further suggests a modulation to G.

Possible harmonization:

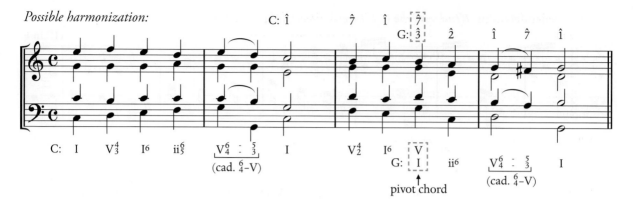

For more on modulating to the dominant key, see A Closer Look.

POINTS FOR REVIEW

- A modulation is a substantial change of key that is confirmed by a cadence.

- Modulations are usually signaled by accidentals, rather than by a new key signature.

- After a modulation has begun, the harmonies and scale degrees are labeled in the new key.

- The key that appears at the start and end of the movement is known as the main key. The keys to which there are modulations are identified by their relationship to the main key.

- In a major-key piece, the most common modulation is to the dominant key (the key of V).

- In modulating between two keys, often the last chord of the first key is the same as the first chord of the new key. This shared chord is known as a pivot chord and must be diatonic to both keys.

- Compared to tonicizations, modulations are changes of key that tend to be more substantial, involve a pivot chord, and have a cadence in the new key.

TEST YOURSELF

1. Identify the accidental needed to modulate between the following keys:

   a. From G to D.

   b. From B♭ to F.

   c. From E to B.

   d. From A to E.

   e. From D♭ to A♭.

   f. From B to F♯.

   g. From E♭ to B♭.

2. a. In a major key signature with two sharps, the main key is _____ and the key of V is _____.

    b. In a major key signature with two flats, the main key is _____ and the key of V is _____.

    c. In a major key signature with four flats, the main key is _____ and the key of V is _____.

3. What chords could serve as a pivot chord between

    a. B♭ major and F major?   b. D major and A major?   c. A major and E major?

4. In each of the following three excerpts, what chord functions as the pivot chord? What is the function of that chord in the main key? In the key of V?

5. Label the Roman numerals.

    Rose Dale, "Barnham" (hymn)

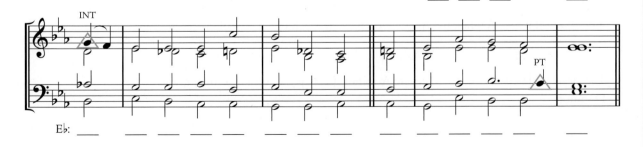

28

Modulation to Closely Related Keys

Modulations to closely related keys—differing from the main key by no more than one sharp or flat—are common.

CLOSELY RELATED KEYS

Modulations can lead to any key, not just the key of the dominant. The most common modulations are those that lead to closely related keys—that is, keys whose signature differs from that of the main key by no more than one sharp or flat.

28.1

Task: **Find the closely related keys of C major.**

- Since C major has no sharps or flats, closely related keys include the relative minor, and the major and minor keys that have one sharp or flat:

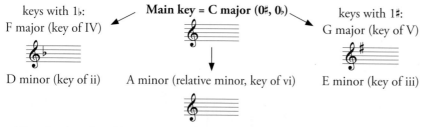

keys with 1♭:
F major (key of IV)

Main key = C major (0♯, 0♭)

keys with 1♯:
G major (key of V)

D minor (key of ii)   A minor (relative minor, key of vi)   E minor (key of iii)

- The closely related keys of C major are A minor, G major, E minor, F major, and D minor.

28.2

Task: **Find the closely related keys of C minor.**

- Since C minor has three flats, closely related keys include the relative major, and the major and minor keys that have four flats and two flats.

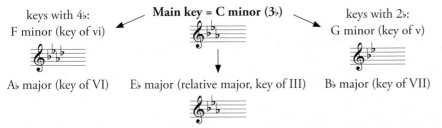

keys with 4♭:
F minor (key of vi)

Main key = C minor (3♭)

keys with 2♭:
G minor (key of v)

A♭ major (key of VI)   E♭ major (relative major, key of III)   B♭ major (key of VII)

- The closely related keys of C minor are E♭ major, F minor, A♭ major, G minor, and B♭ major.

The tonic chord of each closely related key uses notes—without accidentals—from the scale of the main key.

28.3

> The major and minor triads (without accidentals) in a key form the tonic chords of closely related keys.

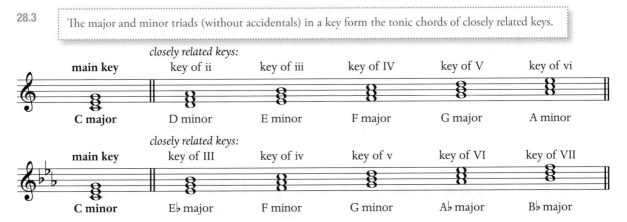

	closely related keys:				
main key	key of ii	key of iii	key of IV	key of V	key of vi
C major	D minor	E minor	F major	G major	A minor

	closely related keys:				
main key	key of III	key of iv	key of v	key of VI	key of VII
C minor	E♭ major	F minor	G minor	A♭ major	B♭ major

MODULATIONS IN MAJOR-KEY PIECES

After a modulation has begun, scale degrees and harmonies are understood in relation to the new key. A modulation to any key requires a cadence. With the exception of modulation from a minor key to its relative major, modulations always involve accidentals or (much less commonly) a new key signature.

28.4 J. F. Schwenke, "Es ist das Heil uns kommen her" ("Salvation unto Us Has Come")

Modulating from D (2♯) to G (1♯) requires C♮.

After the modulation, the harmonies and scale degrees are analyzed in G.

D: I   V⁶   V⁷

G: V   IV⁶ V⁶   I   V⁸⁻⁴₇⁻₃   I

Modulating to the relative minor key requires raising $\hat{7}$ of the new key so that it becomes a leading tone.

28.5 **Franz Schubert, *German Dances*, D. 783, No. 13**

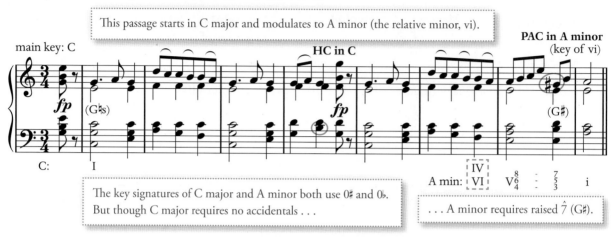

This passage starts in C major and modulates to A minor (the relative minor, vi).

main key: C

HC in C

PAC in A minor
(key of vi)

fp

(G♮s)

fp

(G♯)

C: I

A min: VI | IV | V$^8_6$: $^7_5$ | i | | ^{4} : ^{3}

The key signatures of C major and A minor both use 0♯ and 0♭. But though C major requires no accidentals . . .

. . . A minor requires raised $\hat{7}$ (G♯).

Modulation to other minor keys similarly requires a raised $\hat{7}$, in addition to whatever accidentals are needed to reflect the difference in the key signature of the new key.

28.6 **Edmond Dédé, "Mirliton fin de siècle" ("Kazoo, Turn of the Century")**

Modulating from D major (2♯s) to F♯ minor (3♯s) requires the accidental G♯ (to reflect the different key signature) as well as E♯ (the raised $\hat{7}$ in F♯ minor).

fp

fp

D: I

F♯ min.: VI | I

V^7

6

The D♯ in m. 5 is raised $\hat{6}$ within F♯ minor (part of the ascending melodic minor scale).

(F♯ min.:) i

ii^6 V^7

i

MODULATIONS IN MINOR-KEY PIECES

Within minor-key compositions it is extremely common to modulate to the relative major (III). Although a minor key and its relative major share the same key signature, $\hat{7}$ in minor is almost always raised to form a leading tone. As a result, the prominent and repeated use of $\hat{7}$ that is *not* raised usually indicates a modulation to the relative major, especially if it appears as part of the cadence.

28.7 Henry Purcell, "When Monarchs Unite," from *Dido and Aeneas*

> In the first phrase, $\hat{7}$ is raised to B♮ to form the leading tone in C minor.

> The repeated B♭s in the second phrase signal a modulation to E♭ major.

It is also common in minor keys to modulate to the key of the dominant minor, v. (On the other hand, in minor-key pieces modulations to the key of the dominant major—which is not a closely related key—are rare.)

28.8 Julie Candeille, Piano Sonata in G Minor, Op. 8, No. 2, iii

> In modulating from G minor (2♭) to D minor (1♭), accidentals are needed for both E and C♯ (the leading tone of D minor).

PIVOT CHORDS

Pivot chords are often used to modulate between closely related keys. When one of the keys is minor, the pivot chord may use any of the notes found in the ascending or descending melodic minor scale. Even chords that are less common in simple diatonic passages—such as III, minor v, or subtonic VII—may be used as a pivot chords.

28.9

Task: **Find the pivot chords that may be used in modulating from G major to A minor.**

- Determine the major, minor, and diminished chords in each key, using the notes in the G major and A melodic minor scales.

- Any chord in the main key that uses the same notes as a chord in the new key can be used as a pivot chord.

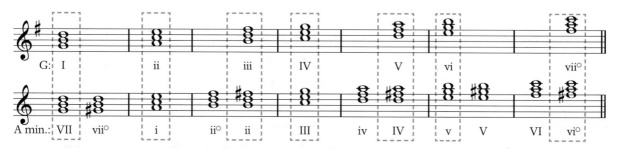

28.10 A. W. Bach, "Zeuch ein zu meinen Toren" ("O Enter Lord")

> Modulation from G major to A minor; pivot chord: IV of G = III of A minor.

28.11 Theophania Cecil, Psalm 51

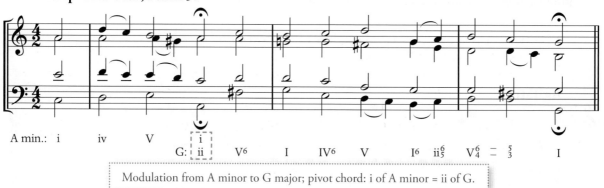

> Modulation from A minor to G major; pivot chord: i of A minor = ii of G.

EXTENDED TONICIZATIONS

Some key changes that do not lead to a cadence in the new key—and thus create tonicizations rather than modulations—nonetheless involve *multiple* harmonies that lead toward a goal chord. These may include chords other than applied dominants, including **S**ubdominant harmonies that relate to the goal chord. The chords within these extended tonicizations may be labeled in relation to the tonicized key.

28.12 Elfrida Andrée, "Visa en vårmorgen" ("View on a Spring Morning")

> In the middle of the phrase (mm. 3–6) the key of D minor is tonicized, but D minor is not confirmed by a cadence.

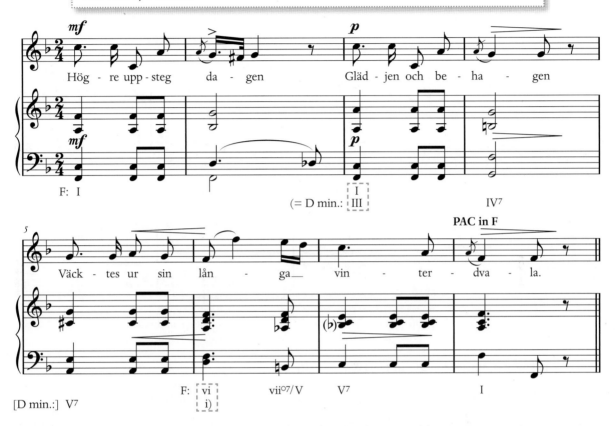

Hög - re upp - steg   da - gen   Gläd - jen och be - ha - gen

F: I   (= D min.: III | I)   IV⁷

Väck - tes ur sin lån - ga— vin - ter - dva - la.

PAC in F

[D min.:] V⁷   F: vi (i)   vii°⁷/V   V⁷   I

Translation: Higher rose the day, joy and the garden were awakened from their long winter hibernation.

MODULATION SCHEMES

Compositions often modulate to several different keys, frequently following a conventional order. In major-key movements composed before 1800, the first modulation is usually to V. In minor-key movements, the first modulation most often is to III (the relative major), though it can also be to v (the dominant minor). In both major and minor keys, the initial modulation normally is followed by modulations to one or more other closely related keys, and then by a return to the main key by the end of the piece.

28.13 Common modulation schemes

major-key piece: **main key** ➔ V ➔ other closely related key(s) ➔ back to **main key**
                              (such as vi or IV)

minor-key piece: **main key** ➔ III ➔ other closely related key(s) ➔ back to **main key**
         OR   (such as iv or v)

                main key ➔ v ➔ other closely related key(s) ➔ back to **main key**
                                       (such as III or iv)

Each key to which there is a modulation is labeled by its relation to the main key. Thus, for instance, in a work in C major a modulation to A minor is labeled as a modulation to the key of vi, even if it is immediately preceded by a modulation to G major.

28.14 J. S. Bach, *Applicatio*

This C-major piece follows a standard modulation scheme: first a modulation to V (G major), then to vi (A minor), and finally back to C.

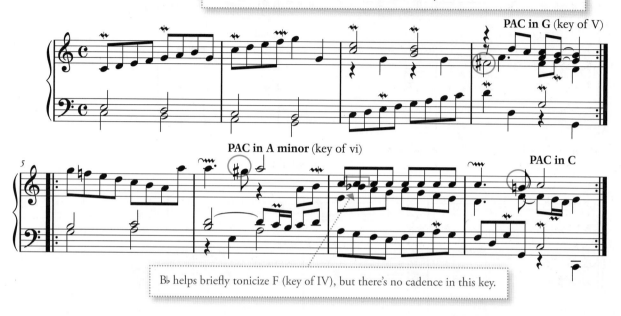

PAC in G (key of V)

PAC in A minor (key of vi)

PAC in C

B♭ helps briefly tonicize F (key of IV), but there's no cadence in this key.

28.15 G. F. Handel, Violin Sonata in E, HWV 373, iii

This C♯-minor movement follows a standard modulation scheme: first a modulation to III (E major), then to iv (F♯ minor), and finally back to C♯ minor.

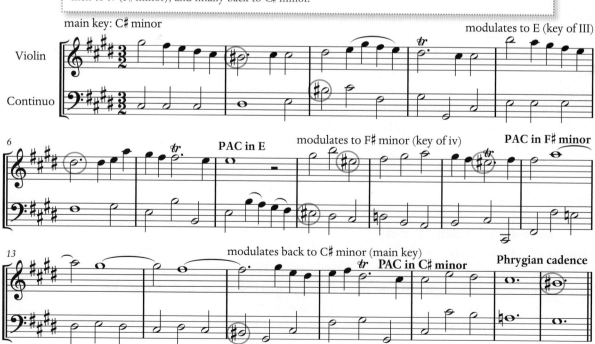

main key: C♯ minor

modulates to E (key of III)

PAC in E

modulates to F♯ minor (key of iv)

PAC in F♯ minor

modulates back to C♯ minor (main key)

PAC in C♯ minor

Phrygian cadence

- It is common to modulate to closely related keys (keys in which the key signature differs from the main key by no more than one sharp or flat).

- In most cases, a modulation is indicated by accidentals, rather than by a change of key signature.

- Modulations to minor keys require not only accidentals that reflect the change of key, but also an accidental that raises $\hat{7}$ in the new key.

- Any major, minor, or diminished chord that occurs in both the main key and the new key (including chords created with different forms of the minor scale) can be used as a pivot chord.

- Tonicization, which does not involve a cadence in the new key, may nonetheless involve a series of harmonies that lead to a goal chord, including chords other than applied dominants.

- The first modulation in a major-key composition is most commonly to the key of V; the first modulation in a minor-key composition is most commonly to the key of III (the relative major), less commonly to v (the minor dominant). The first modulation is often followed by modulations to other closely related keys before the return to the main key.

TEST YOURSELF

1. Identify the closely related key relationships below.
   a. In G major, B minor is the key of _____.   b. In A major, D major is the key of _____.
   c. In G minor, E♭ major is the key of _____.   d. In E minor, B minor is the key of _____.

2. List the closely related keys of the following:
   a. G major   b. B♭ major   c. D minor   d. F♯ minor

3. List the triads that may be used as pivot chords in modulating between the following pairs of keys:
   a. F major and D minor   b. G minor and C minor
   c. A major and C♯ minor   d. E minor and C major

4. List the accidentals required in the following modulations:
   a. From D major to B minor.   b. From A♭ major to D♭ major.
   c. From F major to A minor.   d. From E major to F♯ minor.

5. Supply the missing accidentals in the following passages.

a.

A: I   IV   I   IV
B min.:   III   ii°6   V   i

b.

B♭:   I   ii6
G min.:   iv6   V7   i   V8 – 7   i

c.

G♯ min.:   i   vii°7   i   ii°6   V$_4^6$ — $_3^5$ i
B: vi   V6   I   vii°6

6. Answer the questions about the example below.

    a. To what key is there a motion in measures 2–6 of this excerpt?

    b. Is this best understood as a modulation or extended tonicization, and why?

    c. What applied chord appears in measure 6?

    d. What applied chord appears in measure 7?

George M. Cohan, "Only Forty-Five Minutes from Broadway"

29

Modal Mixture

Modal mixture arises when notes, chords, or passages from the parallel minor are used within a major key, or vice versa.

Parallel Minor in a Major Key
- Borrowed chords resulting from modal mixture
- Common borrowed chords
- vii°7 in major keys

Parallel Major in a Minor Key

PARALLEL MINOR IN A MAJOR KEY

Modal mixture in a major key results from the appearance of notes, chords, or entire passages drawn from the parallel minor. A shift to the parallel minor can have a powerful expressive effect. It is *not* a modulation, however, because a modulation must involve a change of tonic.

29.1 **Franz Schubert, "Thränenregen" ("Rain of Tears")**

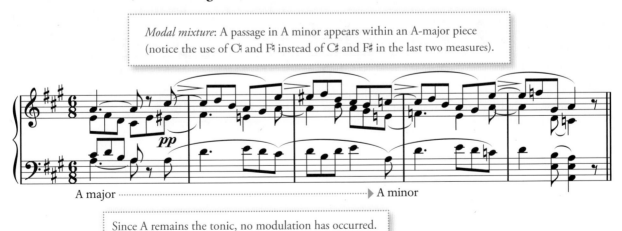

Modal mixture: A passage in A minor appears within an A-major piece (notice the use of C♮ and F♮ instead of C♯ and F♯ in the last two measures).

A major ·········· ▶ A minor

Since A remains the tonic, no modulation has occurred.

BORROWED CHORDS RESULTING FROM MODAL MIXTURE

In a major-key passage, modal mixture may involve only one chord or perhaps just a few harmonies from the parallel minor. In such a case the minor-key harmonies, known as **borrowed chords**, typically use the minor form of either $\hat{3}$ or $\hat{6}$ as one of their chord tones. In each case, the function of the borrowed chord is similar to the diatonic version of the harmony. For instance, within a major key, iv functions like IV, ii°⁶ functions like ii⁶, and so on.

29.2

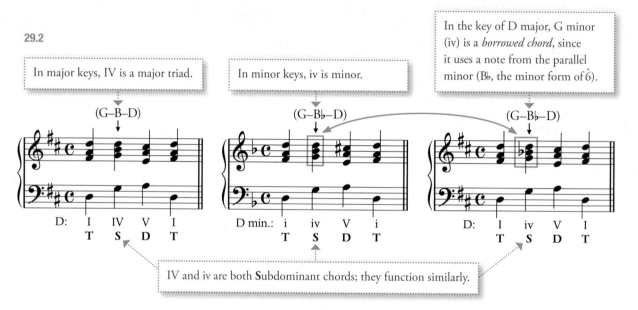

In major keys, IV is a major triad.

In minor keys, iv is minor.

In the key of D major, G minor (iv) is a *borrowed chord*, since it uses a note from the parallel minor (B♭, the minor form of $\hat{6}$).

IV and iv are both **S**ubdominant chords; they function similarly.

29.3 **Antonín Dvořák, Waltz, Op. 54, No. 4**

Borrowed chord in D♭ major: iv instead of IV, with B𝄫 (minor form of $\hat{6}$) instead of B♭.

29.4 Eugène Dédé, "Buenas Noches," Op. 243

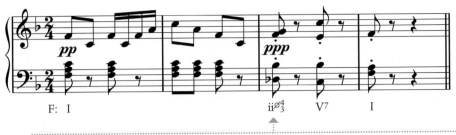

Borrowed chord in F major: ii°$^4_3$ instead of ii$^4_3$, with D♭ (minor form of $\hat6$) instead of D.

29.5 Franz Schubert, "Der Neugierige" ("The Curious One")

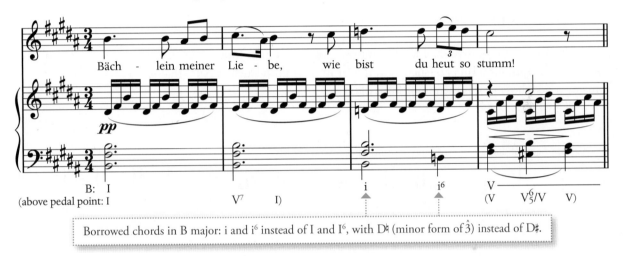

Borrowed chords in B major: i and i⁶ instead of I and I⁶, with D♯ (minor form of $\hat3$) instead of D♯.

Translation: My dear brook, why are you so silent today?

29.6 Scott Joplin, "Euphonious Sounds"

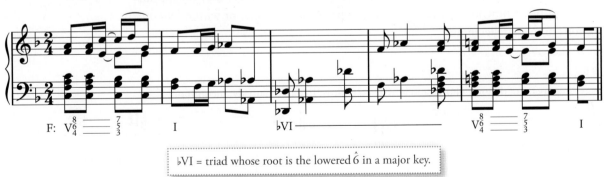

♭VI = triad whose root is the lowered $\hat6$ in a major key.

Borrowed chords use the same voice leading in major keys as they would in their original minor-key context.

29.7

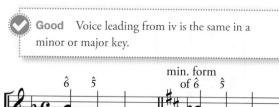

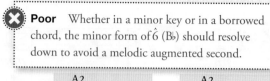

COMMON BORROWED CHORDS

The most common borrowed chords in major use either the minor form of $\hat{3}$ (such as the i triad), the minor form of $\hat{6}$ (such as iv, ii°⁶, or ii°⁷), or both (such as ♭VI—that is, a major triad whose root is the minor form of $\hat{6}$).

29.8

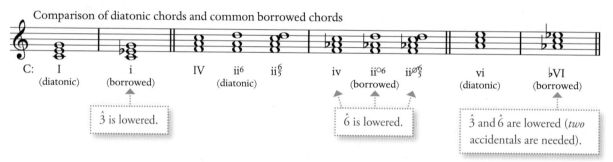

Comparison of diatonic chords and common borrowed chords

Since $\hat{7}$ is usually raised to form a leading tone in minor keys, borrowed chords that use the subtonic $\hat{7}$ are relatively rare. In the few instances where they do appear, they most often function as passing chords, as parts of sequences, or within lengthy sections in the parallel minor.

29.9

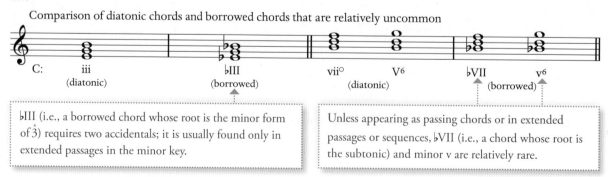

Comparison of diatonic chords and borrowed chords that are relatively uncommon

vii°7 IN MAJOR KEYS

As discussed in Chapter 17, the minor form of $\hat{6}$ may also appear within a major key as part of vii°7.

29.10 **Hélène Riese Liebmann, Grand Piano Sonata, Op. 3, ii**

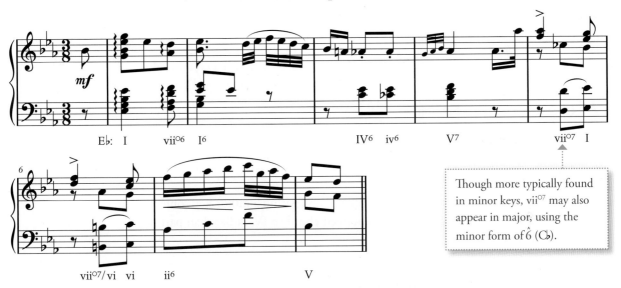

> Though more typically found in minor keys, vii°7 may also appear in major, using the minor form of $\hat{6}$ (C♭).

PARALLEL MAJOR IN A MINOR KEY

Modal mixture can also occur when a minor-key composition includes a passage in the parallel major.

29.11 **Maddalena Lombardini Sirmen, String Quartet in F Minor, Op. 3, No. 5, i**

> A section in F major appears within an F-minor movement.

Unlike major keys, however, minor keys only rarely use borrowed chords in isolation. After all, $\hat{6}$ and $\hat{7}$ are often raised in minor keys anyway (as in the ascending melodic minor scale), and thus chords that use these raised scale degrees—such as IV or V—are usually not considered to be borrowed chords.

29.12 Carl Nielsen, "Alt paa den vilde Hede" ("All on the Wild Heath")

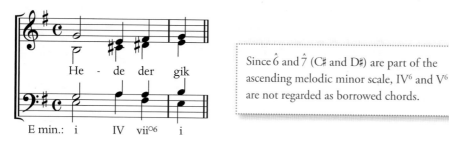

He - de der gik

E min.: i   IV   vii°6   i

> Since $\hat{6}$ and $\hat{7}$ (C♯ and D♯) are part of the ascending melodic minor scale, IV⁶ and V⁶ are not regarded as borrowed chords.

Translation: [All on the wild] heath there went:

Likewise, when it appears in the middle of a phrase within a minor-key context, the major form of $\hat{3}$ usually forms part of an applied chord to IV, rather than part of a borrowed chord.

29.13 Élisabeth Jacquet de la Guerre, Suite in D Minor

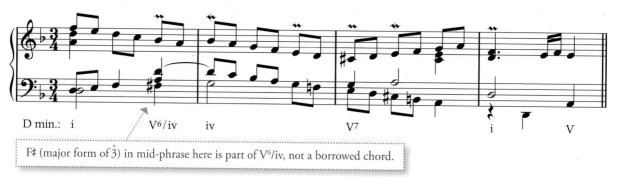

D min.:   i   V⁶/iv   iv   V⁷   i   V

> F♯ (major form of $\hat{3}$) in mid-phrase here is part of V⁶/iv, not a borrowed chord.

The only common instance of a borrowed chord within a minor key arises when the third of a tonic chord is raised at the *end* of a phrase. In this case, the minor form of $\hat{3}$ is replaced by its major form, so that the final tonic chord of the phrase is a major triad rather than a minor one. The raised $\hat{3}$ is known as a **Picardy third**.

29.14 Élisabeth Jacquet de la Guerre, Suite in D Minor

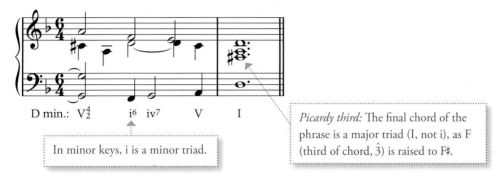

D min.: V_2^4 i^6 iv^7 V   I

In minor keys, i is a minor triad.

Picardy third: The final chord of the phrase is a major triad (I, not i), as F (third of chord, $\hat{3}$) is raised to F♯.

POINTS FOR REVIEW

- **Modal mixture usually occurs when notes or harmonies from the parallel minor appear within a major key. Modal mixture may involve as little as a single note or chord, or as much as an entire section.**

- **Since modulation involves changing tonic notes, moving between parallel major and minor keys is not considered to be a modulation.**

- **Modal mixture that changes the quality of a single harmony creates a *borrowed chord*. The use of modal mixture in a borrowed chord does not change its harmonic function.**

- **The most common borrowed chords are those that use the minor form of $\hat{3}, \hat{6}$, or both within a major key.**

- **Modal mixture may also occur when a section in a major key appears within a minor-key piece.**

- **At the end of a phrase in a minor key, the minor tonic triad may be replaced by a major chord by raising the third of the chord ($\hat{3}$) by a half step. This raised third is known as a *Picardy third*.**

TEST YOURSELF

1. In major keys, which of the following chords involve modal mixture?

   a. iv   b. vi   c. IV   d. ii^6 e. ii^{o6} f. ♭III   g. i   h. iii

2. What accidentals are missing in the following chords (all of which involve modal mixture)?

a.   G: iv   b.   E♭: ♭VI   c.   B: ii^{ø7} d.   F: i   e.   F min.: I   f.   D: vii^{o7}

3. Which of the following statements are true?

   a. Modal mixture may arise when there is a move to the parallel minor key within a major-key piece, or vice versa.

   b. There can be a modulation from D major to D minor.

   c. A borrowed chord in a major key always involves using a flat.

   d. The most common borrowed chords use the minor form of $\hat{3}$, $\hat{6}$, or both within a major-key context.

   e. A Picardy third is found at the end of a phrase, rather than in its middle.

   f. Modal mixture can involve a motion between relative major and minor keys.

4. Which of these shifts between major and minor keys involve modal mixture? Why?

   a. From G major to E minor.

   b. From G major to G minor.

   c. From G major to B minor.

   d. From D minor to D major.

   e. From D minor to F major.

30

♭II⁶: The Neapolitan Sixth

♭II⁶ is a first-inversion major triad built on lowered $\hat{2}$; it has a Subdominant function.

Building ♭II⁶
Harmonic Progression
Voice Leading

BUILDING ♭II⁶

♭II is a major chord whose root is lowered $\hat{2}$. It usually appears in first inversion, as a **♭II⁶**, also known as a **Neapolitan sixth** (or **N⁶**). ♭II⁶ appears most often in minor keys, in place of a diatonic ii°⁶. The root of ♭II⁶ requires an accidental, which may be either a flat or a natural, depending upon the key signature.

30.1

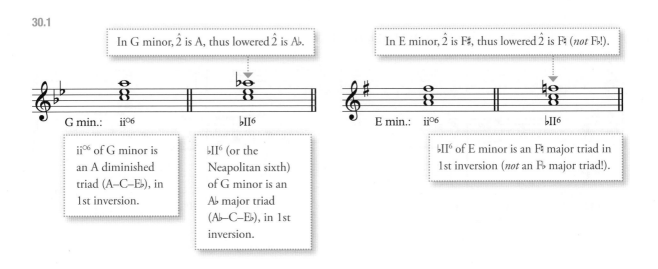

In G minor, $\hat{2}$ is A, thus lowered $\hat{2}$ is A♭.

In E minor, $\hat{2}$ is F♯, thus lowered $\hat{2}$ is F♮ (*not* F♭!).

G min.:   ii°⁶   ♭II⁶

E min.:   ii°⁶   ♭II⁶

ii°⁶ of G minor is an A diminished triad (A–C–E♭), in 1st inversion.

♭II⁶ (or the Neapolitan sixth) of G minor is an A♭ major triad (A♭–C–E♭), in 1st inversion.

♭II⁶ of E minor is an F♮ major triad in 1st inversion (*not* an F♭ major triad!).

HARMONIC PROGRESSION

Like ii°⁶, ♭II⁶ has a **S**ubdominant function. ♭II⁶ may be preceded by any chord that can go before ii°⁶, such as i, iv, or VI, and it usually leads to a **D**ominant harmony such as V, V⁷, or their inversions.

30.2 Franz Schubert, "Klage" ("Lament"), D. 371

> Like ii°⁶, ♭II⁶ can move to V or V⁷.

Translation: I can bear it [no] longer.

30.3 Mel Bonis, Menuet

♭II⁶ also may lead to V via a cadential $^6_4$ or vii°⁷/V.

30.4 W. A. Mozart, Violin Sonata in E Minor, K. 304, i

30.5 J. M. Nunes Garcia, *Missa para o dia da Purificação de Nossa Senhora*

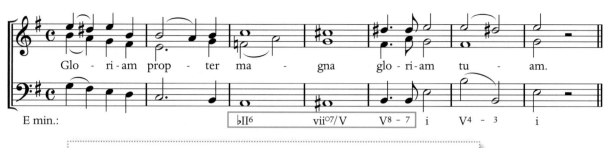

E min.: ♭II⁶　　vii°⁷/V　　V⁸⁻⁷　i　　V⁴⁻³　i

There is a chromatic stepwise ascent in the bass as ♭II⁶ moves through vii°⁷/V to V.

VOICE LEADING

♭II⁶ includes two tendency tones that lead downward: lowered $\hat{2}$ and the minor form of $\hat{6}$. Usually, it is best to double the bass of ♭II⁶ (the third of the chord).

30.6

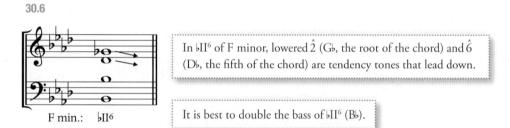

F min.:　♭II⁶

In ♭II⁶ of F minor, lowered $\hat{2}$ (G♭, the root of the chord) and $\hat{6}$ (D♭, the fifth of the chord) are tendency tones that lead down.

It is best to double the bass of ♭II⁶ (B♭).

When it appears in a ♭II⁶–V progression, lowered $\hat{2}$ (the root of ♭II) usually moves *down* toward the leading tone (especially when it appears in the top voice). The motion directly from lowered $\hat{2}$ to $\hat{7}$ creates a melodic diminished third.

30.7

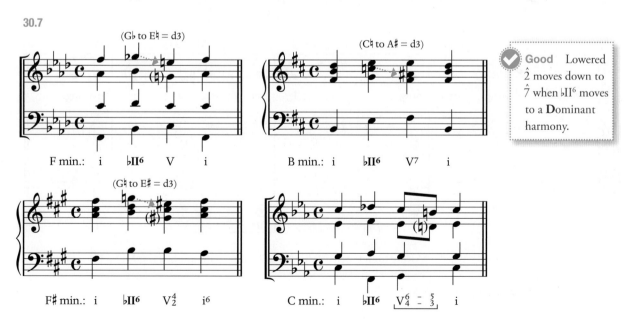

Good Lowered $\hat{2}$ moves down to $\hat{7}$ when ♭II⁶ moves to a **D**ominant harmony.

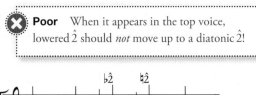

Poor When it appears in the top voice, lowered 2̂ should *not* move up to a diatonic 2̂!

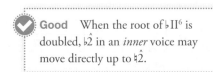

Good When the root of ♭II⁶ is doubled, ♭2̂ in an *inner* voice may move directly up to ♮2̂.

C min.: i ♭II⁶ V⁷ i

Poor A♭–B♮ creates an augmented second!

C min.: i ♭II⁶ V i

30.9 Arthur Sullivan, "A Many Years Ago," from *H.M.S. Pinafore*

Moving from lowered 2̂ directly to 7̂ creates a diminished third (F to D♯).

🔍 For more on ♭II⁶, see A Closer Look.

- ♭II⁶ is a first-inversion major triad, known as the *Neapolitan sixth* (N⁶). The ♭II⁶ almost always appears in minor keys.

- The root of ♭II⁶ requires an accidental, sometimes a flat and sometimes a natural (depending on the key signature).

- ♭II⁶ leads to V, V⁷, or their inversions, sometimes through vii°⁷/V or a cadential $^6_4$.

- It is most common to double the bass of ♭II⁶.

- In the ♭II⁶ to V progression, lowered $\hat{2}$ in the top voice should move *down*.

TEST YOURSELF

1. What accidentals need to be added to the following ii°⁶ chords in order to change them into ♭II⁶ chords?

   F♯ min.: ii°⁶   B♭ min.: ii°⁶   C♯ min.: ii°⁶

2. What notes are in the following chords (from the bass up)?

   a. D minor: ii°⁶: ____, ____, ____ ♭II⁶: ____, ____, ____

   b. B minor: ii°⁶: ____, ____, ____ ♭II⁶: ____, ____, ____

   c. F minor: ii°⁶: ____, ____, ____ ♭II⁶: ____, ____, ____

3. Which of the following chords typically might precede ♭II⁶?

   a. iv   b. V   c. vii°⁶   d. i⁶   e. VI

4. Fill in the blanks:

   a. ♭II⁶ chords usually appear in _____ keys.

   b. ♭II⁶ is also known as a _____.

   c. ♭II⁶ is a _____ (major, minor, or diminished?) triad.

   d. The root of the ♭II⁶ is a tendency tone that usually leads _____.

5. In completing the harmonization below, should the E♭ in the soprano on beat 2 move to an E♮, a C♯, or either?

   D min.: i   ♭II6   V

31 Augmented Sixth Chords

Augmented sixth chords lead to root-position V and contain tendency tones that are a minor second above and below $\hat{5}$.

Types of Augmented Sixth Chords:	A Closer Look
Italian, French, and German	Augmented sixth followed by an applied chord to V
Spelling the German augmented sixth	Augmented sixths resolving to V^7
Harmonic Progressions	German sixths resolving directly to V
Italian and French augmented sixth	Augmented sixth chords leading to harmonies other than V
German augmented sixth	Uncommon types of augmented sixth chords
Harmonies that precede augmented sixth chords	
Augmented sixth chords embellishing V	

Augmented sixth chords are a group of harmonies that drive powerfully toward V. In eighteenth-century music, augmented sixth chords often lead to the dominant chord at climactic cadences. In later styles, augmented sixth chords are used more freely, leading to V at other moments as well.

Unlike most other chords, augmented sixth chords are built not from thirds stacked above a root, but by intervals above the *bass*. The bass of an augmented sixth chord is the minor form of $\hat{6}$, a tendency tone that leads *down* to $\hat{5}$. Augmented sixth chords include raised $\hat{4}$, a tendency tone that leads *up* to $\hat{5}$. These two tendency tones—separated by an augmented sixth—resolve to $\hat{5}$ in opposite directions.

31.1

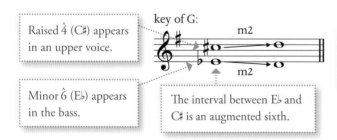

Raised $\hat{4}$ (C♯) appears in an upper voice.

key of G:

Minor $\hat{6}$ (E♭) appears in the bass.

The interval between E♭ and C♯ is an augmented sixth.

E♭ and C♯ are tendency tones that lead to $\hat{5}$ (D) by a melodic minor second.

Raised $\hat{4}$ requires an accidental in both major and minor keys. The minor form of $\hat{6}$ is diatonic in minor keys, but needs an accidental in major keys. In each case, these tendency tones must be spelled as minor seconds above and below $\hat{5}$—*not* as chromatic semitones.

31.2

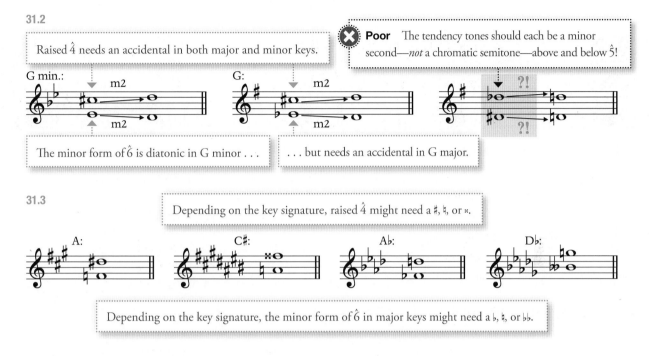

Raised $\hat{4}$ needs an accidental in both major and minor keys.

Poor The tendency tones should each be a minor second—*not* a chromatic semitone—above and below $\hat{5}$!

The minor form of $\hat{6}$ is diatonic in G minor . . .

. . . but needs an accidental in G major.

31.3

Depending on the key signature, raised $\hat{4}$ might need a ♯, ♮, or ×.

Depending on the key signature, the minor form of $\hat{6}$ in major keys might need a ♭, ♮, or ♭♭.

TYPES OF AUGMENTED SIXTH CHORDS: ITALIAN, FRENCH, AND GERMAN

The three most common augmented sixth chords are known as the **Italian augmented sixth** (abbreviated as It⁺⁶), **French augmented sixth** (Fr⁺⁶), and **German augmented sixth** (Ger⁺⁶). In addition to raised $\hat{4}$ and minor $\hat{6}$, these chords all include $\hat{1}$. The Italian augmented sixth includes only these three notes; the French augmented sixth also includes $\hat{2}$; and the German augmented sixth includes the minor form of $\hat{3}$.

31.4

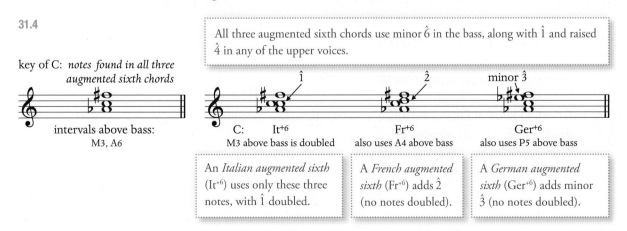

All three augmented sixth chords use minor $\hat{6}$ in the bass, along with $\hat{1}$ and raised $\hat{4}$ in any of the upper voices.

key of C: *notes found in all three augmented sixth chords*

intervals above bass:
M3, A6

C: It⁺⁶
M3 above bass is doubled

Fr⁺⁶
also uses A4 above bass

Ger⁺⁶
also uses P5 above bass

An *Italian augmented sixth* (It⁺⁶) uses only these three notes, with $\hat{1}$ doubled.

A *French augmented sixth* (Fr⁺⁶) adds $\hat{2}$ (no notes doubled).

A *German augmented sixth* (Ger⁺⁶) adds minor $\hat{3}$ (no notes doubled).

SPELLING THE GERMAN AUGMENTED SIXTH

The minor $\hat{3}$ in the German augmented sixth is diatonic in minor keys, but requires an accidental in major keys—either a flat or a natural, depending upon the key signature.

31.5

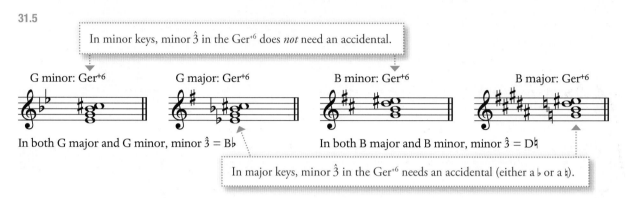

In minor keys, minor $\hat{3}$ in the Ger⁺⁶ does *not* need an accidental.

G minor: Ger⁺⁶   G major: Ger⁺⁶   B minor: Ger⁺⁶   B major: Ger⁺⁶

In both G major and G minor, minor $\hat{3}$ = B♭   In both B major and B minor, minor $\hat{3}$ = D♮

In major keys, minor $\hat{3}$ in the Ger⁺⁶ needs an accidental (either a ♭ or a ♮).

In major keys (but *not* in minor keys), the Ger⁺⁶ may occasionally be spelled with raised $\hat{2}$ instead of minor $\hat{3}$.

31.6

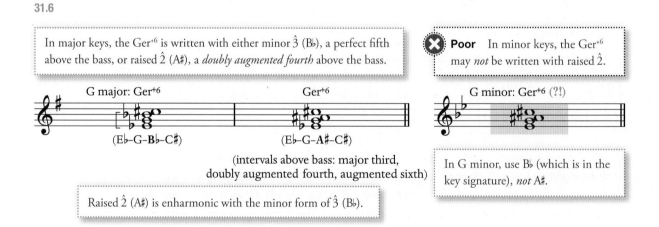

In major keys, the Ger⁺⁶ is written with either minor $\hat{3}$ (B♭), a perfect fifth above the bass, or raised $\hat{2}$ (A♯), a *doubly augmented fourth* above the bass.

❌ **Poor**   In minor keys, the Ger⁺⁶ may *not* be written with raised $\hat{2}$.

G major: Ger⁺⁶   Ger⁺⁶   G minor: Ger⁺⁶ (?!)

(E♭–G–**B♭**–C♯)   (E♭–G–**A♯**–C♯)

(intervals above bass: major third, doubly augmented fourth, augmented sixth)

In G minor, use B♭ (which is in the key signature), *not* A♯.

Raised $\hat{2}$ (A♯) is enharmonic with the minor form of $\hat{3}$ (B♭).

HARMONIC PROGRESSIONS

ITALIAN AND FRENCH AUGMENTED SIXTH

The Italian and French augmented sixth chords may move to a root-position V or V⁷ either directly or through a cadential $^6_4$.

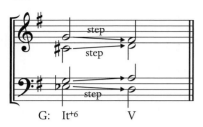
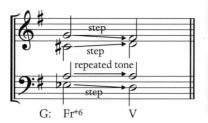

Italian and French augmented sixth chords often move directly to V.

Every voice either repeats or moves by step when a It⁺⁶ or Fr⁺⁶ moves to V.

31.8 Louise Reichardt, "Vaters Klage" ("The Father's Lament")

Translation: Three stars shone in the sky, looking sadly down.

31.9 Hortense de Beauharnais, "Eloigne toi" ("Move away")

Raised $\hat{4}$ (E♯) is in the tenor (raised $\hat{4}$ does *not* need to appear in the soprano).

Translation: Move away, companion of my pain.

31.10   **31.11 Maria Agata Szymanowska, March No. 2**

Italian and French augmented sixth chords can also move through a cadential $^6_4$ to V, with smooth motion in all voices.

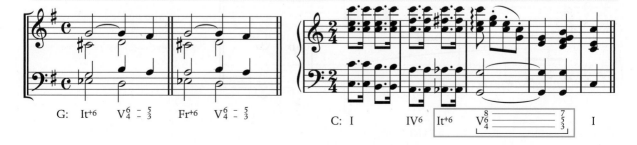

31.12

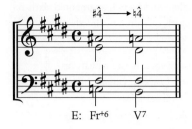

E: Fr⁺⁶   V⁷

When an augmented sixth chord moves directly to V⁷, raised $\hat{4}$ (A♯) slides down by semitone to $\hat{4}$ (A♮).

31.13 Carl Rossini Diton, "All I do, the people keep a' grumbeling"

do in the days of trou-ble, all I do, I do I do, all I do.

E: I   V⁷/ii   V$^4_3$/V   Fr⁺⁶   V⁷   I

GERMAN AUGMENTED SIXTH

A German augmented sixth chord most often leads to V through a cadential $^6_4$.

31.14

A Ger⁺⁶ normally moves to a cadential $^6_4$–V (i.e., V $^{6-5}_{4-3}$), with stepwise motion or repeated notes in all voices.

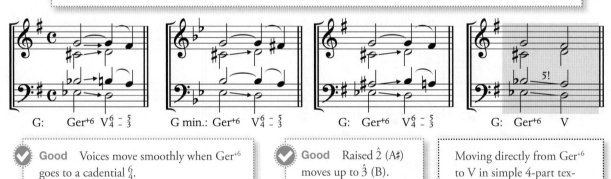

G: Ger⁺⁶ V$^6_4$ – $^5_3$ G min.: Ger⁺⁶ V$^6_4$ – $^5_3$ G: Ger⁺⁶ V$^6_4$ – $^5_3$ G: Ger⁺⁶ V

✅ **Good** Voices move smoothly when Ger⁺⁶ goes to a cadential $^6_4$.

✅ **Good** Raised $\hat{2}$ (A♯) moves up to $\hat{3}$ (B).

Moving directly from Ger⁺⁶ to V in simple 4-part textures creates parallel fifths.

31.15 Frédéric Chopin, Mazurka in A Minor, B. 134

A min.: i⁶   Ger⁺⁶ V$^8_6$ $^{8-7}_{6-5}$ $_{4-3}$ i

Ger⁺⁶ with minor $\hat{3}$ (F–A–C–D♯) moves to a cadential $^6_4$.

31.16 Basile Barès, "Mamie Waltz," Op. 27

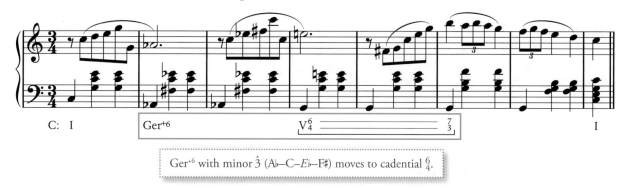

C: I   Ger^{+6} V$^6_4$ ———————— $^7_3$ I

Ger^{+6} with minor $\hat{3}$ (A♭–C–E♭–F♯) moves to cadential $^6_4$.

31.17 Will Marion Cook, "Julep Song"

You may keep all the wine if you think it di-vine: The good old mint ju-lep for me!

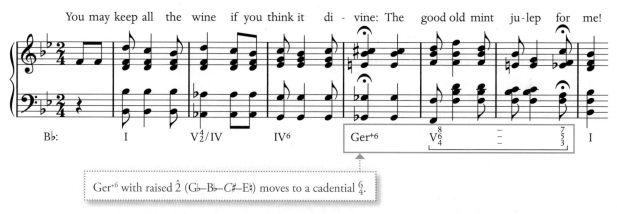

B♭: I   V$^4_2$/IV   IV^6 Ger^{+6} V$^8_6{}_4$ — — $^{7}_{5}_{3}$ I

Ger^{+6} with raised $\hat{2}$ (G♭–B♭–C♯–E♮) moves to a cadential $^6_4$.

HARMONIES THAT PRECEDE AUGMENTED SIXTH CHORDS

Any harmony that may precede V—such as I, IV^6, or vi—may precede an augmented sixth chord.

31.18 Ludwig van Beethoven, Symphony No. 5, i (arr. Liszt)

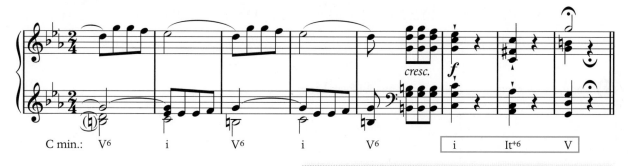

C min.:   V^6 i   V^6 i   V^6 i   It^{+6} V

An augmented sixth chord may be preceded by a tonic chord.

31.19 Hélène de Montgeroult, Etude No. 8 for Piano

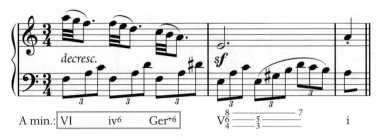

A min.: VI   iv⁶   Ger⁺⁶ │ V⁶₄ — ⁵₃ — ⁷ │ i

> It is particularly common for VI or IV⁶ to precede an augmented sixth chord.

31.20 Fernando Sor, *Leçons progressives* for Guitar, Op. 31, No. 20

A min.: i   V⁴₂/IV   IV⁶   It⁺⁶   V │ V⁴₂   i⁶   V⁴₃ │ i

AUGMENTED SIXTH CHORDS EMBELLISHING V

An augmented sixth chord may also be sandwiched between two root-position V chords, so as to embellish V with neighbor motion in the bass.

31.21 Vincenzo Bellini, "Torna, vezzosa Fillide" ("Return, Charming Phillida")

Fi - li - de mia do - v'è?   do - v'è   Fil - le - mi - a?

A min.: i   Fr⁺⁶ │ V ————————————————
         V   Fr⁺⁶   V   Fr⁺⁶   V

> Fr⁺⁶ embellishes V with E–F–E neighbor motion in the bass.

Translation: Where, Phillida, where?

🔍 For more on augmented sixth chords, see A Closer Look.

POINTS FOR REVIEW

- **The three main types of augmented sixth chords each include minor $\hat{6}$ in the bass, along with $\hat{1}$ and raised $\hat{4}$ in the upper voices.**
    - An Italian augmented sixth (It^{+6}) uses only these three notes, with $\hat{1}$ doubled.
    - A French augmented sixth (Fr^{+6}) also includes $\hat{2}$, with no notes doubled.
    - A German augmented sixth (Ger^{+6}) also includes minor $\hat{3}$ (or sometimes in major keys raised $\hat{2}$), with no notes doubled.

- **When the augmented sixth chord resolves, its tendency tones—minor $\hat{6}$ and raised $\hat{4}$—resolve to $\hat{5}$ in opposite directions.**

- **Italian and French augmented sixth chords move either to root-position V or through a cadential $^6_4$ to V.**

- **A German augmented sixth usually moves through a cadential $^6_4$ to V.**

Summary of the most common types and uses of augmented sixth chords:

key of C: Italian Augmented Sixth	French Augmented Sixth	German Augmented Sixth
$\flat\hat{6}$ in bass; $\hat{1}$, $\sharp\hat{4}$, and $\hat{1}$ in other voices	$\flat\hat{6}$ in bass; $\hat{1}$, $\sharp\hat{4}$, and $\hat{2}$ in other voices	$\flat\hat{6}$ in bass; $\hat{1}$, $\sharp\hat{4}$, and either $\flat\hat{3}$ or $\sharp\hat{2}$ in other voices

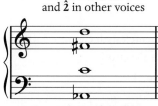 

($\sharp\hat{2}$: major keys only)

moves to root-position V (or cad. $^6_4$–V)	moves to root-position V (or cad. $^6_4$–V)	moves to cadential $^6_4$–V

TEST YOURSELF

1. Name raised $\hat{4}$ and minor $\hat{6}$ in the following keys, and identify which of these notes are not in the key (and thus need accidentals):

    a. F major   b. F minor   c. E major   d. E minor   e. D♭ major

2. What are the notes in the Italian, French, and German augmented sixth chords in these keys?

    a. F major: It^{+6} = _____ Fr^{+6} = _____ Ger^{+6} = _____

    b. F minor: It^{+6} = _____ Fr^{+6} = _____ Ger^{+6} = _____

    c. E major: It^{+6} = _____ Fr^{+6} = _____ Ger^{+6} = _____

    d. E minor: It^{+6} = _____ Fr^{+6} = _____ Ger^{+6} = _____

    e. C♯ minor: It^{+6} = _____ Fr^{+6} = _____ Ger^{+6} = _____

3. Add accidentals to the following harmonies to change them into augmented sixth chords. Identify the augmented sixth chords formed.

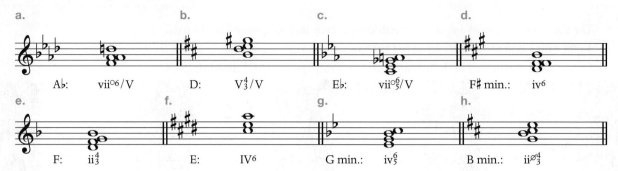

a. Ab: vii°6/V **b.** D: V4/3/V **c.** Eb: vii°6/5/V **d.** F# min.: iv6

e. F: ii4/3 **f.** E: IV6 **g.** G min.: iv6/5 **h.** B min.: ii°4/3

4. The following are augmented sixth chords; label the type of each and identify the keys in which it may appear.

a. **b.** **c.** **d.** **e.**

5. In each example below, which of the two augmented sixth chords is incorrect, is notated incorrectly, or uses incorrect doubling? What is the error?

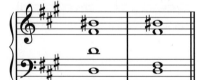
a. F# min.: It+6

b. G min.: Ger+6

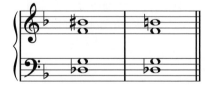
c. F: Fr+6

6. In an augmented sixth chord, must minor $\hat{6}$ appear in a particular voice? If so, which voice? Must raised $\hat{4}$ appear in a particular voice? If so, which voice?

Evocative harmonies can result from chromatic alterations.

Altered Chords

Altered Dominant Chords

♭II in Root Position and in Major Keys

Augmented Sixth Chords with Bass Notes
other than $\hat{6}$

Common-Tone Chromatic Chords

A Closer Look

Chromatic mediants and submediants

In addition to the common chromatic chords discussed in previous chapters, many other harmonies can be created by adding chromatic alterations to diatonic harmonies. These chromatic harmonies either substitute for diatonic chords or serve as embellishing harmonies.

ALTERED CHORDS

Chromatic alterations that do not lead to a change of key usually involve notes from the parallel major or minor key, creating modal mixture (see Chapter 29). It is also possible, however, for such chromatic alterations to involve notes that are *not* in the parallel key. As with modal mixture, these alterations change the quality of chords without necessarily changing their function.

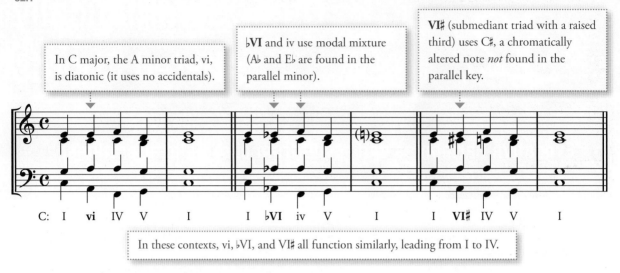

32.1

In C major, the A minor triad, vi, is diatonic (it uses no accidentals).

♭**VI** and iv use modal mixture (A♭ and E♭ are found in the parallel minor).

VI♯ (submediant triad with a raised third) uses C♯, a chromatically altered note *not* found in the parallel key.

C: I vi IV V I I ♭VI iv V I I VI♯ IV V I

In these contexts, vi, ♭VI, and VI♯ all function similarly, leading from I to IV.

A particularly common chromatically altered chord is **III♯**, a major chord whose root is $\hat{3}$ of a major scale and whose third is raised by a half step with an accidental.

32.2

32.3 Frédéric Chopin, Polonaise in A♭, Op. 53

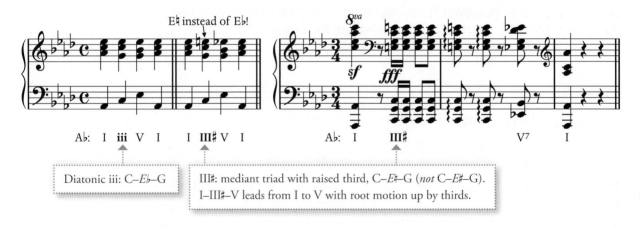

E♮ instead of E♭!

A♭: I iii V I I III♯ V I

A♭: I III♯ V⁷ I

Diatonic iii: C–E♭–G

III♯: mediant triad with raised third, C–E♮–G (*not* C–E♯–G). I–III♯–V leads from I to V with root motion up by thirds.

In many cases, a III♯ at the end of a phrase leads directly to a tonic chord that opens the following phrase.

32.4 Gaetano Donizetti, "Ah! mi fa destin mendico," from *Don Pasquale*

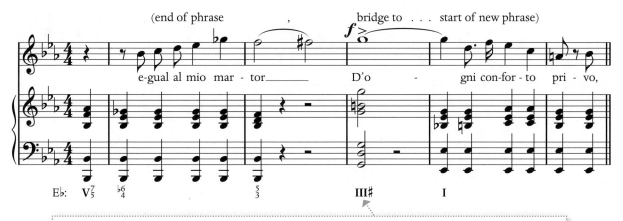

III♯ (G–B♯–D) moves directly to the tonic that starts the next phrase, leading from V to I with root motion down by thirds.

Translation: [Nothing] equals my martyrdom. Deprived of every comfort . . .

ALTERED DOMINANT CHORDS

The fifth of V or V^7 may be raised with an accidental to form an augmented triad (V$^+$) or **augmented seventh chord** (V$^7_{+5}$). Augmented chords may appear over other scale degrees as well, where—because of their instability—they often function as applied dominants. The raised fifth of an augmented chord tends to resolve up by step; as a tendency tone, it should not be doubled in four-part harmony.

32.5

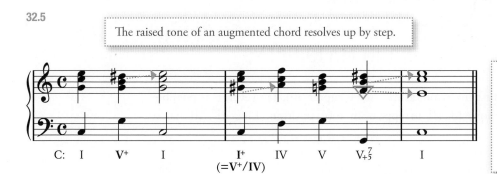

The raised tone of an augmented chord resolves up by step.

When V$^7_{+5}$ resolves to I, the third of I is doubled, since the fifth of V$^7_{+5}$ resolves up and its chordal seventh resolves down.

32.6 Alexandra Thomson, "Eboracum"

The fifth of V^7 is raised to form an augmented V^7 (V$^7_+$).

32.7 Jacob Sawyer, "Welcome to the Era"

G: I   V$^4_3$ I^6 I$^+$ IV   V$^4_3$/ii   ii
                                                (=V$^+$/IV)

> The fifth of I is raised to form an augmented I (I$^+$).

More rarely, the fifth of a dominant seventh chord is lowered. The lowered note is a tendency tone that resolves down by step.

32.8 Agathe Backer Grøndal, Serenade, Op. 15, No. 1

F: V$^4_3$ I
                                        with lowered
                                            fifth

> V^7 with lowered fifth (C–E–G♭–B♭ instead of C–E–G♮–B♭). The lowered fifth, G (= ♭$\hat{2}$), resolves downward to C.

> V$^4_3$ with a lowered fifth has the same pitches as Fr^{+6} built on ♭$\hat{2}$.

♭II IN ROOT POSITION AND IN MAJOR KEYS

♭II usually appears in first inversion, as ♭II^6 (see Chapter 30). However, it is possible (though far less common) for ♭II to appear in root position. Like ♭II^6, ♭II has a **S**ubdominant function.

32.9 Frédéric Chopin, Prelude in C Minor, Op. 28

C min.:   i   VI   ♭II   V^7 i

> The root of ♭II (D♭) is doubled.

> Progressing from ♭II to V produces a dissonant augmented-fourth leap in the bass (D♭–G).

Although ♭II normally appears in minor keys, it may also appear as a borrowed chord within a major key, where it requires two accidentals.

32.10 Clara Schumann, *Einfache Praeludien für Schüler* (*Easy Preludes for Students*), No. 2

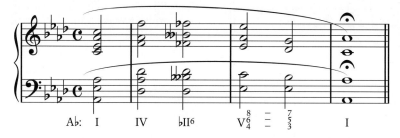

A♭:   I   IV   ♭II⁶   V⁶₄ = ⁷₅₃   I

♭II⁶ is a borrowed chord within major. Since ♭II is a major triad, in a major key both ♭$\hat{2}$ (B♭♭) and the minor form of $\hat{6}$ (F♭) require accidentals.

AUGMENTED SIXTH CHORDS WITH BASS NOTES OTHER THAN $\hat{6}$

Although augmented sixth chords normally use the minor form of $\hat{6}$ in the bass (see Chapter 31), it is possible for one of the other notes within an augmented sixth chord to be used in the bass. An augmented sixth chord with raised $\hat{4}$ in the bass is sometimes referred to as a **diminished third chord**; otherwise, augmented sixth chords with other notes in the bass do not have standardized labels. No matter what note is in the bass of an augmented sixth chord, minor $\hat{6}$ resolves down and raised $\hat{4}$ resolves up.

32.11

G min.:   i   Ger⁺⁶   V⁶⁻⁵₄₋₃   i   i   Ger⁺⁶   V⁶⁻⁵₄₋₃   i
                                              with raised $\hat{4}$ in bass

$\hat{6}$ (E♭) resolves down, and raised $\hat{4}$ (C♯) resolves up.

Ger⁺⁶ with raised $\hat{4}$ in the bass is also sometimes called a "German diminished third chord."

32.12 **Charles A. Tindley Sr. and F. A. Clark, "Stand by Me"**

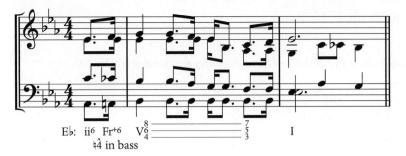

Eb: ii⁶ Fr⁺⁶ V⁸₆ ⁷ ⁵ ₄ ₃ I
       ♮4 in bass

> Fr⁺⁶ with $\hat{4}$ in the bass has the same pitches as a V⁶₅/V with a lowered fifth.

COMMON-TONE CHROMATIC CHORDS

A harmony may be embellished by a chromatic harmony with which it shares a chord tone. The shared tone usually is sustained when the chromatically altered chord resolves to a diatonic harmony, while the other voices are treated as neighbor tones.

32.13 **Pyotr Tchaikovsky,** *Souvenir de Hapsal,* **Op. 2, iii**

F: I   ♭VI⁶   I

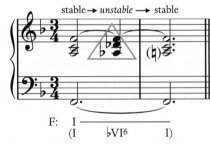

F: I ——————
   (I   ♭VI⁶   I)

> A common tone (F) is sustained as a chromatic harmony embellishes the tonic chord.

32.14 **W. C. Handy, "Joe Turner Blues"**

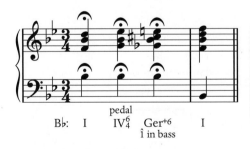

Bb: I   IV⁶₄   Ger⁺⁶   I
          pedal $\hat{1}$ in bass

> Bb is sustained as a common tone while a Ger⁺⁶ (with $\hat{1}$ in the bass) moves directly to I.

A popular instance of an embellishing common-tone chromatic chord is the **common-tone diminished seventh chord**, which results when the root of a triad is sustained while the third and fifth are decorated by chromatic neighbors. This embellishing sonority is labeled simply as a "common-tone °7" rather than with a Roman numeral.

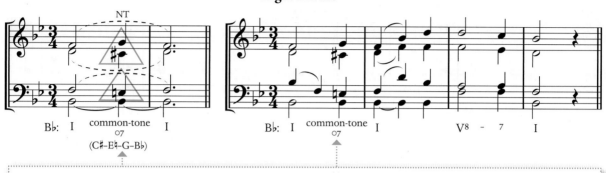

32.15

32.16 Louis Moreau Gottschalk, "Holy Ghost, with Light Divine"

Bb: I common-tone °7 I (C#–E♮–G–Bb)

Bb: I common-tone °7 I V8 – 7 I

Neighbor tones (including chromatic neighbor tones C# and E♮) form a common-tone °7 chord that embellishes I of Bb major.

In many cases, a tone is sustained in the bass while neighbor tones in upper voices form a common-tone diminished seventh chord.

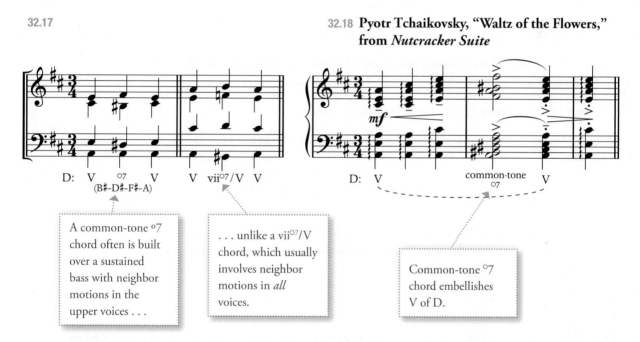

32.17

32.18 Pyotr Tchaikovsky, "Waltz of the Flowers," from *Nutcracker Suite*

D: V °7 V V vii°7/V V (B#–D#–F#–A)

D: V common-tone °7 V

A common-tone °7 chord often is built over a sustained bass with neighbor motions in the upper voices . . .

. . . unlike a vii°7/V chord, which usually involves neighbor motions in *all* voices.

Common-tone °7 chord embellishes V of D.

However, a common-tone diminished seventh chord can also result from other types of embellishments, such as passing tones. Furthermore, the common tone within this chord might appear in a voice other than the bass.

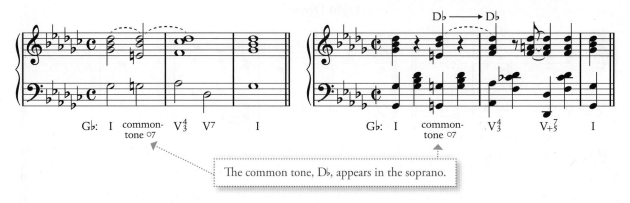

32.19   32.20 **Jelly Roll Morton, "King Porter Stomp"**

The common tone, D♭, appears in the soprano.

🔍 For more about chromatic mediants and submediants, see A Closer Look.

POINTS FOR REVIEW

- The third and fifth of any harmony may be raised or lowered with an accidental, changing the quality of the chord, although not its function.

- ♭II may appear in root position, in either a major or minor key.

- Augmented sixth chords may appear with a note other than the minor form of $\hat{6}$ in the bass.

- A harmony may be decorated by a chromatic chord with which it shares one or more common tones.

- A common-tone diminished seventh chord results from a major triad whose third and fifth are decorated by chromatic lower neighbor tones while the root of the chord is sustained.

TEST YOURSELF

1. What are the notes of the following chords (from the bass up)?

   a. A major: III♯   b. B♭ major: III♯   c. G♭ major: III♯   d. F major: V⁺
   e. B major: IV⁺   f. G major: ♭II   g. E major: ♭II   h. A major: V^7_{+5}
   i. D major: Fr⁺⁶ with raised $\hat{4}$ in bass   j. B minor: Ger⁺⁶ with $\hat{1}$ in bass

2. For each of the following, name the major key and the chord.

a.   b.   c.   d.   e.

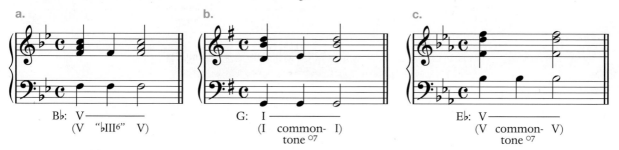

3. In each of the following, a diatonic chord is embellished by a chromatic harmony with which it shares a common tone. What are the missing notes?

a.   b.   c.

         Bb: V———————   G: I———————   Eb: V———————
          (V "bIII6" V)   (I common- I)   (V common- V)
                                tone °7   tone °7

4. Which of the following chords is an applied vii°7? Which is a common-tone diminished seventh chord?

    D: V   ?   V   I   V6   ?   V6   I

5. Answer the following questions about this excerpt from Irving Berlin's "I Like It":

  a. Is the first chord a common-tone °7 or an applied °7?

  b. Is the chord on the last beat of the first measure a common-tone °7 or an applied °7?

  c. What is the chord on the last beat of the second measure?

     a. ___   b. ___   c. ___

33

Chromatic Sequences

Chromaticism within sequences creates new harmonic possibilities, including motion to distant keys.

Applied Chords in Sequences
    Applied chords in descending fifth sequences
    Applied chords in other sequences

Other Chromatic Sequential Patterns
Strict Chromatic Sequences
Equal Division of the Octave

Chromaticism often embellishes diatonic sequences. In more extreme cases, chromatic patterns can even create sequences for which there is no diatonic model, sequences that lead outside the key, or both.

APPLIED CHORDS IN SEQUENCES

APPLIED CHORDS IN DESCENDING FIFTH SEQUENCES

Accidentals added to sequences can create applied chords that lead to the next harmony in the sequence. Applied chords are particularly common in descending fifth sequences in which chord roots alternate moving up a fourth and down a fifth.

33.1

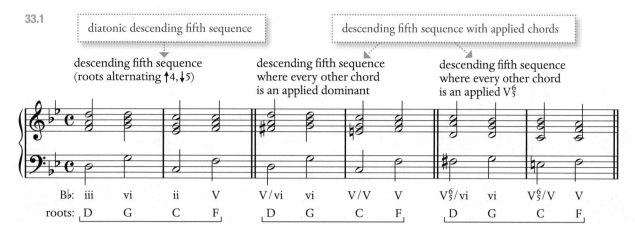

It is even possible for *every* chord in a descending fifth sequence to be an applied chord of the next harmony.

33.2

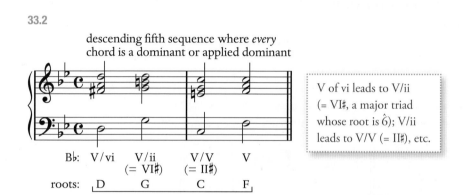

V of vi leads to V/ii (= VI♯, a major triad whose root is $\hat{6}$); V/ii leads to V/V (= II♯), etc.

A descending fifth sequence can also involve a series of applied dominant seventh chords. If so, the leading tone in each applied dominant does not need to ascend to the root of the goal chord as expected, but rather can slide down by semitone to become the dissonant seventh of the following chord.

33.3

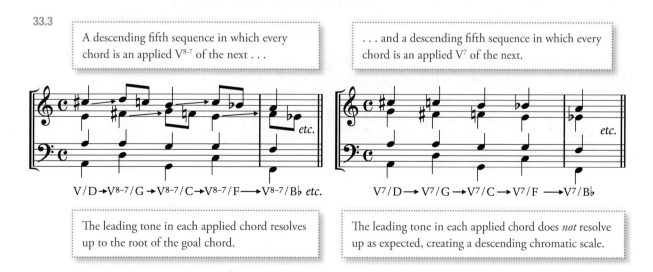

A descending fifth sequence in which every chord is an applied V^{8-7} of the next . . .

. . . and a descending fifth sequence in which every chord is an applied V^7 of the next.

The leading tone in each applied chord resolves up to the root of the goal chord.

The leading tone in each applied chord does *not* resolve up as expected, creating a descending chromatic scale.

33.4 Clara Rogers, "A Match"

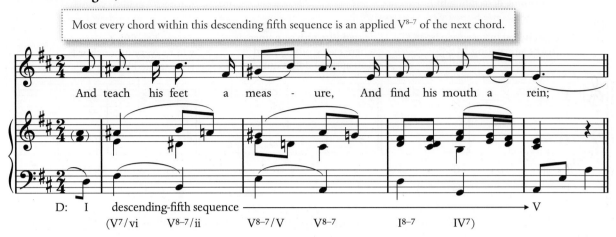

Most every chord within this descending fifth sequence is an applied V^{8-7} of the next chord.

APPLIED CHORDS IN OTHER SEQUENCES

Applied chords can appear in other types of sequences as well, especially those in which roots alternate moving down a third and up a fourth.

33.5

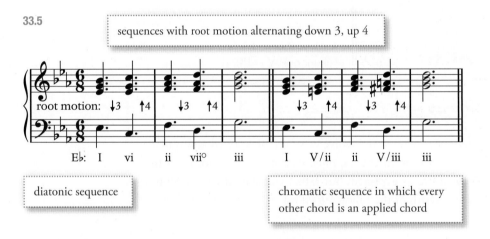

sequences with root motion alternating down 3, up 4

diatonic sequence

chromatic sequence in which every other chord is an applied chord

33.6 Ludwig van Beethoven, Piano Sonata in E♭, Op. 81a, iii

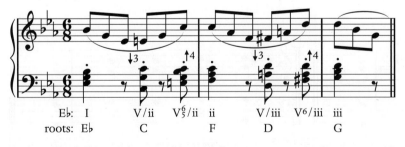

OTHER CHROMATIC SEQUENTIAL PATTERNS

Chords in sequences can be chromatically embellished in other ways as well, without necessarily creating applied chords. In many cases, a chromatically embellished sequence can be understood as a variant of a diatonic sequence.

33.7

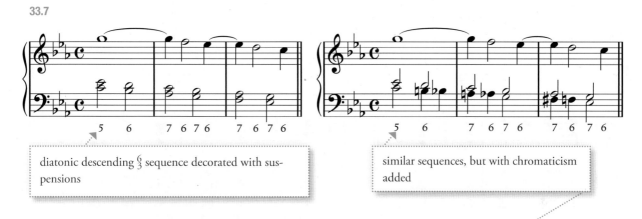

diatonic descending $^6_3$ sequence decorated with suspensions

similar sequences, but with chromaticism added

33.8 Antonio Vivaldi, Sonata in C Minor for Violin and Basso Continuo, RV 6, iv

In more extreme cases, however, the chromaticism serves such an essential role that the resulting harmonic pattern does not directly correspond to a diatonic sequence.

33.9 R. Nathaniel Dett, *Magnolia Suite*, No. 4

This descending chromatic sequence does not directly correspond to any diatonic sequential pattern.

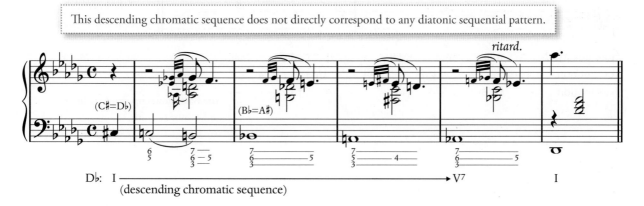

STRICT CHROMATIC SEQUENCES

A diatonic sequence moves up or down the same number of scale steps with each repetition of the sequential pattern. At each stage of the diatonic sequence, the precise number of semitones by which the pattern is transposed varies according to the scale. In a **strict chromatic sequence**, on the other hand, the sequential pattern always moves up or down by the same number of semitones. A particularly common strict chromatic sequence is a descending fifth sequence in which the roots move by perfect fifth between every chord of the sequence.

33.10

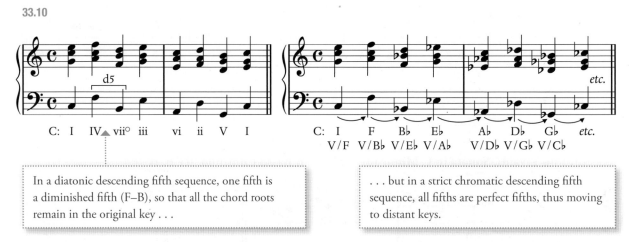

In a diatonic descending fifth sequence, one fifth is a diminished fifth (F–B), so that all the chord roots remain in the original key . . .

. . . but in a strict chromatic descending fifth sequence, all fifths are perfect fifths, thus moving to distant keys.

Strict chromatic sequences can involve other root patterns as well, such as those in which roots alternately move down a third and up a fourth.

33.11

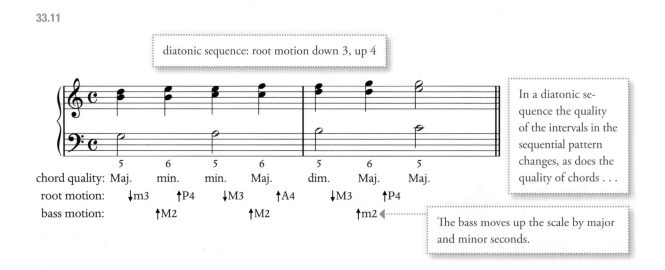

diatonic sequence: root motion down 3, up 4

In a diatonic sequence the quality of the intervals in the sequential pattern changes, as does the quality of chords . . .

The bass moves up the scale by major and minor seconds.

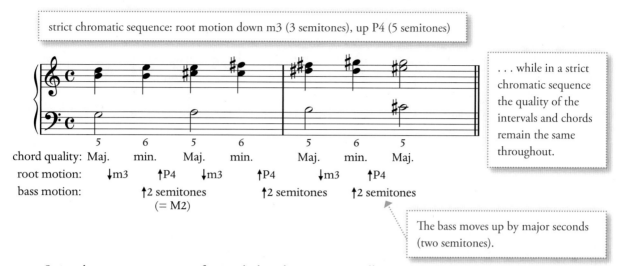

strict chromatic sequence: root motion down m3 (3 semitones), up P4 (5 semitones)

. . . while in a strict chromatic sequence the quality of the intervals and chords remain the same throughout.

chord quality: Maj. min. Maj. min.   Maj. min. Maj.

root motion: ↓m3 ↑P4 ↓m3 ↑P4   ↓m3 ↑P4

bass motion: ↑2 semitones   ↑2 semitones   ↑2 semitones
                (= M2)

The bass moves up by major seconds (two semitones).

Strict chromatic sequences often include enharmonic respelling.

33.12 Frédéric Chopin, *Nouvelle Etude* **No. 2**

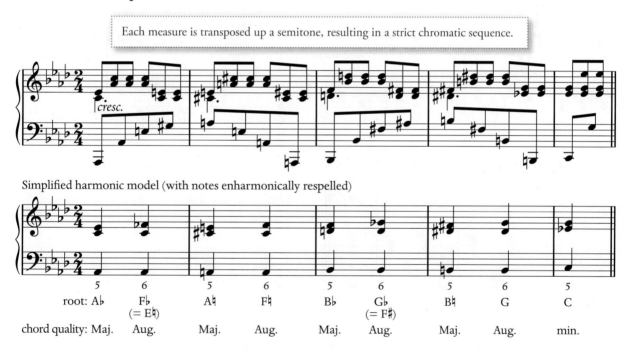

Each measure is transposed up a semitone, resulting in a strict chromatic sequence.

Simplified harmonic model (with notes enharmonically respelled)

5	6	5	6	5	6	5	6	5

root: A♭ F♭   A♮ F♮   B♭ G♭   B♮ G   C
      (= E♮)   (= F♯)

chord quality: Maj. Aug. Maj. Aug. Maj. Aug. Maj. Aug. min.

Strict chromatic sequences became increasingly popular during and after the nineteenth century.

EQUAL DIVISION OF THE OCTAVE

If the sequential pattern is repeated enough times, a strict chromatic sequence returns to its starting harmony.

33.13

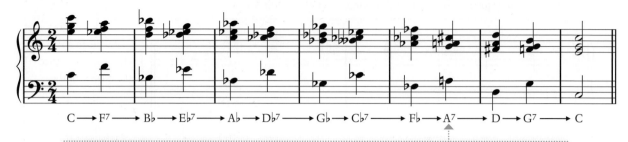

$C \longrightarrow F^7 \longrightarrow B\flat \longrightarrow E\flat^7 \longrightarrow A\flat \longrightarrow D\flat^7 \longrightarrow G\flat \longrightarrow C\flat^7 \longrightarrow F\flat \longrightarrow A^7 \longrightarrow D \longrightarrow G^7 \longrightarrow C$

> To return to the beginning point in a complete descending fifth sequence, one chord will need to be enharmonically respelled. Here, B♭♭ is respelled as A♮.

A strict chromatic sequence that returns to its starting harmony results in an **equal division of the octave**.

33.14 **Georges Bizet, "The Ball," from *Jeux d'enfants* (*Children's Games*)**

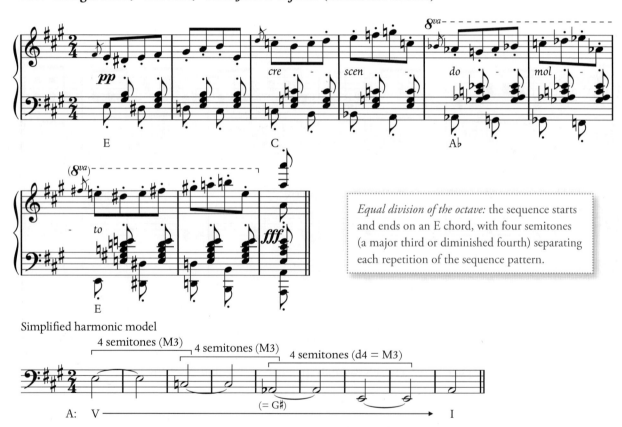

> *Equal division of the octave:* the sequence starts and ends on an E chord, with four semitones (a major third or diminished fourth) separating each repetition of the sequence pattern.

Simplified harmonic model

- Chromaticism can vary diatonic sequences or create entirely new harmonic patterns.

- Chromatic alterations can create applied dominants in sequences.

- In a descending fifth sequence in which every chord is an applied dominant seventh, the leading tone in each chord slides down by half step to become the seventh of the next chord instead of resolving up by step.

- In strict chromatic sequences each segment of the sequence is transposed by the same number of semitones.

- Strict chromatic sequences that return to the first chord of the sequence create an equal division of the octave.

TEST YOURSELF

1. Add the missing accidentals in the following sequences, and identify each sequence type (descending fifth or "down 3, up 4").

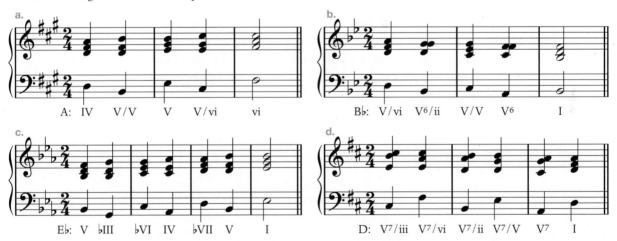

2. In the sequence (d) above, what chord tone (root, third, fifth, or seventh) is missing from every other chord?

3. In a sequence involving a series of applied dominant sevenths, how should each leading tone move?

4. In a sequence involving a series of applied dominant sevenths, how should each chordal seventh resolve?

34

Chromatic Modulation

Modulations between distantly related keys take place through a variety of chromatic techniques.

Pivot Chords Involving Mixture

Common-Tone Modulation

Enharmonic Modulation

    Enharmonically reinterpreted diminished seventh chords

    Enharmonic reinterpretations of German augmented sixth chords

Other Types of Modulation

Chromatic Key Schemes

Distantly related keys have signatures that differ by more than one accidental. Before the nineteenth century, modulations to distantly related keys occurred primarily in the unstable middle sections of movements, such as the development in sonata form (see Chapter 39). But during and after the nineteenth century, modulations to distantly related keys became increasingly common.

PIVOT CHORDS INVOLVING MIXTURE

A modulation between closely related keys often involves a pivot chord that is diatonic to both keys (see Chapters 27 and 28). In moving between distantly related keys, on the other hand, the pivot chord often is diatonic to only *one* of the keys, functioning within the other key as a chromatic chord.

34.1

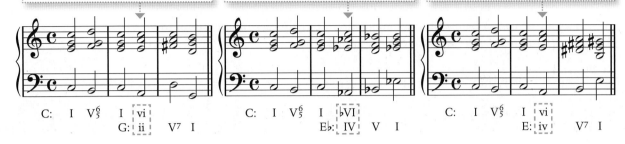

Modulation between closely related keys: the pivot chord is diatonic to both keys.

Modulation to a distant key: the pivot chord is diatonic in the second key (E♭) but involves modal mixture in the original key (C).

Modulation to a distant key: the pivot chord is diatonic in the original key (C) but involves modal mixture in the second key (E).

34.2 Johann Strauss Jr., Overture to *Die Fledermaus*

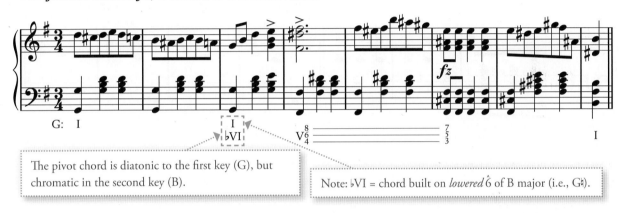

The pivot chord is diatonic to the first key (G), but chromatic in the second key (B).

Note: ♭VI = chord built on *lowered* $\hat{6}$ of B major (i.e., G♮).

34.3 Harry T. Burleigh, "In Christ there is no East nor West"

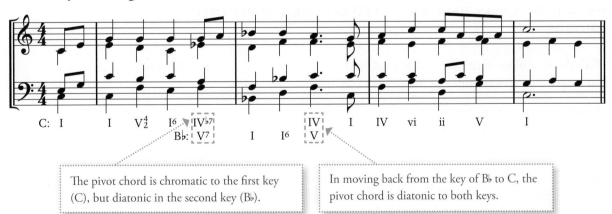

The pivot chord is chromatic to the first key (C), but diatonic in the second key (B♭).

In moving back from the key of B♭ to C, the pivot chord is diatonic to both keys.

COMMON-TONE MODULATION

In a **common-tone modulation**, the last chord before the modulation shares just one tone with the first chord after the modulation, so that only a single tone—rather than the entire chord—serves as a pivot. Especially when the shared tone is highlighted in the melody or bass, a common-tone modulation can help ease the transition to a distantly related key, even if there is no pivot chord.

34.4 **Clara Schumann, "Walzer"**

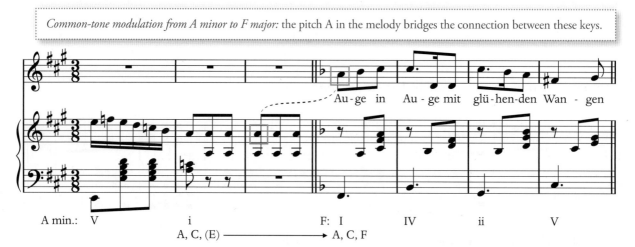

Common-tone modulation from A minor to F major: the pitch A in the melody bridges the connection between these keys.

Translation: Face-to-face with glowing cheeks . . .

ENHARMONIC MODULATION

ENHARMONICALLY REINTERPRETED DIMINISHED SEVENTH CHORDS

With the possibility of enharmonic equivalence, any diminished seventh chord might function as vii°7 in four different minor keys and their parallel majors.

34.5

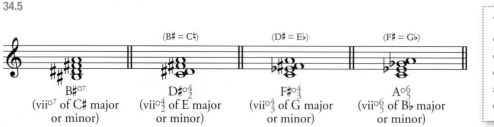

> Though these four diminished seventh chords are spelled differently, they are enharmonically equivalent.

Sometimes an enharmonically reinterpreted diminished seventh chord is used as a pivot chord, so that a vii°7 introduced in one key resolves as vii°7 in another key.

34.6

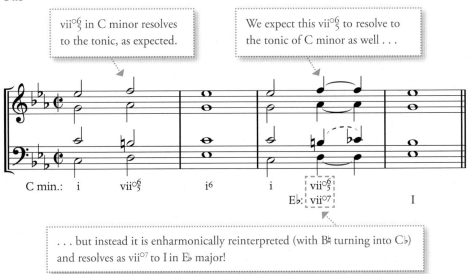

vii°⁶₅ in C minor resolves to the tonic, as expected.

We expect this vii°⁶₅ to resolve to the tonic of C minor as well . . .

C min.:   i   vii°⁶₅   i⁶   i   vii°⁶₅
                                      E♭: vii°⁷   I

. . . but instead it is enharmonically reinterpreted (with B♮ turning into C♭) and resolves as vii°⁷ to I in E♭ major!

When enharmonically reinterpreting a diminished seventh chord in moving from one key to another, composers usually don't bother to spell the chord to reflect its function in both keys. Rather, they simply spell the notes of the diminished seventh chord as it would appear in the key to which it is leading.

34.7 Gioachino Rossini, "Ah! Se puoi così lasciarmi," from *Mosè in Egitto*

Modulation from the key of A to C (♭III, i.e., the key whose tonic is the lowered $\hat{3}$ of A) through an enharmonically reinterpreted °7 chord (vii°⁶₅/ V in A = vii°⁷/ V in C).

cor!   di   tua   man   pria m'apri il pet-to,

vii°⁶₅ of E   = vii°⁷ of G!
(F♯, A, C, D♯)   (F♯, A, C, E♭)

Translation: (heart!) Then pierce this breast

The vii°⁶₅ of E has the same pitches (enharmonically respelled) as vii°⁷ of G.

Simplified harmonic model

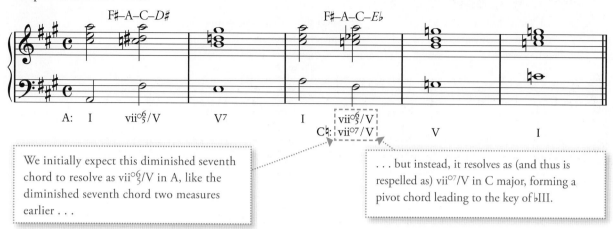

We initially expect this diminished seventh chord to resolve as vii°⁶₅/V in A, like the diminished seventh chord two measures earlier . . .

. . . but instead, it resolves as (and thus is respelled as) vii°⁷/V in C major, forming a pivot chord leading to the key of ♭III.

ENHARMONIC REINTERPRETATIONS OF GERMAN AUGMENTED SIXTH CHORDS

German augmented sixth chords may also be enharmonically reinterpreted, since a German augmented sixth is enharmonically equivalent to a dominant seventh chord.

34.8

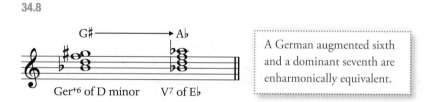

A German augmented sixth and a dominant seventh are enharmonically equivalent.

This enharmonic reinterpretation can lead to a distant modulation when a harmony introduced as a German augmented sixth resolves as a dominant seventh chord.

34.9

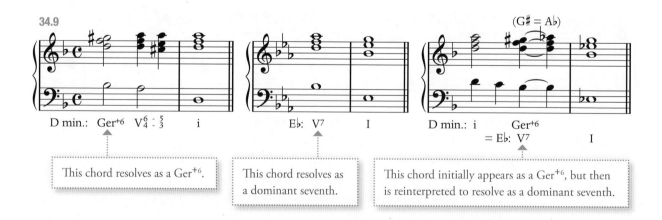

This chord resolves as a Ger⁺⁶.

This chord resolves as a dominant seventh.

This chord initially appears as a Ger⁺⁶, but then is reinterpreted to resolve as a dominant seventh.

34.10 **Joseph Haydn, Symphony No. 55, i**

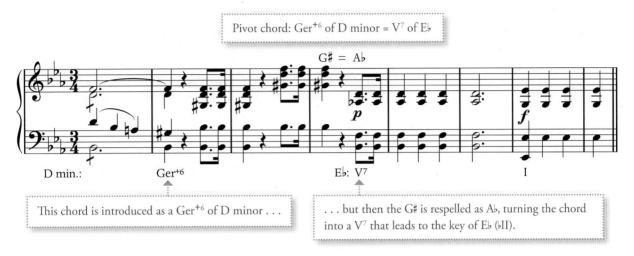

Pivot chord: Ger^{+6} of D minor = V^7 of E♭

G♯ = A♭

D min.:   Ger^{+6} E♭: V^7 I

This chord is introduced as a Ger^{+6} of D minor . . .

. . . but then the G♯ is respelled as A♭, turning the chord into a V^7 that leads to the key of E♭ (♭II).

The reinterpretation can go in the other direction as well, with a dominant seventh chord reinterpreted as a German augmented sixth.

34.11 **Joseph Haydn, Symphony No. 55, i**

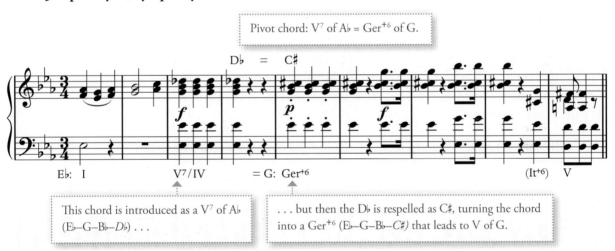

Pivot chord: V^7 of A♭ = Ger^{+6} of G.

D♭ = C♯

E♭: I   V^7/IV   = G: Ger^{+6} (It^{+6})   V

This chord is introduced as a V^7 of A♭ (E♭–G–B♭–D♭) . . .

. . . but then the D♭ is respelled as C♯, turning the chord into a Ger^{+6} (E♭–G–B♭–C♯) that leads to V of G.

OTHER TYPES OF MODULATION

Not every modulation or tonicization is approached smoothly. It is certainly possible for a tonal center to shift abruptly, without the use of a pivot chord, enharmonically reinterpreted pivot chord, or common tone. Changes of key may also be organized as part of a sequence.

34.12 Antonín Dvořák, Symphony No. 8, Op. 88, iv

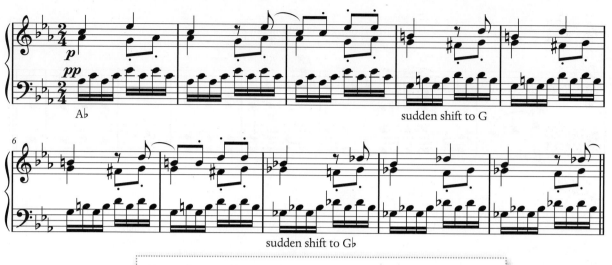

Ab

sudden shift to G

sudden shift to Gb

Abrupt changes of key—with no pivot chords or common tones—follow a sequential pattern of descending semitones Ab to G to Gb.

CHROMATIC KEY SCHEMES

In music composed after 1800, modulations between distantly related keys became increasingly popular. Modulations involving chromatic mediants or chromatic submediants—such as modulations in a major-key piece to the keys of III♯ or VI♯— are particularly common.

34.13 Will Marion Cook, *Clorindy, or the Origin of the Cakewalk* (arr. Meacham)

This passage starts in B♭ (2♭) and moves via a chromatic pivot to cadence in the key of D (III♯, 2♯).

In more extreme cases, a modulation may lead to a key whose tonic is not a note in the original key, as in a modulation from I to ♭III or ♭VI.

34.14 Franz Schubert, "Kennst du das Land" ("Do You Know the Place")

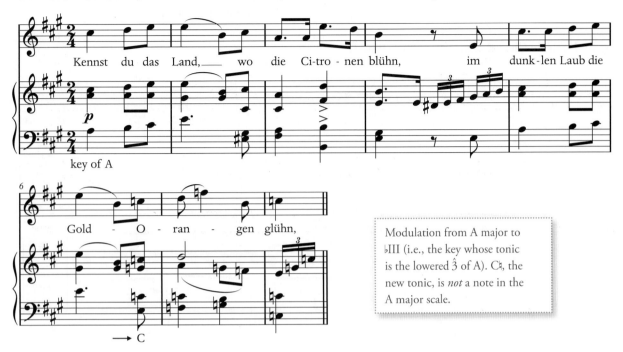

> Modulation from A major to
> ♭III (i.e., the key whose tonic
> is the lowered $\hat{3}$ of A). C♮, the
> new tonic, is *not* a note in the
> A major scale.

Translation: Do you know the place where lemon trees grow, where amid dark leaves the gold-colored orange glows . . . ?

Successive modulations or tonicizations by the same interval can link between keys that are very distantly related to each other.

34.15 Basile Barès, "Basile's Galop"

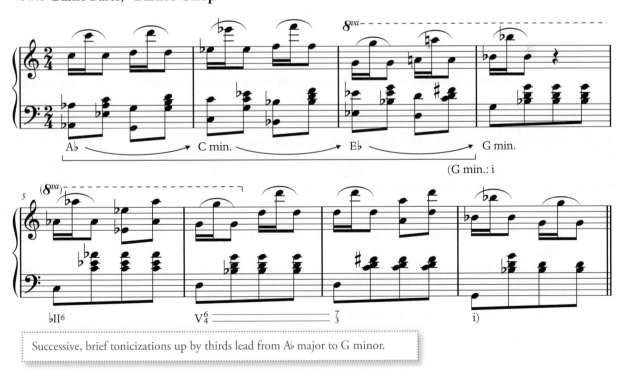

Successive, brief tonicizations up by thirds lead from A♭ major to G minor.

If repeated enough times, successive modulations or tonicizations by the same interval can return to the original key. This creates an **equal division of the octave**.

34.16 **Frédéric Chopin,** *Nouvelle Etude* **No. 2**

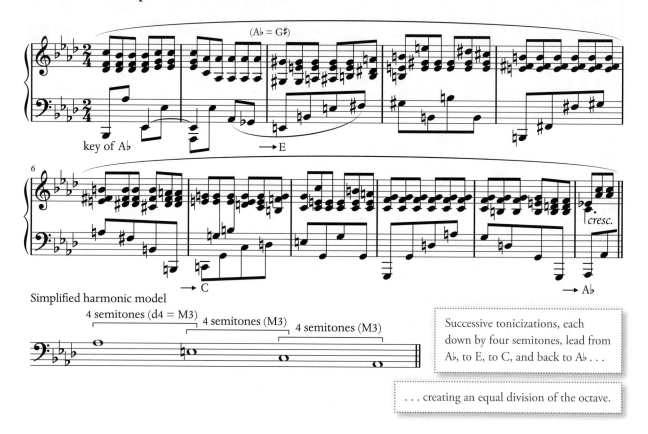

Simplified harmonic model

Successive tonicizations, each down by four semitones, lead from Ab, to E, to C, and back to Ab . . .

. . . creating an equal division of the octave.

POINTS FOR REVIEW

- **Distantly related keys are those whose key signatures differ by more than one sharp or flat.**

- **In a modulation between distantly related keys, the pivot chord can involve mixture in either the original key or the new key.**

- **A common-tone modulation involves a shared tone in the chords before and after the modulation.**

- **Each diminished seventh chord is enharmonically equivalent to three other diminished seventh chords and can function as vii°⁷ in four different keys and their parallels. An enharmonically reinterpreted diminished seventh chord can be a pivot chord.**

- A German augmented sixth chord is enharmonically equivalent to a dominant seventh chord. An enharmonically reinterpreted German augmented sixth chord or enharmonically reinterpreted dominant seventh chord can be a pivot chord.

- An abrupt modulation may involve a sudden shift to a key that is not prepared by a pivot chord or common tone.

- In music composed after 1800, modulation schemes that involve keys that are distantly related became increasingly common.

- Repeated sequential modulation or tonicization by the same interval can lead to a distantly related key or may create an equal division of the octave.

TEST YOURSELF

1. Identify these chromatic pivot chords, each of which involves mixture within either the first or the second key.

   a. ♭VI of D major = _____ in E♭ major

   b. iv of E major = ii of _____ major.

   c. _____ of C major = V of A♭ major

   d. iv of _____ major = vi of D♭ major

2. Identify the common tones of the following pairs of chords.

   a. I of A major and I of F major

   b. I of E major and V^7 of C major

   c. V of A major and V^7 of F major

3. vii°7 of D major is enharmonically equivalent to
   a. vii°$^6_5$ of _____; b. vii°$^4_3$ of _____; and c. vii°$^4_2$ of _____.

4. vii°7 of E major is enharmonically equivalent to
   a. vii°$^6_5$ of _____; b. vii°$^4_3$ of _____; and c. vii°$^4_2$ of _____.

5. For each of the following, identify the key of the enharmonically equivalent V^7 or Ger^{+6}.

a. Ger^{+6} of E = V^7 of _____   b. Ger^{+6} of G = V^7 of _____   c. V^7 of D = Ger^{+6} of _____   d. V^7 of E = Ger^{+6} of _____

part

five

Form

35

Sentences and Other Phrase Types

Many phrases begin with a stable opening followed by increased momentum toward a cadence.

Sentences	Sentence Length
Basic Idea—Repeated or Varied	Sentence-Like Phrases

SENTENCES

A phrase is the basic unit of tonal music (see Chapter 6). Phrases conclude with a cadence and do not include a cadence in the middle. Typically, the first half of a phrase begins in a stable fashion, and its second half becomes more active as it leads to a cadence.

One of the most common phrase layouts is a **sentence**. A sentence is typically eight measures, divided into two halves. The opening four measures—the **presentation**—consist of a repeated two-measure melodic segment known as the **basic idea**. Within the presentation, the tonic is usually embellished in a straightforward manner. In the next four measures—the **continuation**—an intensified sense of momentum leads to a cadence. The pace usually quickens in the continuation, often with faster rhythms and more-frequent changes of harmony than in the presentation, and with **fragmentation**, in which a part of the basic idea, or a shorter new idea, is repeated, perhaps sequentially or in varied form.

35.1
EIGHT-MEASURE SENTENCE

4 MEASURES		4 MEASURES
Presentation (relatively stable)		Continuation
2 measures basic idea	**2 measures** repetition (or varied repetition) of basic idea	Momentum increases, leading to cadence (PAC, IAC, or HC)

35.2 Joseph Haydn, Symphony No. 21, iii

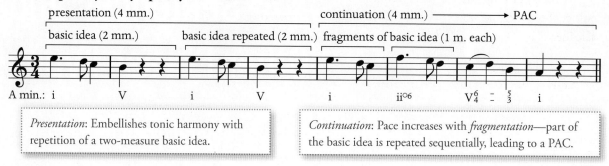

Presentation: Embellishes tonic harmony with repetition of a two-measure basic idea.

Continuation: Pace increases with *fragmentation*—part of the basic idea is repeated sequentially, leading to a PAC.

BASIC IDEA—REPEATED OR VARIED

During the presentation, the basic idea may be repeated exactly, or varied by transposition or elaboration.

35.3 Maria Hester Park, Piano Sonata in C, Op. 2, No. 3, ii

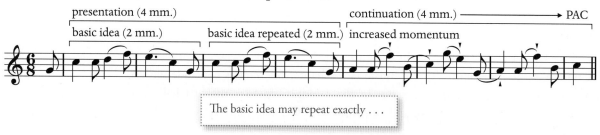

The basic idea may repeat exactly . . .

35.4 J. Rosamond Johnson, "The Old Flag Never Touched the Ground"

. . . or it may be transposed . . .

35.5 Ignatius Sancho, Minuets, Book II, No. 7

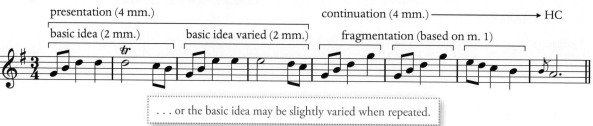

. . . or the basic idea may be slightly varied when repeated.

A basic idea and its varied repetition can be harmonized differently from one another. For instance, where the varied repetition involves transposition, often the basic idea is harmonized with I and its varied repetition, with V.

35.6 Ludwig van Beethoven, Piano Sonata in F Minor, Op. 2, No. 1, i

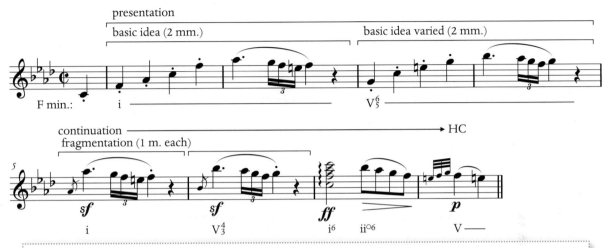

The basic idea is harmonized with **T**onic; its varied repetition is a transposition and is harmonized with **D**ominant; harmonies change more rapidly during the continuation.

In many other instances, a basic idea harmonized with a I–V progression is answered by a varied repetition harmonized with V–I.

35.7 Mildred and Patty Hill, "Good Morning to All"

The basic idea is harmonized I–V; its varied repetition is harmonized V–I.

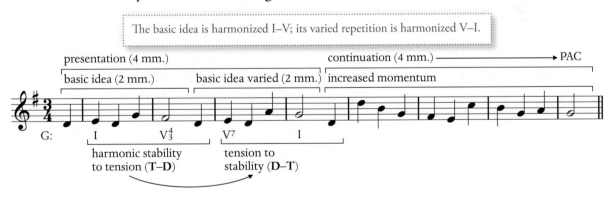

SENTENCE LENGTH

Although most sentences are eight measures long, sentences that are twice as short or long are also possible—provided that the relative proportions of the segments are similar to those of an eight-measure sentence.

35.8 Maria Frances Parke, Piano Sonata in F, Op. 1, No. 1, ii

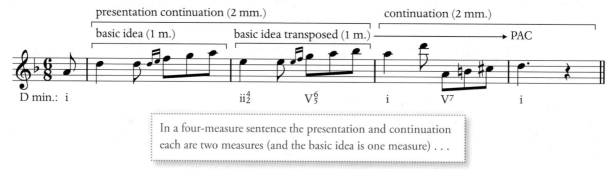

> In a four-measure sentence the presentation and continuation each are two measures (and the basic idea is one measure) . . .

35.9 Richard Rodgers, "I'm in Love with a Wonderful Guy," from *South Pacific*

> . . . and in a sixteen-measure sentence the presentation and continuation each are eight measures (and the basic idea is four measures).

In other situations, the strict proportions of a sentence may be altered by compressing or expanding the segments of the phrase. For instance, a measure or group of measures may be repeated, or a melodic figure inserted in the middle or at the end of a phrase, so that a segment is stretched beyond its normal length.

35.10 W. A. Mozart, "Dove sono," from *The Marriage of Figaro*

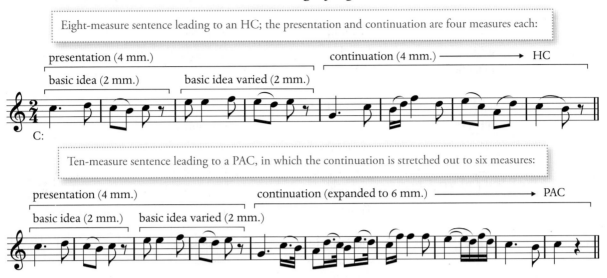

Eight-measure sentence leading to an HC; the presentation and continuation are four measures each:

presentation (4 mm.)   continuation (4 mm.) ⟶ HC

basic idea (2 mm.)   basic idea varied (2 mm.)

Ten-measure sentence leading to a PAC, in which the continuation is stretched out to six measures:

presentation (4 mm.)   continuation (expanded to 6 mm.) ⟶ PAC

basic idea (2 mm.)   basic idea varied (2 mm.)

SENTENCE-LIKE PHRASES

In addition to sentences, there are other types of phrase layouts. For instance, a phrase may begin with a basic idea that is followed by a new idea (a **contrasting idea**) rather than by a repetition of the basic idea. A phrase with such a layout is similar to a sentence, since it begins with a relatively stable segment followed by an active passage that leads to a cadence.

35.11 Fernando Sor, Sonata for Guitar, Op. 22, Trio

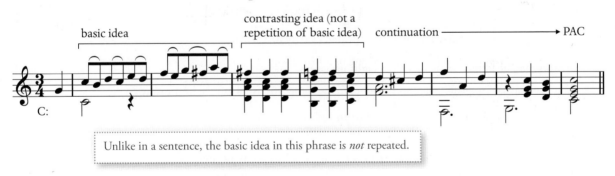

basic idea   contrasting idea (not a repetition of basic idea)   continuation ⟶ PAC

Unlike in a sentence, the basic idea in this phrase is *not* repeated.

To be sure, it is not always so easy to determine whether a phrase is properly regarded as a sentence or merely sentence-like. This is especially so when it is unclear whether what follows the basic idea is best understood as a varied repetition or as a contrasting idea, or when the proportions of the phrase seem to radically depart from what is typically found in a sentence.

35.12 **George Gershwin, "I've Got Rhythm," from *Girl Crazy***

Whether this is labeled as a sentence or sentence-like depends on whether measures 3–4 can be understood as a varied repetition of the basic idea.

35.13 **"We Wish You a Merry Christmas"**

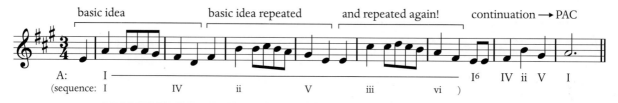

Is this an oddly proportioned sentence, with a six-measure presentation followed by a two-measure continuation? Or is this better understood as a sentence-like phrase?

POINTS FOR REVIEW

- **A sentence is a phrase that is usually eight measures long, divided into two halves: the first half (*presentation*) consists of a repeated two-measure segment (*basic idea*); the second half (*continuation*) increases momentum as it leads to a cadence.**

- **In the presentation, the basic idea may be repeated exactly or varied.**

- **Sentences may be longer or shorter than eight measures.**

  - Four- or sixteen-measure sentences maintain the proportions of an eight-measure sentence.

  - Sentences of other lengths may be understood as compressed or expanded.

- **In addition to the sentence, other phrase layouts are possible; many of these other layouts resemble sentences, in that they begin stably and increase in momentum leading to a cadence.**

1. Determine whether each melody below is a sentence, and explain why.

36

Periods and Other Phrase Pairs

Phrase pairs are classified by the cadences at the end of each phrase and the relationship between the openings of the two phrases.

PERIODS

QUESTION AND RESPONSE

Two successive phrases—each with its own cadence—may combine to form a **phrase pair**. In many phrase pairs, a harmonically unstable cadence at the end of the first phrase (HC or IAC) seems to pose a question that is answered by a harmonically stable cadence at the end of second phrase (PAC). Such a pair of phrases is called a **period**.

36.1 Ludwig van Beethoven, Symphony No. 9, iv

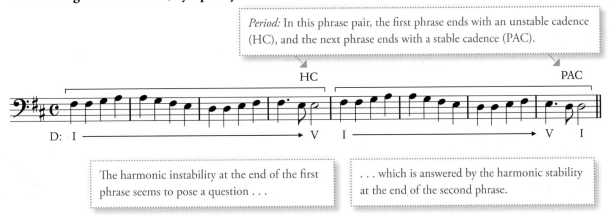

Period: In this phrase pair, the first phrase ends with an unstable cadence (HC), and the next phrase ends with a stable cadence (PAC).

The harmonic instability at the end of the first phrase seems to pose a question . . .

. . . which is answered by the harmonic stability at the end of the second phrase.

The first phrase of a period, which leads to the unstable cadence, is called the **antecedent**. The second phrase, which leads to the stable cadence, is the **consequent**.

36.2 Alicia Scott, "Annie Laurie"

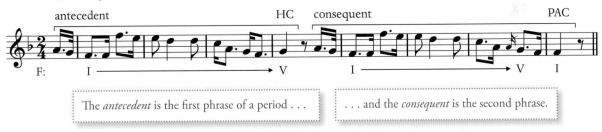

The *antecedent* is the first phrase of a period . . .

. . . and the *consequent* is the second phrase.

CADENCES WITHIN A PERIOD

Typically, the antecedent of a period ends with a half cadence (HC), and the consequent concludes with a perfect authentic cadence (PAC).

36.3 Joseph Boulogne, String Quartet in C Minor, Op. 1, No. 4, ii

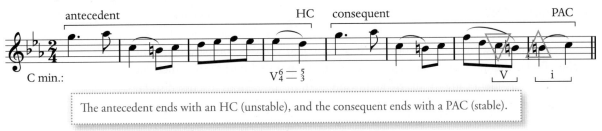

The antecedent ends with an HC (unstable), and the consequent ends with a PAC (stable).

It is also possible for the antecedent to end with an imperfect authentic cadence (IAC), which is relatively unstable compared to the PAC at the end of the consequent.

36.4 Henry Bishop, "Home, Sweet Home"

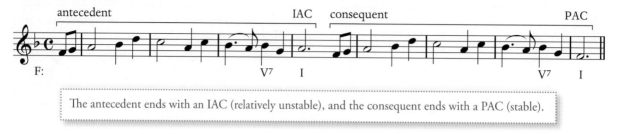

The antecedent ends with an IAC (relatively unstable), and the consequent ends with a PAC (stable).

The PAC at the end of a period may appear in the original key, or (if the consequent phrase modulates) in a new key.

36.5 Pyotr Tchaikovsky, "The Doll's Funeral"

This period does not modulate: it ends with a PAC in the original key.

36.6 Elisabetta de Gambarini, Menuet in A, Op. 2, No. 5

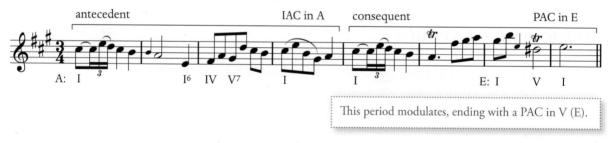

This period modulates, ending with a PAC in V (E).

PARALLEL PERIOD

Periods are classified by how the openings of their two phrases compare with one another. By far the most common type of period is the **parallel period**, in which the two phrases start identically (or nearly identically). All of the periods discussed so far in this chapter are parallel periods.

36.7 "Greensleeves"

Parallel period: Both phrases of the period begin the same way.

36.8 Queen Lili'uokalani, "Aloha Oe"

SEQUENTIAL AND CONTRASTING PERIODS

In a **sequential period**, the melody at the opening of the antecedent returns transposed at the start of the consequent, where it is set with different harmonies. (In contrast, in a parallel period, both the antecedent and consequent begin with the same notes and harmonies.)

36.9 Edvard Grieg, "Watchman's Song," from *Lyric Pieces*, Op. 12

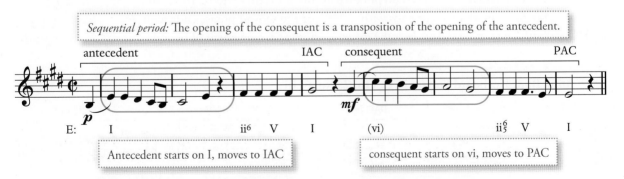

Sequential period: The opening of the consequent is a transposition of the opening of the antecedent.

Antecedent starts on I, moves to IAC

consequent starts on vi, moves to PAC

The two phrases of a sequential period often mirror one another harmonically. While the antecedent starts in a harmonically stable manner (on I) and leads to an unstable cadence, the consequent begins unstably (on a chord other than the tonic) and leads to a stable PAC.

36.10 Jesús González Rubio, "Jarabe tipatío"

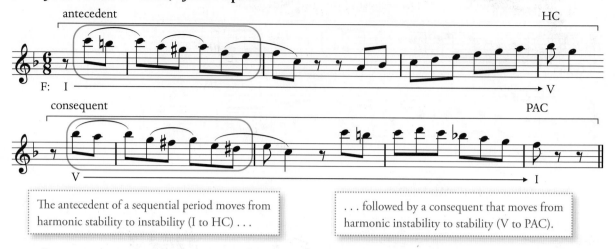

> The antecedent of a sequential period moves from harmonic stability to instability (I to HC) . . .

> . . . followed by a consequent that moves from harmonic instability to stability (V to PAC).

In a **contrasting period**, the two phrases begin much differently from one another.

36.11 Ignatius Sancho, "Friendship Source of Joy"

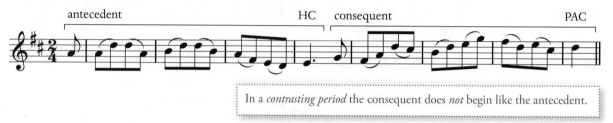

> In a *contrasting period* the consequent does *not* begin like the antecedent.

PAIRED PHRASES THAT ARE NOT PERIODS

Because of their cadential layouts, certain phrase pairs do not form periods. This is the case when the first phrase of a pair ends with a PAC, or the second phrase ends with an HC, or both. Such phrase pairs lack the question–answer arrangement of periods.

36.12 Anna Bon, Keyboard Sonata in C, Op. 2, No. 6, iii

> Though the two phrases begin similarly, this is *not* a parallel period, since the first phrase ends with a PAC (rather than an HC or IAC) and the second phrase with an HC (rather than a PAC).

PHRASES WITHIN PHRASE PAIRS

SENTENCES WITHIN PERIODS AND OTHER PHRASE PAIRS

Within a period (or any phrase pair), each of the two phrases may be a sentence or sentence-like.

36.13 **Sophia Dussek, Harp Sonata in G, Op. 2, No. 2, ii**

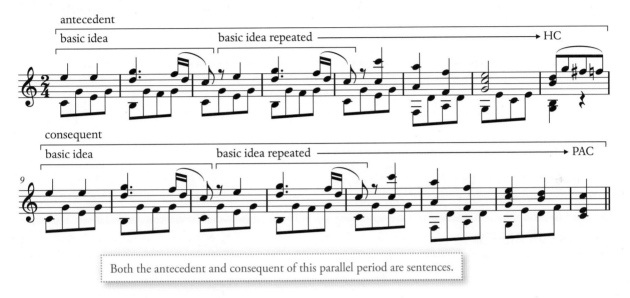

Both the antecedent and consequent of this parallel period are sentences.

RELATIVE LENGTH OF PHRASES

Typically, the two phrases within a period (or any phrase pair) are the same length as one another, around four or eight measures each. However, it is also possible for one or both of the phrases to be expanded or compressed, in which case one of the phrases (usually the second one) might be longer than the other.

36.14 J. M. Nunes Garcia, Overture in D, CPM 232

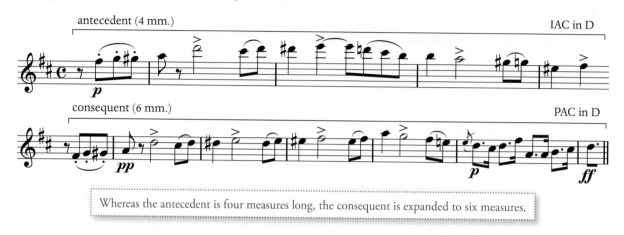

Whereas the antecedent is four measures long, the consequent is expanded to six measures.

For more on periods and other phrase pairs, see A Closer Look.

POINTS FOR REVIEW

- **Two successive phrases may combine to form a *phrase pair*.**

- **A *period* is a phrase pair in which the first phrase ends with an HC or IAC, and the second phrase ends with a PAC (either in the original key or in a new key).**

- **The first phrase of a period is the *antecedent*, the second phrase the *consequent*.**
  - In a *parallel period*, the antecedent and consequent begin with same notes (or nearly the same notes).
  - In a *sequential period*, the melody at the start of the antecedent is transposed at the start of the consequent, with different harmonies.
  - In a *contrasting period*, the antecedent and consequent begin much differently from each other.

- **Phrase pairs with other cadential layouts—and which thus do not form periods—are also possible.**

- **Each phrase within a period or other phrase pair may be a sentence.**

For each of the following phrase pairs, consider the cadences and identify which are periods and which are not, and why. Which periods are parallel? Sequential? Contrasting? In which is there an expansion?

37

Binary Form

Binary form organizes a composition into two parts.

Binary Form
  Beginning each part
Rounded Binary Form
Balanced Binary Form

Simple Binary Form
Relative Lengths of Sections
A Closer Look
  Other terminology associated with binary form

BINARY FORM

In **binary form** an entire movement is divided into two parts, each of which is usually repeated. Each part of a binary form consists of one or more phrases and ends with a cadence. The first part may end conclusively with an authentic cadence in the main key. Usually, however, it is harmonically open-ended, closing with either a half cadence in the main key or an authentic cadence in another key (most often, the key of V or—in minor-key pieces—the relative major). The second part of a binary form almost always ends with a perfect authentic cadence in the main key.

37.1
BINARY FORM

‖ FIRST PART ‖	‖ SECOND PART ‖
Ends with a PAC in the new key, or HC in the main key, or PAC (or IAC) in the main key.	Ends with a PAC in the main key.

BEGINNING EACH PART

The two parts of binary form often begin differently. The first part typically opens in a relatively stable way, embellishing the tonic harmony. The second part, on the other hand, usually begins in an unstable fashion. For instance, the second part might start with a sustained dominant harmony, with a sequence, or with a series of tonicizations, possibly (in longer binary forms) leading to a modulation and cadence in a new key.

37.2 Fernando Sor, Menuetto for Guitar, Op. 5, No. 1

The first part begins stably, embellishing the tonic with a simple progression.

The end of the first part is harmonically open-ended, with a PAC in V.

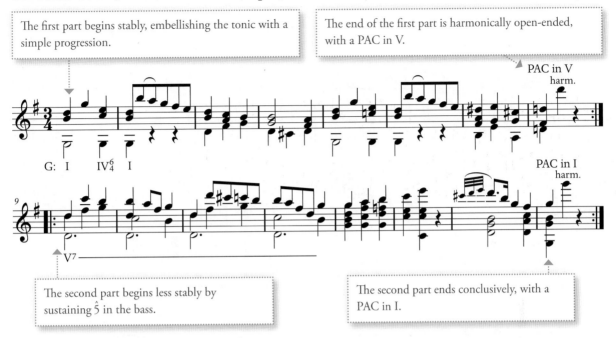

The second part begins less stably by sustaining $\hat{5}$ in the bass.

The second part ends conclusively, with a PAC in I.

37.3 François Couperin, "Les brinborions"

The opening of the first part embellishes the tonic, while the second part begins with a sequence.

The end of the first part is harmonically open-ended, with an HC in I . . .

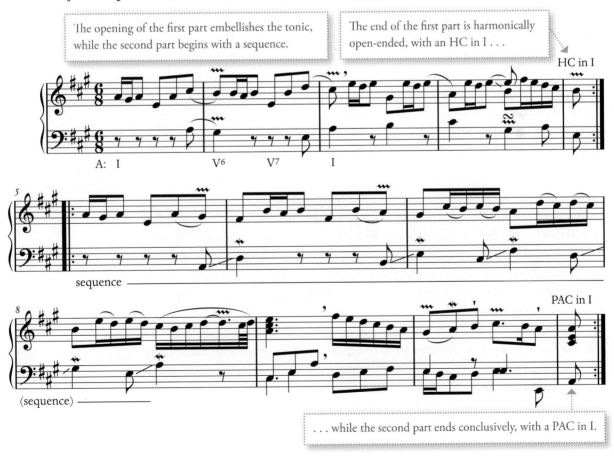

. . . while the second part ends conclusively, with a PAC in I.

The first part opens firmly in the tonic key; the second part opens with a modulation to iii.

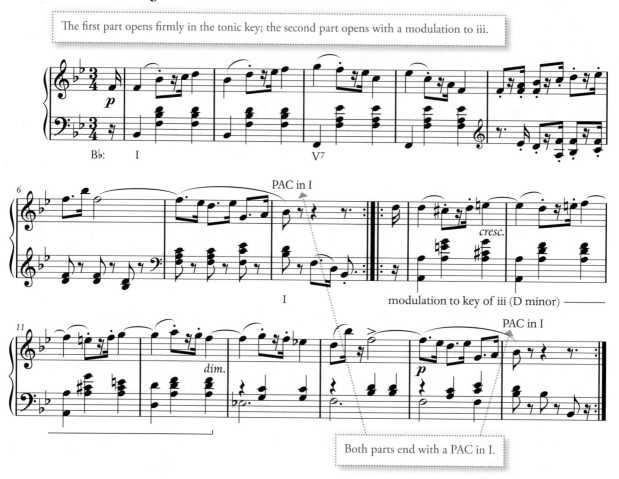

Both parts end with a PAC in I.

ROUNDED BINARY FORM

Sometimes the opening from the first part of a binary form returns in the original key in the middle of the second part, forming a **rounded binary form**. To be classified as rounded binary, the opening measures from the first part must be repeated either exactly or varied only slightly, so that there is a clear sense of a return. In some cases the entire opening part returns within the second part; at other times only the start of the opening part returns. In every rounded binary, however, the return of the opening must be in the original key.

Letters often are used to designate formal sections; thus rounded binary is labeled ‖: A :‖ B A :‖ or ‖: A :‖ B A′ :‖. The section designated as **B** contrasts with the opening section, which is labeled as **A**. The repetition of a letter (in this case, **A**) specifies a repetition of that earlier section; a prime mark (′) indicates that the repetition is varied.

37.5
ROUNDED BINARY FORM (OPENING RETURNS IN MIDDLE OF SECOND PART)

FIRST PART		SECOND PART	
‖: A	:‖	‖: B	A (or A') :‖
		• Contrasts with the **A** section. • Often ends on V of the main key.	• Begins and ends in the main key. • If **A**: the entire **A** section returns exactly (or almost exactly). • If **A'**: Either only the opening of **A** returns, or the entire **A** returns in a much varied form.

37.6 **Leopoldine Blahetka, "Erinnerungen an Holland" ("Remembrances of Holland"), Op. 33**

The *entire* first section returns in the tonic key at the end of the second part; this is *rounded binary* (‖: A :‖: B A :‖).

37.7 **Franz Schubert, Minuet in F, D. 41, No. 1**

The **A** section is eight measures long and ends in C major; **A'** is shorter (only four measures) and ends in F major . . .

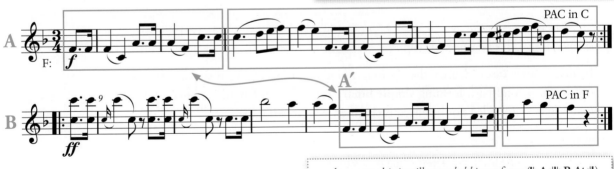

. . . however, this is still *rounded binary* form (‖: A :‖: B A' :‖), since **A** and **A'** both begin the same way (in the main key).

BALANCED BINARY FORM

In a **balanced binary form**, only the *ending* of the first part (*not* its beginning) returns in the main key at the end of the second part. Almost always, the first part finishes with a segment that leads to a PAC in a new key (such as V or the relative major). This concluding segment then returns transposed to the main key at the end of the second part, where it now leads to a PAC in I.

37.8
BALANCED BINARY FORM (ENDING OF FIRST PART RETURNS AT END OF SECOND PART)

FIRST PART	SECOND PART
‖: A :‖	‖: B :‖
First part usually ends with a PAC in the new key.	The ending segment of the first part returns, transposed to the main key, now leading to a PAC in the main key.

37.9 W. A. Mozart, Minuet, K. 1f

The *opening* of the first part doesn't return in the main key in the second part, so this is not rounded binary form . . .

. . . but the *ending* of the first part does return—now transposed to the main key—to end the second part, thus this is balanced binary form.

SIMPLE BINARY FORM

In many other cases, neither the opening nor the closing of the first part returns within the second part, forming **simple binary form**. Put differently: a binary form that is neither rounded nor balanced is classified as simple binary.

37.10
SIMPLE BINARY FORM (NEITHER ROUNDED NOR BALANCED)

FIRST PART	SECOND PART
‖: A :‖	‖: B :‖
	Although the second part is related to the first part, neither the opening nor the ending of the first part returns in the second part.

37.11 Niccolò Paganini, Caprice for Violin, Op. 1, No. 24

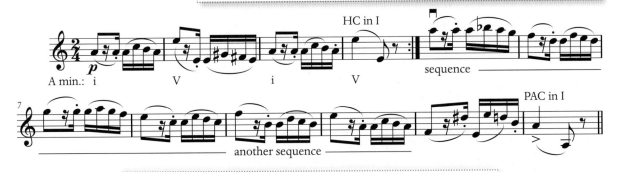

Although the two parts share similar melodic and rhythmic material, neither the opening nor the ending of the first part returns in the second part . . .

. . . thus, since this is neither rounded nor balanced, it is simple binary form.

RELATIVE LENGTHS OF SECTIONS

In many binary-form pieces, both parts are about the same length.

37.12 Antonín Dvořák, Minuet, Op. 28, No. 2, iii

The two parts of this binary form are each eight measures long.

More often than not, however, the second part of a binary form is considerably longer than the first part, often twice as long or even longer.

37.13 Robert Schumann, "Valse Allemande," from *Carnaval*, Op. 9

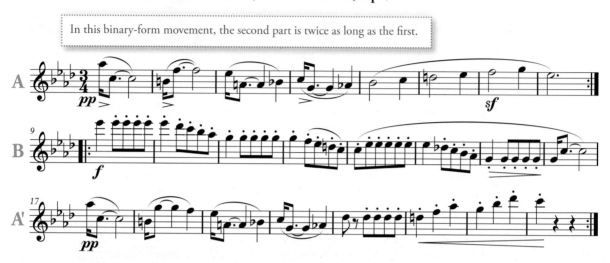

In this binary-form movement, the second part is twice as long as the first.

For more on binary form, see A Closer Look.

POINTS FOR REVIEW

- Binary form is divided into two parts; usually both parts are repeated.

- The first part ends with an authentic cadence in the tonic key, a half cadence in the tonic key, or a perfect authentic cadence in another key. The second part usually ends with a perfect authentic cadence in the tonic key.

- The first part typically begins with an embellishment of the tonic, and the second part typically begins in a relatively unstable harmonic fashion.

- In a *rounded binary form*, the opening of the first part returns in the tonic key in the middle of the second part.

- In a *balanced binary form*, the ending of the first part returns (transposed to the tonic key) at the end of the second part (but the opening of the first part does not return in the tonic key).

- A *simple binary form* is one in which neither the opening nor the ending of the first part returns in the middle of the second part.

- The second part of a binary form may be about the same length as the first part, or it may be considerably longer than the first part.

1. Are the following statements true or false?

   a. In a rounded binary form, material from the opening measures must return (either exactly or slightly varied) in the tonic key.

   b. In every case, if the last measures of both parts of a binary form are similar, the form will be classified as balanced binary form.

   c. In a simple binary form, the two parts have little in common.

   d. In a binary form, usually both parts are repeated.

2. Would you classify each of the following as a rounded, balanced, or simple binary form?

38 Ternary and Rondo Forms

In ternary and rondo forms, a main section recurs one or more times in the tonic key, alternating with one or more contrasting sections.

TERNARY FORM

Ternary form involves three sections in which the first and last sections are similar to one another, with a contrasting section sandwiched in the middle. The resulting form could be described either as **ABA** or **ABA'** (depending on whether the opening section is varied when it returns), with the **B** often taking the form of a departure or digression. A three-part composition in which the main section is not restated at the end (**ABC** format) lacks this sense of departure and return and thus is *not* in ternary form.

KEYS AND CADENCES

In a ternary form, both the **A** and **B** sections usually consist of multiple phrases. The two **A** sections usually begin and end in the tonic key (though the first **A** section may modulate to another key, so that it begins and ends in different keys). Furthermore, both **A** sections typically conclude with a perfect authentic cadence. The **B** section is often either in a different key or in the parallel major or minor. The **B** section usually starts and ends in the same key, and it may conclude with either a perfect authentic cadence or a half cadence. Sometimes a short passage known as a **bridge** leads from the end of the **B** section to the second **A** section.

TERNARY FORM

A *main section*	B *contrasting section*	A (OR A') *return of main section*
• Usually multiple phrases. • Starts in the tonic key. • Ends with a PAC, usually in the tonic key.	• Often in a new key or In the parallel major or minor key. • Usually starts and ends in the same key. • Ends with a PAC or HC. • A short bridge may lead to the return of **A**.	• Can be varied. • Starts and ends in the tonic key. • Ends with a PAC.

38.2 **Robert Schumann, "Volksliedchen" ("Folk Song")**

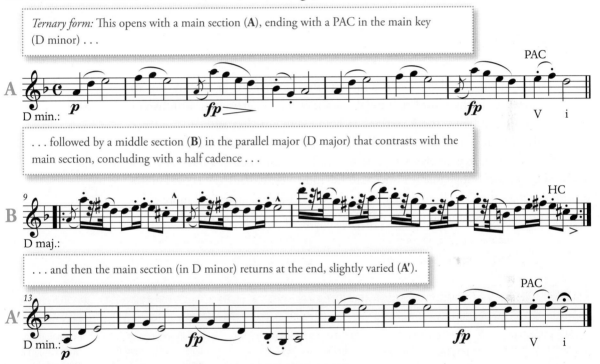

Ternary form: This opens with a main section (**A**), ending with a PAC in the main key (D minor) . . .

. . . followed by a middle section (**B**) in the parallel major (D major) that contrasts with the main section, concluding with a half cadence . . .

. . . and then the main section (in D minor) returns at the end, slightly varied (**A'**).

TERNARY FORM VERSUS ROUNDED BINARY FORM

In many ways, ternary form and rounded binary form are similar to one another. Nonetheless, certain features tend to distinguish ternary from rounded binary. In particular, the **A** and **B** section tend to be more self-contained and independent of each other in ternary form than in rounded binary, and they are more likely to be separated by a strong cadence. Also, in ternary form the second **A** section will more likely be either the same length as or longer than the first **A** section, while in rounded binary the second **A** section is generally either the same length as the first or abbreviated. Most notably, the two parts of a typical rounded binary form are almost always grouped together by repeat signs, ‖: **A** :‖: **B A** :‖. Conversely, while there may be repeats within the **A** or **B** section of a ternary form, the **B** and second **A** section generally are not repeated together as a unit.

TERNARY VERSUS ROUNDED BINARY FORM

TERNARY FORM	ROUNDED BINARY FORM
ABA or **ABA'**	‖: A :‖: B A :‖ or ‖: A :‖: B A' :‖
• Though there might be repeats *within* **A** or **B**, these sections are *not* repeated together. • The **A** section typically starts and ends in the same key, as does the **B** section. **A** typically ends with a PAC. • The **B** section is usually substantial and may end with a PAC. • The second **A** section is often the same length as or even longer than the first **A** section.	• Repeats usually divide the form into two parts. • The first **A** section and the **B** section each often start and end in different keys; the first **A** section may end with an HC. • The **B** section may be relatively short and unstable, and it rarely ends with a PAC. • The second **A** section may be the same length as or considerably shorter than the first **A**.

RONDO FORM

In **rondo form**, the initial **A** section returns (either unchanged or slightly varied) two or more times in the tonic key throughout a movement, alternating with two or more contrasting sections. The **A** sections each end with a perfect authentic cadence in the tonic key; the **B** and **C** sections (the contrasting sections) end either with a half cadence in the tonic key, or else with a perfect authentic cadence in a non-tonic key followed by a short bridge that leads back to the tonic key. Usually the **B** section is a bit simpler than the **C** section, which tends to be less stable, longer, and more complex. A common type of rondo form, **ABACA**, is known as a **five-part rondo**.

38.4

FIVE-PART RONDO

A *main section*	B *contrasting section*	A (or A') *main section*	C *another* *contrasting section*	A *main section*
• Starts and ends (with PAC) in the tonic key.	• Relatively simple. • May be in a closely related key. • Ends with a PAC or HC. • A short bridge may lead to return of **A**.	• Starts and ends (with PAC) in the tonic key. • May be shorter than first **A**.	• Usually longer and more complex than **B** section. • Usually in a closely related key that is different from the key of the **A** or **B** section. • Ends with a PAC or HC. • A short bridge may lead to return of **A**.	• Starts and ends (with PAC) in the tonic key.

38.5 Jean-Joseph Mouret, Fanfare

In this typical **ABA′ CA** rondo form, the middle **A′** section is half as long as the outer ones (8 mm. vs. 16 mm.), and the **C** section is longer and more complex than **B**.

(bridge leads from C to final A)

Other types of rondo forms may involve more alternations between the main section in the tonic key and contrasting sections.

38.6

SOME OTHER POSSIBLE SCHEMES FOR MOVEMENTS IN RONDO FORM

ABACAB'A	ABACB'A	ABAB'A	ABACADA . . . (etc.)
Seven-part rondo form: The first **B** section is in a related key (such as V or the relative major) and the second **B** section is in the tonic key. (This is sometimes called *sonata rondo*: see Chapter 39.)	Variant of seven-part rondo.	Variant of five-part rondo.	Sometimes found in French Baroque movements; ends with return of **A** in the tonic key.

 For additional forms, see A Closer Look.

POINTS FOR REVIEW

- In ternary form, a contrasting section appears between statements of a main section: ABA (or ABA').

- Both A sections of ternary form usually start and end in the tonic key (though sometimes the first A section modulates to another key). Both conclude with a PAC, and they are often around the same length.

- The B section of a ternary form is usually either in a non-tonic key or in the parallel major or minor. It often starts and ends in the same key.

- In rondo form, a main section in the tonic key alternates with two or more contrasting sections; some schemes include ABACA, ABACAB'A, and ABACADA.

1. Which of the following are examples of ternary form?

   a. **ABA**   b. **ABA′**   c. **ABC**

2. In an **ABA′** ternary form, which of the sections are almost always in the tonic key?

3. In an **ABA′** ternary form, which sections usually end with a PAC?

4. In which key do the **A** sections of a rondo form usually appear: in the tonic key, the dominant key, another key, or in any of these keys?

5. What type of cadence usually appears at the end of the **A** sections of a rondo?

6. In an **ABACA** rondo, which is usually longer, the **B** section or the **C** section, or are they usually around the same length?

Sonata form—consisting of an exposition, a development, and a recapitulation—organizes many instrumental works.

ELEMENTS OF SONATA FORM

Many instrumental works from the second half of the eighteenth century through the nineteenth century (including symphonies, chamber works, and sonatas) are in **sonata form**. Sonata form resembles a large rounded binary form. The first part, which is usually repeated, consists of the **exposition**. The exposition starts in the tonic key and modulates to a secondary key (a key other than the tonic). The second part of a sonata form movement—which may be repeated as well—consists of two sections, each of which is about as long and substantial as the exposition. The first of these sections is the **development**, which tonicizes various keys before returning to the tonic key. The last section is the **recapitulation**, which starts and ends in the tonic key.

39.1
SONATA FORM

FIRST PART *(usually repeated)*		SECOND PART *(often repeated in works composed before 1800)*	
‖: **Exposition** :‖		‖: **Development**	**Recapitulation** :‖
Like **A** of rounded binary; begins in the tonic key, ends in a secondary key.		Like **B** of rounded binary; tonicizes various keys and ends by returning to the tonic key.	Like **A′** of rounded binary; about the same length as **A**.

These three main sections—exposition, development, and recapitulation—themselves are made up of smaller subsections. Although few individual works contain all the characteristic features associated with sonata form, those movements that contain at least most of these features may be regarded as being in sonata form.

EXPOSITION

A sonata form exposition usually consists of two halves. The first half of the exposition starts with a **primary theme** (also known as a *first theme* or *main theme*) that establishes the tonic key. This is followed by a **transition** that leads to a strong half cadence (HC). The second half of the exposition begins and ends in a secondary key. In major-key movements, the secondary key is usually V; in minor-key movements, the secondary key is usually III (the relative major). The opening section of the exposition's second half is the **secondary theme** (also known as the *second theme* or *subordinate theme*). Following a perfect authentic cadence (PAC) at the end of the secondary theme, a **closing section** wraps up the exposition.

39.2

FIRST HALF OF EXPOSITION *Begins in the tonic key; ends with an HC either in the tonic key or a new key*		SECOND HALF OF EXPOSITION *Begins and ends in a secondary key*	
primary theme	*transition* ————————➤	*secondary theme*	*closing section*
Ends with HC, PAC, or IAC in the tonic key.	Starts in the tonic key, leads to a strong HC.	Ends with a PAC in a secondary key.	Wraps up the exposition, ends with a PAC in a secondary key.

PRIMARY THEME AND TRANSITION

The primary theme establishes the tonic key with one or more phrases and concludes with either an authentic cadence or a half cadence in this key. The transition that follows starts in the tonic key and leads to a half cadence. In some expositions, the half cadence at the end of the transition is in the tonic key. In most expositions, however (especially in the late eighteenth century and later), the transition modulates to end with a half cadence in the secondary key. The transition typically is more energetic and unstable than the primary theme, involving increased momentum leading to the half cadence at its conclusion.

39.3 **W. A. Mozart, Piano Sonata in G, K. 283, ii (mm. 1–8)**

primary theme
(relatively stable, starts and ends in tonic key)

p legato

PAC in I

f

First half of exposition: The *primary theme* (mm. 1–4) establishes the tonic key (C) . . .

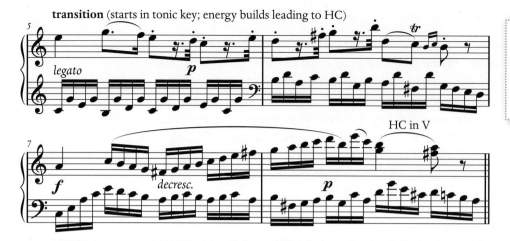

transition (starts in tonic key; energy builds leading to HC)

HC in V

> . . . the *transition* (mm. 5–8) creates momentum leading to an HC in V, the secondary key (G).

The primary theme and transition may begin similarly, though they always end differently. In many cases, there is a *phrase overlap* between these sections, in which the last chord of the primary theme is also the first chord of the transition. As a result, often there is no sharp break between the end of the primary theme and the start of the transition.

39.4 Franz Schubert, Sonata for Violin and Piano in D, D. 384, i (mm. 27–31)

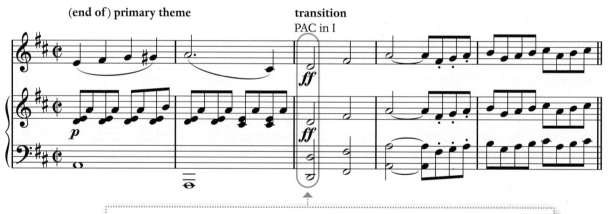

(end of) primary theme

transition
PAC in I

Phrase overlap: The last chord of the primary theme is also the first chord of the transition.

END OF TRANSITION

The end of the transition is usually strongly demarcated. Typically, the transition ends with a **medial caesura**, a pause or break that marks the end of the exposition's first half and dramatically sets the stage for the secondary theme. The medial caesura may consist of a brief rest in all voices, a sudden thinning of the texture, or some other dramatic change that clearly separates the end of the transition from the start of the ensuing secondary theme.

39.5 Joseph Boulogne, String Quartet in C Minor, Op. 1, No. 4, i (mm. 19–22)

A rest in all parts creates a *medial caesura* that starkly separates the end of the transition from the beginning of the secondary theme.

39.6 Hélène Reise Liebmann, Cello Sonata Op. 11 in B♭, i (mm. 31–34)

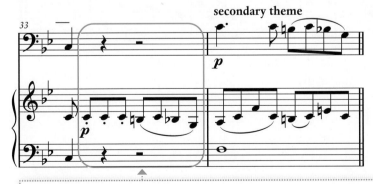

A sudden decrease in texture separates the end of the transition from the start of the secondary theme.

SECONDARY THEME AND CLOSING SECTION

The secondary theme immediately follows the medial caesura. The secondary theme may present completely new material, or it may be a variant of the primary theme. The secondary theme ends with a perfect authentic cadence in the secondary key. After this cadence, the closing section begins and confirms the conclusion of the exposition with one or more perfect authentic cadences in the secondary key.

39.7 Joseph Haydn, Piano Sonata in C, Hob. XVI:10, i: Exposition (mm. 1–21)

This exposition starts in the tonic key and ends with a secondary theme and closing section in V.

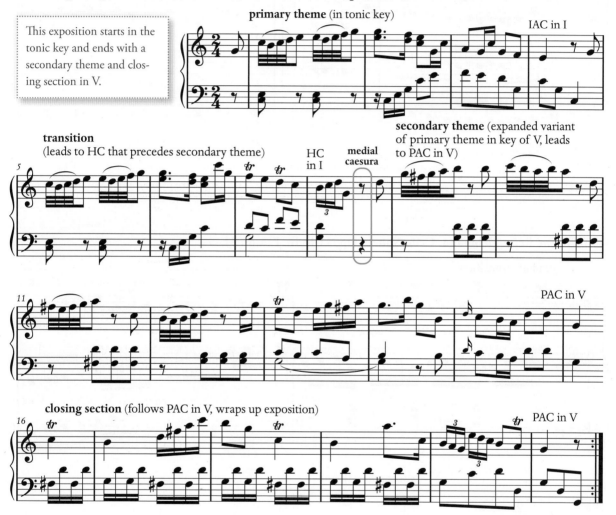

DEVELOPMENT

There is a wider range of possibilities for the development. Soon after it begins, the development usually builds momentum with tonicizations and sequences that involve fragments of themes from the exposition, along with other thematic fragments. The development often ends with a cadence in a key other than the tonic key or secondary key. This cadence is followed by a **retransition**, a passage that leads back to the tonic key. Alternately, the development section may end with a dramatic half cadence in the tonic key that prepares for the upcoming recapitulation.

39.8

Development begins stably . . .	. . . it then continues with fragments and variants of themes, using sequences and tonicizations . . .	. . . and ends with either:
		• PAC in a new key, followed by a retransition leading to the recapitulation, or
		• a strong HC in the tonic key.

39.9 Joseph Haydn, Piano Sonata in C, Hob. XVI:10, i: Development (mm. 22–38)

The development section involves various thematic fragments, sequences, and tonicizations, eventually leading back to the tonic key.

RECAPITULATION

The recapitulation mostly repeats the music from the exposition, except that the recapitulation both starts *and* ends in the tonic key, with the secondary theme and closing section now transposed to the tonic. The transition is the only section that is usually greatly altered when it reappears in the recapitulation. This is especially so when the transition of the exposition ends with a half cadence in the secondary key: in such a case, the transition must be changed in the recapitulation so as to end with a half cadence in the tonic key.

39.10

FIRST HALF OF RECAPITULATION *Begins and ends in the tonic key*		SECOND HALF OF RECAPITULATION *Begins and ends in the tonic key (often a transposition of the second half of the exposition)*	
primary theme	*transition* ⟶	*secondary theme*	*closing section*
Often the same as or similar to the primary theme of the exposition.	Starts and ends in the tonic key; often differs greatly from the transition of the exposition.	Ends with a PAC in the tonic key.	Ends with a PAC in the tonic key.

39.11 Joseph Haydn, Piano Sonata in C, Hob. XVI:10, i: Recapitulation (mm. 39–59)

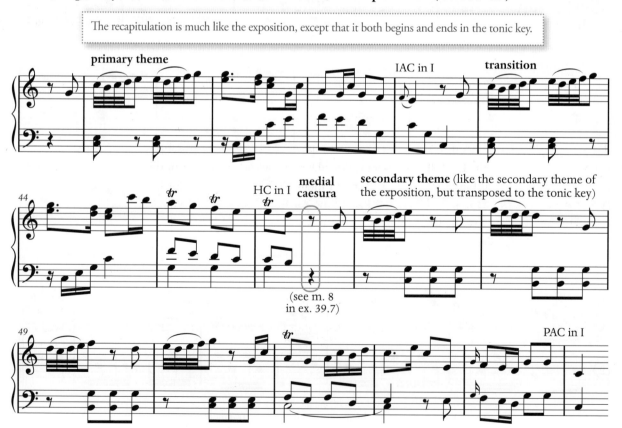

The recapitulation is much like the exposition, except that it both begins and ends in the tonic key.

closing theme (like the closing section of the exposition, but transposed to the tonic key)

INTRODUCTION AND CODA

Some sonata form movements open with an **introduction**. The introduction is in a slower tempo than the rest of the movement, and unlike the exposition, it is not repeated. Sonata form movements may also include a **coda**, a concluding section that follows the closing section of the recapitulation. In movements where the development and recapitulation are repeated, the coda is not included within the repeat.

39.12

Introduction	‖: Exposition :‖	‖: Development/Recapitulation :‖	Coda
Optional, slower than the rest of the movement, *not* repeated; ends with an HC in the tonic key.			Optional, in the tonic key; follows the end of the recapitulation; *not* repeated.

SONATA RONDO

The seven-part **ABACABA** rondo is often referred to as a **sonata rondo**. This is especially so if the first **A** and **B** sections are structured like a sonata form exposition, the middle **C** section resembles a sonata form development section, and the following **A** and **B** sections are structured like a recapitulation. Sonata rondos are particularly common in fast final movements of multi-movement works.

39.13

SONATA RONDO

A	B	A′	C	A″	B′	A‴
Starts in the tonic key, ends with an HC (like a primary theme + transition).	In a secondary key (like a secondary theme + closing section).	In the tonic key.	In a new key, or tonicizes various keys (like a development).	Starts in the tonic key, ends with an HC.	In the tonic key (like a secondary theme + closing section).	In the tonic key.
Exposition			**Development**	**Recapitulation**		

- Sonata form movements are made up of two large parts: the first part includes just the *exposition* (which is usually repeated); the second part includes the *development* and *recapitulation* (this second part may also be repeated).

- The exposition includes (1) a *primary theme* in the tonic key; (2) a *transition* that ends with an HC in either the tonic key or a new key, followed by a break known as a *medial caesura*; then (3) a *secondary theme* that begins and ends (with a PAC) in the new key, which is usually followed by (4) a *closing section* in the new key.

- The recapitulation revisits the material of the exposition, with the secondary theme and closing section now transposed to the tonic key. In many cases, the material of the transition is significantly revised for the recapitulation so as to end with a half cadence in the tonic key.

EXPOSITION
Starts in the tonic key; ends in a secondary key, usually repeated

1. **Primary theme**: starts and ends in the tonic key; ends with a PAC, IAC, or HC.
2. **Transition**: might modulate, ends with an HC in the tonic key or an HC in a secondary key.

3. **Secondary theme**: in a secondary key, ends with a PAC.
4. **Closing section**: in a secondary key, wraps up the exposition, ends with a PAC.

DEVELOPMENT
Tonicizes various keys, ends by returning to the tonic key, sometimes repeated together with the recapitulation

RECAPITULATION
Starts and ends in the tonic key

1. **Primary theme**: like the primary theme of the exposition.
2. **Transition**: often a much-revised version of the transition from the exposition, ends with an HC in the tonic key.

3. **Secondary theme**: in the tonic key, ends with a PAC.
4. **Closing section**: in the tonic key, wraps up the recapitulation, ends with a PAC.

- Some sonata form movements also include a slow introduction at the beginning of the movement, and a coda following the recapitulation; neither the introduction nor the coda is repeated.

- A sonata rondo is a seven-part rondo in which the opening sections are structured like a sonata form exposition, the middle section is like a development, and the sections toward the end are structured like a recapitulation.

1. In what order do the following appear?

   coda, development, exposition, introduction, recapitulation

2. In what order do the following appear within both the exposition and recapitulation?

   closing section, primary theme, secondary theme, transition

3. The medial caesura appears at the end of the _____ and precedes the _____.

4. In what key is the primary theme presented in the exposition: the tonic key or the secondary key? In what key does it appear in the recapitulation?

5. What types of cadences, in what keys, are typically found at the end of the primary theme?

6. What types of cadences, in what keys, are typically found at the end of the transition in the exposition? In the recapitulation?

7. In what key does the secondary theme appear in the exposition? In what key does it appear in the recapitulation?

8. What types of cadences, in what keys, are typically found at the end of the secondary theme in the exposition? In the recapitulation?

9. Which of the following statements is true?

   a. The primary and secondary themes always have contrasting melodies.

   b. The primary and secondary themes always have similar melodies.

   c. The melodies of the primary and secondary themes can either contrast with or be similar to one another.

part
six

Post-Tonal Theory

40 Collections and Scales I: Diatonic and Pentatonic

Post-tonal music is often based on one or more familiar scales or collections.

In previous chapters, we have been primarily concerned with tonal harmony and voice leading. Tonal harmony is functional, with chords progressing according to well-established norms toward cadential goals. Tonal voice leading requires special treatment of tendency tones, especially leading tones and dissonances, and avoids parallel perfect consonances. Starting around 1900, many composers in the Western classical tradition began to write music that does not observe the norms of tonal harmony and voice leading. We will refer to this sort of music as **post-tonal**.

COLLECTIONS AND SCALES

A **collection** is a group of notes, distinct in content, but without regard to the **order** of the notes (which comes first, which comes second, and so on). When a collection is written out in ascending order within an octave, starting on a principal tone, it is a **scale** (and the principal tone is $\hat{1}$). Post-tonal music sometimes uses familiar major and minor scales, but in the absence of traditional functional harmony, it can be hard or even impossible to figure out which pitch is $\hat{1}$. We will often have to see which pitch is emphasized by, for example, duration ($\hat{1}$ sounds for the longest), metrical placement ($\hat{1}$ appears on strong beats), and register ($\hat{1}$ is placed in the bass). In post-tonal music based on the diatonic scale, $\hat{1}$ can sometimes be ambiguous.

DIATONIC SCALES

The seven white notes of the piano form a **diatonic collection**. There are twelve different transpositions of the diatonic collection, and we can identify them by their traditional key signatures—for example, the "2-sharp collection," abbreviated as $DIA_{2\sharp}$, or the "3-flat collection," abbreviated as $DIA_{3\flat}$.

40.1

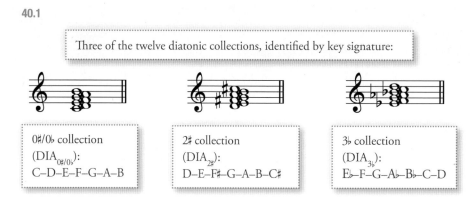

Three of the twelve diatonic collections, identified by key signature:

| 0♯/0♭ collection $(DIA_{0\sharp/0\flat})$:
C–D–E–F–G–A–B | 2♯ collection $(DIA_{2\sharp})$:
D–E–F♯–G–A–B–C♯ | 3♭ collection $(DIA_{3\flat})$:
E♭–F–G–A♭–B♭–C–D |

There are seven different ways of writing a diatonic collection as a **scale**, beginning on any of its seven notes. In post-tonal music, the first (primary) degree of the scale is called the **centric tone**. The seven scales of the 0♯/0♭ collection correspond to the seven **diatonic modes**. Each diatonic scale (mode) has its own distinctive **interval ordering**, which we will count in semitones.

40.2

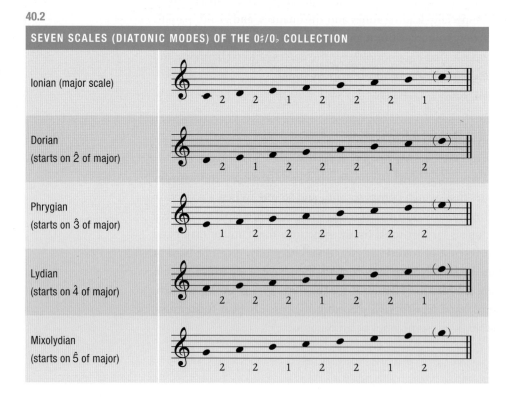

SEVEN SCALES (DIATONIC MODES) OF THE 0♯/0♭ COLLECTION

Ionian (major scale)	2 2 1 2 2 2 1
Dorian (starts on 2̂ of major)	2 1 2 2 2 1 2
Phrygian (starts on 3̂ of major)	1 2 2 2 1 2 2
Lydian (starts on 4̂ of major)	2 2 2 1 2 2 1
Mixolydian (starts on 5̂ of major)	2 2 1 2 2 1 2

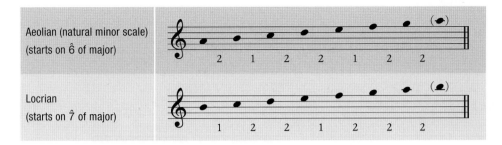

Passages based on a diatonic collection or scale can be labeled in two ways: the collection and centric tone (2♯ collection on E) or the scale name (E Dorian).

40.3

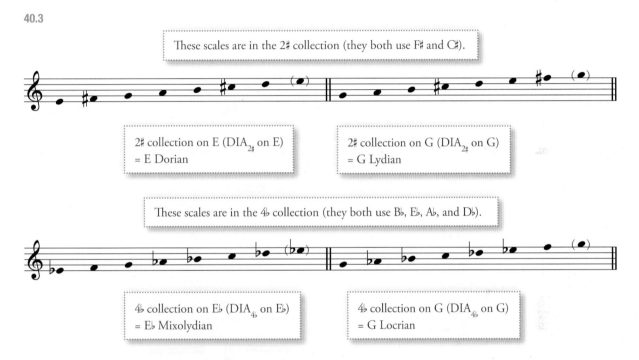

40.4 **Maurice Ravel, Sonata for Violin and Cello, iii**

When more than one diatonic collection or scale is in use, something like a modulation can take place, either by moving between diatonic collections, changing the principal tone (1̂), or both.

40.5 John Adams, *Phrygian Gates*

Starts in the 5♯ collection on E (E Lydian) . . .

. . . and then moves to the 0♯/0♭ collection on E (E Phrygian). It thus keeps its centric tone, but changes its diatonic collection.

E is identified as the centric tone because it is the lowest pitch.

40.6 Igor Stravinsky, *Petrushka*

Starts in the 0♯/0♭ collection on G (G Mixolydian) . . .

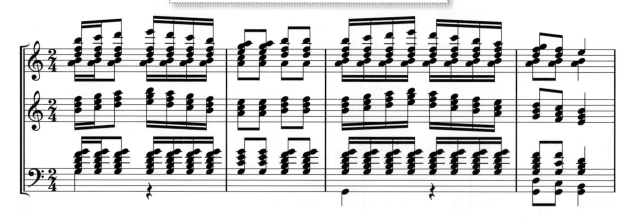

> . . . and then moves to the 1♯ collection on A (A Dorian). It thus changes both its centric tone and its diatonic collection.

The diatonic collection contains lots of triads and seventh chords. But in post-tonal music, composers often extract other harmonies.

A diatonic collection spans a seven-note segment of the circle of fifths. Motion among diatonic collections can be measured by the number of fifths moved in a clockwise (sharpward, +) or counter-clockwise (flatward, –) direction.

40.7

John Adams, *Phrygian Gates*

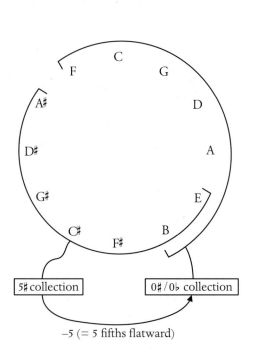

Igor Stravinsky, *Petrushka*

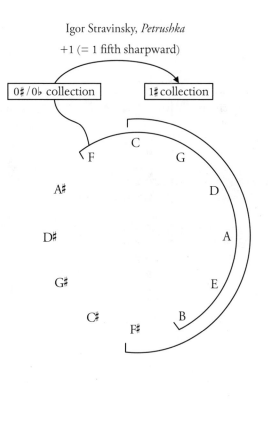

PENTATONIC SCALES

The five black keys on the piano form a **pentatonic collection**. There are twelve different transpositions of the pentatonic collection.

40.8

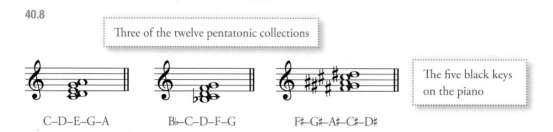

Three of the twelve pentatonic collections

The five black keys on the piano

C–D–E–G–A B♭–C–D–F–G F♯–G♯–A♯–C♯–D♯

A pentatonic collection can be arranged as a scale in five different ways, each with a distinctive pattern of major seconds (two semitones) and minor thirds (three semitones) (note that the pentatonic collection contains no semitones or tritones). We identify pentatonic collections by naming the lowest note in the "major" interval ordering: 2–2–3–2–3 and, if possible, the centric tone ($\hat{1}$).

40.9

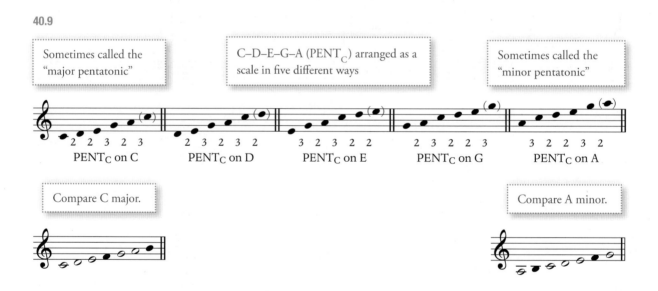

Sometimes called the "major pentatonic"

C–D–E–G–A (PENT$_C$) arranged as a scale in five different ways

Sometimes called the "minor pentatonic"

2 2 3 2 3   2 3 2 3 2   3 2 3 2 2   2 3 2 2 3   3 2 2 3 2

PENT$_C$ on C   PENT$_C$ on D   PENT$_C$ on E   PENT$_C$ on G   PENT$_C$ on A

Compare C major.

Compare A minor.

40.10 Jessie Montgomery, *Source Code* (for string quartet)

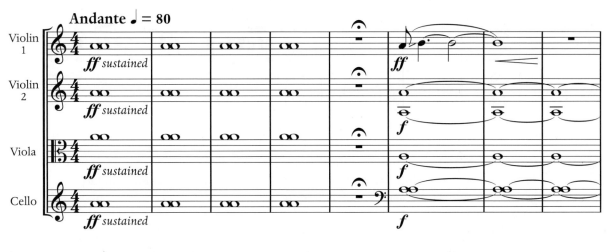

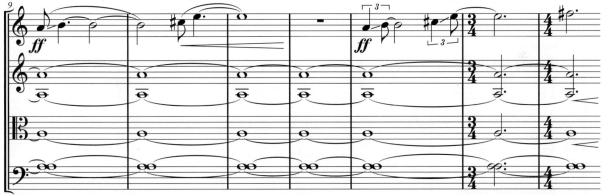

Over sustained As, first in unison and then in octaves, the first violin ascends through PENT$_A$ on A: A–B–C♯–E–F♯.

40.11 Béla Bartók, *Bluebeard's Castle*

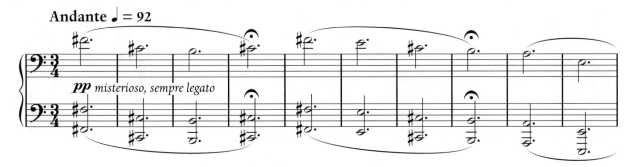

PENT_A on F♯: F♯–A–B–C♯–E. F♯ is the first note in the first two phrases and the goal in the bass of the fourth phrase. In the fourth phrase, the melody introduces notes from outside the pentatonic collection.

40.12 **Kaija Saariaho,** *L'amour de loin*

PENT_E on F♯: F♯–G♯–B–C♯–E. F♯ is in the bass, sustained throughout the passage.

RELATING DIATONIC AND PENTATONIC SCALES

The pentatonic and diatonic collections are related in two important ways. First, they are **complementary**: the seven notes missing from a given pentatonic collection form a diatonic collection and vice versa (like the black and white notes of the piano keyboard).

40.13 **György Ligeti, "Désordre," from Etudes, Book 1**

In the piano right hand—the 0♯/0♭ collection on B (DIA$_{0♯/0♭}$): B–C–D–E–F–G–A

In the piano left hand—PENT$_{F♯}$ on D♯: D♯–F♯–G♯–A♯–C♯

The second relationship between pentatonic and diatonic is one of **inclusion**: every diatonic collection contains three pentatonic collections; every pentatonic collection can be expanded into a diatonic collection with the addition of two notes. Every diatonic collection is a seven-note segment of the circle of fifths; every pentatonic collection is a five-note segment of the circle of fifths.

40.14

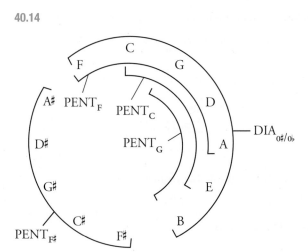

40.15 Tan Dun, *Elegy: Snow in June*

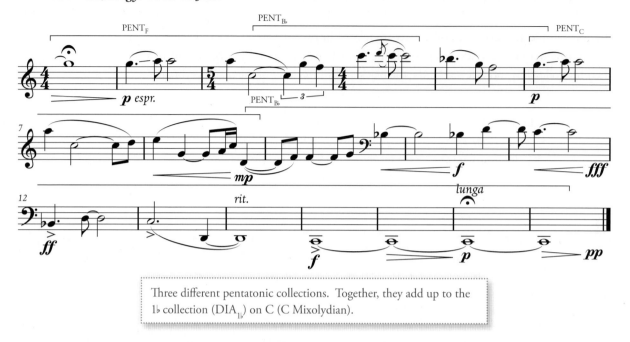

Three different pentatonic collections. Together, they add up to the 1♭ collection (DIA$_{1♭}$) on C (C Mixolydian).

🔍 For more on diatonic and pentatonic scales, see A Closer Look.

POINTS FOR REVIEW

- **A collection is a group of notes. When a collection is written out in ascending order within an octave, starting on a centric tone, it is a scale.**

- **To determine the centric tone, look for a pitch that is emphasized with duration, accent, or registral position.**

- **A diatonic collection is any transposition of the seven white notes of the piano.**
  - There are twelve diatonic collections, and each can be arranged as a scale in seven ways (corresponding to the traditional modes).
  - On the circle of fifths, any seven consecutive notes are a diatonic collection.

- **A pentatonic collection is any transposition of the five black notes of the piano.**
  - There are twelve pentatonic collections, and each can be arranged as a scale in five ways.
  - On the circle of fifths, any five consecutive notes are a pentatonic collection.

- **The diatonic and pentatonic collections are complementary: the notes missing from a diatonic collection form a pentatonic collection and vice versa.**

- **Each diatonic collection includes (contains) three pentatonic collections.**

1. Identify the following scales:

a.

b.

c.

d.

e.

2. Write out the following scales using letter names:

   a. $DIA_{3\sharp}$ on E (E Mixolydian)

   b. $PENT_F$ on G

   c. $PENT_{A\flat}$ on E♭

   d. $DIA_{2\sharp}$ on G (G Lydian)

   e. $DIA_{1\flat}$ on G (G Dorian)

3. Which pentatonic collection is the complement of each of these diatonic collections?

   a. $DIA_{3\sharp}$

   b. $DIA_{4\flat}$

   c. $DIA_{1\sharp}$

4. Which diatonic collection is the complement of each of these pentatonic collections?

   a. $PENT_F$

   b. $PENT_G$

   c. $PENT_{F\sharp}$

5. Name the three pentatonic collections contained in each of these diatonic collections.

   a. $DIA_{2\sharp}$

   b. $DIA_{3\flat}$

   c. $DIA_{6\sharp}$

Collections and Scales II: Octatonic, Hexatonic, and Whole-Tone

41

In addition to the diatonic and pentatonic collections, post-tonal music uses octatonic, hexatonic, and whole-tone collections.

Composers of post-tonal music have often made use of nontraditional collections, including octatonic, hexatonic, and whole-tone. These are more symmetrical than the diatonic collection. They have the same intervals reading from bottom to top and top to bottom, and the same intervals repeat from many points in the scale. Thus, they have fewer than twelve distinct forms. Using the notes of some of these collections, it is possible to write traditional harmonies (triads and seventh chords); all of them may be used to produce new, nontraditional harmonies.

OCTATONIC SCALES

There are three **octatonic collections**. Each octatonic collection consists of two diminished seventh chords a semitone apart. Any two octatonic collections have four notes in common (one of the diminished seventh chords). The abbreviation for an octatonic collection identifies it by one of the semitones it uniquely contains, beginning on C, C♯, or D. For example, $OCT_{C\sharp D}$ is the octatonic collection that contains C♯ and D. When working with octatonic scales, assume enharmonic equivalence; note spelling is for convenience only.

41.1 The three octatonic collections

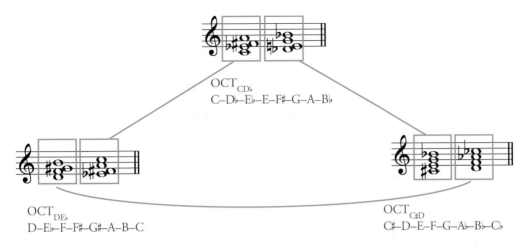

OCT$_{CD\flat}$
C–D♭–E♭–E–F♯–G–A–B♭

OCT$_{DE\flat}$
D–E♭–F–F♯–G♯–A–B–C

OCT$_{C\sharp D}$
C♯–D–E–F–G–A♭–B♭–C♭

An octatonic scale alternates semitones (1) and whole tones (2). It has only two interval orderings: one that starts with 1 and one that starts with 2.

41.2 Some octatonic scales

OCT$_{C\sharp D}$ on E
(scale in 1–2 ordering)

OCT$_{DE\flat}$ on F♯
(scale in 2–1 ordering)

OCT$_{CD\flat}$ on E
(scale in 2–1 ordering)

41.3 Olivier Messiaen, *Quartet for the End of Time*

OCT$_{C\sharp D}$ on E: E–F–G–A♭–B♭–B–C♯–D

The octatonic collection contains many triads and seventh chords, related by transposition at the minor third or the tritone.

41.4

All of these seventh chords (and the triads they contain) are included in OCT_CD♭.

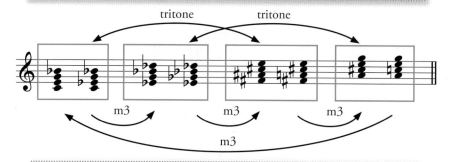

Major and minor triads (and dominant and minor seventh chords) extracted from OCT_CD♭ are related by minor third or tritone.

41.5 Igor Stravinsky, *Petrushka*

OCT_CC♯ on either C or F♯

C major and F♯ major triads, related at the tritone, are arpeggiated together.

41.6 Igor Stravinsky, *Symphony of Psalms*

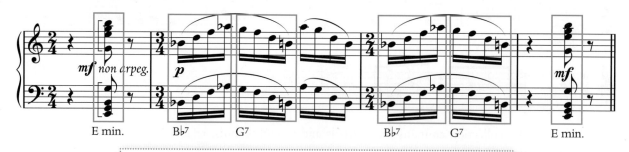

All the notes come from OCT_C♯D on E: E–F–G–A♭–B♭–B♮–(C♯)–D. The triads and seventh chords have roots related by minor third or tritone.

HEXATONIC SCALES

There are four **hexatonic collections**. Each hexatonic collection consists of two augmented triads a semitone apart. Any two hexatonic collections either share an augmented triad or have no notes in common.

41.7 **The four hexatonic collections**

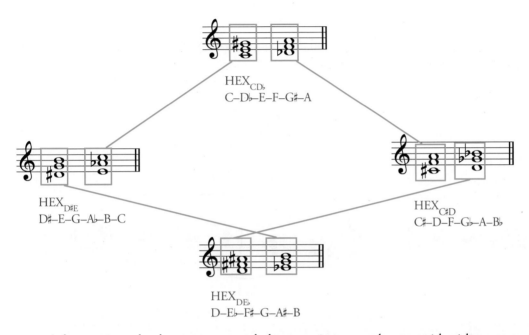

A hexatonic scale alternates one and three semitones, and starts with either 1 or 3. The abbreviation for a hexatonic collection identifies it by one of the semitones it uniquely contains, beginning on C, C♯, D, or D♯. For example, HEX$_{C\sharp D}$ is the hexatonic collection that contains C♯ and D.

41.8 **Some hexatonic scales**

41.9 Kaija Saariaho, *Sept papillons* (for solo cello), iii

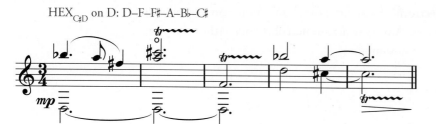

HEX$_{C\sharp D}$ on D: D–F–F♯–A–B♭–C♯

The hexatonic collection contains three major and three minor triads, with roots related by major third.

41.10

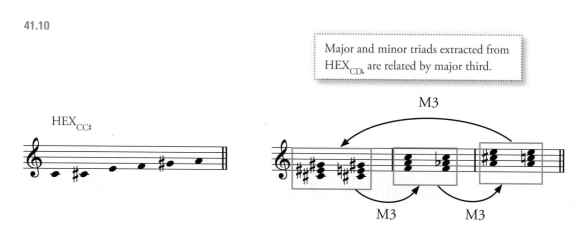

HEX$_{CC\sharp}$

Major and minor triads extracted from HEX$_{CD\flat}$, are related by major third.

M3

M3   M3

41.11 Ursula Mamlok, *Panta Rhei*, iii

HEX$_{C\sharp D}$: C♯–D–F–F♯–A–B♭   F♯ maj.   B♭ maj.   D maj.(+E)

Violin

Cello

Piano

B♭ min.   D min.

Five triads (F♯ major, B♭ minor, B♭ major, D minor, and D major) appear within this hexatonic passage.

The four hexatonic collections can be divided into two complementary pairs. Within each complementary pair, each hexatonic collection contains all the notes excluded by the other, and together they contain all twelve notes.

41.12

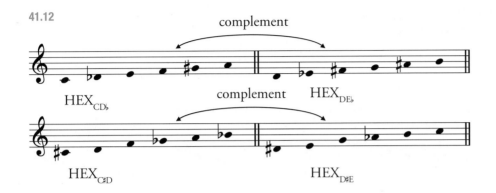

41.13 Milton Babbitt, String Quartet No. 2

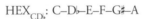

Violin 1 and Viola share HEX$_{CD\flat}$: Violin 2 and Cello share the complementary collection, HEX$_{DE\flat}$. Together, the quartet plays all twelve notes.

WHOLE-TONE SCALES

There are only two **whole-tone collections**, and each has only one scalar ordering: 2–2–2–2–2–(2). WT$_C$ contains the note C, and WT$_{C\sharp}$ contains the note C♯. Because the whole-tone collection is so symmetrical, it is often difficult to determine a centric tone (1̂).

41.14

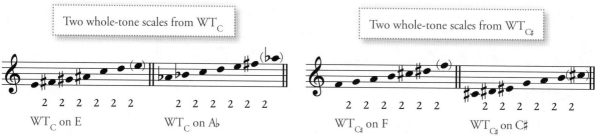

41.15 Claude Debussy, *Voiles*

WT$_C$ on B♭ (because of the emphasis on B♭ in the bass). Two descending whole-tone scales move in parallel major thirds with an octave leap in the middle.

Unlike the other scales we have discussed, the whole-tone scale contains no consonant triads or familiar seventh chords (although it does feature an augmented triad built on each of its notes—these augmented triads are a whole step apart).

41.16

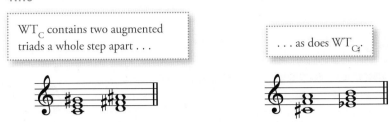

WT$_C$ contains two augmented triads a whole step apart . . .

. . . as does WT$_{C\sharp}$.

The two whole-tone collections are complementary: each contains the notes excluded by the other and, together, they contain all twelve notes.

41.17 Thomas Adès, Mazurka No. 3

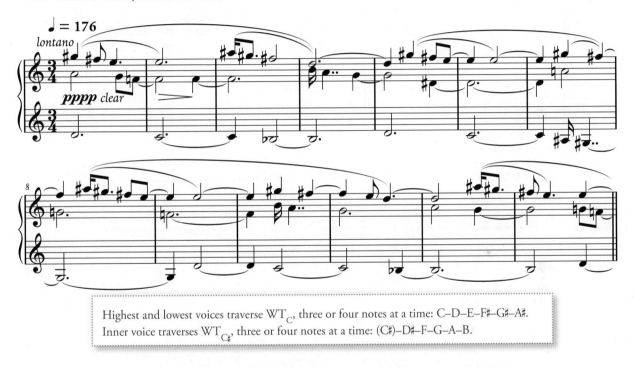

Highest and lowest voices traverse WT$_C$, three or four notes at a time: C–D–E–F♯–G♯–A♯.
Inner voice traverses WT$_{C\sharp}$, three or four notes at a time: (C♯)–D♯–F–G–A–B.

INTERACTION BETWEEN SCALES

Each of the collections we have discussed has a distinctive quality determined by the intervals that dominate it. Diatonic and pentatonic collections feature many perfect fourths and fifths; octatonic collections feature minor thirds and tritones; hexatonic collections feature major thirds; whole-tone collections feature major seconds, major thirds, and tritones. When music shifts from one of these collections to another, some shared elements may remain, but the sound of the music changes.

The octatonic and diatonic collections have particularly strong affinities. Both are rich in triads, which can function as pivots between them.

41.18 Igor Stravinsky, *Symphony of Psalms*

At first, we hear an E minor triad in the context of $OCT_{C\sharp D}$ on E: E–F–G–A♭–B♭–B–(C♯)–D. . . .

. . . Later, the E minor triad comes back, but now the context is $DIA_{0\sharp}$ on E (E Phrygian): E–F–G–A–B–C–D.

The E minor triad is common to both collections and functions as a pivot in the modulation between them.

A change in collection can mark a formal division in the music.

41.19 Claude Debussy, *Voiles*

From a whole-tone collection on B♭: B♭–C–D–E–F♯–A♭ . . .

> . . . to a pentatonic collection also on B♭: B♭–D♭–E♭–G♭–A♭.

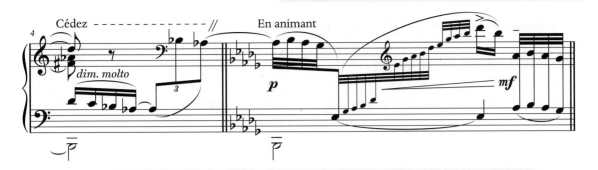

> B♭ is the centric tone in both collections. They also share F♯ and A♭. These three common tones smooth the modulation between the contrasting collections.

Or a change in collection can be a source of harmonic contrast.

41.20 **Joan Tower,** *Vast Antique Cubes*

> Ascending scale through OCT$_{C♯D}$

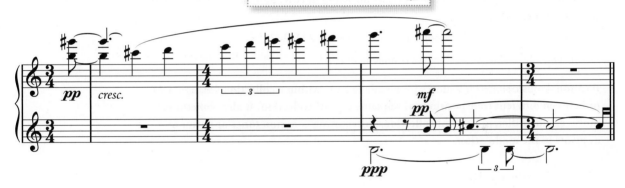

> The ascending scale returns, but now through WT$_{C♯}$. The scale is doubled in parallel major thirds.

For more on the octatonic, hexatonic, and whole-tone scales, see A Closer Look.

POINTS FOR REVIEW

- **There are three octatonic collections, each consisting of two diminished seventh chords.**
  - Octatonic collections can be arranged as scales of alternating semitones and whole tones (1–2–1–2–1–2–1 or 2–1–2–1–2–1–2).
  - Octatonic collections contain major and minor triads, and dominant and minor seventh chords. These chords are related by transposition at the minor third and the tritone.
  - Any two octatonic collections share a diminished seventh chord in common.

- **There are four hexatonic collections, each consisting of two augmented triads related by semitone.**
  - Hexatonic collections can be arranged as scales of alternating semitones and minor thirds (1–3–1–3–1–3 or 3–1–3–1–3–1).
  - Hexatonic collections contain major and minor triads related by transposition at the major third.
  - Any two hexatonic collections either share an augmented triad or are complementary.

- **There are two whole-tone collections, each consisting of two augmented triads related by whole tone.**
  - Whole-tone collections have only one scalar ordering: 2–2–2–2–2.
  - The two whole-tone collections are complementary.

- **Post-tonal music sometimes moves from scale to scale within a collection (changing 1̂) or between different transpositions of the same type of collection. It also sometimes moves among different types of collections, often using common tones or harmonies as pivots in the modulation.**

TEST YOURSELF

1. Identify the following scales

   a.

   b.

c.

d.

e.

2. Write out the following scales using letter names.

   a. HEX$_{C\sharp D}$ on F

   b. OCT$_{C\sharp D}$ on F

   c. OCT$_{DE\flat}$ on F

   d. WT$_C$ on E

   e. HEX$_{CD\flat}$ on A

3. Each of the following harmonies are contained by at least two collections. What are they?

   a. C^7 (C–E–G–B♭)

   b. E major triad (E–G♯–B)

   c. C♯–E–G–B♭

   d. F–A–C♯

chapter 42

Triadic Post-Tonality

Some post-tonal music uses major and minor triads in nontraditional ways.

Triadic Transformation
    L, P, R, and SLIDE
    Chains and maps

Parallel Motion (Planing)

Triads with Added Notes

Bitonal and Bi-triadic Music

A Closer Look
    Triadic chains
    Traditional progressions recomposed

In tonal music, triadic progressions are defined by chord function (**T**onic, **D**ominant, or **S**ubdominant), and voice leading typically follows well-defined guidelines (for example, dissonances must resolve). Post-tonal music often still uses triads, but they are not usually constrained by tonal norms.

TRIADIC TRANSFORMATION

L, P, R, AND SLIDE

A **triadic transformation** is a nontraditional way of relating one major or minor triad to another. The most common transformations of triads keep one or two common tones and move the remaining note or notes by semitone or whole tone. They also involve a change of quality: a major triad goes to minor or vice versa. The four principal transformations are called **L** (for **L**eading-tone exchange), **P** (for **P**arallel), **R** (for **R**elative), and **SLIDE**.

42.1 Triadic transformations

	TRANSFORMATION		EXAMPLE (STARTING ON C MAJOR)
L (Leading-tone exchange)	Hold two notes forming a minor third in common. The remaining voice moves by semitone.	The third of a major triad becomes the root of a minor triad (and vice versa).	C+ ←—L—→ E−
P (Parallel)	Hold two notes forming a perfect fifth in common. The remaining voice moves by semitone.	Major and minor triads share the same root.	C+ ←—P—→ C−
R (Relative)	Hold two notes forming a major third in common. The remaining voice moves by whole tone.	The root of a major triad becomes the third of a minor triad (and vice versa).	C+ ←—R—→ A−
SLIDE	Hold the third of the triads in common. Root and fifth move by semitone.	Major and minor triads share the same third.	C+ ←—SLIDE—→ C♯−

In post-tonal music, + and − are used to identify major and minor triads, respectively. Do not confuse a + used to label a major triad with the symbol for an augmented triad.

42.2 Alfred Schnittke, *Hymnus II*

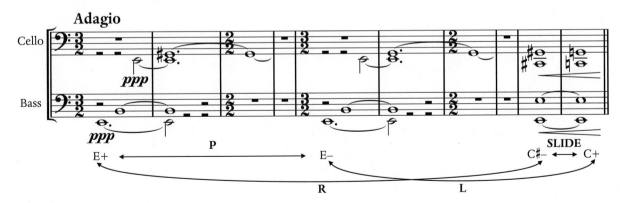

42.3 Suzanne Farrin, "Unico spirto," from *Dolce la morte*

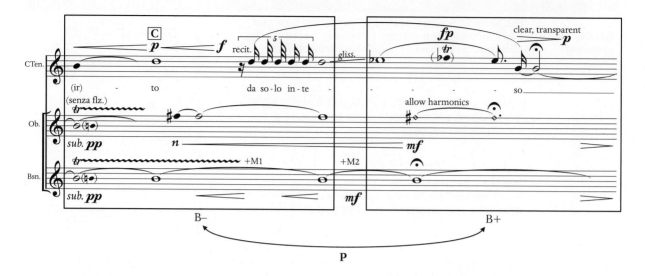

CHAINS AND MAPS

Sometimes triadic transformations are linked into chains that span three or more chords. Among the most common chains are **L–P** and **P–SLIDE**. These chains eventually lead back to the chord they started on, but music rarely traverses a chain in its entirety. Still, it can be revealing to trace a series of triads against a hypothetical complete chain.

42.4 Ellen Taaffe Zwilich, Chamber Concerto for Trumpet and Five Players

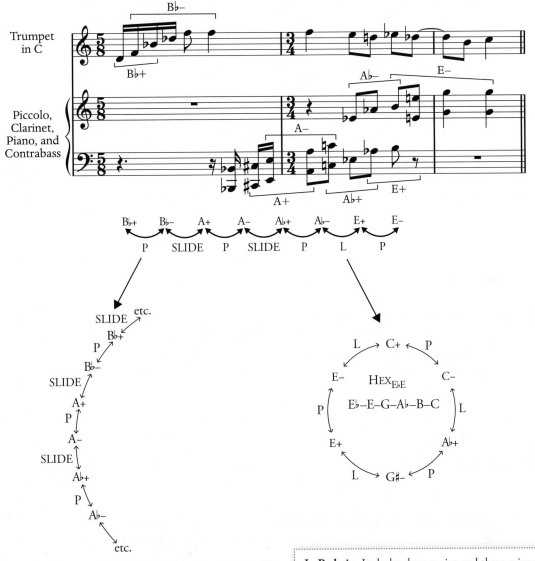

P–SLIDE chain. Complete chain has 24 links (including 12 major and 12 minor triads).

L–P chain. Includes three major and three minor triads, all of which are part of a single hexatonic collection. There are four L–P chains, one for each hexatonic collection.

The major and minor triads and all the triadic transformations can be visualized on a single map (a chart with rows and columns and pathways) called a ***Tonnetz*** (German for "network of tones"). Within each row of the map, triads are related by transposition at the minor third; within each column of the map, triads are related by transposition at the major third. The map wraps around on itself both vertically and horizontally.

42.5 *Tonnetz*

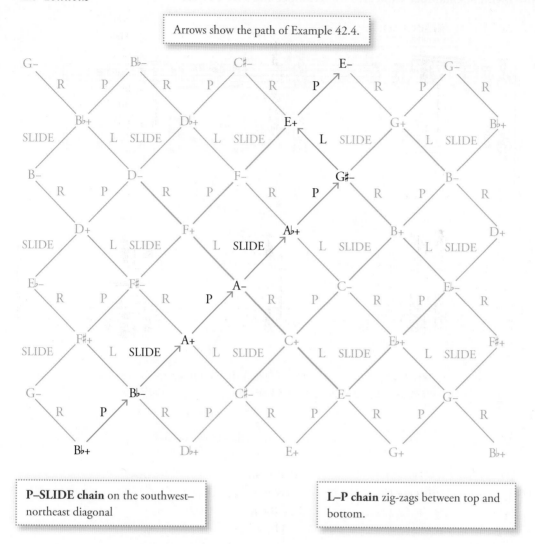

Arrows show the path of Example 42.4.

P–SLIDE chain on the southwest–northeast diagonal

L–P chain zig-zags between top and bottom.

All the progressions discussed so far in this chapter, and many more similar progressions of triads, can be traced as simple, consistent, directed motions on this map.

PARALLEL MOTION (PLANING)

Triads are often used in parallel or similar motion to amplify a melody, a procedure called **planing**. The melody often traverses a familiar scale, and may do so directly, in scale order, or in some more elaborate way. Traditional voice-leading rules that prohibit parallel fifths and octaves are set aside.

42.6 Claude Debussy, *Canope*

Trés calme et doucement triste

Melody in PENT$_C$: C–D–E–G–A. Triads follow in parallel motion. Total collection is DIA$_{1b}$ (with one exceptional B♮).

42.7 Béla Bartók, *Bluebeard's Castle*

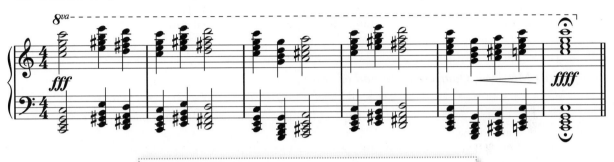

Melody traverses PENT$_C$ on C: C–D–E–G–A. Triads are all major.

TRIADS WITH ADDED NOTES

Harmonies of four or more notes can often be understood as triads with added tones. As long as the triadic root and fifth are clearly audible, pretty much any tone or tones can be added without changing the basic triadic identity of the harmony. Sometimes the added tones can be thought of as extensions of the triad by stacking thirds on top (sevenths, ninths, elevenths, thirteenths). But often in post-tonal music, the added tones cannot be easily understood in this tertian manner (i.e., as a stack of thirds).

42.8

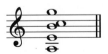

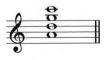

An A minor triad with added 7th and 9th. Stack of thirds: A–C–E–G–B

Possibly an A minor triad with added 7th and 11th and missing 5th. Stack of thirds(?): A–C–(E)–G–(B)–D.

42.9 Igor Stravinsky, *Symphonies of Wind Instruments*

$DIA_{0\sharp/0\flat}$ on C: C–D–E–F–G–A–B. The progression hints at an underlying I^6–vii^{o6}–I progression in C major.

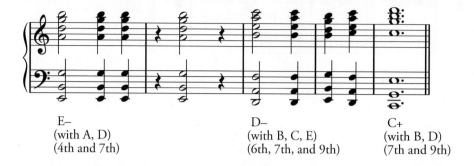

E–
(with A, D)
(4th and 7th)

D–
(with B, C, E)
(6th, 7th, and 9th)

C+
(with B, D)
(7th and 9th)

42.10 Olivier Messiaen, *Quartet for the End of Time*

$OCT_{C\sharp D}$ on E: E–F–G–G$\sharp$–A$\sharp$–B–C$\sharp$–D. Triads have roots related by minor third and tritone.

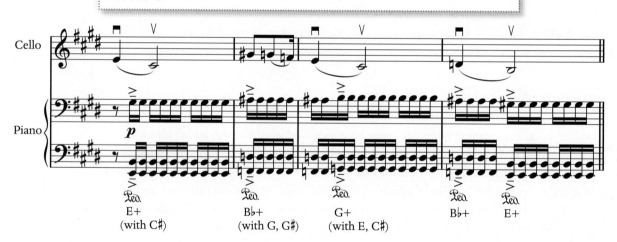

Cello

Piano

E+
(with C$\sharp$)

B$\flat$+
(with G, G$\sharp$)

G+
(with E, C$\sharp$)

B$\flat$+

E+

BITONAL AND BI-TRIADIC MUSIC

Some post-tonal music approaches a state of **bitonality**—sounding in two keys at the same time. If the two keys are closely related, the triads in each key will clash only mildly.

42.11 **Darius Milhaud, "Corcovado," from *Saudades do Brasil***

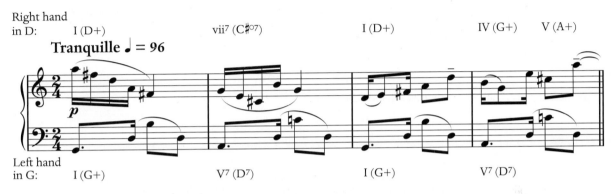

Much post-tonal music is more accurately described as **bi-triadic**—built around a clash between two triads. The competing triads may be in a relationship like **L**, **P**, **R**, or **SLIDE**, or they may be related by a semitone or tritone or some other interval. The more dissonant the interval, the more severe the clash.

42.12 **Alfred Schnittke, *Hymnus II***

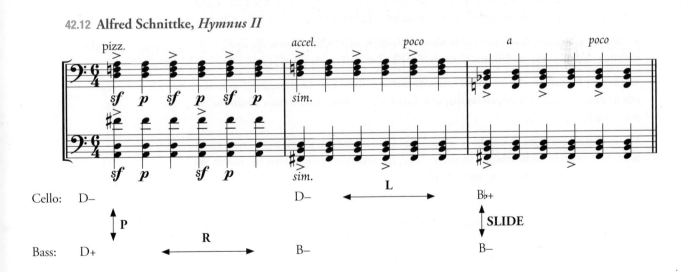

42.13 Igor Stravinsky, *The Rite of Spring*, "Dance of the Young Girls"

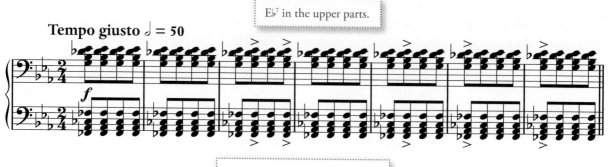

E♭⁷ in the upper parts.

Tempo giusto ♩ = 50

F♭+ triad in the lower parts

For more on chains of triads, see A Closer Look.

POINTS FOR REVIEW

- **Triadic transformations connect a major triad with a minor triad, and vice versa.**
  - **L**-related triads share a common minor third.
  - **R**-related triads share a common major third.
  - **P**-related triads share a common perfect fifth.
  - **SLIDE**-related triads share a common chordal third.
- **Triads may be connected in transformational chains (L–P and P–SLIDE are the most common), and these chains may be visualized on a *Tonnetz*.**
- **Triads are sometimes used in parallel motion, usually to amplify a melody, and without regard to the traditional concern for parallel perfect consonances.**
- **Triads may be encrusted with added tones. Sometimes these may be thought of as tertian extensions (sevenths, ninths, elevenths, and thirteenths). Other non-tertian additions are also possible.**
- **Music that seems to be in two keys at the same time is bitonal; music based on a clash between two triads is bi-triadic. In such a case, the triads may be related by one of the triadic transformations, or in some other way.**

TEST YOURSELF

1. Are the following statements true or false?
   a. A triadic transformation connects a major triad to a minor triad.
   b. A triadic transformation connects a minor triad to a minor triad.

c. Triads related by a triadic transformation share one or two tones.

d. The tones that are not shared in a triadic transformation may be connected by any interval.

2. Match the triadic transformation with its description.

L   Triads share a common chordal third, with the remaining two notes moving by semitone (like C major and C♯ minor).

P   Triads share a major third, with the remaining note moving by whole tone (like C major and A minor).

R   Triads share a minor third, with the remaining note moving by semitone (like C major and E minor).

SLIDE   Triads share a perfect fifth, with the remaining note moving by semitone (like C major and C minor).

3. Write the next two triads in the following transformational chains:

                      P   L   P   L

a. A+ (A–C♯–E) ⟷ A– (A–C–E) ⟷ F+ (F–A–C) ⟷ _____ ⟷ _____

                    SLIDE   P   SLIDE   P

b. G♯– (G♯–B–D♯) ⟷ G+ (G–B–D) ⟷ G– (G–B♭–D) ⟷ _____ ⟷ _____

4. When triads are used in parallel motion (planing), is it okay to write parallel fifths and octaves?

5. The following chords are triads with added notes. Identify the triads and calculate the added tones according to their interval above the root of the triad.

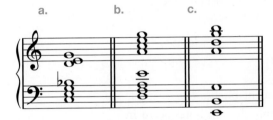

    a.   b.   c.

6. The following chords are bi-triadic. Identify the two triads in each, and name the relationship between them (whether triadic transformation or simple transposition).

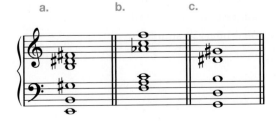

    a.   b.   c.

Intervals (counted in semitones) are the basic units of post-tonal harmony.

Pitch and Pitch Intervals
    Enharmonic equivalence
    Ordered and unordered pitch intervals
    Intervallic motives

Pitch Class and Pitch-Class Intervals
    Octave equivalence
    Ordered and unordered pitch-class intervals
    Interval inversion and interval class

A Closer Look
    Interval cycles
    Cyclic harmonies

PITCH AND PITCH INTERVALS

ENHARMONIC EQUIVALENCE

Tonal music distinguishes between enharmonically equivalent pitches (for example A♯ and B♭). The difference in spelling has a musical meaning: the two notes occur in different diatonic scales and have different melodic tendencies. The same is true for intervals: in tonal music, enharmonically equivalent intervals (for example, a minor third from G to B♭ and an augmented second from G to A♯) have different musical meanings. In post-tonal music, however, spelling is largely a matter of convenience: notes and intervals that are enharmonically equivalent are understood to be musically equivalent. Accordingly, we will usually identify post-tonal intervals simply by distance in semitones.

43.1

> In analyzing tonal music, these intervals are labeled differently.

minor 3rd   augmented 2nd

3 semitones   3 semitones

> But in analyzing post-tonal music, these intervals are labeled the same way, as three semitones apart.

43.2 Anton Webern, "Wie bin ich froh!" Op. 25, No. 1

major 7th   diminished 8ve   major 7th

11 semitones   11 semitones   11 semitones

> Whether spelled as major sevenths or diminished octaves, these intervals are all labeled as eleven semitones.

43.3

TRADITIONAL NAME	NO. OF SEMITONES
perfect unison	0
minor 2nd	1
major 2nd, diminished 3rd	2
minor 3rd, augmented 2nd	3
major 3rd, diminished 4th	4
augmented 3rd, perfect 4th	5
augmented 4th, diminished 5th	6
perfect 5th, diminished 6th	7
augmented 5th, minor 6th	8
major 6th, diminished 7th	9
augmented 6th, minor 7th	10
major 7th, diminished 8ve	11
perfect octave	12
minor 9th	13
major 9th	14
minor 10th	15
major 10th	16

ORDERED AND UNORDERED PITCH INTERVALS

The interval between two pitches can be labeled in two ways:

- An **ordered pitch interval (opi)** identifies the number of semitones between the pitches *and* the direction (up or down) from the first note to the second (using plus and minus signs). Identify an interval this way when you are interested in both its size and direction.

- An **unordered pitch interval (upi)** identifies the number of semitones alone, without regard to direction or which pitch comes first. Identify an interval this way when you are interested only in the distance between two pitches.

43.4

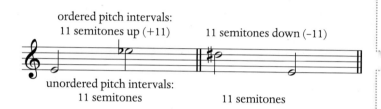

Ordered pitch intervals indicate distance (in semitones) and direction from the first note to the second note (+ = up; − = down).

Unordered pitch intervals indicate only distance, *not* direction, and thus which note comes first is irrelevant.

43.5 Anton Webern, "Wie bin ich froh!" Op. 25, No. 1

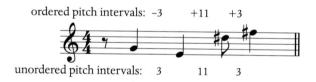

INTERVALLIC MOTIVES

Two or more intervals (ordered or unordered pitch intervals) may be combined into a distinctive musical shape called a **motive**. The intervals within a motive are enclosed within angle brackets: <first interval, second interval, third interval, etc.>.

43.6 Anton Webern, "Wie bin ich froh!" Op. 25, No. 1

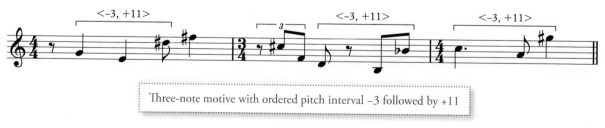

Three-note motive with ordered pitch interval −3 followed by +11

43.7 Igor Stravinsky, "Music to hear," from *Three Shakespeare Songs*

Three-note motive with unordered pitch intervals 8 and 10 moving in opposite directions with either interval coming first

PITCH CLASS AND PITCH-CLASS INTERVALS

OCTAVE EQUIVALENCE

Because octave-related pitches sound roughly equivalent, music notation gives them the same name: a B♭ is a B♭ regardless of register. A *pitch* is a specific point on the continuum of audible sound (the eighty-eight keys of the piano keyboard, for example, correspond to eighty-eight different pitches). A **pitch class (pc)** is group of pitches related by octave, and thus with the same (or enharmonic) name.

43.8

Although these are different pitches, they are the same *pitch class*, since they all are C♯/D♭.

43.9 Shulamit Ran, *Verticals* for piano

The circled notes are different pitches, but the same pitch classes: D♯, G♯, and A.

There are twelve pitch classes, and it can be helpful to visualize them on the **pitch-class clockface**.

43.10

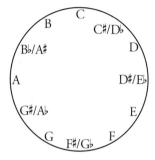

Instead of letter names, the twelve pitch classes can also be represented by **numbers** 0–11, with C as 0 (zero).

43.11

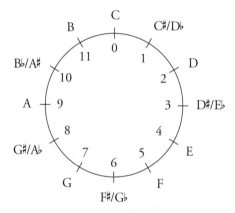

ORDERED AND UNORDERED PITCH-CLASS INTERVALS

A pitch-class interval is the distance between two pitch classes.

43.12

> Although these are different *pitch intervals* (the pitches are separated by different numbers of semitones) they are the same *pitch-class interval*, since they all involve a motion from G to B♭/A♯.

An **ordered pitch-class interval (opci)** is the distance *from* one pitch class *to* another. To find the pitch-class interval using letter names, use the staff or the pitch clockface. Using the staff, you can write the notes within the same octave with the first note as the lower note, then count the semitones upward from the first note to the second.

43.13

Task: **Use the staff to figure out the ordered pitch-class intervals from A to C♯, F♯ to E, and E♭ to B.**

Alternatively, you can use the pitch-class clockface. Circle the two notes on the pitch-class clockface, then count the semitones from the first note to the second, moving clockwise.

43.14

Task: **Use the pitch-class clockface to figure out the ordered pitch-class intervals from A to C♯, F♯ to E, and E♭ to B.**

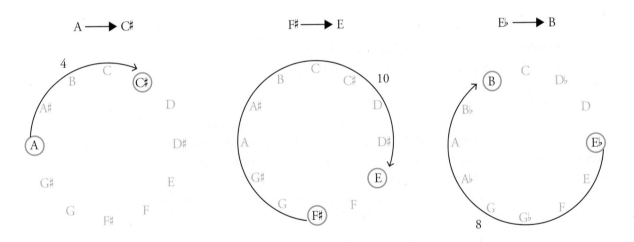

To find the pitch-class interval between two pitch classes using numbers, subtract the first pitch class from the second. If you get a negative number, just add 12. That's because in the world of octave-equivalent pitch classes, adding or subtracting 12 is the same as going up or down an octave: it doesn't change the pitch class or the pitch-class interval.

Task: **Use pitch-class numbers to figure out the ordered pitch-class intervals from A to C♯, F♯ to E, and E♭ to B.**

Notes:	A ⟶ C♯	F♯ ⟶ E	E♭ ⟶ B
Pitch-class numbers:	9 ⟶ 1	6 ⟶ 4	3 ⟶ 11
Subtract the first note from the second:	1 − 9 = −8	4 − 6 = −2	11 − 3 = ⑧
Add 12 if necessary:	−8 + 12 = ④	−2 + 12 = ⑩	

Subtract the first note from the second. Then, if you get a negative number, add 12.

43.16 **Igor Stravinsky, "Music to hear," from** *Three Shakespeare Songs*

Although the bracketed notes form different pitch intervals, they form the same successions of *ordered pitch-class intervals*: either <8, 2, 1> or <4, 10, 11>. These are intervallic motives.

An **unordered pitch-class interval (upci)** is the shortest distance between two pitch classes, without regard to which comes first. Whereas ordered pitch-class intervals are always calculated upward (or clockwise) from the first note to the second, unordered pitch-class intervals are calculated as the shortest distance between two pitch classes, either up or down. To find the unordered pitch-class interval between two pitch-classes using numbers, find the pitch-class interval from the first note to the second and from the second to the first. The smaller of the two ordered pitch-class intervals is the unordered pitch-class interval.

To find the unordered pitch-class interval using the staff, write the notes within the same octave in two ways—with either note as the lower note. The smaller of the two intervals is the unordered pitch-class interval.

43.17

Task: **Use the staff to figure out the unordered pitch-class intervals between A and C♯, F♯ and E, and E♭ and B.**

To find the unordered pitch-class interval using the pitch-class clockface, first circle the two notes on the pitch-class clockface. Then choose the shortest route between them, either clockwise or counterclockwise, and count the semitones.

43.18

Task: **Use the pitch-class clockface to figure out the unordered pitch-class intervals between A and C♯, F♯ and E, and E♭ and B.**

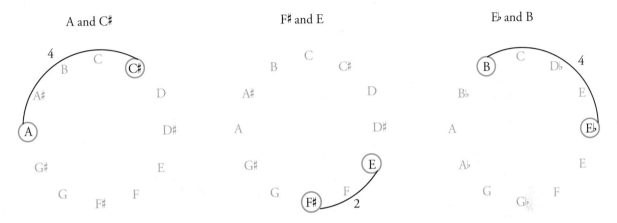

You can also determine the unordered pitch-class interval between two notes by comparing the two possible ordered pitch-class intervals—that is, the two values depending on which note is first. Find the two ordered pitch-class intervals by subtracting the first number from the second and the second from the first. The unordered pitch-class interval is the smaller of the two values.

43.19

Task: **Use pitch-class numbers to figure out the unordered pitch-class intervals between A and C♯, F♯ and E, and E♭ and B.**

Notes:	A and C♯	F♯ and E	E♭ and B
Pitch-class numbers:	9 and 1	6 and 4	3 and 11
Subtract the first note from the second:	1 − 9 = −8 = ④	4 − 6 = −2 = 10	11 − 3 = 8
Subtract the second note from the first:	9 − 1 = 8	6 − 4 = ②	3 − 11 = −8 = ④

Ordered pitch-class intervals give more specific information. Unordered pitch-class intervals permit greater generalization.

43.20 Igor Stravinsky, "Music to hear," from *Three Shakespeare Songs*

The bracketed notes have the same unordered pitch-class intervals in the same order: <4, 2, 1>. <4, 2, 1> is an intervallic motive.

INTERVAL INVERSION AND INTERVAL CLASS

There are eleven different ordered pitch-class intervals, containing between 1 and 11 semitones. Using **interval inversion**, we can relate every interval larger than a tritone to an interval smaller than a tritone [for example, a major third (4) and a minor sixth (8)]. Ordered pitch-class intervals that combine to make up an octave (that sum to 12) are related by interval inversion.

43.21 Pairs of ordered pitch-class intervals related by interval inversion (sum to 12)

1 and 11	2 and 10	3 and 9	4 and 8	5 and 7	6 and 6

With interval inversion, the eleven ordered pitch-class intervals can be reduced to only six unordered pitch-class intervals, containing 1–6 semitones. An unordered pitch-class interval is also called an **interval class (ic)**. Just as a pitch class contains many pitches, an interval class contains—and can be realized by—many different pitch intervals. For pitch intervals that are negative or larger than 12, add or subtract 12 as needed to bring them into range. (Adding or subtracting an octave does not change the identity of a pitch-class interval.)

An interval can be understood and described in different ways, ranging from more concrete to more abstract. Ultimately, every interval belongs to one of the six interval classes.

43.22

Interval inversion

EXAMPLE	SOME ORDERED PITCH INTERVALS	ORDERED PITCH-CLASS INTERVAL	INTERVAL CLASS (UNORDERED PITCH-CLASS INTERVAL)	ORDERED PITCH-CLASS INTERVAL	SOME ORDERED PITCH INTERVALS	EXAMPLE
A–B♭	+1, –11 +13, –23	1	1	11	–1, +11 –13, +23	B♭–A
A–B	+2, –10 +14, –22	2	2	10	–2, +10 –14, +22	B–A
A–C	+3, –9 +15, –21	3	3	9	–3, +9 –15, +21	C–A
A–C#	+4, –8 +16, –20	4	4	8	–4, +8 –16, +20	C#–A
A–D	+5, –7 +17, –19	5	5	7	–5, +7 –17, +19	D–A
A–E♭	+6, –6 +18, –18	6	6	6	–6, +6 –18, +18	E♭–A

There are four different ways of describing an interval in post-tonal music. Choose the one that best reflects the musical relationship you are describing.

43.23

	DIRECTION IS IMPORTANT	DIRECTION IS NOT IMPORTANT
OCTAVE POSITION IS IMPORTANT	Ordered pitch intervals	Unordered pitch intervals
OCTAVE POSITION IS NOT IMPORTANT— OCTAVE EQUIVALENCE ASSUMED	Ordered pitch-class intervals	Unordered pitch-class intervals (interval class)

To learn about interval cycles, see A Closer Look.

POINTS FOR REVIEW

- Intervals in post-tonal music are counted in semitones, and enharmonic equivalence is assumed.

- An ordered pitch interval is the number of semitones between two pitches and the direction (up or down) from the first pitch to the second.

- An unordered pitch interval is the number of semitones between two pitches, without regard to direction or which pitch comes first.

- A pitch class is a collection of pitches related by one or more octaves (octave equivalence). Pitches in a pitch class have the same (or enharmonic) letter name.

- Pitch classes may be identified by numbers 0–11 (C = 0; C♯/D♭ = 1, D = 2, and so on).

- An ordered pitch-class interval is the number of semitones from one pitch class to another, counting upward (or clockwise on the pitch-class clockface).

- An unordered pitch-class interval or interval class is the shortest distance between two pitch classes (counting up or down, clockwise or counterclockwise, without regard to which pitch comes first).

- Pairs of ordered pitch-class intervals are related by inversion (1 and 11, 2 and 10, 3 and 9, 4 and 8, 5 and 7, 6 and 6). Each of these complementary pairs represents one unordered pitch-class interval (interval class).

- Intervals may be combined into recognizable shapes called motives. The intervals involved may be any of the four types discussed in this chapter: ordered and unordered pitch or pitch-class intervals.

TEST YOURSELF

1. Which of the following pairs of notes are enharmonic equivalents?
   a. A♭/G♯
   b. A♯/B♭
   c. E♭/F♭
   d. B♯/C
   e. F♯/G♭
   f. E♯/F♭

2. Give the number of semitones in these diatonic intervals:
   a. minor second
   b. perfect fifth
   c. augmented fourth
   d. major ninth
   e. augmented sixth

3. Identify these intervals in four ways: as ordered pitch intervals, unordered pitch intervals, ordered pitch-class intervals, and unordered pitch-class intervals.

	ORDERED PITCH INTERVALS	UNORDERED PITCH INTERVALS	ORDERED PITCH-CLASS INTERVALS	UNORDERED PITCH-CLASS INTERVALS

4. Identify the interval class to which each of these ordered pitch intervals belongs:

a. −9

b. +14

c. −11

d. +28

e. +3

f. +18

g. −8

h. +14

i. −7

chapter 44   Pitch-Class Sets: Trichords

Collections of notes (pitch-class sets), and especially collections of three notes (trichords), are basic harmonic, melodic, and motivic units in much post-tonal music.

Pitch-Class Sets	A Closer Look
Transposition	Interval-class content
Inversion	Common tones under transposition
Set Class	Composing-out
Composing with Pitch-Class Sets	

Just as triads are the basic building blocks of traditional tonal music, pitch-class sets are the basic harmonic units in post-tonal music. Pitch-class sets are related in a variety of ways, and may be presented as melodies, motives, chords, or some combination of these. They may be of any size, but three-note sets (trichords) are especially common and useful for study.

PITCH-CLASS SETS

A **pitch-class set** is an unordered collection of pitch classes. If the set contains three notes, it is called a **trichord**.

44.1

> The same trichord written in three different ways. The trichord consists of its three pitch classes: A♭/G♯, E♭/D♯, and D. The order, register, and spelling of the notes does not matter.

For convenience, we write the notes of a pitch-class set in **normal form**: in ascending order within an octave (like a scale), with the smallest possible interval between the lowest and highest notes.

44.2

> To figure out the *normal form* of this trichord . . .

> . . . first arrange the notes in ascending order within an octave in three different ways, starting on each of the three different notes. . . .

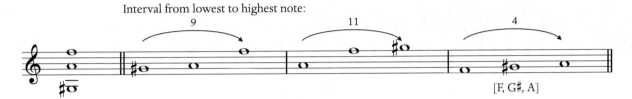

Interval from lowest to highest note:

[F, G♯, A]

> . . . and the one with the smallest interval from lowest to highest is the normal form—in this case, [F, G♯, A]. Normal forms are written in square brackets.

44.3 Anton Webern, Five Movements for String Quartet, Op. 5, No. 2

Viola

Violin II

Cello

> Both groups of notes consist only of G, B, and C♯, but the notes occur in different registers and in a different order.

> The notes of this trichord can be arranged in ascending order in three ways:
>
> 6
> G–B–C♯
>
> 8
> B–C♯–G
>
> 10
> C♯–G–B
>
> Normal form is [G, B, C♯]—smallest interval from lowest to highest.

TRANSPOSITION

To **transpose** a pitch-class set, move each note in the set by the same ordered pitch-class interval (upward on the staff; clockwise on the pitch-class clockface). Transpositions are labeled with the letter T plus a subscript number that indicates the **interval of transposition**. For instance, T_3 means "transpose each note in a set upward (or clockwise) by three pitch-class semitones."

44.4

Task: **Transpose [F, G♯, A] by three semitones (T_3).**

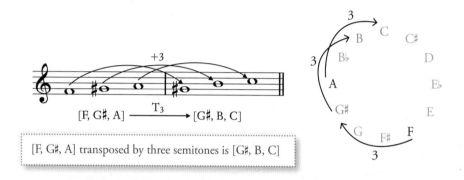

[F, G♯, A] transposed by three semitones is [G♯, B, C]

If two sets are related by transposition, their normal forms will have the same intervals in the same order.

44.5

The first trichord is transposed six semitones to the second trichord, or T_6 . . .

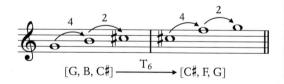

. . . thus the normal forms of these trichords have the same intervals in the same order: <4, 2>.

44.6

Task: **Figure out if the circled trichords (in Chen Yi's *Northern Scenes*) are related by transposition. If so, indicate the interval of transposition.**

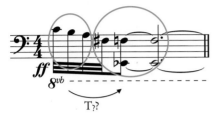

1. Put each trichord into its normal form (ascending within an octave with the smallest interval from lowest to highest note):

[A, B, C]   [E♭, F, F♯]

2. Figure out if the two sets have the same intervals in the same order; if so, they are related by transposition:

> Both trichords have the same intervals in the same order: <2, 1>. They are thus related by transposition.

3. Figure out the interval of transposition. It will be the ordered pitch-class interval from the first note of the first set to the first note of the second set. Corresponding notes of the two sets will be related by this interval:

> Six semitones from A to E♭
> Six semitones from B to F
> Six semitones from C to F♯

> The circled trichords are related by transposition at T_6.

[A, B, C] [E♭, F, F♯]

T_6

We can also use the pitch-class numbers to transpose sets and, if two sets are related by transposition, to calculate the interval of transposition. To transpose a set, add the interval of transposition to each note in the set. You will need to subtract 12 from any number larger than 11.

44.7

Task: **Transpose [C♯, F, G] by T₁₀, using pitch-class numbers.**

1. Write out the set using numbers:

   [C♯, F, G] = [1, 5, 7]

2. Add the interval of transposition (10) to each note in the set:

   1 + 10 = 11

   5 + 10 = 15

   7 + 10 = 17

3. Subtract 12 from any numbers greater than 11:

   11

   15 − 12 = 3

   17 − 12 = 5

4. The results can be translated into pitch names:

   [C♯, F, G]   [B, E♭, F]

   [1, 5, 7]   [11, 3, 5]

   T_{10}

   To calculate the interval of transposition, subtract a note in the first set from the corresponding note in the second set. You may need to add 12 to be sure your subtraction results in a number between 0 and 11. Adding or subtracting 12 does not change the identity of a pitch class—it is the same as moving a note up or down by an octave.

44.8

Task: **Using pitch-class numbers, figure out the interval of transposition for two sets related by transposition: [A, C♯, D] and [E, G♯, A].**

1. Write out the sets using numbers:

   [9, 1, 2] and [4, 8, 9]

2. Subtract the first note in the first set from the first note in the second set:

   4 − 9 = −5

3. If the subtraction results in a negative number, add 12 to produce a number between 0 and 11.

   −5 + 12 = 7

4. Confirm the result by subtracting the other corresponding notes:

   The second note in each set: 8 − 1 = 7

   The third note in each set: 9 − 2 = 7

5. The results can be translated into pitch names:

   [A, C♯, D]   [E, G♯, A]

   [9, 1, 2]   [4, 8, 9]

   T_7

INVERSION

Pitch-class sets can also be **inverted**. The inversion of a pitch-class set flips its intervals upside down.

44.9

> The lowest interval in the first set (1) becomes the highest interval in the second set; the highest interval in the first set (3) becomes the lowest interval in the second set. The sets are thus related by inversion.

Pitch-class inversion (I) can be visualized on the pitch-class clockface: each note inverts onto its **complement**, reflected across an axis that runs through C and F♯. Each pitch class is related by inversion to its complement.

44.10

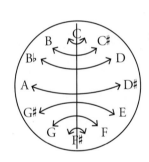

C is its own complement.   C ◄ I ► C

B and C♯ are complements.   B ◄ I ► C♯

B♭ and D are complements.   B♭ ◄ I ► D

A and D♯ are complements.   A ◄ I ► D♯

G♯ and E are complements.   G♯ ◄ I ► E

G and F are complements.   G ◄ I ► F

F♯ is its own complement.   F♯ ◄ I ► F♯

Sets related by inversion are mirror images of each other on the pitch-class clockface.

44.11

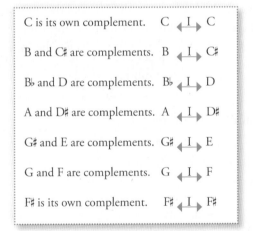

[A, B♭, C♯] ◄——I——► [B, D, D♯]

Inversion (I) means "invert around C." That is, every pitch class that is a certain number of semitones below C in the original set is swapped with a pitch class the same number of semitones above C in the inverted set, and vice versa. *Do not confuse the inversion of a pitch-class set with the familiar inversion of a triad (as in its first and second inversions)—these are not the same thing!*

44.12

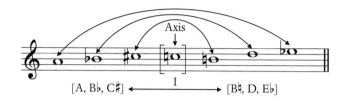

A is three semitones below C . . .

B♭ is two semitones below C . . .

C♯ is one semitone above C . . .

. . . E♭ is three semitones above C.

. . . D is two semitones above C.

. . . B is one semitone below C.

After a set is inverted (I), it can also be transposed in the usual way (T_n). Thus, for instance, T_9I means "first invert the pitch-class set around C (I) and then transpose up 9 semitones (T_9)." Inversion (T_nI) is thus a compound operation comprising inversion (I) followed by transposition (T_n). In the expression T_nI, n is called the **index of inversion**. Remember: In the compound operation T_nI, invert first, then transpose.

44.13

Task: **Invert and transpose the trichord [F, G♯, A] by T_9I.**

1. Invert the trichord (I):

   [F, G♯, A] inverts to [D♯, E, G].

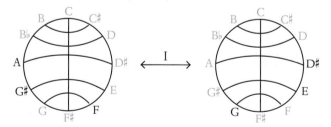

2. Transpose the inverted trichord up 9 semitones.

   [D♯, E, G] transposed up 9 semitones is [C, C♯, E].

$$[F, G♯, A] \xleftrightarrow{\quad T_9I \quad} [C, C♯, E]$$

Note that inversion works in both directions. If T_9I relates [F, G♯, A] to [C, C♯, E], it also relates [C, C♯, E] to [F, G♯, A]. That is why the arrows that connect I-related sets are double-headed.

44.14

Task: **Figure out if two sets are related by inversion and, if so, identify the index of inversion.**

1. Put the sets in normal form and compare the intervals. If they have same intervals in reverse order, they are related by inversion.

<2, 3> and < 3, 2> are the same intervals in reverse order, so these sets are related by inversion.

2. Invert one set by replacing each note with its complement. (It doesn't matter which set you start with because the inversion will be the same either way.) Write it in reverse order (it will now be in normal form) and compare it to the other set (the sets are now related by transposition).

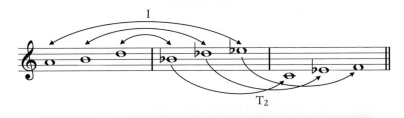

When inverted, A becomes E♭, B becomes D♭, and D becomes B♭.

3. The original sets are related by inversion at T_2I.

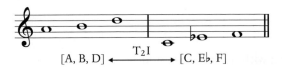

Task: **Determine if the circled sets (in Hale Smith's *Three Brevities* for Solo Flute, No. 2) are related by inversion, and if so, find the index of inversion.**

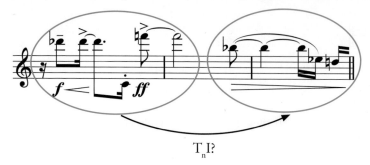

$$T_nI?$$

1. Put the sets in normal form and compare the intervals. If the same intervals occur in reverse order, the sets are related by inversion:

1	4		4	1

   [C, Db, F]   [Bb, D, Eb]

2. Invert either of the sets:

   [C, Db, F] inverts to [G, B, C].

3. Compare the newly inverted first set with the original second set (they are now related by transposition):

   $$[G, B, C] \xrightarrow{T_3} [Bb, D, Eb]$$

4. The original sets are related by inversion at T_3I.

   $$[C, Db, F] \xleftrightarrow{T_3I} [Bb, D, Eb]$$

We can use the pitch-class numbers to invert sets and, if two sets are related by inversion, to calculate the index of inversion. To invert a set, subtract each note from the index of inversion. You may need to add 12 to the result to avoid negative numbers.

44.16

Task: **Invert [C♯, D, F♯] by T_5I, using pitch-class numbers.**

1. Write out the set using numbers:

   [C♯, D, F♯] = [1, 2, 6]

2. Subtract each note from the index of inversion (5), starting with the last note. Add 12 if needed to avoid negative numbers:

   $5 - 6 = -1$, then $-1 + 12 = 11$
   $5 - 2 = 3$
   $5 - 1 = 4$

3. The results can be translated into pitch names:

[C♯, D, F♯]   [B, D♯, E]

[1, 2, 6]   [11, 3, 4]

T_5I

 To calculate the index of inversion for two sets in normal form, add the first note in the first set to the last note in the second set. You may need to subtract 12 to arrive at a number between 0 and 11.

44.17

Task: **Using pitch-class numbers, figure out the index of inversion for two sets related by inversion: [E♭, G, B♭] and [A, C, E].**

1. Write out the sets using numbers:

[E♭, G, B♭]   [A, C, E]

[3, 7, 10]   [9, 0, 4]

2. Add the first note in the first set to the last note in the second set:

3 + 4 = 7

3. Confirm the result by adding the other corresponding notes:

The second note in the first set and the second note in the second set: 7 + 0 = 7

The last note in the first set and the first note in the second set: 10 + 9 = 19; 19 − 12 = 7

4. The results can be translated into pitch names:

[E♭, G, B♭]   [A, C, E]

[3, 7, 10]   [9, 0, 4]

T_7I

SET CLASS

All the pitch-class sets related by transposition or inversion make up a **set class**. For a familiar example, the twelve major triads (related to each other by transposition) and the twelve minor triads (also related to each other by transposition) together form a set class of twenty-four members. (The minor triads are related to the major triads by inversion—one has the same intervals reading from bottom to top as the other reading from top to bottom.)

 Set classes are named with their **prime form**. The prime form of a trichord is a string of three numbers starting on 0, and written without spaces or commas and enclosed in parentheses—for example, (025). To find the prime form of a set class:

	EXAMPLE 1	EXAMPLE 2	EXAMPLE 3
1. Start with a set in normal form.	[G, G♯, B]	[G, B, C♯]	[G, B, D]
2. Extract the succession of intervals.	G → G♯ → B 1 3	G → B → C♯ 4 2	G → B → D 4 3
3. Arrange the two intervals so the smaller is on the left.	1 3	2 4	3 4
4. Starting with 0, write the string of three numbers that replicates that pattern of intervals.	0 → 1 → 4 1 3 Prime form = (014)	0 → 2 → 6 2 4 Prime form = (026)	0 → 3 → 7 3 4 Prime form = (037)

There are twelve **trichord classes**, each with its own distinctive intervallic profile and musical sound, and its own prime form. Every possible combination of three notes belongs to one of these twelve trichord classes.

PRIME FORM	REPRESENTATIVE SETS (WRITTEN IN NORMAL FORM STARTING ON C)	IN RELATION TO FAMILIAR SCALES
(012)	<1, 1>	*Chromatic trichord* (any three consecutive notes of the chromatic scale).
(013)	<1, 2> <2, 1>	*Octatonic trichord* (any three consecutive notes of the octatonic scale). Also occurs four times in the diatonic scale.
(014)	<1, 3> <3, 1>	*Hexatonic trichord* (any three consecutive notes of the hexatonic scale).
(015)	<1, 4> <4, 1>	Occurs in both diatonic and hexatonic scales.
(016)	<1, 5> <5, 1>	Occurs in both diatonic and octatonic scales.
(024)	<2, 2>	*Whole-tone trichord* (any three consecutive notes of the whole-tone scale). Also occurs three times in the diatonic scale.

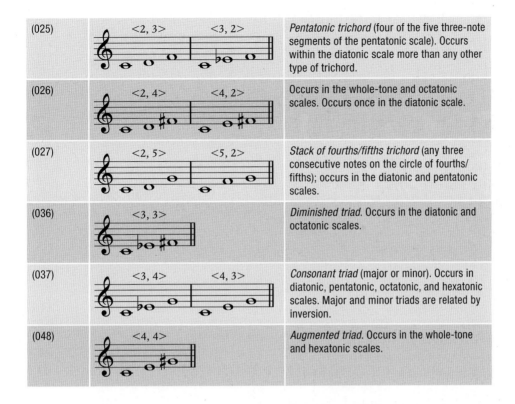

(025)	<2, 3> <3, 2>	*Pentatonic trichord* (four of the five three-note segments of the pentatonic scale). Occurs within the diatonic scale more than any other type of trichord.
(026)	<2, 4> <4, 2>	Occurs in the whole-tone and octatonic scales. Occurs once in the diatonic scale.
(027)	<2, 5> <5, 2>	*Stack of fourths/fifths trichord* (any three consecutive notes on the circle of fourths/fifths); occurs in the diatonic and pentatonic scales.
(036)	<3, 3>	*Diminished triad.* Occurs in the diatonic and octatonic scales.
(037)	<3, 4> <4, 3>	*Consonant triad* (major or minor). Occurs in diatonic, pentatonic, octatonic, and hexatonic scales. Major and minor triads are related by inversion.
(048)	<4, 4>	*Augmented triad.* Occurs in the whole-tone and hexatonic scales.

COMPOSING WITH PITCH-CLASS SETS

Many post-tonal pieces use pitch-class sets as the basic harmonic units and relate them with transposition or inversion. To analyze this music, we have three principal tasks:

- Identify sets belonging to the same set class. Circle them, and label them with their normal and prime forms.
- Connect sets with arrows and label the arrows with the relevant T_n or $T_n I$.
- Try to account for the composer's choice of these particular T_n and $T_n I$. What is the musical motivation for the choice, and what are the musical consequences?

There are three fairly common strategies composers use to relate sets belonging to the same set class:

- *Common tones.* Frequently, composers connect sets related by T_n or $T_n I$ that share notes in common.
- *Motivic transposition.* Composers may transpose a set by an interval it contains—an interval may thus be heard simultaneously within and between the sets.
- *Larger referential collections.* The combination of trichords at particular T_n or $T_n I$ may result in a familiar large collection, such as the diatonic, octatonic, hexatonic, or whole-tone collections.

44.20 George Crumb, "Gargoyles," from *Makrokosmos,* Vol. 2, No. 8

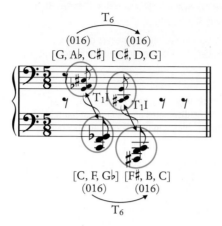

These four sets are all members of set-class (016). Within each hand, the sets are related by transposition at T$_6$. The tritone is thus heard both within and between the sets. This interval of transposition produces two common tones: G–C♯ in both right-hand sets; C–F♯ in both left-hand sets.

44.21 Charles Wuorinen, Twelve Short Pieces, No. 3

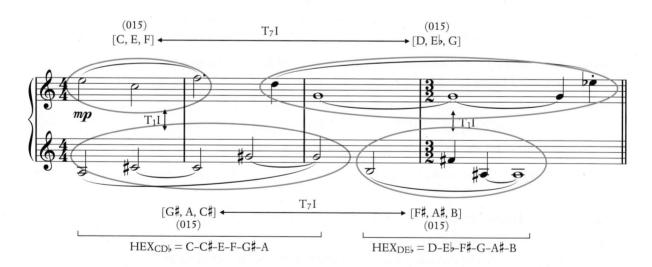

These four sets are all members of set-class (015). Combining sets between right and left hands via T$_1$I results in two complementary hexatonic collections.

44.22

Task: **Analyze a passage of music by identifying sets belonging to the same set class, relating them by transposition (T_n) and inversion (T_nI), and explaining the choice of n (interval of transposition or index of inversion).**

Elisabeth Lutyens, Two Bagatelles, Op. 48, No. 1

1. Listen to and play the passage repeatedly to establish the music in your mind and your fingers.

2. Find an obvious three-note group that might be a basic structural unit (you might have to try out several possibilities before you find one that makes sense for the piece). Put it in normal form and get to know its intervallic identity:

> This three-note chord might be a point of entry into the passage. [C, Eb, E] contains interval-classes 1, 3, and 4. It is from set-class (014).

3. Start to look for other sets in the same set class, related to this one by transposition or inversion. Look for audible groups of notes that occur near each other in time or in register. Identify the T_n or T_nI, and try to explain the choice.

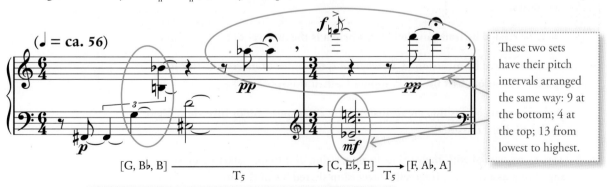

> These two sets have their pitch intervals arranged the same way: 9 at the bottom; 4 at the top; 13 from lowest to highest.

> The same transposition, T_5, that takes us from [G, Bb, B] to [C, Eb, E] also takes us from [C, Eb, E] to [F, Ab, A].

4. Look for less obvious but still musically viable groups of notes that belong to the same set class, and try to relate them to each other and to the more-obvious groups. Groupings may overlap; notes may belong to more than one group.

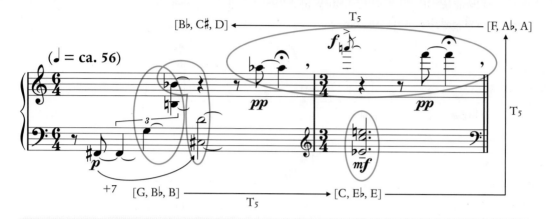

These four forms of (014) are related by T_5. This may relate to the first melodic gesture in the bass, by the complementary interval, seven semitones from F♯ to C♯.

 For more on trichords, see A Closer Look.

POINTS FOR REVIEW

- A pitch-class set is an unordered collection of notes. A trichord is a pitch-class set with three notes.

- A normal form is a convenient way of writing a pitch-class set: in ascending order within an octave, and with the smallest possible interval between the lowest and highest notes.

- Sets may be related by transposition (T_n), where n is the interval of transposition.

- Sets may be related by inversion (T_nI), where n is the index of inversion. This is a compound operation: first invert (I) around C, then transpose (T_n).

- A set class consists of sets that are related by either transposition or inversion. There are twelve trichord classes.

- Set classes are named with their prime form, a string of numbers starting on 0, arranged to make clear the intervallic succession shared by all the members of the set class.

1. Figure out the normal form for these trichords. Write your answer using letter names separated by commas within square brackets.

    a. B♭–A–C♯

    b. E♭–C–B♭

    c. C♯–F♯–A

    d. D–G♯–A

    e. D–E–E♭

2. Transpose these sets as indicated.

    a. [A, B♭, C♯] by T_8

    b. [G♯, C♯, D] by T_4

    c. [B♭, C, E♭] by T_6

    d. [D, E♭, E] by T_2

    e. [F, A♭, C] by T_{11}

3. Identify the T_n that connect each of these pairs of sets.

    a. [A, B♭, C♯] ⟶ [G, A♭, B]

    b. [F♯, A, C♯] ⟶ [D, F, A]

    c. [D, F♯, G♯] ⟶ [C♯, F, G]

    d. [G, A, B♭] ⟶ [D, E, F]

    e. [F, G, B] ⟶ [B, C♯, F]

4. Invert these sets as indicated. Write your answer in normal form.

    a. [A, B♭, C♯] by T_3I

    b. [F♯, A, C♯] by T_8I

    c. [B♭, C, E♭] by T_5I

    d. [B, C, D] by T_9I

    e. [G♯, A♯, C] by T_0I

5. Identify the T_nI that connects these pairs of sets. The sets are given in normal form.

    a. [A, B♭, C♯] ⟶ [F♯, A, B♭]

    b. [G♯, C♯, D] ⟶ [G, A♭, D♭]

    c. [A, B, C] ⟶ [A, B♭, C]

    d. [F♯, A, C♯] ⟶ [G, B, D]

    e. [D, F♯, G] ⟶ [B, C, E]

6. Identify the prime form for these sets given in normal form. Write your answer as a string of three integers, starting on 0, with no spaces or commas, and enclosed within parentheses.

    a. [A, B♭, C♯]

    b. [B♭, D♭, E♭]

    c. [F♯, A, C♯]

    d. [D, E♭, E]

45

Inversional Symmetry

Post-tonal music often features groups of notes that move toward, away from, or balance around a central note or notes.

Wedge Progressions
Inversional Symmetry in Pitch
Inversional Symmetry in Pitch Class

A Closer Look
   Axes of pitch-class symmetry
   Inversionally symmetrical set classes
   (trichords)

Inversional symmetry—an arrangement of notes in register so that the intervals from bottom to top are the same as the intervals from top to bottom—is an important organizing principle in much post-tonal music. Harmonies often balance symmetrically around a central tone or tones, which may take on the role of a traditional tonic. Music may move toward or away from central tones, and the central tones may change, in the manner of traditional modulation. Previous chapters considered the idea of centricity, where a tone could be defined as the principal note in a collection or scale. Inversional symmetry provides a different source of centricity.

WEDGE PROGRESSIONS

In some post-tonal music, notes move symmetrically outward from a central pitch or pitches in an **expanding wedge progression**.

45.1 **Béla Bartók, Bagatelle, Op. 6, No. 2**

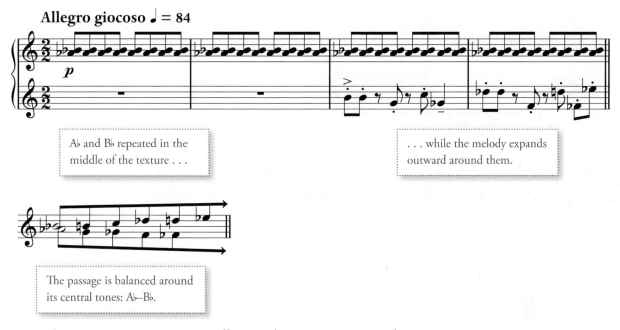

Ab and Bb repeated in the middle of the texture . . .

. . . while the melody expands outward around them.

The passage is balanced around its central tones: Ab–Bb.

Or notes may move symmetrically inward in a **contracting wedge progression**.

45.2 **Béla Bartók, String Quartet No. 5, i**

Convergence on Bb creates a strong cadential effect. Bb is the central tone—a sort of tonic.

45.3 Ruth Crawford Seeger, "In Tall Grass"

Alto

Bees   and a hon-ey-comb

> Melody converges on A from above and below.

INVERSIONAL SYMMETRY IN PITCH

Without necessarily expanding or contracting in a consistent way, pitches may balance around a central pitch: every pitch is as far above the center as a corresponding pitch is below it, and vice versa. The **inversional partners** balance around the central pitch **axis of symmetry**, also called an **inversional axis**.

> Around a sustained B, we hear F♯, seven semitones above, soon balanced by E, seven semitones below. B is the axis of symmetry; E and F♯ are inversional partners.

45.4 Suzanne Farrin, "Unico spirto," from *Dolce la morte*

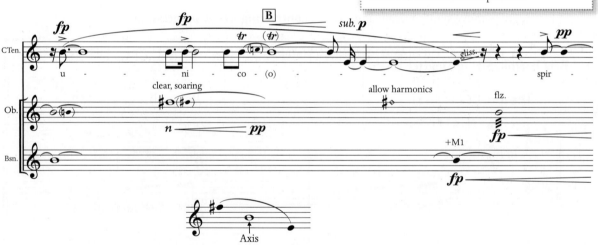

CTen.

u - - - - - - ni - - co - (o) - spir -

Ob.

Bsn.

Axis

45.5 Ross Lee Finney, Fantasy for Solo Violin, i

Adagio ma non troppo ♩ = ca. 66

Axis

> The notes are balanced above and below the central D (the *axis of symmetry*). Each note is heard together with its *inversional partner*.

These axes of symmetry may act as **centric tones**. A shift in the axis of symmetry from one pitch to another can thus have the effect of a modulation from one center to another. The axis may involve a single note or a pair of notes a semitone apart. Music that is inversionally symmetrical in pitch will have the same pitch intervals from bottom to top and top to bottom.

45.6 Béla Bartók, "Subject and Reflection," *Mikrokosmos* **No. 141**

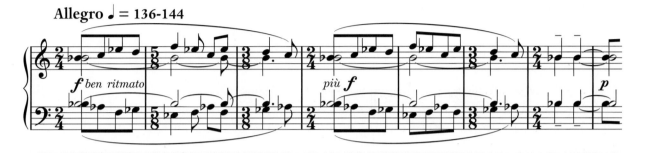

> The "subject" in one voice is balanced against its "reflection" in the other, around the axis B♮, sustained in the middle.

> A bit later in the piece, the subject and reflection both change and so does the axis of symmetry: Now the melodies balance around B, a semitone higher.

45.7

***Task:* Figure out if a harmony in Anton Webern's Five Movements for String Quartet, Op. 5, No. 2 is inversionally symmetrical in pitch and if so, identify its axis of symmetry. Focus on the four-note chord in the viola and cello.**

1. Write the notes of the chord on a staff from lowest to highest and identify the pitch intervals between adjacent notes. The four-note chord is inversionally symmetrical in pitch—the same intervals from bottom to top and top to bottom:

2. Locate the axis right in the middle. In this case, the axis pitches, D/E♭, are not present in the chord, but they are heard in the violins, two and three octaves higher:

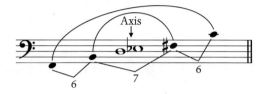

INVERSIONAL SYMMETRY IN PITCH CLASS

A pitch-class set is inversionally symmetrical if it inverts onto itself, that is, if there is a way to invert the set that results in the same pitch classes as the original set. An inversionally symmetrical set can be written as an intervallic *palindrome*—its intervals are the same reading from left to right and right to left.

45.8

> These three sets are written as intervallic palindromes (the same intervals reading from left to right and right to left).

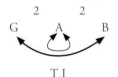
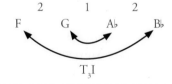
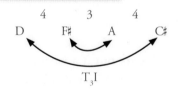

> Inversionally symmetrical sets are related to themselves by inversion. These sets invert onto themselves at the T_nI shown.

An inversionally symmetrical pitch-class set can be arranged in register as a palindrome (the same intervals from bottom to top and top to bottom), but it does not need to be arranged that way. Even if it is not arranged symmetrically in pitch (**pitch symmetry**), it is still symmetrical in pitch class (**pitch-class symmetry**).

45.9

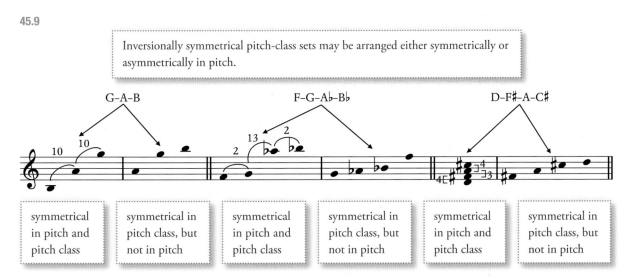

Inversionally symmetrical pitch-class sets may be arranged either symmetrically or asymmetrically in pitch.

| symmetrical in pitch and pitch class | symmetrical in pitch class, but not in pitch | symmetrical in pitch and pitch class | symmetrical in pitch class, but not in pitch | symmetrical in pitch and pitch class | symmetrical in pitch class, but not in pitch |

Pitch-class symmetry is easiest to see on the pitch-class clockface. The notes balance around a central axis, which cuts across the circle at two points a tritone apart, passing either through a note or between two notes. Around that axis, each note is balanced against its inversional partner. Identify pitch-class axes of symmetry by connecting to two tritone-related *poles* with a dash.

45.10

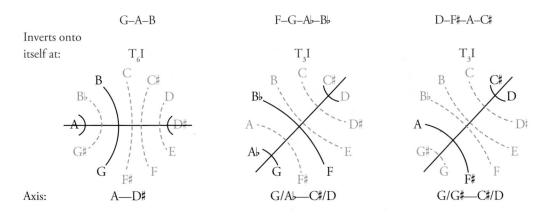

Task: **Figure out if a harmony from Tania León's "Oh Yemanja" (from *Scourge of Hyacinths*) is symmetrical and if so, identify its axis of symmetry.**

1. Indicate the notes of the harmony on a pitch-class clockface. This passage uses only five notes:

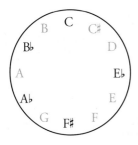

2. Identify the axis around which the notes balance (bearing in mind that a note might balance itself):

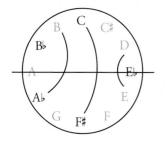

This harmony is symmetrical around E♭—A. It is not arranged symmetrically in register (pitch), but E♭ is strongly emphasized as the bass note. It is a centric tone in two senses: as a sort of tonic note and as an inversional axis.

The inversional axis may change within the music. This is like a change in centric tone or modulation.

45.12 Ruth Crawford Seeger, "Rat Riddles"

Each of the three phrases is organized around a different inversional axis. Notes are slurred to their inversional partners. The third phrase begins as an expanding wedge.

The distances between the axes can be measured in pitch-class intervals: <−3, +1>.

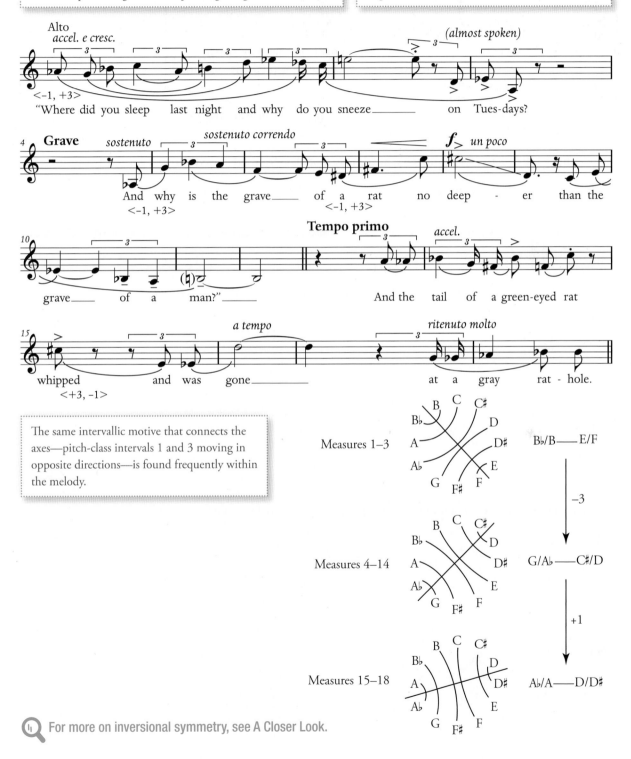

The same intervallic motive that connects the axes—pitch-class intervals 1 and 3 moving in opposite directions—is found frequently within the melody.

🔍 For more on inversional symmetry, see A Closer Look.

POINTS FOR REVIEW

- In a wedge progression, notes move symmetrically to or from a central pitch or pitches.

- In pitch symmetry, notes that are inversional partners balance around a central pitch axis of symmetry (a single pitch or a pair of pitches a semitone apart). Music that is inversionally symmetrical in pitch has the same pitch intervals from bottom to top and top to bottom.

- In pitch-class symmetry, notes that are inversional partners balance around an inversional axis on the pitch-class clockface.

- In either pitch or pitch-class symmetry, music may modulate from axis to axis.

TEST YOURSELF

1. Name the note or notes from which the following inversional wedges expand.

   a.

B	C	C♯	D	D♯
A	G♯	G	F♯	F

   b.

D♯	E	F	F♯	G
C	B	B♭	A	A♭

2. Name the note or notes toward which the following inversional wedges contract.

   a.

F	E	E♭	D	C♯
G	A♭	A	B♭	B

   b.

D	D♭	C	B	B♭
E♭	E	F	F♯	G

3. Are the following collections of pitches inversionally symmetrical? If so, name the axis of symmetry.

a.   b.   c.   d.   e.

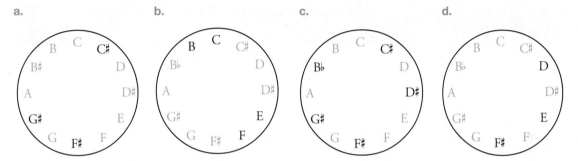

4. Are the following collections of pitch classes inversionally symmetrical? If so, name the axis of symmetry.

a.   b.   c.   d.

46 Twelve-Tone Serialism

Many post-tonal works are based on an ordered series of all twelve pitch classes.

Until now, we have focused mostly on unordered collections of notes (large collections like diatonic, octatonic, and hexatonic, and small collections like trichords). In addition, some post-tonal music also makes use of ordered lines of notes, known as **series**, especially series that consist of the twelve pitch classes stated once each (a **twelve-tone series**).

TWELVE-TONE SERIES

A series (sometimes called a **row)** of the twelve pitch classes forms the basis for a style of post-tonal music called **twelve-tone music**. The series functions as the source for the intervals, harmonies, melodies, and motives of a twelve-tone work. A series may be realized musically in a variety of ways—as a melody, a group of harmonies, or some combination of these.

A twelve-tone series uses all twelve notes of the chromatic scale in a specific order. Usually each of the twelve notes occurs only once (although a note might be repeated before it moves on to the next note).

46.1 Arnold Schoenberg, String Quartet No. 4

This series is realized as a single-line melody. Some notes of the series are repeated, but none recur until all twelve have been presented.

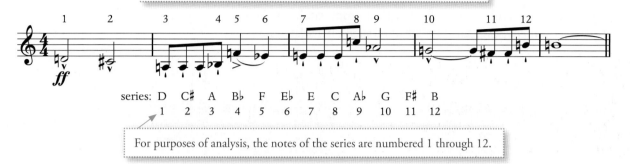

series: D C# A Bb F Eb E C Ab G F# B
        1   2 3   4 5   6 7 8   9 10 11 12

For purposes of analysis, the notes of the series are numbered 1 through 12.

46.2 Luigi Dallapiccola, "Simbolo," from *Quaderno musicale di Annalibera*

The first two notes of the series alternate as an ostinato in the bass. The remaining notes are presented as chords of two or three notes. The registral arrangement of pitches within the chords does not necessarily follow the ordering of the series.

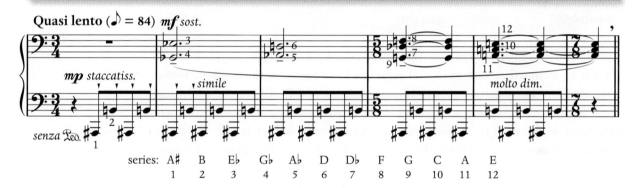

series: A# B Eb Gb Ab D Db F G C A E
         1 2   3   4   5 6   7 8 9 10 11 12

46.3 Elisabeth Lutyens, Two Bagatelles, Op. 48, No. 1

The series is presented as isolated single notes interspersed with chords of two or three notes.

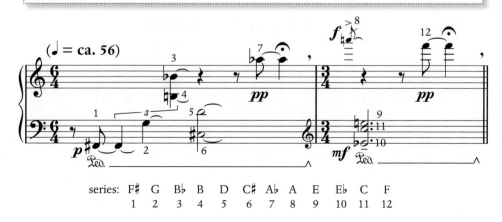

series: F# G Bb B D C# Ab A E Eb C F
         1 2   3 4 5   6   7 8 9 10 11 12

BASIC OPERATIONS

The pitches of a series can be inverted, retrograded (played backwards), or both. This results in four basic orderings (Prime, Inversion, Retrograde of the Prime, and Retrograde of the Inversion), each of which can be transposed. Each of these pitch orderings also has a distinctive associated profile of ordered pitch-class intervals.

46.4

	PITCH	INTERVAL
Prime (P)	The original presentation of the twelve-note series.	A distinctive succession of eleven ordered pitch-class intervals.
Inversion (I)	The notes are inverted.	Each interval is replaced, in order, by its complement (1 becomes 11, 2 becomes 10, and so on).
Retrograde of the Prime (RP) (often called Retrograde [R])	The notes are written in reverse order.	The order of the intervals is reversed, and each interval is replaced by its complement.
Retrograde of the Inversion (RI)	The notes are both inverted and written in reverse order.	The intervals occur in reverse order.

One statement of the series, usually the first one in the piece, is designated P, and the rest are analyzed in relation to it. A subscript letter identifies the first note in the series. P_D, for example, is the prime ordering that starts on D. RP_D is the retrograde form that *ends* on D because it is P_D backwards. Pitch-class numbers can also be used to name series forms: P_5 is the prime ordering that starts on pitch-class 5 (F); RI_8 is the retrograde of the inverted ordering that starts on pitch-class 8 (G♯); and so on. Ordinal numbers are used to designate the position of each note in the series as seen in the ordering of P and I—the numbers for RP and RI run backwards.

46.5 Arnold Schoenberg, Piano Concerto

This is a P-form of the series—the basic idea for the piece, with a particular ordering of the twelve notes and associated intervals. Individual tones of the series and small groups of notes are repeated in the melody.

An RI-form follows. The same intervals as P, but in reverse order. The numbers run backwards, because RI is the retrograde of I. Again, individual notes and small groups of notes repeat in the melody.

opci		8	2	8	5	2	6	8	11	3	4	7
RI$_{G\sharp}$	E	C	D	B♭	E♭	F	B	G	F♯	A	C♯	G♯
	12	11	10	9	8	7	6	5	4	3	2	1

An RP-form, with numbers running backwards. Compared to P, the intervals are *complementary* and in reverse order. Compared to RI, the intervals are complementary and in the same order, because RP and RI are inversions of each other.

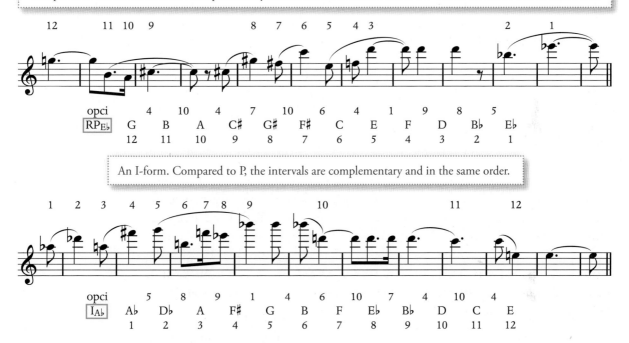

opci		4	10	4	7	10	6	4	1	9	8	5
RP$_{E\flat}$	G	B	A	C♯	G♯	F♯	C	E	F	D	B♭	E♭
	12	11	10	9	8	7	6	5	4	3	2	1

An I-form. Compared to P, the intervals are complementary and in the same order.

opci		5	8	9	1	4	6	10	7	4	10	4
I$_{A\flat}$	A♭	D♭	A	F♯	G	B	F	E♭	B♭	D	C	E
	1	2	3	4	5	6	7	8	9	10	11	12

46.6

Task: **Given a twelve-tone series (from Webern's "Wie bin ich froh!" Op. 25, No. 1), write out the I$_F$ form.**

| G | E | D♯ | F♯ | C♯ | F | D | B | B♭ | C | A | G♯ |

1. Identify the original row as Prime, starting on G (P$_G$).

2. Write out the intervals:

	9	11	3	7	4	9	9	11	2	9	11
P$_G$	G	E	D♯	F♯	C♯	F	D	B	B♭	C	A	G♯

3. Write out the intervals for an I-form (remember that the I-form has complementary intervals in the same order).

| 3 | 1 | 9 | 5 | 8 | 3 | 3 | 1 | 10 | 3 | 1 |

4. Starting on the designated note (F), write out the I_F form of the series, observing the I-form's succession of intervals:

		3	1	9	5	8	3	3	1	10	3	1
I_F	F	G♯	A	F♯	B	G	B♭	C♯	D	C	E♭	E

46.7

Task: **Figure out the relationship between two forms of the series (in Schoenberg's String Quartet No. 4). Assume that the first of the two is a P-form.**

P_D	D	C♯	A	B♭	F	E♭	E	C	A♭	G	F♯	B
?	B♭	E♭	D	C♯	A	F	F♯	E	B	C	A♭	G

1. Write out the intervals for both series:

		11	8	1	7	10	1	8	8	11	11	5
P_D	D	C♯	A	B♭	F	E♭	E	C	A♭	G	F♯	B

		5	11	11	8	8	1	10	7	1	8	11
?	B♭	E♭	D	C♯	A	F	F♯	E	B	C	A♭	G

2. Compare the intervals. These two successions have the same intervals in reverse order, so the second series must be an RI-form. It is the retrograde of the inversion that starts on G, so the second series form is RI_G.

RI_G	B♭	E♭	D	C♯	A	F	F♯	E	B	C	A♭	G
	12	11	10	9	8	7	6	5	4	3	2	1

Like trichords and other smaller sets, series forms can be related by transposition or inversion. To figure out the interval of transposition or index of inversion, compare any pair of corresponding notes. If you are using pitch-class numbers, subtraction will give the interval of transposition and addition will give the index of inversion. Note that I_n refers to a series form (like I_F) and $T_n I$ refers to an operation performed on sets or series (like $T_5 I$).

46.8

Task: **Using pitch-class numbers and addition, figure out how the P_C and I_F forms of the series (in Schoenberg's String Quartet No. 4) are related.**

1. Write out the series in both letter names and pitch-class numbers:

P_C (pitch-class numbers):	0	11	7	8	3	1	2	10	6	5	4	9
P_C (letter names):	C	B	G	A♭	E♭	D♭	D	B♭	F♯	F	E	A

I_F (letter names):	F	F♯	B♭	A	D	E	E♭	G	B	C	D♭	A♭
I_F (pitch-class numbers):	5	6	10	9	2	4	3	7	11	0	1	8

2. Add the corresponding pitch-class numbers (first to first, second to second, and so on). The sum is the index number (T_nI).

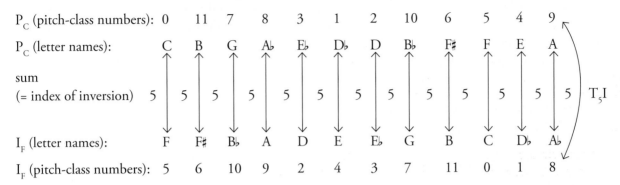

P_C (pitch-class numbers): 0 11 7 8 3 1 2 10 6 5 4 9

P_C (letter names): C B G A♭ E♭ D♭ D B♭ F♯ F E A

sum (= index of inversion) 5 5 5 5 5 5 5 5 5 5 5 5 5 T_5I

I_F (letter names): F F♯ B♭ A D E E♭ G B C D♭ A♭

I_F (pitch-class numbers): 5 6 10 9 2 4 3 7 11 0 1 8

P_C and I_F are related at T_5I.

46.9

Task: **Using pitch-class numbers and subtraction, figure out how the $P_{F\sharp}$ and P_G forms of the series (in Lutyens's Two Bagatelles, Op. 48, No. 1) are related.**

1. Write out the series in both letter names and pitch-class numbers.

P_F♯ (pitch-class numbers): 6 7 10 11 2 1 8 9 4 3 0 5

P_F♯ (letter names): F♯ G B♭ B D C♯ A♭ A E E♭ C F

P_G (letter names): G A♭ B C E♭ D A B♭ F E C♯ F♯

P_G (pitch-class numbers): 7 8 11 0 3 2 9 10 5 4 1 6

2. Subtract the corresponding pitch-class numbers (first from first, second from second, and so on). The difference is the interval of transposition (T_n).

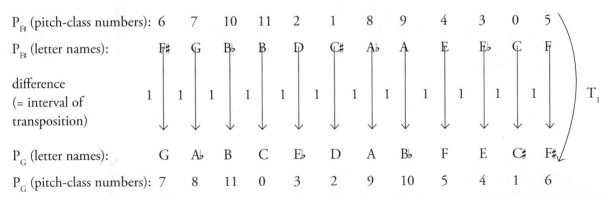

P_F♯ (pitch-class numbers): 6 7 10 11 2 1 8 9 4 3 0 5

P_F♯ (letter names): F♯ G B♭ B D C♯ A♭ A E E♭ C F

difference (= interval of transposition) 1 1 1 1 1 1 1 1 1 1 1 1 T_1

P_G (letter names): G A♭ B C E♭ D A B♭ F E C♯ F♯

P_G (pitch-class numbers): 7 8 11 0 3 2 9 10 5 4 1 6

$P_{F\sharp}$ and P_G are related at T_5I.

Unlike trichords and other smaller sets, where the notes do not occur in any specified order, series forms can also be related by retrograde. We have already seen that the labels RP_n and RI_n refer to the retrogrades of series forms P_n and I_n. In addition, when comparing a P or I form to an RP or RI form, you can use the labels RT_n (retrograde of a transposition) or RT_nI (retrograde of an inversion) to describe the transformations that relate series forms.

46.10

Task: **Using pitch-class numbers and addition, figure out how the P_F and $RI_{E\flat}$ forms of the series (in Dallapiccola's *Quaderno musicale di Annalibera*) are related.**

1. Write out the series in both letter names and pitch-class numbers.

P_F (pitch-class numbers):	5	4	0	9	7	1	2	10	8	3	6	11
P_F (letter names):	F	E	C	A	G	D♭	D	B♭	A♭	E♭	F♯	F
$RI_{E\flat}$ (letter names):	A	D	F	C	B♭	F♯	G	D♭	B	A♭	E	E♭
$RI_{E\flat}$ (pitch-class numbers):	9	2	5	0	10	6	7	1	11	8	4	3

2. Add the corresponding pitch-class numbers (first to last, second to second-to-last, and so on). The sum is the index number.

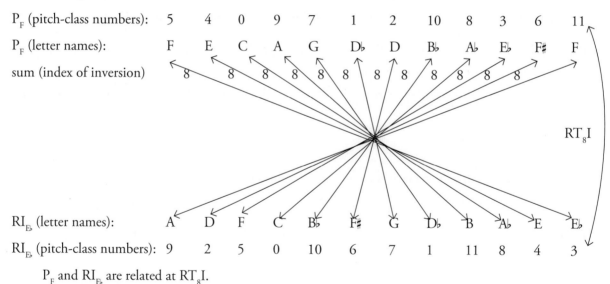

P_F and $RI_{E\flat}$ are related at RT_8I.

TWELVE-BY-TWELVE MATRIX

Any of the four forms of the series (P, I, RP, and RI) can be transposed to start on any of the twelve pitch classes. Any series can thus be presented in forty-eight different ways: twelve primes, twelve inversions, twelve retrogrades, and twelve retrograde-inversions. We can show the forty-eight forms of the row in a compact format called a **twelve-by-twelve** (12×12) **matrix**, which may be filled in with either letter names or pitch-class numbers.

The twelve I-forms are read from top to bottom. The subscript indicates the first note in the series.

The twelve P-forms are read from left to right. The subscript indicates the first note in the series.

The twelve RP-forms are read from right to left. The subscript indicates the last note in the series.

	I_D	$I_{C\sharp}$	I_A	$I_{B\flat}$	I_F	$I_{E\flat}$	I_E	I_C	$I_{A\flat}$	I_G	$I_{F\sharp}$	I_B	
$P_D \rightarrow$	D	C♯	A	B♭	F	E♭	E	C	A♭	G	F♯	B	$\leftarrow RP_D$
$P_{E\flat} \rightarrow$	E♭	D	B♭	B	F♯	E	F	C♯	A	A♭	G	C	$\leftarrow RP_{E\flat}$
$P_G \rightarrow$	G	F♯	D	E♭	B♭	A♭	A	F	C♯	C	B	E	$\leftarrow RP_G$
$P_{F\sharp} \rightarrow$	F♯	F	C♯	D	A	G	A♭	E	C	B	B♭	E♭	$\leftarrow RP_{F\sharp}$
$P_B \rightarrow$	B	B♭	F♯	G	D	C	C♯	A	F	E	E♭	A♭	$\leftarrow RP_B$
$P_{C\sharp} \rightarrow$	C♯	C	A♭	A	E	D	E♭	B	G	F♯	F	B♭	$\leftarrow RP_{C\sharp}$
$P_C \rightarrow$	C	B	G	A♭	E♭	C♯	D	B♭	F♯	F	E	A	$\leftarrow RP_C$
$P_E \rightarrow$	E	E♭	B	C	G	F	F♯	D	B♭	A	A♭	C♯	$\leftarrow RP_E$
$P_{A\flat} \rightarrow$	A♭	G	E♭	E	B	A	B♭	F♯	D	C♯	C	F	$\leftarrow RP_{A\flat}$
$P_A \rightarrow$	A	A♭	E	F	C	B♭	B	G	E♭	D	C♯	F♯	$\leftarrow RP_A$
$P_{B\flat} \rightarrow$	B♭	A	F	F♯	C♯	B	C	A♭	E	E♭	D	G	$\leftarrow RP_{B\flat}$
$P_F \rightarrow$	F	E	C	C♯	A♭	F♯	G	E♭	B	B♭	A	D	$\leftarrow RP_F$
	RI_D	$RI_{C\sharp}$	RI_A	$RI_{B\flat}$	RI_F	$RI_{E\flat}$	RI_E	RI_C	$RI_{A\flat}$	RI_G	$RI_{F\sharp}$	RI_B	

The twelve RI-forms are read from bottom to top. The subscript indicates the last note in the series.

46.12

Task: Write a 12×12 matrix for the series from Luytens's Two Bagatelles, Op. 48, No. 1.

$P_{F\sharp}$	F♯	G	B♭	B	D	C♯	A♭	A	E	E♭	C	F

1. Write the given P-form across the top row of the matrix. In that row of the chart, $P_{F\sharp}$ is read from left to right; $RP_{F\sharp}$ is read from right to left.

2. Down the first column, write the I-form that starts with F♯ (the first note of the P-form in the first row). In that column of the chart, $I_{F\sharp}$ is read from top to bottom; $RI_{F\sharp}$ is read from bottom to top.

$I_{F\sharp}$												
$P_{F\sharp}$ F♯	G	B♭	B	D	C♯	A♭	A	E	E♭	C	F	**$RP_{F\sharp}$**
F												
D												
C♯												
B♭												
B												
E												
E♭												
A♭												
A												
C												
G												
$RI_{F\sharp}$												

3. Fill in the P-forms (from left to right), starting with whatever note appears in the first column. The P-forms are related by transposition and will have the same succession of intervals. To transpose a series, transpose each note in turn by the required interval. In the second row of the chart, for example, F is a semitone lower than F♯, so every note in P_F will be a semitone lower than the corresponding note in $P_{F\sharp}$. As a way of checking your work, note that the first pitch class in the original P will run diagonally from the upper-left-hand corner to the lower-right-hand corner.

	$I_{F\sharp}$	I_G	$I_{B\flat}$	I_B	I_D	$I_{C\sharp}$	$I_{A\flat}$	I_A	I_E	$I_{E\flat}$	I_C	I_F	
$P_{F\sharp}$	F♯	G	B♭	B	D	C♯	A♭	A	E	E♭	C	F	**$RP_{F\sharp}$**
P_F	F	F♯	A	B♭	C♯	C	G	A♭	E♭	D	B	E	**RP_F**
P_D	D	E♭	F♯	G	B♭	A	E	F	C	B	A♭	C♯	**RP_D**
$P_{C\sharp}$	C♯	D	F	F♯	A	A♭	E♭	E	B	B♭	G	C	**$RP_{C\sharp}$**
$P_{B\flat}$	B♭	B	D	E♭	F♯	F	C	C♯	A♭	G	E	A	**$RP_{B\flat}$**
P_B	B	C	E♭	E	G	F♯	C♯	D	A	A♭	F	B♭	**RP_B**
P_E	E	F	A♭	A	C	B	F♯	G	D	C♯	B♭	E♭	**RP_E**
$P_{E\flat}$	E♭	E	G	A♭	B	B♭	F	F♯	C♯	C	A	D	**$RP_{E\flat}$**
$P_{A\flat}$	A♭	A	C	C♯	E	E♭	B♭	B	F♯	F	D	G	**$RP_{A\flat}$**
P_A	A	B♭	C♯	D	F	E	B	C	G	F♯	E♭	A♭	**RP_A**
P_C	C	C♯	E	F	A♭	G	D	E♭	B♭	A	F♯	B	**RP_C**
P_G	G	A♭	B	C	E♭	D	A	B♭	F	E	C♯	F♯	**RP_G**
	$RI_{F\sharp}$	**RI_G**	**$RI_{B\flat}$**	**RI_B**	**RI_D**	**$RI_{C\sharp}$**	**$RI_{A\flat}$**	**RI_A**	**RI_E**	**$RI_{E\flat}$**	**RI_C**	**RI_F**	

TWELVE-COUNTING A PIECE

You can get a basic sense of a twelve-tone piece by doing what is called a **twelve-count**. That involves identifying the forms of the series with a label (e.g., $P_{E\flat}$ or RI_G) and using integers 1–12 to indicate the order position of each note within the series. For this task, it is helpful to have a 12×12 matrix handy.

46.13 **Arnold Schoenberg, String Quartet No. 4, iii (matrix in Example 46.11)**

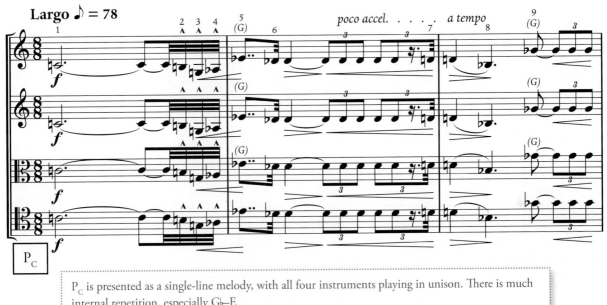

P_C is presented as a single-line melody, with all four instruments playing in unison. There is much internal repetition, especially G♭–F.

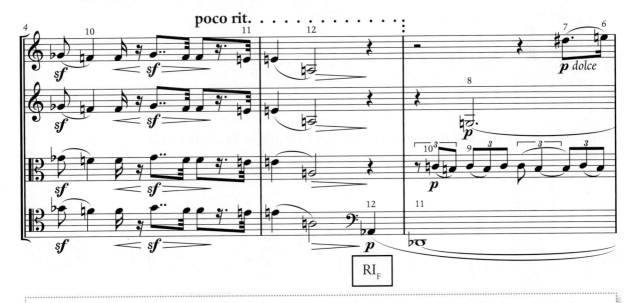

The notes of RI_F are distributed among the four instruments: the lower instruments share the first five notes; the first violin has the last seven. RI_F begins with a descending 7, the same interval P_C ended with. Note the internal repetition of B–C.

The first six notes of RP$_C$ are shared by the lower instruments; the first violin plays the last six. Note the internal repetition of A–B♭ and E–D.

Two series forms played simultaneously: I$_D$ shared by viola and second violin, and P$_A$ in its entirety in the cello.

46.14 **Elisabeth Lutyens, Two Bagatelles, Op. 48, No. 1 (matrix in Example 46.12)**

Two statements of P$_{F♯}$, mostly as chords.

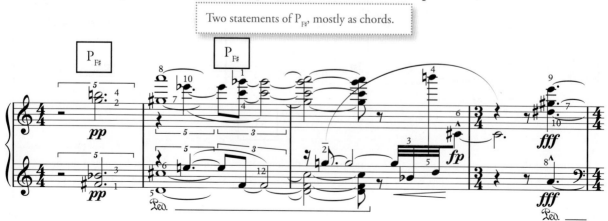

The piece ends with RP$_G$ and I$_F$. The beginning of RP$_G$ overlaps with the end of the previous P$_{F\sharp}$.

Only a single note cannot be accounted for as part of a series form: the left hand *sforzando* F♯ with the circle around it. Although it lacks a serial explanation, it resonates strongly with other prominent F♯s, functioning almost as a centric tone for this music.

SUBSETS

Within a series, composers often use the smaller groupings of notes (called **subsets**), treating them as pitch-class sets. No matter how the series is transposed, inverted, retrograded, or retrograde-inverted, the set classes of its subsets remain the same. The smallest groupings—adjacent collections of two and three notes (**dyads** and trichords)— are the easiest for the ear to grasp.

46.15 Anton Webern, "Wie bin ich froh!" Op. 25, No. 1

The series contains a lot of two-note groups that correspond to unordered pitch-class intervals 1 and 3. Among the trichords, four are members of set-class (014).

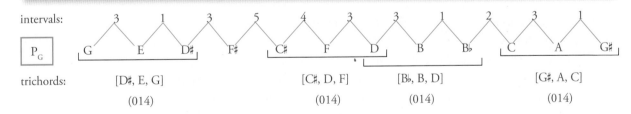

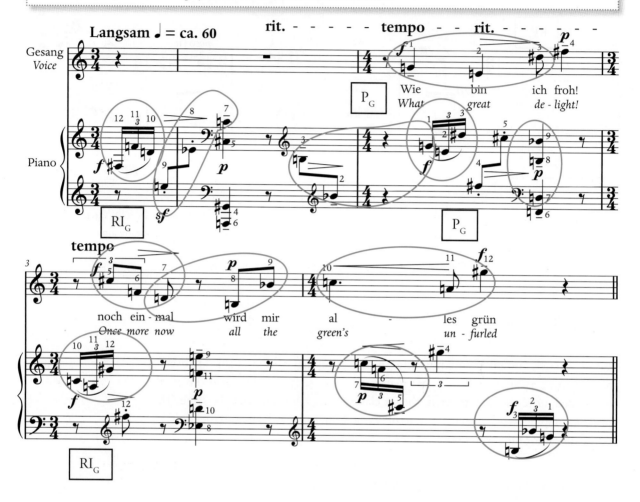

INVARIANCE

Sometimes it is not only the types of dyads or trichords that are repeated among the different series forms, but the actual pitch classes. This is known as **invariance**: certain collections of pitch classes are held **invariant** (i.e., are still found together) even when the series is transposed or inverted. The recurrence of pitch-class sets between different forms of the series gives the listener a coherent path through the music, and one that is relatively easy to follow.

46.16 Arnold Schoenberg, String Quartet No. 4, iii

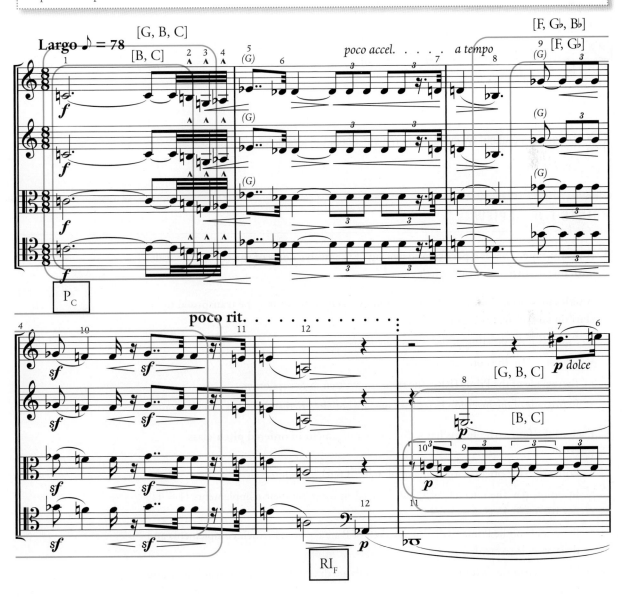

The dyads [B, C] and [F, G♭] are held invariant in the series forms P_C and RI_F, as are the trichords [G, B, C] and [F, G♭, B♭]. As the music moves through these series forms, these dyads and trichords are heard again and again, usually in prominent positions.

To learn more about twelve-tone serialism, see A Closer Look.

POINTS FOR REVIEW

- **A twelve-tone series is a particular ordering of the twelve notes of the chromatic scale, with one occurrence of each pitch class.**

- **A series may occur in four different orderings, each of which may be transposed to start on any of the twelve pitch classes:**
  - Prime (P): An ordering of the twelve pitch classes.
  - Inversion (I): The notes are inverted.
  - Retrograde of the Prime (RP): The notes are written in reverse order.
  - Retrograde of the Inversion (RI): The notes are both inverted and written in reverse order.

- **Each of the four series forms has a distinct arrangement of ordered pitch-class intervals.**
  - Prime (P): The original arrangement of ordered pitch-class intervals.
  - Inversion (I): The intervals of P are replaced in order by their complements (1 = 11, 2 = 10, 3 = 9, 4 = 8, 5 = 7, 6 = 6).
  - Retrograde of the Prime (RP): The intervals of P are replaced by their complements and their order is reversed.
  - Retrograde of the Inversion (RI): The intervals are the same as in P, but heard in reverse order.

- **A 12×12 matrix is a convenient way of presenting the forty-eight series forms.**

- **Subsets are smaller groupings of notes within a series. The set classes of the subsets remain the same in all the forms of the series.**

- **Invariant pitch-class sets remain even when the series is transposed or inverted.**

TEST YOURSELF

1. Given $P_{C\sharp}$ (from Webern, Quartet, Op. 22), write the specified series forms:

$P_{C\sharp}$	C♯	B♭	A	C	B	E♭	E	F	F♯	G♯	D	G

a. I_D

b. RP_G

c. $RI_{G\sharp}$

2. Are these statements about series ordered pitch-class intervals true or false?

a. Two series related by transposition have the same intervals, in the same order.

b. A P-form and an RI-form of a series have the same intervals, in reverse order.

c. A P-form and an I-form of a series have complementary intervals, in reverse order.

3. All four trichordal subsets of this series (from Babbitt, String Quartet No. 2) are the same trichord type. Identify the normal and prime form of each trichord.

A C A♭	E C♯ F	D♯ B D	F♯ B♭ G

4. In each of the following series, identify the invariant pitch-class sets.

a. Circle the trichords that occur in both series forms (from Schoenberg, String Quartet No. 4).

D	C♯	A	B♭	F	E♭	E	C	A♭	G	F♯	B
G	A♭	C	B	E	F♯	F	A	C♯	D	E♭	B♭

b. Circle the dyads that occur in both series forms (from Webern, Quartet Op. 22).

C♯	B♭	A	C	B	E♭	E	F	F♯	G♯	D	G
D	F	F♯	E♭	E	C	B	B♭	A	G	C♯	G♯

47

Form

Post-tonal music uses a variety of formal designs, some traditional and widely shared, others unique to the individual work.

Traditional Phrase Types	Sonata Form
Sentence	Moment Form
Period	Collage Form
	Form as Process

In most post-tonal music, form is unique to the individual piece, emerging from the underlying musical processes of the work. However, many composers continue to employ traditional forms adapted to new musical contexts. In the absence of traditional tonal harmony, we will necessarily be using terms like *phrase* and *cadence* in a somewhat imprecise way—looking to contour, phrase slurs, rests, dynamics, and other cues to impart the feel of a phrase or a cadence.

TRADITIONAL PHRASE TYPES

SENTENCE

The sentence is a common phrase type in post-tonal music, although without the traditional harmonic arrangement and proportions (see Chapter 35).

47.1 Arnold Schoenberg, Piano Piece, Op. 33b (right hand)

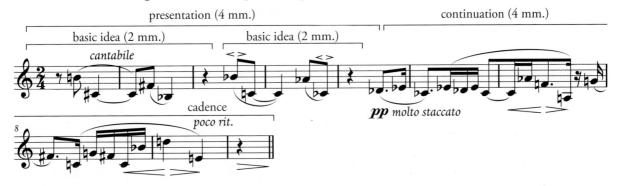

47.2 Ruth Crawford, *Diaphonic Suite* No. 1 for Oboe, i

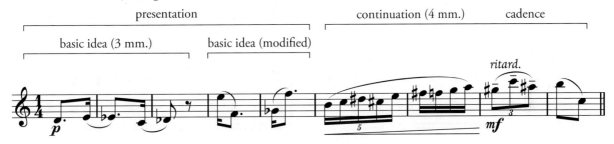

In a **dissolving sentence**, the identity of the basic idea is weakly formed and the continuation evaporates without leading to a secure cadence.

47.3 Béla Bartók, String Quartet No. 5, ii

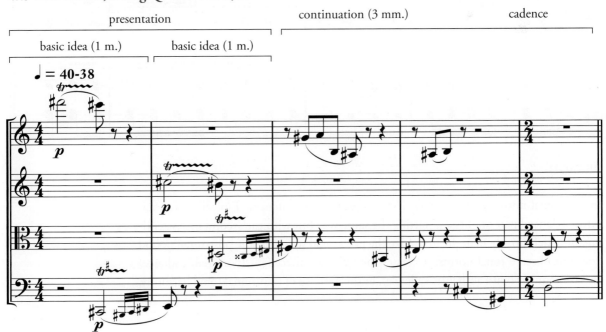

In an **immobilized sentence**, instead of a developmental push toward a cadence, a harmonically immobile continuation, produced through static and exact repetitions of the basic idea, leads to an abrupt cadence that may feel tacked on.

47.4 Igor Stravinsky, "Russian Dance," from _Petrushka_

PERIOD

In post-tonal music, periods are far less common than sentences. Typically, they feature a balanced pair of phrases, starting the same way but with the second phrase ending more definitively than the first. Like the post-tonal sentence, the post-tonal period does not observe tonal norms: it creates the _effect_ of antecedent (with half cadence) and consequent (with authentic cadence), in the absence of traditional tonal harmony.

47.5 Sergey Prokofiev, Sonata for Flute, Op. 94, i

The passage is in a sort of D major, although with many unusual harmonic moves. There are two four-measure phrases. The first (antecedent) ends in an odd sort of half cadence. The second (consequent) begins in the same way (although a step lower) and ends with a stronger cadence back in the tonic.

SONATA FORM

Post-tonal compositions that are written in historically oriented styles tend to draw on traditional forms, including binary, ternary, and sonata form. Post-tonal sonata form is used primarily as a way of arranging themes: an exposition with two contrasting themes, a development full of motivic play and rhythmic drive, and a recapitulation in which the two themes are heard again, although not necessarily in their original order or at their original transposition level.

47.6 Igor Stravinsky, Octet, i

Fanfare-like first theme, centered on E♭.

Gentle second theme ("cantabile, tranquillo") centered on D (a semitone below the tonic, E♭).

Second theme recapitulated first, centered on E (a semitone above the tonic, E♭).

The first theme recapitulated last, on the tonic E♭.

MOMENT FORM

Many styles of post-tonal music cultivate extremes of formal fragmentation. A piece is divided into short formal units, but these seem to have little in common, and are not smoothly connected. A particular extreme of fragmentation is called **moment form**, because each musical chunk is designed to be maximally self-contained—a discrete moment in time.

47.7 Igor Stravinsky, Three Pieces for String Quartet, ii

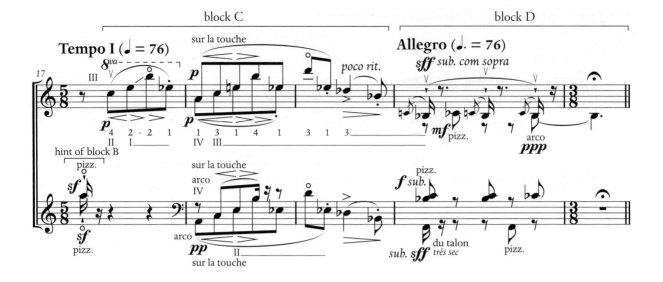

COLLAGE FORM

In **collage form**, musical passages that might traditionally have succeeded each other in time are heard simultaneously, in polyphonic layers. Often, some of the layers are quotations of earlier works.

47.8 **Luciano Berio, Sinfonia, iii**

This movement layers simultaneous quotations from many late-nineteenth-century and early-twentieth-century works, including Mahler's Second Symphony, Ravel's *La valse*, and Strauss's *Der Rosenkavalier*

FORM AS PROCESS

In some cases, in which the process of the piece is entirely systematic, form and process are no longer distinguishable: the form is the process.

47.9 **Steve Reich,** *Piano Phase*

> In this piece, each measure is repeated the number of times indicated above the score. The two parts begin in unison, but after each measure, the lower part accelerates until it is one sixteenth note ahead of where it started.

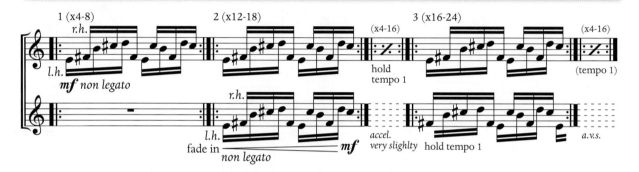

> The process continues until the two parts are back in phase, in the thirteenth measure of the piece (only three measures are shown here).

POINTS FOR REVIEW

- **Traditional phrase types, like sentences and periods, occur in post-tonal music in the absence of traditional tonal harmony.**

- **Some post-tonal music makes use of traditional larger forms, like sonata form.**

- **Moment form and collage form are post-tonal forms where blocks of music are juxtaposed.**

- **In some works, a consistent compositional process defines the musical form.**

TEST YOURSELF

Are the following statements true or false?

1. A dissolving sentence has two clearly articulated statements of the basic idea.

2. A dissolving sentence may lead only weakly to a cadence.

3. In an immobilized sentence, the basic idea may be stated more than twice.

4. An immobilized sentence leads convincingly to an expected cadence.

5. A post-tonal period has an antecedent phrase that leads to the dominant and a consequent phrase that leads to the tonic.

6. In post-tonal music, composers use features other than harmony (like phrasing, articulation, and dynamics) to create a sense of phrase and cadence.

7. Post-tonal sonata forms have a first theme in the tonic key and a second theme in some other key.

8. Post-tonal sonata forms are often built around two contrasting themes.

9. In moment form, each section is clearly and smoothly connected to the next.

10. In musical forms based entirely on process, there is a systematic and predictable working out of a basic musical idea.

Test Yourself Answers

CHAPTER 0: NOTATION OF PITCH AND RHYTHM

1.

2.

3.

4.

CHAPTER 1: SCALES

1.

1.

M3   M6   P5   d5   m3 (m10)   P4 (P11)   d7   P5

2.

M3   d7   P5   P8   m6   M7   P4   m7

3. (**a**) G–D = P5

   (**b**) E♭–A = A4

   (**c**) E–C♯ = M6

   (**d**) F♯–A = m3

4. (**a**) A♯–E = d5

   (**b**) A–G♭ = d7

   (**c**) D–A = P5

   (**d**) F♯–B♯ = A4

CHAPTER 3: TRIADS AND SEVENTH CHORDS

1.

C♯ minor   F♯ diminished   D augmented   G minor   A♭ major

2.

E♭m   A°   B♭+   G♯m   A

3.

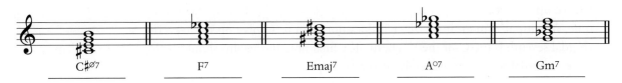

C♯ø7   F7   Emaj7   A°7   Gm7

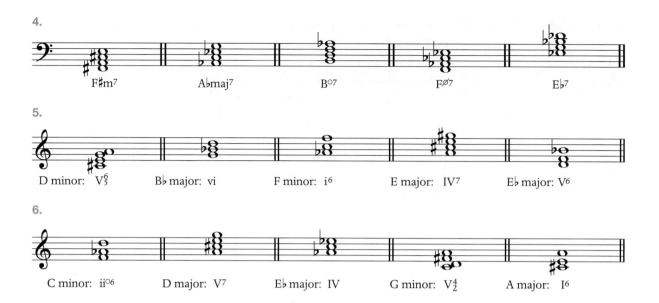

4. F♯m⁷ | A♭maj⁷ | B°⁷ | F∅⁷ | E♭⁷

5. D minor: V⁶₅ | B♭ major: vi | F minor: i⁶ | E major: IV⁷ | E♭ major: V⁶

6. C minor: ii°⁶ | D major: V⁷ | E♭ major: IV | G minor: V⁴₂ | A major: I⁶

CHAPTER 4: FOUR-PART HARMONY

1. (**a**) Soprano. (**b**) Soprano and alto. (**c**) Bass: it should always be stemmed downward in SATB format. (**d**) The root of the chord (E♭) is doubled. (**e**) IV⁶₃ or IV⁶ (first inversion)

2. (**b**) and (**d**).

CHAPTER 5: VOICE LEADING

1. Excerpt (**b**), because the upper voices either repeat their notes, move stepwise, or use the melodic interval of a third. The one big leap of a melodic fourth in the soprano voice—in the beginning of the second measure—is a chord skip, occurring when the chord repeats. The big leaps in the bass voice are also normal. In excerpt (**a**) the upper voices use mostly large melodic leaps; particularly egregious is the leap of a melodic seventh.

2. (**a**) similar; (**b**) contrary; (**c**) stationary; (**d**) parallel; (**e**) oblique.

3. (**a**) and (**c**). In (**b**) the octave and fifth are approached in stationary motion; in (**d**) the octave between the tenor and soprano likewise is approached in stationary motion. In the upper voices of (**e**), the interval of a perfect fifth (F–C in the first chord and C–G in the second) appear between two different pairs of voices.

4. (**a**) F♯ is the leading tone; there is no chordal seventh. The leading tone must resolve up to G because it is in an outer voice (soprano). (**b**) C♯ is the leading tone. Because it is in an inner voice it does not need to resolve up by step. The chordal seventh is the G of the V⁷ chord. The final note in the alto should be F♯, since a chordal seventh must resolve down by step.

5. **(b)**, **(c)**, and **(e)** contain faulty motion to perfect intervals. **(b)** The perfect fifth between soprano and alto on the third beat is arrived at by parallel motion. **(c)** The compound octave between the bass and soprano is arrived at by similar motion between outer voices, with the soprano arriving by leap. **(e)** The octave between alto and tenor is arrived at by similar motion from a dissonant interval (F–G).

6.

CHAPTER 6: HARMONIC PROGRESSION

1. **(a)** HC. **(b)** PAC. **(c)** IAC. **(d)** PAC.

2. A normal half cadence ends with a root-position V triad, not an inversion (m. 4). A normal authentic cadence ends with a root-position V (or V^7) to I, not with an inversion of V or V^7 to I (mm. 7–8).

3. **(a) T–D–T**. **(b) T–D–T** (with the **T**onic and **D**ominant harmonies repeated). **(c)** Neither (faulty **T–D–S–T** progression). **(d) T–S–D–T**.

4. **(a)** Good: **T–S–D–T** pattern, without voice-leading errors. **(b)** Good: **T–D–T** pattern, without voice-leading errors. **(c)** Poor: the final chord is not a root-position I or V; the end of the progression is **D–S**; there are parallel fifths between the second and third chords. **(d)** Poor: the third note of the melody, B, is $\hat{2}$ and is not in I^6. **(e)** Poor: voice-leading errors (parallel octave between the first two chords, as well as between the last two chords, and a doubled leading tone). **(f)** Good: **T–D–T** pattern, with no voice-leading errors. **(g)** Good: **T–S–D–T** pattern, with no voice-leading errors. **(h)** Poor: contains a **D**ominant that is followed by a **S**ubdominant harmony, and the melody note A is not in IV.

CHAPTER 7: MELODIC ELABORATION

1. I–IV–V–I. The notes of the chords are arpeggiated in the treble clef.

2. **(a)** approached by step, left by step **(b)** approached by step, left by leap **(c)** approached by leap, left by step **(d)** approached by common tone, left by step **(e)** approached by common tone, left by step **(f)** approached by leap, left by step **(g)** approached by step, left by common tone

3. **(a)** unaccented; PT **(b)** accented; PT **(c)** accented; PT **(d)** accented; SUS **(e)** unaccented; NT **(f)** unaccented; INT **(g)** unaccented; ANT **(h)** accented; RET.

CHAPTER 8: SPECIES COUNTERPOINT

1. First species

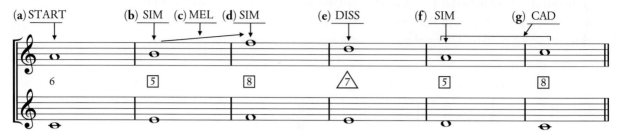

2. Second species

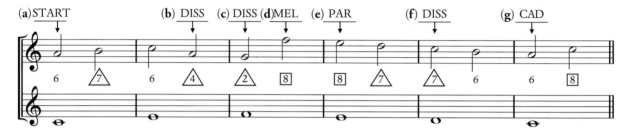

3. Fourth species

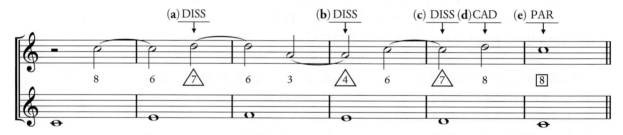

CHAPTER 9: I AND V

1. (**a**) I = E♭, G, B♭; V = B♭, D, F

    (**b**) I = E, G♯, B; V= B, D♯, F♯

    (**c**) i = E, G, B; V= B, D♯, F♯

2. The excerpt in (**b**) is better than (**a**), since the melodic intervals of the upper voices are smoother. The excerpt in (**d**) is better than (**c**), since in (**c**) the leading tone (G♯) does not resolve up to the tonic when V progresses to I, even though it is in the soprano. In (**d**), the leading tone is in the alto, and thus does not need to resolve up to the tonic.

3.

F: I V I

4. (a) E♯ **(b)** B♮ **(c)** B♯ **(d)** F𝄪 **(e)** E♮ **(f)** C♯

5. (a) $\hat{7}$ of G minor is F, which should be raised by a half step to F♯ in order to form a leading tone. **(b)** The leading tone (which in E major is D♯) should not be doubled. **(c)** There are too many leaps between the first two chords, which creates faulty parallel octaves and fifths. In **(d)**, the leading tone (C♯) should resolve up to D in the top voice when V goes to I.

CHAPTER 10: THE DOMINANT SEVENTH CHORD: V⁷

1. (a) D–F♯–A–C **(b)** B–D♯–F♯–A **(c)** B♭–D–F–A♭ **(d)** A♭–C–E♭–G♭.

2. (a) E minor; add D♯ **(b)** F♯ minor; add E♯ **(c)** F minor; add E♮ **(d)** C minor; add B♮ **(e)** B minor; add A♯ **(f)** D♯ minor; add C𝄪

3. (a) and **(b)**. The last note in the alto could be either E♭ or A♭ (in the latter instance, the fifth of the I chord is omitted, and the root is tripled).

(c) and **(d)**. The notes in the alto and tenor in the first chord could either be, respectively, B and G♯, or G♯ and E (in the latter instance, the fifth of V⁷ is omitted, and its root is doubled).

(e) The note in the tenor in the second chord should be A (since this note is needed for V⁷). (The seventh of V⁷ on the downbeat does not yet need to resolve, since the V⁷ is repeated.) The note in the third chord in the tenor should be G♯, since the seventh of V⁷ does need to resolve down by step when V⁷ progresses to I. The last note in the alto should be E; using a G♯ in the alto in the last chord would produce improper doubling, and a B in the last chord would create parallel fifths.

4. (a), **(b)**, and **(c)**. Each of these could be labeled either as V–V⁷–I or V⁸⁻⁷–I. They also each could be labeled as a V–I in which there is a passing tone in one of the voices.

5. (a) G major. The voice leading here is good: the motion of a perfect fifth to a diminished fifth (G–D to F♯–C) is fine. In the last chord, the root of I is tripled and the fifth (D) is omitted; this is also fine.

(b) B♭ major. The voice leading has problems: the chordal seventh in the second chord (E♭) does not resolve down by step; it must do so, even though it is in an inner voice. Also, the third (d) is missing from the final I chord. In four-part harmony, you may omit a fifth from a triad, but not a third.

(c) D minor. The voice leading here is good. In the second chord, the root of V^7 is doubled and the fifth (A) is omitted; this is fine.

(d) E♭ major. The voice leading has problems: there are parallel fifths between the bass and alto in the last two chords. Also, the spacing between the alto and tenor in the last chord is more than an octave, which is less than ideal.

CHAPTER 11: I⁶ AND V⁶

1. (a) Either G, B♭, or D, since any note of i⁶ may be doubled. (b) Either B or E, since you may double the root or the fifth of V⁶. You may not double the third of the chord, G♯, since that is the leading tone. (c) Either G or C. You may not double the E, which is the leading tone.

2. Any of these chords may follow I⁶.

3. I, V, or V⁷ may follow V⁶; I⁶ may not, since it would not allow the leading tone in the bass to resolve up by step in an outer voice.

4. Of these chords, only I normally follows V⁷.

5. (a) Bass C should be C♯, since you should raise $\hat{7}$ in a minor key. (b) The leading tone (D♯) is doubled in the second chord. (c) There are parallel octaves (A to C♯) between the bass and alto beats 2–3: notice that the half note (A) in the alto on beat 1 is sustained through beat 2, thus forming an octave with the bass on this beat. (d) V⁷–V⁶ should be avoided, since it prevents resolution of the chordal seventh (E♭) of V⁷. (e) V⁶ to I⁶ should be avoided, since it does not allow the leading (F♯) to resolve up by step in an outer voice.

CHAPTER 12: V⁶₅ AND V⁴₂

1. (a) V⁶₅. (b) It may be followed by I, not by I⁶, since then the leading tone in the bass could not resolve up by step. It may be followed by either V⁷ or V⁴₂, not by V or V⁶: V⁷ in any inversion chord may not lead to a V triad, since then the chordal seventh would not be able to resolve down. (c) Any of these chords could precede V⁶₅.

2. (a) V⁴₂. (b) V⁴₂ must lead directly to i⁶, since the prominent chordal seventh in the bass of V⁴₂ must resolve down by step. (c) Any of these chords could precede V⁴₂.

3. (a) The G in m. 1 could be harmonized with V⁶₅, but not V⁴₂: V⁴₂ of D major uses G in the bass, and thus V⁴₂ would double the chordal seventh. The E in m. 2 could be harmonized with either V⁶₅ or V⁴₂. The C♯ in m. 3 could be harmonized with V⁴₂: V⁶₅ of D major uses C♯ in the bass, and thus V⁶₅ would double the leading tone. (b) The E in m. 4 cannot be harmonized with either V⁶₅ or V⁴₂, since it is part of the cadence: the cadence in this measure should be harmonized V–I or V⁷–I. (c) A voice exchange could be used in m. 2, with the motion from F♯ to D in the melody set with a motion from D to F♯ in the bass.

4. (a) C♯, E, G, A (b) F♯, A, C, D (c) D♭, E♭, G, B♭ (d) B, C♯, E♯, G♯ (e) F, G, B♭, D.

5. **(a)** The chordal seventh (F) doesn't resolve properly; a diminished fifth moves to a perfect fifth (B♮–F to C–G). **(b)** V_2^4 may not move to V^7. **(c)** V_5^6 should resolve to I, not I^6, because the leading tone in the bass must resolve up by step. **(d)** V_2^4 should resolve to I^6 because the chordal seventh must resolve down by step.

CHAPTER 13: V_3^4 AND vii$^{\circ 6}$

1. **(a)** V_3^4 = D, F♯, A, C; bass = A. vii$^{\circ 6}$ = F♯, A, C; bass = A.

   (b) V_3^4 = F, A, C, E♭; bass = C. vii$^{\circ 6}$ = A, C, E♭; bass = C.

   (c) V_3^4 = B, D♯, F♯, A; bass = F♯. vii$^{\circ 6}$ = D♯, F♯, A; bass = F♯.

   (d) V_3^4 = B, D♯, F♯, A; bass = F♯. vii$^{\circ 6}$ = D♯, F♯, A; bass = F♯ (same as in E major).

2. **(a)** V_5^6 **(b)** V_3^4 **(c)** V_2^4 **(d)** vii$^{\circ 6}$

3. **(a)** There are no faulty parallel fifths here. The perfect fifth to diminished fifth between the alto and soprano in the first two chords (E♭/B♭–D/A♭) is fine, because it is a diminished fifth, not a perfect fifth, that is approached in parallel motion. The chordal seventh (A♭) properly resolves down by step.

   (b) There is a faulty (parallel) approach to the perfect fifth between the alto and soprano in the third chord. The chordal seventh of the V^7 (C) is treated improperly also: it does not resolve down by step.

   (c) The diminished fifth to perfect fifth between the alto and soprano in the second and third chords is fine, as is the upward motion of the chordal seventh (E♭), since these are allowed when V_3^4 moves to I^6.

CHAPTER 14: APPROACHING THE DOMINANT: IV, ii^6, AND ii$_5^6$

1. **(a)**, **(b)**, **(c)**, **(f)**, **(h)**, and **(i)** are correct. **(d)** is poor—V^6 may not progress to ii$_5^6$. **(e)** is poor—V may not progress to ii^6. **(g)** is poor—vii$^{\circ 6}$ is a **D**ominant harmony, and thus may not progress to IV.

2. **(a)** iv, quality = minor **(b)** ii$^{\circ 6}$, quality = diminished **(c)** ii$^{\varnothing 6}_5$, quality = half-diminished.

3. **(a)** root; $\hat{1}$ **(b)** any note: root, third, or fifth; $\hat{1}$, $\hat{3}$, $\hat{5}$ **(c)** root; $\hat{5}$ **(d)** root or fifth; $\hat{5}$ or $\hat{2}$ (not the third, which is the leading tone) **(e)** root; $\hat{4}$ **(f)** root or third (= bass); $\hat{2}$ or $\hat{4}$

4. **(a)** D; $\hat{1}$ **(b)** A♭; $\hat{4}$ **(c)** B♭; $\hat{1}$ **(d)** D; $\hat{4}$ **(e)** C♯; $\hat{1}$ **(f)** G; $\hat{4}$

5. **(a)** True. **(b)** False: $\hat{4}$ must resolve down by step only if it is a chordal seventh of V^7. **(c)** True. **(d)** True.

6. **(a)** Parallel fifths between bass and alto. **(b)** Chordal seventh within ii$_5^6$ (D) does not resolve down by step. **(c)** Melodic augmented second between A♭ and B♮. **(d)** Parallel octaves between bass and alto. **(e)** $\hat{7}$ is not raised in a minor key.

CHAPTER 15: EMBELLISHING V: CADENTIAL $^6_4$

1. (a) B and G (b) B♭; G and E♭ (c) A; F and D (d) B; G and E

2. (a) C, F, A (b) F♯, B, D♯ (c) D, G, B♭ (d) E, A, C

3.

a.

B♭: V$^6_4$ – $^5_3$
(cad. $^6_4$–V)

b.

F♯ min.: V$^6_4$ – $^5_3$

c.

G: V$^6_4$ – $^5_3$

4. (c) and (d). In (c), the cadential $^6_4$ follows a **Dominant** harmony (V^6). In (d), the cadential $^6_4$ appears on a weaker beat (beat 2) than the notes of the V triad that follow it on beat 3.

CHAPTER 16: LEADING TO THE TONIC: IV

1. All are typical progressions, except for (d): I–IV^6–I is uncommon.

2. $\hat{3}$–$\hat{4}$–$\hat{3}$, $\hat{5}$–$\hat{6}$–$\hat{5}$, and $\hat{1}$–$\hat{1}$–$\hat{1}$.

3. All of these could be harmonized with I–IV–I except for (b), since the second note, B♭, is not in the IV chord of the key of A♭. Though the melodic line of (c), $\hat{5}$–$\hat{4}$–$\hat{3}$, is not among the most typical for a I–IV–I progression, it nonetheless would be possible to harmonize this with I–IV–I.

4. (a) I–ii^6–V: half cadence. (b) iv–V–i: imperfect authentic cadence. (c) i–iv–i: plagal cadence. (d) I^6–V–I: perfect authentic cadence.

CHAPTER 17: THE LEADING-TONE SEVENTH CHORD: vii°⁷ AND vii⌀⁷

1. (a) B♭ (b) C♯ (c) C♮ (d) D♯ (e) No accidental is needed for a vii⌀⁷ chord in a major key.

2. (a) vii°⁷; chordal seventh = F♮; leading tone = G♯

   (b) vii°$^4_3$; chordal seventh = D♭; leading tone = E♮

   (c) vii⌀$^6_5$; chordal seventh = B; leading tone = C♯

   (d) vii°$^4_2$; chordal seventh = E♭; leading tone = F♯

   (e) vii⌀⁷; chordal seventh = C♯; leading tone = D♯

3. (a) vii°$^4_3$; leads to I^6. (b) vii°⁷; leads to i (root position). (c) vii°$^6_5$; leads to i^6 (root-position i would produce faulty parallel fifths with the tenor voice). (d) vii°$^4_2$; leads to V^7 (because the chordal seventh is in the bass, vii°$^4_2$ cannot lead to i or i^6).

4. **(a)** B♭, because the chordal seventh of vii°7 (C♭) must resolve down by step.

(b) A, because the leading tone in vii°̸7 (G♯) should resolve up by step.

(c) D, even though this would double the third of a root-position I. The E♭ within the vii°7 cannot move up to F, since this would cause faulty parallel fifths—that is, a diminished fifth (A–E♭) moving to a perfect fifth (B♭–F).

(d) F, even though this would double the third of a root-position I. The E within the vii°7 cannot move down to D, since this would cause faulty parallel fifths—that is, a diminished fifth (E–B♭) moving to a perfect fifth (D–A).

CHAPTER 18: APPROACHING V: IV⁶, ii, ii⁷, AND IV⁷

1. **(a)** I–ii–V–I is good; I–V–ii–I is poor, since V should not progress to ii (**D**ominant moving to **S**ubdominant), and ii should not progress to I.

   (b) Although both of these progressions are acceptable, I–IV–ii–V is more standard, since in moving from one **S**ubdominant harmony to another, the bass usually moves down by a third (IV–ii). The I–ii–IV–V progression is less typical, since when moving between ii and IV the bass moves up by third.

   (c) Both of these progressions are good.

   (d) I–ii–ii⁷–V–I is good; I–ii⁷–ii–V–I is poor, since it involves a **S**ubdominant seventh chord that leads to a **S**ubdominant triad.

2. **(a)** The first progression is good (the doubled G is fine); the second of these progressions is problematic, since the minor form of $\hat{6}$ is doubled and moves up rather than down, giving rise to a faulty melodic augmented second between E♭ and F♯.

   (b) The first progression is faulty, since the seventh of the ii⁷ (D) does not resolve down by step. The second progression is good; note that the fifth (E) is omitted from the V⁷ chord—this is fine.

   (c) The first progression is good: the seventh of IV⁷ (G) does resolve down by step, although this resolution is momentarily delayed by the cadential $^6_4$ (which is fine). The second progression is faulty, since the seventh of IV⁷ does not resolve down, but rather moves up to A♭.

3. **(a)** False. It is not good to double the bass of iv⁶. The bass of iv⁶ is the minor form of $\hat{6}$, which is a tendency tone; doubling it would give rise to voice-leading errors.

   (b) True.

   (c) False. ii° should not appear in root position.

   (d) True.

   (e) False.

   (f) True.

1. (**a**) All of these harmonies—even ii^7—may directly follow vi: vi may lead to any **S**ubdominant harmony.

   (**b**) vi often leads to I^6, but it is not common for vi to be followed directly by a root-position I.

   (**c**) vi may occasionally lead to V or V^6 (or even to V^7 or V$^6_5$); though less common, the vi–V or vi–V^6 progression is not faulty.

2. IV or ii^6 does not normally precede vi: a IV–vi or ii^6–vi progression would involve an unusual root motion up by third.

3. (**a**) V–vi and (**b**) V^7–vi may form part of a standard deceptive cadence, but the progressions found in (**c**)–(**e**) may not: a deceptive cadence must involve a root-position V (not V in inversion) and a root-position vi (not vi in inversion). The progression I–vi is a good progression, but it does not form a deceptive cadence, which must involve V or V^7 to vi.

4. The progressions found in (**a**), (**b**), (**d**), and (**e**) display good, standard voice leading. Although (**c**) is less typical (since when V moves to vi, normally the third of vi is doubled), this voice leading nonetheless is fine. The progression found in (**f**), on the other hand, does not have good voice leading: the C♯–B♭ in the alto creates a faulty melodic augmented second. The C♯ here should have ascended to D, doubling the third of VI.

CHAPTER 20: VOICE LEADING WITH EMBELLISHING TONES

1. (**a**), (**b**), (**c**) are faulty; (**d**) and (**e**) are fine.

   (**a**) There are parallel octaves between the bass and tenor (the use of a passing tone does not remove these faulty parallels).

   (**b**) The neighbor tone in the alto forms parallel fifths with the bass (D–A, C–G).

   (**c**) The embellishing tones create parallel octaves between the bass and alto (F–E) on the first two beats.

   (**d**) If the chord on the second beat were omitted, there would have been parallel fifths between the tenor and soprano (F–C, G–D). The chord skips on the second beat avert this problem, however.

   (**e**) The passing tones here do not either create or avert faulty parallel octaves or fifths, thus this is fine.

2. (**a**) F, A, D (no note is doubled)

   (**b**) F, G, C (the bass C should be doubled)

   (**c**) C, D, F (no note is doubled)

   (**d**) B, D, A–G

   (**e**) D, G, with either D or G doubled (the "2" in the figure indicates that the bass C is dissonant and thus may not be doubled)

1. **(a)** True. **(b)** False. The leading tone within the iii triad can descend. **(c)** True. **(d)** True. **(e)** False. iii should be rarely—if ever—used within basic melody harmonization exercises, and iii⁶ should never be used in such contexts. **(f)** False. vii°⁶ is a common chord; you should not use a *root-position* vii° triad in four-part harmony exercises. **(g)** True—although such a progression is not often found in simple harmonic contexts.

2. **a.** **b.**

CHAPTER 22: SEQUENCES

1. (a) True. (b) False. (c) True. (d) False. (e) False.

2.

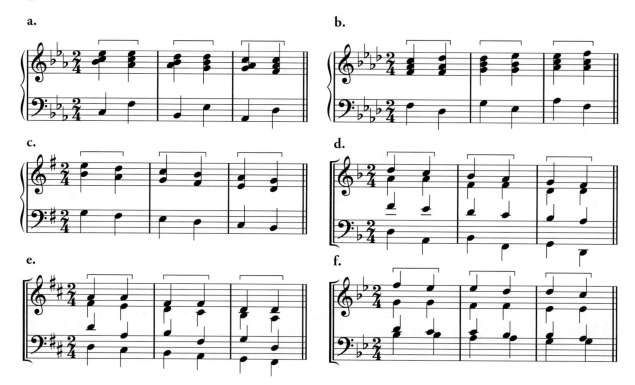

CHAPTER 23: OTHER $^6_4$ CHORDS

1. (a) True. (b) False: I^6_4 does not function like I or I^6. (c) False: A passing or arpeggiated I^6_4 need not be followed by V or V^7. (d) False: A passing, pedal, or arpeggiated I^6_4 usually appears on a weak beat. (e) False: A pedal $^6_4$ may follow V or V^7. (f) False: Usually the bass is doubled, but unless it is a cadential $^6_4$, other notes may be doubled.

2.

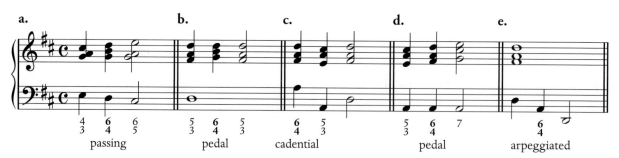

f.

arpeggiated   arpeggiated

g.

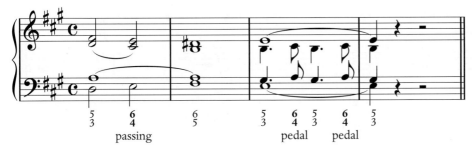

passing   pedal   pedal

CHAPTER 24: OTHER EMBELLISHING CHORDS

1.

D: I^6 ii$^6_5$ I^6 ii^7 V^7 I

2. ii$^6_5$–I^6 (m. 1, beat 1 to beat 2) is an unusual chord succession. The ii is a neighboring chord, a byproduct of a neighboring tone in the bass.

3. I–V^6–IV^6–V (or V^7).

4. V (or V^7)–vi (or IV^6) –V^6 (or V$^6_5$)–I.

5. I–IV^6–I^6

CHAPTER 25: APPLIED DOMINANTS OF V

1. (**a**), (**d**), (**e**), or (**f**). V/V may not be followed by I, IV, ii^6. V/V must be followed by a **D**ominant harmony (V or V^6; V^7, cadential $^6_4$–V) or by another V/V.

2. (**a**), (**b**), (**c**), (**d**), and (**e**) all are correct. Any chord that may precede V may also precede V/V.

3. (**a**) C♯ (**b**) A♮ (**c**) E♮ (**d**) E♮ and G♮ (**e**) A♯ (**f**) A♯ and C♯.

4. (**a**) G (**b**) E (**c**) F♯ (**d**) F♯ (**e**) B♭ (**f**) B♭.

5. **(a)** G, B♮, D; B♮ requires an accidental. **(b)** E, G♯, B; G♯ requires an accidental. **(c)** F♯, A♯, C♯; A♯ requires an accidental. **(d)** D♯, F✕, A♯; F✕ requires an accidental.

6. **(a)** G, B♮, D♮, F; B♮ and D♮ require accidentals. **(b)** E, G♯, B♮, D; G♯ and B♮ require accidentals. **(c)** F♯, A♯, C♯, E; A♯ and C♯ require accidentals. **(d)** D♯, F✕, A♯, C♯; F✕ and A♯ require accidentals. Compare with question (5): notice that V⁷/V uses the same notes in parallel major and minor keys, but in minor keys V/V requires two accidentals.

7.

8. **(a)** the third chord (V/V) **(b)** E♮ **(c)** it slides down

CHAPTER 26: OTHER APPLIED CHORDS

1. **(a)**, **(b)**, or **(d)**: Much as V may be followed by I, I⁶, or another V, so V/ii may be followed by ii, ii⁶, or another V/ii.

2. **(a)** G♯ **(b)** B♮ **(c)** B♯ **(d)** G♯ and B♮ **(e)** B♮ and A♭ **(f)** F♯

3. **(a)** D♯ **(b)** E♭ **(c)** no accidentals needed **(d)** A♮ **(e)** F♯ and A♮: **(f)** no accidentals needed

4. **(a)** C♯ **(b)** A♯ **(c)** G♯ **(d)** D **(e)** D♯ **(f)** B

5. **(a)** V/ii or V⁷/ii **(b)** V⁷/IV **(c)** V/vi or V⁷/vi **(d)** V/V or V⁷/V

CHAPTER 27: MODULATION TO THE DOMINANT KEY

1. **(a)** C♯ **(b)** E♮ **(c)** A♯ **(d)** D♯ **(e)** G♮ **(f)** E♯ **(g)** A♮

2. **(a)** The main key is D; the key of V is A. **(b)** The main key is B♭; the key of V is F. **(c)** The main key is A♭; the key of V is E♭.

3. **(a)** B♭ major; D minor, F major, G minor **(b)** D major; F♯ minor, A major, B minor **(c)** A major; C♯ minor, E major, F♯ minor

4. **(a)** The third chord of m. 1 (B♭ major) is I in B♭ and IV in F.

   (b) The fourth chord of m. 1 (E minor) is vi in G and ii in D. You could also read the third chord of m. 1 (G major) as the pivot chord: I in G and IV in D.

   (c) The first chord of m. 3 (C♯ minor) is vi in E and ii in B. You also arguably could read the third chord of m. 2 (B major) as the pivot chord: V in E and I in B.

5.

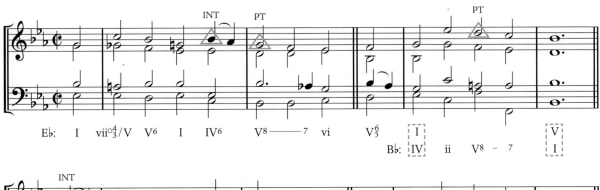

CHAPTER 28: MODULATION TO CLOSELY RELATED KEYS

1. (**a**) iii; (**b**) IV; (**c**) VI; (**d**) v

2. (**a**) A minor, B minor, C major, D major, E minor

   (**b**) C minor, D minor, E♭ major, F major, G minor

   (**c**) F major, G minor, A minor, B♭ major, C major

   (**d**) A major, B minor, C♯ minor, D major, E major

3. (**a**) F major, G minor, A minor, B♭ major, C major, D minor, E diminished

   (**b**) G minor, B♭ major, C minor, E♭ major, F major

   (**c**) A major, C♯ minor, E major; F♯ minor

   (**d**) E minor, G major, A minor, C major

4. (**a**) A♯; in B minor, the note G♯ might also appear as part of an ascending melodic minor scale. (**b**) G♭. (**c**) B♮ and G♯; in the key of A minor, the note F♯ might also appear as part of an ascending melodic minor scale. (**d**) D♮ and E♯; in the key of F♯ minor, the note D♯ might also appear as part of an ascending melodic minor scale.

5.

a.

A: I   IV   I   ⌐IV⌐
B min.:   ⌐III⌐   ii°6   V   i

b.

Bb: I   ⌐ii6⌐
G min.:   ⌐iv6⌐   V7   i   V8 – 7   i

c.

G# min.: i   vii°7   ⌐i⌐   ⌐ii°6⌐   V$^6_4$ – $^5_3$ i
B: ⌐vi⌐   V6   I   ⌐vii°6⌐

6. (**a**) C minor. (**b**) An extended tonicization, because it only appears for a few measures in the middle of a phrase and is not confirmed by a cadence. (**c**) V $\frac{4}{3}$/vi. (**d**) V⁷/V (or V/V and V$^6_5$/V).

CHAPTER 29: MODAL MIXTURE

1. (**a**), (**e**), (**f**), and (**g**) involve mixture; these chords will need an accidental within a major key. The other chords (**b**), (**c**), and (**d**) are diatonic chords within their keys—that is, they do not involve mixture, and do not need an accidental.

2. (**a**) Eb (**b**) Cb and Gb (**c**) G♮ (**d**) Ab (**e**) A♮ (**f**) B♮

3. (**a**) True. (**b**) False. A move from D major to D minor is not a modulation, since the tonic does not change. (**c**) False. A borrowed chord in a major key often involves a lowered $\hat{3}$ or $\hat{6}$. However, this chromatic alteration does not always involve the use of a flat: it might also involve the use of a natural or a double flat. (**d**) True. (**e**) True. (**f**) False. Modal mixture involves motion between parallel major and minor keys.

4. (**a**) No modal mixture, because this is a modulation to the relative minor. (**b**) Modal mixture, because this is a shift to the parallel minor (with no modulation). (**c**) No modal mixture, because this is a modulation to the key of iii. (**d**) Modal mixture because this is a shift to the parallel major (with no modulation). (**e**) No modal mixture, because this is a modulation to the relative major.

1. (a) G♮ (b) C♭ (c) D♮

2. (a) ii°⁶ = G, B♭, E; ♭II⁶ = G, B♭, E♭

    (b) ii°⁶ = E, G, C♯; ♭II⁶ = E, G, C

    (c) ii°⁶ = B♭, D♭, G; ♭II⁶ = B♭, D♭, G♭

3. (a) (d) and (e) may precede ♭II⁶; (b) and (c) may not precede ♭II⁶, since they function as **D**ominants.

4. (a) minor (b) Neapolitan sixth (c) major (d) downward

5. As ♭$\hat{2}$ in the top voice, the E♭ should move down to C♯, not up to E♮.

CHAPTER 31: AUGMENTED SIXTH CHORDS

1. (a) ♯$\hat{4}$ = B♮; minor $\hat{6}$ = D♭. Both require accidentals. (b) ♯$\hat{4}$ = B♮; minor $\hat{6}$ = D♭. B♮ requires an accidental. (c) ♯$\hat{4}$ = A♯; minor $\hat{6}$ = C♮. Both require accidentals. (d) ♯$\hat{4}$ = A♯; minor $\hat{6}$ = C. A♯ requires an accidental. (e) ♯$\hat{4}$ = G♮; minor $\hat{6}$ = B♭♭. Both require accidentals.

2. (a) It⁺⁶ = D♭, F, B♮; Fr⁺⁶ = D♭, F, G, B♮; Ger⁺⁶= D♭, F, A♭, B♮ (or D♭, F, G♯, B♮).
    (b) It⁺⁶ = D♭, F, B♮; Fr⁺⁶ = D♭, F, G, B♮; Ger⁺⁶ = D♭, F, A♭, B♮ (or D♭, F, G♯, B♮).
    (c) It⁺⁶ = C♮, E, A♯; Fr⁺⁶ = C♮, E, F♯, A♯; Ger⁺⁶ = C♮, E, G♮, A♯ (or C♮, E, F×, A♯).
    (d) It⁺⁶ = C, E, A♯; Fr⁺⁶ = C, E, F♯, A♯; Ger⁺⁶ = C, E, G, A♯. (e) It⁺⁶ = A♮, C♯, F×; Fr⁺⁶ = A♮, C♯, D♯, F×; Ger⁺⁶ = A♮, C♯, E, F×.

3. (a) Adding F♭ turns this chord into an It⁺⁶ (b) B♭, Fr⁺⁶ (c) C♭, Ger⁺⁶ (d) B♯, It⁺⁶ (e) D♭ and B♮, Fr⁺⁶ (f) C♮ and A♯, It⁺⁶ (g) C♯, Ger⁺⁶ (f) E♯, Fr⁺⁶

4. (a) Key of D major or D minor, It⁺⁶ (b) Key of A major or A minor, Fr⁺⁶

    (c) Key of G major or G minor, Ger⁺⁶ (d) Key of C major (*not* C minor), Ger⁺⁶

    (e) Key of E major or E minor, It⁺⁶

5. (a) The first of the chords has incorrect doubling: in an It⁺⁶, you should double the tonic, *not* the bass note (which is a tendency tone).

    (b) The first chord is misspelled: an augmented sixth chord requires raised $\hat{4}$—*not* lowered $\hat{5}$—in an upper voice.

    (c) The first chord has a wrong note: raised $\hat{4}$ of F is B♮, *not* B♯.

6. In a standard augmented sixth chord, minor $\hat{6}$ must appear in the bass; raised $\hat{4}$ may appear in any upper voice (tenor, alto, or soprano).

CHAPTER 32: OTHER CHROMATICALLY ALTERED CHORDS

1. (a) C♯, E♯, G♯ (b) D, F♯, A (c) B♭, D♮, F (d) C, E, G♯ (e) E, G♯, B♯ (f) A♭, C, E♭ (g) F♮, A, C♯ (h) E, G♯, B♯, D (i) G♯, B♭, D, E (j) B, D, E♯, G

2. (a) F: ♭II (b) E: Ger⁺⁶ with $\hat{1}$ in the bass (c) E♭: V⁺ (d) D: III♯ (or V/vi) (e) A: IV⁺

3.

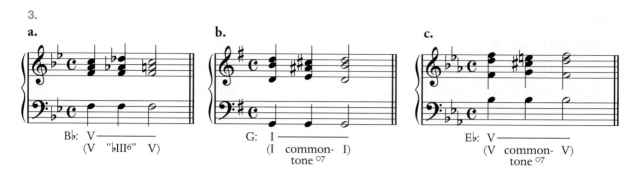

a.

Bb: V————
(V "bIII6" V)

b.

G: I————
(I common- I)
tone °7

c.

Eb: V————
(V common- V)
tone °7

4. The first diminished seventh chord is an applied vii°7 of V; the second is a common-tone diminished seventh chord that embellishes V.

5. (**a**) common tone °7 (**b**) applied °7 (**c**) V$^7_{+5}$

CHAPTER 33: CHROMATIC SEQUENCES

1.

a.   down 3, up 4

A: IV   V/V   V   V/vi   vi

b.   descending fifth

Bb: V/vi V6/ii   V/V   V6   I

c.   down 3, up 4

Eb: V bIII   bVI IV   bVII V   I

d.   descending fifth

D: V7/iii V7/vi   V7/ii V7/V   V7   I

2. The fifth of every other chord is omitted.

3. The leading tones within the applied dominant sevenths slide down by semitone to the seventh of the following chord instead of resolving up by step.

4. The chordal sevenths must resolve down by step, even within an inner voice and even within a sequence.

CHAPTER 34: CHROMATIC MODULATION

1. (a) V (b) G (c) ♭III (d) F
2. (a) A (b) B (c) E
3. (a) B (b) A♭ (c) F
4. (a) D♭ or C♯ (b) B♭ (c) G
5. (a) F (V⁷ of F = C, E, G, B♭)

   (b) A♭ (V⁷ of A♭ = E♭, G, B♭, D♭)

   (c) C♯ (Ger⁺⁶ of C♯ = A, C♯, E, F𝄪) or D♭ (Ger⁺⁶ of D♭ = B♭♭, D♭, F♭, G♮)

   (d) E♭ (Ger⁺⁶ of E♭ = C♭, E♭, G♭, A♮)

CHAPTER 35: SENTENCES AND OTHER PHRASE TYPES

1. (a) This is a standard sentence, with a presentation in mm. 1–4 (mm. 1–2, basic idea; mm. 3–4, strict repetition) followed by a continuation in mm. 5–8 leading to a cadence. (b) In this standard sentence, the basic idea in mm. 1–2 is repeated in varied form (transposed up a step) in mm. 3–4. (c) This is sentence-like, but *not* a sentence. What is clearly a contrasting idea appears in mm. 3–4; there is no repetition of the basic idea. (d) This is clearly *not* a sentence: a sentence consists of a single phrase, and thus cannot have a cadence in its middle. (e) This standard sentence is four measures long, rather than the more typical eight measures: the presentation is in mm. 1–4 (basic idea in m. 1, varied repetition in m. 2) followed by a continuation leading to a half cadence in mm. 3–4. (f) This is a standard sentence that is extended to 12 measures as a result of an evaded cadence in m. 8 and rhythmic expansions in the subsequent measures. (g) Whether this is a sentence or merely sentence-like depends on whether mm. 3–4 are understood as a variant of mm. 1–2 (in which case this phrase would be called a sentence) or a contrasting idea (in which case this phrase would be considered sentence-like); one could reasonably argue for either of these interpretations.

CHAPTER 36: PERIODS AND OTHER PHRASE PAIRS

1. Parallel period, with HC in I and PAC in I.
2. Parallel period, with HC in I and PAC in V.
3. Contrasting period, with HC in I and PAC in I; the consequent phrase is motivically new.
4. Parallel period; the first phrase ends with an IAC, which is less stable than the PAC at the end of the following phrase.
5. Parallel period with an expansion; the consequent phrase is extended by two measures.
6. Not a period, since the first phrase ends with a PAC.
7. Sequential period; the consequent phrase starts a step higher.

CHAPTER 37: BINARY FORM

1. (**a**) True. (**b**) False: If the opening of the **A** section returns in the tonic key in the middle of the second part, it is classified as rounded binary, even if the endings of the two parts are the same. A binary form is classified as balanced binary only if it cannot be classified as rounded binary. (**c**) False: The two parts of a simple binary might share motives and other features, even though there is no large return of material from the first part within the second part. (**d**) True.

2. (**a**) Balanced binary: The opening measures do not return in the tonic key within the second part, so this is not rounded binary. On the other hand, the last four measures of the first part return—slightly varied and transposed to the tonic key—as the last four measures of the second part; this is typical of balanced binary. (**b**) Rounded binary: Although at a different dynamic level ($\boldsymbol{f}$ as opposed to $\boldsymbol{mf}$), four measures from the end of the second part there is a clear return—in the tonic key—of the first two measures. Note that the last two measures of the second part are a varied repetition of the last two measures of the first part. Even so, this is *not* a balanced binary form, since in balanced binary the opening does not return in the tonic key in the middle of the second part. (**c**) Simple binary: Although the two parts share musical materials in common, the opening measures do not return in the tonic key within the second part, and the two parts end differently. (**d**) Rounded binary: Material from mm. 1–2 return in the middle of the second part in mm. 13–14. Note that mm. 13–16 are also similar to mm. 5–8; however, since the opening measures of the first part so clearly return in the tonic key within the middle of the second part, this is classified as rounded binary.

CHAPTER 38: TERNARY AND RONDO FORMS

1. (**a**) **ABA** and (**b**) **ABA′** are examples of ternary form, *not* (**c**) **ABC**.

2. The **A** and **A′** sections are usually in the tonic key (though it is possible for the first **A** section to end in a different key). The **B** section may also be in the tonic key (or in the parallel key), but often it is not.

3. Both the **A** and **A′** sections usually end with a PAC; the **B** section may end with a PAC (either in the tonic key or in another key), but it may also end with an HC.

4. The **A** sections of a rondo are almost always in the tonic key.

5. The **A** sections of a rondo usually end with a PAC in the tonic key.

6. In an **ABACA** rondo, the **C** section is usually longer than the **B** section.

CHAPTER 39: SONATA FORM

1. Introduction, exposition, development, recapitulation, coda

2. Primary theme, transition, secondary theme, closing section.

3. The medial caesura appears at the end of the transition and precedes the secondary theme.

4. The primary theme appears in the tonic key in both the exposition and recapitulation.

5. The primary theme typically ends with an HC or PAC in the tonic key in both the exposition and recapitulation.

6. The transition typically ends with an HC in the tonic key or the secondary key in the exposition and an HC in the tonic key in the recapitulation.

7. The secondary theme appears in the secondary key in the exposition (usually the key of V, or—in minor-key movements—in the relative major), and in the primary key in the recapitulation.

8. The secondary theme typically ends with a PAC in the secondary key in the exposition and a PAC in the primary key in the recapitulation.

9. (c) The melodies of the primary and secondary themes can either contrast with or be similar to one another.

CHAPTER 40: COLLECTIONS AND SCALES I: DIATONIC AND PENTATONIC

1. (a) $PENT_{Ab}$ on Bb (b) $DIA_{2\sharp}$ on A (A Mixolydian) (c) DIA_{5b} on F (F Phrygian) (d) $PENT_{C\sharp}$ on C♯ (e) DIA_{3b} on F (F Dorian)

2. (a) E–F♯–G♯–A–B–C♯–D–(E) (b) G–A–C–D–F–(G) (c) Eb–F–Ab–Bb–C–(Eb) (d) G–A–B–C♯–D–E–F♯–(G) (e) G–A–Bb–C–D–E–F–(G)

3. (a) $PENT_{Eb}$ (b) $PENT_{D}$ (c) $PENT_{C\sharp}$

4. (a) $DIA_{5\sharp}$ (b) DIA_{5b} (c) $DIA_{0\sharp/0b}$

5. (a) $PENT_{G}$, $PENT_{D}$, $PENT_{A}$ (b) $PENT_{Ab}$, $PENT_{Eb}$, $PENT_{Bb}$ (c) $PENT_{B}$, $PENT_{F\sharp}$, $PENT_{C\sharp}$

CHAPTER 41: COLLECTIONS AND SCALES II: OCTATONIC, HEXATONIC, AND WHOLE-TONE

1. (a) $OCT_{C\sharp D}$ on E (b) WT_{C} on F♯ (c) HEX_{DEb} on F♯ (d) $HEX_{C\sharp D}$ on Bb (e) OCT_{DEb} on Eb

2. (a) F–F♯–A–Bb–C♯–D–(F) (b) F–G–Ab–Bb–B–C♯–D–E–(F) (c) F–F♯–G♯–A–B–C–D–Eb–(F) (d) E–F♯–G♯–A♯–C–D–(E) (e) A–C–Db–E–F–G♯–(A)

3. (a) DIA_{1b}, OCT_{CDb} (b) $DIA_{3\sharp}$, $DIA_{4\sharp}$, $DIA_{5\sharp}$, $PENT_{E}$, $OCT_{C\sharp D}$, $HEX_{D\sharp E}$ (c) OCT_{CDb}, $OCT_{C\sharp D}$ (d) HEX_{CDb}, $HEX_{C\sharp D}$, $WT_{C\sharp}$

CHAPTER 42: TRIADIC POST-TONALITY

1. (a) True (b) False (c) True (d) False

2. L-related triads share a minor third; P-related triads share a perfect fifth; R-related triads share a major third; SLIDE-related triads share a chordal third.

3. (a) F– (F–Ab–C), Db+ (Db–F–Ab) (b) F♯+ (F♯–A♯–C♯), F♯– (F♯–A–C♯)

4. Yes.

5. (a) C+ (with added seventh and ninth) (b) D– (with added seventh, ninth, and fourth) (c) E– (with added seventh and fourth)

6. (a) E+ and B+, related by transposition by P5 (b) F+ and F–, related by P (c) G+ and G♯–, related by SLIDE

CHAPTER 43: INTERVALS

1. (a), (b), (d), and (e) are enharmonic equivalents.

2. (a) 1 (b) 7 (c) 6 (d) 14 (e) 10

3.

	ORDERED PITCH INTERVALS	UNORDERED PITCH INTERVALS	ORDERED PITCH-CLASS INTERVALS	UNORDERED PITCH-CLASS INTERVALS
	+7	7	7	5
	−16	16	8	4
	−2	2	10	2
	10	10	10	2
	−18	18	6	6

4. (a) 3 (b) 2 (c) 1 (d) 4 (e) 3 (f) 6 (g) 4 (h) 2 (i) 5

CHAPTER 44: PITCH-CLASS SETS: TRICHORDS

1. (a) [A, B♭, C♯] (b) [B♭, C, E♭] (c) [F♯, A, C♯] (d) [G♯, A, D] (e) [D, E♭, E]

2. (a) [F, G♭, A] (b) [C, F, F♯] (c) [E, F♯, A] (d) [E, F, F♯] (e) [E, G, B]

3. (a) T_{10} (b) T_8 (c) T_{11} (d) T_7 (e) T_6

4. (a) [D, F, F♯] (b) [G, B, D] (c) [D, F, G] (d) [G, A, B♭] (e) [C, D, E]

5. (a) T_7I (b) T_9I (c) T_9I (d) T_8I (e) T_6I

6. (a) (014) (b) (025) (c) (037) (d) (012)

CHAPTER 45: INVERSIONAL SYMMETRY

1. (**a**) A♯ (**b**) D♭/D

2. (**a**) C (**b**) G♯/A

3. (**a**) Yes, B (**b**) Yes, B♭/B (**c**) Yes, A (**d**) No (**e**) No

4. (**a**) Yes, C♯—G. (**b**) Yes, D—G♯. (**c**) Yes, D—G♯. (**d**) Yes, E—B♭.

CHAPTER 46: TWELVE-TONE SERIALISM

1. (**a**) D F F♯ E♭ E C B B♭ A G C♯ G♯

   (**b**) C♯ G♯ D C B B♭ A F F♯ D♯ E G

   (**c**) D G C♯ E♭ E F F♯ B♭ A C B G♯

2. (**a**) True, (**b**) True, (**c**) False; they have complementary intervals in the same order.

3.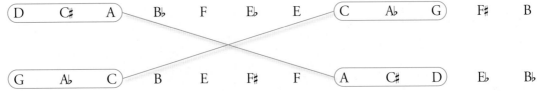

| A | C | A♭ | | E | C♯ | F | | D♯ | B | D | | F♯ | B♭ | G |

Normal order:　　[A♭, A, C]　　　　[C♯, E, F]　　　　[B, D, D♯]　　　　[F♯, G, B♭]

Prime form:　　　　(014)　　　　　　(014)　　　　　　(014)　　　　　　(014)

4. **a.**

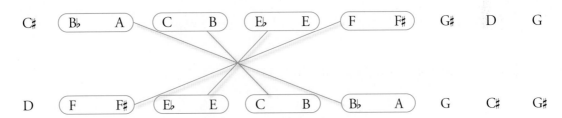

b.

CHAPTER 47: FORM

| 1. False | 2. True | 3. True | 4. False | 5. False |
| 6. True | 7. False | 8. True | 9. False | 10. True |

♭II⁶ First-inversion major triad whose root is lowered $\hat{2}$; functions as a **S**ubdominant and occurs most often in minor keys. Also called *Neapolitan sixth*.

♭III Major triad occurring by modal mixture in a major key, using the minor form of $\hat{3}$ (in the bass) and the minor form of $\hat{7}$.

III♯ Major triad whose root is $\hat{3}$ of a major scale and whose third is raised $\hat{5}$.

♭VI Major triad occurring by modal mixture in a major key, using the minor form of $\hat{6}$ (in the bass) and the minor form of $\hat{3}$.

V⁹, V⁹₇ Chord that uses the notes of V⁷ plus a major or (in a minor key or using modal mixture) a minor ninth above the bass.

VI♯ Major triad whose root is $\hat{6}$ of a major scale and whose third is raised $\hat{1}$.

5–6 sequence See *ascending sequence*.

accented Sounding on a relatively strong beat or part of the beat or appearing at the same time (most of) the notes of the chord are sounded.

accented neighbor tone Neighbor tone that coincides with the onset of a chord.

accented passing tone Passing tone that coincides with the onset of a chord.

accidental Any of the signs for sharp, flat, double sharp, or double flat, placed immediately before the notehead on the staff to indicate whether the pitch is to be raised or lowered (generally, for that measure only), or natural, which cancels a sharp or flat.

aggregate Collection consisting of all twelve pitch classes.

alto clef C clef 𝄡 indicating that the third line from the bottom of the staff is middle C; used for viola and also called *viola clef*.

anacrusis Note or group of notes forming an incomplete measure and leading to a downbeat; sometimes called a pickup or (if a single beat) an upbeat.

antecedent In a period, the first phrase, which ends with a half cadence or imperfect authentic cadence, requiring an "answer" by the second, *consequent* phrase.

anticipation (ANT) Chord tone that arrives before the beat, as an unaccented non-chord tone, approached by step and left by common tone.

applied dominant Chord that has been chromatically altered to act as V of a note being tonicized. Also called *secondary dominant*.

appoggiatura Accented embellishing tone.

arpeggiated ⁶₄ Second-inversion triad that results from a chord skip in the bass.

arpeggiation The statement of chord tones in succession instead of together.

ascending 5–6 sequence Harmonic sequence, most often occurring in a three-voice texture, in which the bass line ascends by step, with each bass note of the sequence supporting a $\overset{5}{3}$ triad followed by a $\overset{6}{3}$ triad; a variant of the sequence in which chord roots alternately move down 3, up 4, with every chord in first inversion.

ascending fifth sequence Harmonic sequence involving major and minor chords whose roots alternately move up by a fifth and down by a fourth.

ascending melodic minor See *melodic minor scale*.

asymmetrical binary form Binary form in which the two halves are different lengths.

asymmetrical period Period in which the antecedent and consequent are different lengths.

augmentation dot Dot following a notehead that increases the duration by one half the value of the note.

augmented interval Interval a semitone larger than a perfect or major interval; for example, C–G♯, augmented fifth (A5); B♭–D♯, augmented third (A3).

augmented second (A2) Second that is three semitones in size; characteristic distance between $\hat{6}$ and $\hat{7}$ in a harmonic minor scale.

augmented sixth chord Three- or four-note harmony built on two tendency tones that drive to a resolution to V (directly or through a cadential ⁶₄); includes the minor form of $\hat{6}$ in the bass (leading down to $\hat{5}$), raised $\hat{4}$ in an upper voice (leading up to $\hat{5}$), plus one or two other notes; see also *Italian augmented sixth*, *French augmented sixth*, and *German augmented sixth*.

augmented triad Triad built of a major third and an augmented fifth.

authentic cadence (AC) Cadence consisting of V or V⁷ moving to I; may be perfect (melody ends on $\hat{1}$) or imperfect (melody ends on $\hat{3}$ or $\hat{5}$).

axis of symmetry The central pitches or pitch classes around which a collection of notes balances.

balanced binary form See *binary form*.

barline Vertical line on the staff separating measures.

basic idea See *sentence*.

bass The lowest voice; the bottom note of a chord.

bass clef (F clef) 𝄢 symbol indicating that the fourth line from the bottom of the staff is F below middle C.

basso ostinato Continuous variation in which the same bass line is repeated with each variation.

beam Horizontal line connecting the stems of two or more notes to indicate durations shorter than a quarter note: a single beam indicates eighth notes, a double beam indicates sixteenth notes, and so forth.

beat Regular pulsation at a moderate speed.

binary form Form of a movement or piece divided into two parts, each of which is usually repeated; the first part may be harmonically open-ended (ending with an unstable cadence or a modulation to V or to the relative major), while the second part concludes with an authentic cadence in the main key. In *rounded binary form*, the opening of the first part returns in the middle of the second part, exactly or nearly so and in the main key, creating a sense of return. In *balanced binary form*, the two parts only *conclude* with the same music; generally, the first part ends with a perfect authentic cadence in V or the relative key, and the second part repeats the concluding segment, but transposed to the tonic. Simple binary form does not contain these repetitions.

bitonality Music simultaneously in two different keys.

bi-triadic harmony Harmony that consists of two contrasting triads.

borrowed chord A chord that uses notes more normally found in the parallel key, such as, in a major key, a chord using the minor form of $\hat{3}$ or $\hat{6}$; a form of modal mixture.

bridge Brief passage (sometimes shorter than a phrase) that follows the cadence at the end of a large section and leads to the beginning of the next section.

C clef 𝄡 symbol indicating the staff line that is middle C; see *alto clef, tenor clef*.

cadence Harmonic conclusion of a phrase; cadence types include *authentic, half, Phrygian, plagal*, and *deceptive cadences*.

cadential $^6_4$ Harmony that decorates V with accented embellishing tones, using notes of the tonic chord ($\hat{5}$, $\hat{1}$, and $\hat{3}$), with $\hat{5}$ in the bass.

cantus firmus In species counterpoint, a melody in whole notes.

centric tone The primary degree of a scale ($\hat{1}$); a tone that functions as a tonic; in some cases, the tone (or tones) that form an axis of inversional symmetry.

chord position The arrangement of a chord depending on which note is in the bass.

chord progression *Harmonic progression*.

chord skip Melodic leap between chord tones while a chord is repeated or sustained.

chord symbol Representation of the root and quality of a chord, as Gm (G minor triad), E°7 (E diminished seventh chord).

chordal dissonance A note of a chord (such as the seventh of a seventh chord) that is dissonant with the root or the bass and thus has a strong tendency to move downward.

chordal seventh The seventh of a seventh chord; in four-part harmony, a tendency tone that should resolve down.

chromatic embellishing tone Embellishing tone that is altered to move by half step.

chromatic mediant Non-diatonic harmony whose root is the mediant ($\hat{3}$).

chromatic neighbor tone Neighbor tone that is approached and left by half step and uses an accidental.

chromatic passing tone Passing tone that requires an accidental and that leads between two notes that are a major second apart.

chromatic submediant Non-diatonic harmony whose root is the submediant ($\hat{6}$).

circle of fifths Major keys (or minor keys) on each of the twelve chromatic tones, organized in an arrangement a fifth apart, and showing the progression of key signatures; also, the *circle of fifths progression*.

circle of fifths progression See *descending fifth sequence*.

clef Symbol that associates lines and spaces on the staff with specific pitches. See also *treble clef, bass clef, C clef, alto clef, tenor clef*.

closing section In sonata form, section that usually ends both the exposition and recapitulation, following the perfect authentic cadence that marks the end of the secondary theme.

coda Concluding section of a movement; in sonata form, it follows the recapitulation.

collage form The stratification of the musical texture into discrete layers, some of which may be quotations of earlier works.

collection Group of notes, distinct in content, but without regard to the order in which the notes occur.

combinatoriality The combination of a pitch-class set with one or more transposed or inverted forms of itself (or its complement) to create an aggregate.

common-tone diminished seventh chord Embellishing chromatic diminished seventh chord resulting from a sustained root and embellishing notes in other voices.

common-tone modulation Modulation between two keys in which one tone shared by two chords is used as a pivot between the keys.

complement The relationship of each pitch class to its inversional partner with respect to the inversional axis C–F♯ (i.e., C and C, B and C♯, B♭ and D, A and E♭, A♭ and E, G and F, F♯ and F♯).

complementary The relationship of two collections that have no notes in common and together contain all twelve notes: each contains the notes the other excludes (for example, the white and black notes of the piano).

composing-out Compositional technique in which brief motives are expanded over greater time spans.

compound interval Interval larger than an octave; identified by the number of steps or by its simple-interval equivalent (e.g., tenth or compound third).

compound meter Meter in which the basic time unit is a dotted-note value; indicated in the upper number of a time signature by 6, 9, or a larger multiple of 3.

compound ternary form Ternary form in which each of the three sections is itself in binary or ternary form (as in a minuet and trio).

consequent In a period, the second phrase, which ends with a perfect authentic cadence and which answers the "question" posed by the first, *antecedent* phrase.

consonant interval Interval that is relatively stable; generally, major or minor third or sixth, perfect unison, octave, fifth, and (in some contexts) fourth.

continuation See *sentence*.

continuous binary form Binary form in which the first half does not end with a perfect authentic cadence (PAC) in the home key.

continuous period Period in which the antecedent ends with a half cadence (HC) and the consequent does not begin on I.

continuous variation form A theme and variations in which the theme (and each variation) consists of a single phrase that may end with a half cadence or elide with the start of the next variation.

contracting wedge progression A pattern of notes moving symmetrically inward toward a central pitch or pitches.

contrapuntal cadence A phrase ending in which an inverted V, inverted V7, or vii°6 moves to I.

contrary motion Voice leading between two voices in which the voices move in opposite directions.

contrasting idea In a sentence-like phrase, statement of a new idea (usually about two measures long) that follows the *basic idea*; takes the place of the repetition (or varied repetition) that occurs within the presentation of a sentence.

contrasting period   Period in which the second (consequent) phrase does not begin like the first (antecedent).

cross relation   An occurrence of a scale degree and its chromatic variant appearing in two different voices in successive chords.

cyclic harmony   A collection of notes that is a continuous segment of an interval cycle, an entire interval cycle, or a combination of two or more interval cycles.

deceptive cadence (DC)   Cadence in which V (or V⁷) moves to a root-position vi (or VI) instead of the expected I.

descending fifth sequence   Common harmonic sequence involving chords whose roots alternately move up by fourth and down by fifth; also called *circle of fifths progression*. In its diatonic version, it can circle through the chords built on all seven scale tones; in its chromatic version, it uses applied dominant chords and can arrive at a distant key.

descending melodic minor   See *melodic minor scale*.

development   In sonata form, the beginning of the second part, often involving a wide variety of intensifying techniques, including tonicizations, sequences, and fragmentation of themes from the exposition. It may conclude with a cadence in a key other than the main or secondary key, followed by a retransition to the tonic key; or it may prepare the recapitulation with a half cadence in the tonic.

diatonic   Staying within the key and using the notes of the scale.

diatonic collection   The seven white notes of the piano or any transposition of them. There are twelve diatonic collections.

diatonic modes   The seven ways of writing a diatonic collection as a scale, beginning on any of its seven notes.

diminished interval   Interval a semitone smaller than a perfect or minor interval; for example, B–F, diminished fifth (d5); B–D♭, diminished third (d3).

diminished third chord   "Inversion" of an augmented sixth chord with the raised $\hat{4}$ in the bass, creating a diminished third with the minor form of $\hat{6}$.

diminished seventh chord   Seventh chord constructed of a diminished triad and a diminished seventh.

diminished triad   Triad built of a minor third and a diminished fifth.

direct fifths   *Similar fifths*.

direct octaves   *Similar octaves*.

dissolving sentence   Sentence in which the basic idea is weakly formed and the continuation evaporates without leading to a secure cadence.

dissonant interval   Interval that is relatively unstable; generally, seconds, sevenths, diminished and augmented intervals, and (in some contexts) perfect fourth.

dominant   The fifth note in a scale ($\hat{5}$); also, the name of the chord (V) based on that tone, or (as **Dominant**) any of a group of chords that function as dominants, including vii° and V⁷ chords.

dominant key   The key in which the dominant chord of a composition's main key is tonic: for example, in a G-major composition, the key of D major.

dominant seventh chord (⁷)   Seventh chord built on the dominant ($\hat{5}$) note of a scale, containing two tendency tones ($\hat{7}$ and the chordal seventh, $\hat{4}$) and functionally leading strongly to the tonic; also, the *chord quality* of a chord constructed of a major triad plus a minor seventh.

double flat ♭♭   Accidental lowering a natural note by a whole step.

double neighbor   Four-note embellishing figure in which the first and fourth notes are the same and are embellished by tones a step above and below in the middle two notes.

double period   Period in which both the antecedent and consequent themselves form phrase pairs.

double sharp ×   Accidental raising a natural note by a whole step.

doubling   In four-part harmony, the appearance of the same chord tone (perhaps separated by one or more octaves) in two voices.

downbeat   First beat of a measure.

duple meter   Meter with a two-beat grouping (one strong and one weak beat).

dyad   Pitch-class set consisting of two notes or an unordered collection of two pitch classes.

échappée   *Escape tone*.

eighth note   Note written as a solid notehead with a stem and a flag or beam, representing the duration half as long as a quarter note and twice as long as a sixteenth note.

embellishing tone   Note that decorates a chord tone and does not belong to the harmony; classified by whether the non-chord tone appears on or off the beat (accented or unaccented) and how it is approached and left.

enharmonic equivalents   Notes that have different names ("spellings") but sound the same pitch.

enharmonic intervals   Intervals with the same number of semitones but spanning a different number of scale degrees (letter names), as C–D♯ (A2) and C–E♭ (m3).

enharmonic modulation   Modulation to a distant key brought about by enharmonically reinterpreting (or respelling) a chord, as when an augmented sixth chord is reinterpreted as a V⁷ (or vice versa).

equal division of the octave   Repetition of a strict chromatic sequence to return to its starting point, in the process dividing the octave into smaller intervals of the same size, as by three major thirds or four minor thirds.

escape tone   Embellishing tone that is approached by step and left by leap in the opposite direction. Also called *échappée*.

evaded cadence   Technique for extending a phrase by averting a perfect authentic cadence, as when I⁶ is substituted for the expected appearance of I.

expanding wedge progression   Pattern of notes moving symmetrically outward from a central pitch or pitches.

exposition   First part of sonata form. In the exposition the *primary theme* establishes the tonic key; a transition leads to the *secondary theme* in the secondary key and ends with a perfect authentic cadence (PAC) in this key (usually V or, in minor, III), which is then usually followed by a closing section.

F clef   See *bass clef*.

fifth   Interval between two tones spanning five scale steps (letter names), as C–G or $\hat{1}$–$\hat{5}$; in a chord, the fifth above the root.

figured bass   Keyboard notation in which a bass line is given, with *figures* to indicate upper voices.

figures   Arabic numerals, written vertically below bass note, used to indicate chords or intervals above the bass note.

first inversion   Chord position in which the third is in the bass; indicated $\frac{6}{3}$ or ⁶ for a triad, $\frac{6}{5}$ for a seventh chord.

first theme   *Primary theme*.

first-species counterpoint   Species counterpoint in which the new melody is written in whole notes against the cantus firmus, using only consonant intervals between the melodies.

five-part rondo form   Rondo form in which there are two sections that contrast with the main-key **A** section (**ABACA**).

flag Short line attached to an individual note stem indicating a duration shorter than a quarter note: a single flag indicates an eighth note, a double flag indicates a sixteenth note, and so forth.

flat ♭ Sign (accidental or in the key signature) lowering a natural note by a half step.

four-part harmony Texture of four voices; each chord uses four notes, with mostly the same basic rhythm in all four parts, as in a typical hymn.

fourth Interval between two tones spanning four scale steps (letter names), as C–F or $\hat{1}$–$\hat{4}$.

fourth-species counterpoint Species counterpoint in which the new melody is written in pairs of half notes that are tied across the barline, with dissonances allowed only on the first half of the measure, as suspensions.

fragmentation Technique in which a portion of a previous melodic idea is repeated two or more times, perhaps transposed and presented sequentially.

French augmented sixth (Fr⁺⁶) *Augmented sixth chord* that uses the minor form of $\hat{6}$ in the bass and $\hat{1}$, $\hat{2}$, and raised $\hat{4}$ in the upper voices.

fully diminished seventh chord (°⁷) *Diminished seventh chord.*

function Category of chords—*Tonic, **D**ominant,* or *Subdominant*—that can play a similar role in harmonic progressions.

G clef See *treble clef.*

German augmented sixth (Ger⁺⁶) *Augmented sixth chord* that uses the minor form of $\hat{6}$ in the bass, $\hat{1}$, the minor form of $\hat{3}$ (in major keys, sometimes spelled as raised $\hat{2}$), and raised $\hat{4}$ in the upper voices.

grand staff Paired treble and bass clef staves joined by a vertical line and brace.

ground bass Continuous variation in which the same bass line is repeated with each variation.

half cadence (HC) Cadence ending on V.

half note Note written as an open notehead with a stem, representing the duration half as long as a whole note and twice as long as a quarter note.

half step *Semitone.*

half-diminished seventh chord (ø⁷) Seventh chord constructed of a diminished triad and a minor seventh.

harmonic interval Distance (or relationship) between two tones sounding together.

harmonic minor scale Alteration of the minor scale with raised $\hat{7}$ to create a leading tone; there are three half steps, $\hat{2}$–$\hat{3}$, $\hat{5}$–$\hat{6}$, and $\hat{7}$–$\hat{8}$, and an augmented second, $\hat{6}$–$\hat{7}$.

harmonic progression Series of chords that follow each other in a logical manner, with one chord leading to the next.

harmonic sequence See *sequence.*

harmonize To supply bass and harmonies for the notes of a melody.

hexachord Pitch-class set consisting of six notes or an unordered collection of six pitch classes.

hexatonic collection Collection of notes consisting of two augmented triads a semitone apart, arrangeable as a scale of alternating intervals 1 and 3. There are four content-distinct hexatonic collections.

hexatonic cycle L-P chain (progression of triads that uses the triadic transformations L and P in succession); all of the triads belong to the same hexatonic collection.

hidden fifths *Similar fifths.*

hidden octaves *Similar octaves.*

home key *Main key.*

IH-combinatoriality The combination of a hexachord with an inverted form of itself to create an aggregate.

immobilized sentence Sentence in which the basic idea is repeated literally, often more than once, and a harmonically static continuation leads to an abrupt cadence.

imperfect authentic cadence (IAC) Somewhat unstable cadence, consisting of V or V⁷ moving to I, ending with $\hat{3}$ or $\hat{5}$ in the melody (soprano voice).

inclusion Collection contained within a larger collection, as, for example, the C major chord is included within a C major scale.

incomplete neighbor tone (INT) *Embellishing tone* that is approached by leap and moves by step to a chord tone, or that is approached by step and left by leap.

index of inversion The ordered pitch-class interval by which a previously inverted pitch-class set or series is transposed. In the abbreviation T_nI, n is the index of inversion. Using pitch-class numbers, the index of inversion for two sets or series is the sum of any pair of inversional partners.

interrupted period Period in which the antecedent ends with a half cadence (HC) and the consequent begins on I.

interval Distance between two tones, whether sounding together (harmonic interval) or in succession (melodic interval).

interval class Unordered pitch-class interval. There are six interval classes.

interval-class content The interval classes formed by the notes in a pitch-class set.

interval-class vector Way of writing the interval-class content of a pitch-class set as a string of six numbers, representing the number of times each of the six interval classes occurs in the set.

interval cycle The pattern that results when a pitch class is transposed repeatedly by a single interval, leading to a return of the original pitch class.

interval inversion Ordered pitch-class intervals that combine to make up an octave, like 1 and 11, 2 and 10, 3 and 9, 4 and 8, and 5 and 7; 6 is its own inversion.

interval of transposition The ordered pitch-class interval by which a pitch-class set or series is transposed. In the abbreviation T_n, n is the interval of transposition.

interval quality The "flavor" of an interval in terms of number of half steps; in a major key, seconds, thirds, sixths, and sevenths, are major (large) or minor (small); fourths are perfect or augmented (larger), while fifths are perfect or diminished (smaller).

introduction Opening section of a movement; in sonata form, a (usually slow) passage preceding the exposition that is not repeated with the exposition.

invariance Preservation of a collection of pitch classes when a twelve-tone series is transposed or inverted.

invariant Collection of pitch classes that is preserved when a twelve-tone series is transposed or inverted.

inversion (1) For intervals, the interval created when the lower note becomes the upper note (and vice versa); (2) for chords, the arrangement of the chord in which a note other than the root is in the bass.

Inversion (I) Ordering of a twelve-tone series. Related to the Prime form (P) by inversion (T_nI) where n indicates the level of transposition; related to the Retrograde form (RP) by retrograde (RT_nI); related to the Retrograde-Inverted form (RI) by retrograde (RT_n).

inversion (T_nI) An operation that inverts the notes of a set or series with respect to the inversional axis C—F♯ and then transposes them; in the abbreviation T_nI, n is the index of inversion.

inversional axis   The central pitches or pitch classes around which a collection of notes balances. Among the pitch classes, there are twelve potential inversional axes.

inversional partners   Pair of notes that balance symmetrically around an inversional pitch or pitch-class axis of symmetry.

inversional symmetry   Property of a collection of notes arranged in register so that the intervals from bottom to top are the same as the intervals from top to bottom.

Italian augmented sixth (It⁺⁶)   *Augmented sixth chord* built on the minor form of $\hat{6}$ in the bass, with $\hat{1}$ and raised $\hat{4}$ in the upper voices.

key   The particular major or minor scale used as the basis of a piece or passage of music.

key of V   *Dominant key.*

key signature   The sharps or flats needed for a major or minor scale or key, generally indicated immediately after the clef.

keyboard format   Notation of four-part harmony in which soprano, alto, and tenor are all written on the treble staff (played by the right hand), the bass on the bass staff (left hand).

L   Triadic transformation in which the two notes forming a minor third are held in common while the remaining note moves by semitone. The third of a major triad becomes the root of a minor triad, and vice versa.

lament bass   Descending chromatic bass line from $\hat{1}$ to $\hat{5}$, commonly used in minor keys, often used to express grief and mourning.

leading tone   The seventh note in a major scale ($\hat{7}$), a half step below the tonic, an important tendency tone that often appears as the third of the dominant chord. In minor keys, the leading tone requires an accidental.

ledger line   Short horizontal line written above or below the staff to extend the staff for higher or lower notes.

lower neighbor   Neighbor tone that is a step below the note it embellishes.

L-P chain   Progression of triads connected by alternating L and P triadic transformations.

L-P-R chain   Progression of triads that uses the triadic transformations L, P, and R in succession.

main key   The key that begins and ends a movement or piece; also known as home key or tonic key.

main theme   *Primary theme.*

major interval   The larger natural size of a second, third, sixth, or seventh.

major scale   Scale built of whole and half steps, in which the two half steps are $\hat{3}$–$\hat{4}$ and $\hat{7}$–$\hat{8}$.

major seventh chord (M7)   Seventh chord constructed of a major triad plus a major seventh.

major triad   Triad built of a major third and a perfect fifth above a root.

measure   One unit of a meter, consisting of a strong beat (downbeat) followed by weak beats.

medial caesura   In sonata form, a pause, break, or other textural demarcation that follows the cadence marking the end of the transition within the exposition or recapitulation and that immediately precedes the secondary theme.

mediant   The third note in a scale ($\hat{3}$); also, the name of the chord (III or iii) based on that note.

melodic interval   Distance (or relationship) between two tones sounding in succession.

melodic minor scale   Minor scale with raised $\hat{6}$ and $\hat{7}$ (leading tone) in the ascending form, natural $\hat{6}$ and $\hat{7}$ in the descending form.

melodic sequence   See *sequence.*

meter   Grouping of beats into a regular pattern of strong and weak beats.

middle C   The C roughly in the middle of the piano keyboard, notated one ledger line below the treble staff or one ledger line above the bass staff.

minor interval   The smaller natural size of a second, third, sixth, or seventh.

minor scale   Natural minor scale, with half steps $\hat{2}$–$\hat{3}$ and $\hat{5}$–$\hat{6}$; see also *harmonic minor scale* and *melodic minor scale.*

minor seventh chord (m7)   Seventh chord constructed of a minor triad plus a minor seventh.

minor triad   Triad built of a minor third and a perfect fifth above a root.

modal mixture   The use of elements drawn from the parallel key, recognizably sounding minor in a major key, or sounding major in a minor key.

modified strophic form   Song form in which the music repeats in a varied fashion with each verse of the text.

modulation   Change of key that is confirmed by a cadence.

modulating period   Period in which the consequent modulates to a new key; also called *progressive period.*

moment form   The fragmentation of the musical form into discrete units having no evident connection with each other.

motive   Combination of pitches or pitch classes and their intervals to form a distinctive musical shape.

N6   *♭II⁶.*

natural   White key of the piano; one of the seven notes A–G, with no sharp or flat; also, the accidental ♮ that cancels a sharp or flat.

natural interval   Any interval built on white keys (naturals).

natural minor scale   Minor scale with no accidentals, with half steps $\hat{2}$–$\hat{3}$ and $\hat{5}$–$\hat{6}$.

natural seventh chord   Any seventh chord built on white keys (naturals).

natural triad   Any triad built on white keys (naturals).

Neapolitan sixth   *♭II⁶.*

neighbor chord   Embellishing sonority resulting either from a neighbor tone in the bass (and possibly embellishing tones in other voices) or from neighbor tones in the upper voices above a stationary bass.

neighbor motion   See *neighbor tone.*

neighbor tone (NT)   Embellishing tone that leaves a chord tone by step and returns to it.

normal form   Set written in ascending order within an octave, with the smallest possible interval between the lowest and highest notes.

oblique motion   Voice leading between two voices in which one voice moves up or down while the other remains on the same pitch.

octave (8ve)   Interval between two notes spanning eight scale steps and having the same letter name, as C–C or $\hat{1}$–$\hat{8}$.

octatonic collection   The combination of two diminished seventh chords, arrangeable as a scale of alternating whole tones and semitones; there are three content-distinct octatonic collections.

octave doubling   Enrichment of harmonic texture by doubling a voice in parallel octaves.

open-score choral format, open-score format   Notation for four-part harmony in which each voice is written on a separate staff, with the tenor part most often written in treble clef but sounding an octave lower.

ordered pitch interval (opi)   The number of semitones between two pitches and their direction (up or down).

ordered pitch-class interval (opci)   The distance counted in semitones between two pitch classes, where the order of the pitch classes (first and second) is specified.

P   Triadic transformation in which the two notes forming a perfect fifth are held in common while the remaining note moves by semitone; as between major and minor triads sharing the same root and fifth.

P-SLIDE chain   Progression of triads connected by alternating P and SLIDE triadic transformations.

parallel $^6_3$ chords   Harmonic sequence, most often occurring in a three-voice texture, in which a first-inversion chord ($^6_3$) is repeatedly transposed by step.

parallel fifths   Fifths approached in parallel motion, permitted in four-part harmony only under extremely special circumstances.

parallel keys   The pair of major and minor keys sharing the same tonic.

parallel motion   Voice leading between two voices in which the voices move in the same direction and the same distance, so that the intervallic distance between the two voices stays the same.

parallel octaves   Octaves approached in parallel motion, forbidden in four-part harmony.

parallel period   Period in which the two phrases start identically (or nearly identically).

parallel unisons   Unisons approached in parallel motion, forbidden in four-part harmony.

passing $^6_4$ Second-inversion triad whose bass is a passing tone.

passing chord   Embellishing sonority resulting from a passing tone in the bass (and possibly embellishing tones in other voices).

passing V⁶   Passing chord commonly occurring between I and vi or I and IV⁶, as a result of bass stepwise motion.

passing IV⁶   Passing chord commonly occurring between V and V⁶ (or inversions of V⁷), as a result of stepwise bass motion.

passing motion   See *passing tone*.

passing tone (PT)   Embellishing tone that moves stepwise between two chord tones; may be accented or unaccented.

pedal $^6_4$ Second-inversion harmony that results when a root-position chord is embellished by motion in the upper voices, with the bass sustaining the root.

pedal point   Embellishment of a harmony in which one note (usually the bass) is sustained, while the other voices move, forming different harmonies above or around it; most commonly, a device to embellish a sustained I or V.

pentatonic collection   The five black notes of the piano, or any transposition of them; there are twelve pentatonic collections.

perfect authentic cadence (PAC)   The most stable cadence, consisting of V or V⁷ moving to I, ending with $\hat{1}$ in the melody (soprano voice).

perfect intervals   Unisons, octaves, and most fourths and fifths; in any major key, there is one augmented fourth and one diminished fifth; all others are perfect.

period   Phrase pair in which a first phrase (antecedent) leads to an unstable cadence, answered by a second phrase (consequent) that concludes with an authentic cadence.

phrase   Basic unit of tonal music, often around four or eight measures long, that concludes with a cadence.

phrase overlap   Technique of connecting phrases in which the last chord of one phrase also serves as the first chord of the next.

phrase pair   The combination of two successive phrases, often about the same length, each with its own cadence.

Phrygian cadence   Half cadence that consists of a iv⁶–V progression.

Picardy third   The use of raised $\hat{3}$ within a minor key to create a major tonic triad at the end of a phrase (especially, at the end of a piece), the most common use of modal mixture in minor.

pitch   Specific points on the continuum of audible sound; pitches are measured by the frequency of vibrations.

pitch class   Group of pitches related by octave and thus with the same (or enharmonic) name.

pitch-class clockface   Circular arrangement of the twelve pitch classes, with pitch-class C occupying the twelve o'clock position.

pitch-class numbers   The assignment to each of the twelve pitch classes of a number from 0 to 11; C = 0, C♯/D♭ = 1, D = 2, and so on.

pitch-class set   An unordered collection of pitch classes.

pitch-class symmetry   The balanced arrangement of pitch classes symmetrically around a central pitch class or pitch classes.

pitch symmetry   The balanced arrangement of pitches symmetrically above and below a central tone or tones.

pivot chord   In a modulation, chord that is shared by both keys and is used as a means of transitioning from one key to the next.

plagal cadence   IV–I motion occurring at the end of a phrase.

planing   The use of triads in parallel or similar motion.

position   *Chord position.*

post-tonal   Music in the Western classical tradition written after 1900 that does not observe the norms of tonal harmony and voice leading.

presentation   See *sentence*.

Prime (P)   An ordering of a twelve-tone series. The twelve levels of transposition are indicated as T_n. Related to the Inverted form (I) by inversion (T_nI); related to the Retrograde-Prime form (RP) by retrograde (RT_n); related to the Retrograde-Inverted form (RI) by retrograde inversion (RT_nI).

prime form   Conventional way of naming set classes as a string of numbers starting with 0.

primary theme   Opening theme of sonata form exposition and recapitulation, establishing the tonic key and ending with a cadence in the tonic key. Also called *first theme* or *main theme*.

progressive period   *Modulating period.*

quadruple meter   Meter with a four-beat grouping (one strong and three weaker beats).

quality   See *interval quality*; *triad quality*; *seventh-chord quality*.

quarter note   Note written as a solid notehead with a stem, and most often used to represent one beat; its duration is half as long as a half note and twice as long as an eighth note.

R   (1) Triadic transformation in which the two notes forming a major third are held in common while the remaining note moves by whole tone. The root of a major triad becomes the third of a minor triad, and vice versa. (2) *Retrograde* (RP or R).

range   Scope of a voice or instrument defined by its lowest and highest notes.

realize   To compose a passage based on indicated chords according to Roman numerals or figures.

recapitulation   The last section of a piece in sonata form, in which the primary theme and secondary theme are repeated in the main key.

reinterpreted half cadence   A cadence that is initially heard as a perfect authentic cadence (PAC) in V, but later understood as a half cadence (HC) in the home key.

relative keys   The pair of major and minor keys sharing a key signature.

rest A duration of silence; notated with signs equivalent to whole note, half note, and so forth.

Retrograde (RP or R) An ordering of a twelve-tone series. May occur at twelve levels of transposition (T_n). Related to the Inverted form (I) by retrograde-inversion (RT_nI); related to the Prime form (P) by retrograde (RT_n); related to the Retrograde-Inverted form (RI) by inversion (T_nI).

retardation (RET) Accented embellishing tone that is approached by common tone and resolves up by step; sometime called an "upward resolving suspension."

retransition In sonata form, passage at the end of the development section that leads back to the tonic key of the recapitulation; the retransition usually follows a cadence in a non-tonic key (such as the key of vi) that appears near the end of the development.

Retrograde-Inversion (RI) An ordering of a twelve-tone series. May occur at twelve levels of transposition (T_n). Related to the Inverted form (I) by retrograde (RT_n); related to the Retrograde-Prime form (RP) by inversion (T_nI); related to the Prime form (P) by retrograde inversion (RT_nI).

Roman numeral Designation of a chord according to the scale degree on which it is built as well as its quality (e.g., ii indicates a minor triad built on $\hat{2}$; ♭III indicates a major triad built on lowered $\hat{3}$).

Romanesca Harmonic sequence in which the chord roots move alternately down a fourth and up a second.

rondo form Multipart form of a movement or piece in which the first section, in the main key, returns after each of two or more contrasting sections, such as **ABACA** or **ABACABA**.

root The pitch on which a triad or other chord is built.

root position The arrangement of a chord in which the root is in the bass; indicated $\frac{5}{3}$ or no figures for a triad, $\frac{7}{3}$ or 7 for a seventh chord.

rounded binary form See *binary form*.

row *Series*.

SATB (chorale) format Notation of four-part harmony in which soprano and alto are written on the treble staff, tenor and bass on the bass staff.

scale Collection of notes, typically arranged in ascending order, organized with reference to a central pitch (tonic), and used as the basis for a musical composition.

scale degree The step within a scale, indicated as a name or number (e.g., "tonic" or $\hat{1}$).

scale-degree name The name of the step within a scale, as "mediant."

scale-degree number The number of a step within a scale, as $\hat{3}$.

second Interval between two tones spanning two scale steps (letter names), as C–D or $\hat{1}$–$\hat{2}$.

second inversion Chord position in which the fifth is in the bass; indicated $\frac{4}{3}$ for a seventh chord, $\frac{6}{4}$ for a triad (and considered dissonant in this form).

second theme *Secondary theme*.

secondary dominant *Applied dominant*.

secondary theme In sonata form, the theme in the secondary key of the exposition, which ends with a PAC in the secondary key, and which generally is restated in the tonic key when it returns in the recapitulation. Also called *second theme* or *subordinate theme*.

second-species counterpoint Species counterpoint in which the new melody is written in half notes, with dissonances allowed only on the second half of the measure, as passing or neighbor tones.

sectional binary form Binary form in which the first part ends with a perfect authentic cadence (PAC) in the home key.

sectional period Period in which the antecedent ends with an imperfect authentic cadence (IAC).

sectional variation form Theme and variations in which the theme (and each variation) involves two or more phrases, usually structured in binary form.

semitone Distance between two adjacent notes on the piano; commonly, the smallest distance between two notes in Western music. There are twelve semitones in an octave.

sentence Phrase layout typically consisting of eight measures, divided into two halves, *presentation* and *continuation*; the presentation consists of a melodic basic idea (usually about two-measures long) that is repeated, elaborating the tonic. In the continuation, the momentum is intensified in a drive to a cadence, often with *fragmentation* of the basic idea or a new idea.

series The ordered presentation of a line of pitch classes; also called a *row*.

set class The collection of pitch-class sets related by either transposition or inversion.

sequence Harmonic or melodic pattern in which a segment of music is repeated one or more times in succession, transposed in a regular manner, whether diatonically or (using accidentals) chromatically.

sequential period Period in which the consequent (second phrase) begins with a transposed version of the antecedent (first phrase).

seven-part rondo form Rondo form of the shape **ABACAB′A**, in which the first **B** section is generally in V or the relative major, while the second **B** section is in the main key. Often called sonata rondo when the sections are structured like a sonata form's exposition (**AB**), development (**C**), and recapitulation (**A′B**).

seventh Interval between two tones spanning seven scale steps (letter names), as C–B or $\hat{1}$–$\hat{7}$.

seventh chord Four-note chord constructed of a triad plus a seventh over its root; in figured bass, $\frac{7}{3}$, abbreviated to 7.

seventh-chord quality The "flavor" of seventh chord depending on the qualities of the triad and the seventh, as a *minor seventh chord* (minor triad, minor seventh).

sharp (♯) Sign (accidental or in the key signature) raising a natural note by a half step.

similar fifths Fifths approached in similar motion, permitted in four-part harmony with certain restrictions.

similar motion Voice leading between two voices in which the voices move in the same direction but different distances.

similar octaves Octaves approached in similar motion, permitted in four-part harmony with certain restrictions.

simple binary form See *binary form*.

simple interval Interval smaller than an octave.

simple meter Meter in which the basic time unit is not a dotted-note value (compare *compound meter*).

sixteenth note Note written as a solid notehead with a stem and a double flag or beam, representing the duration half as long as an eighth note and twice as long as a thirty-second note.

sixth Interval between two tones spanning six scale steps (letter names), as C–A or $\hat{1}$–$\hat{6}$.

SLIDE A triadic transformation in which the chordal third of two triads is held in common while the root and fifth move by semitone, as between a major and minor triad that share the same chordal third.

sonata form Extended musical form resembling a large rounded binary form, consisting of two large parts: *exposition*, which modulates to a secondary key (most often V or the relative major), and is usually repeated, and *development* and *recapitulation*, which may also be repeated as one part. There may also be a slow *introduction* at the beginning, and a *coda* at the end.

sonata rondo   See *seven-part rondo form*.

spacing   Distance between adjacent voices in four-part harmony.

species counterpoint   Traditional method for learning voice leading, particularly the treatment of dissonant embellishing tones and perfect consonances, by writing melodies to go with a cantus firmus; the different species are categorized as first through fifth species, depending on the time values in the new melody.

staff   Arrangement of five horizontal lines on which pitches are indicated.

stationary motion   Voice leading between two voices in which both remain on the same pitch.

strict chromatic sequence   Sequence in which a musical segment is transposed the same number of semitones with each repetition of the sequential pattern.

strophic form   Song form in which the same music is used for each verse of the text.

subdominant   The fourth note in a scale ($\hat{4}$); also, the name of the chord (IV or iv) based on that tone, or (as *Subdominant*) any of a group of chords that function as subdominants, including ii⁶, ii⁶₅, ii⁷, and Neapolitan sixth chords.

submediant   The sixth note in a scale ($\hat{6}$); also, the name of the chord (VI or vi) based on that tone.

subordinate theme   *Secondary theme* of sonata form.

subset   A smaller grouping within a larger one as, for example, a dyad or a trichord within a twelve-tone series.

subtonic   The seventh note in a scale ($\hat{7}$) as it occurs in natural minor, a whole step below the tonic, or the name of the chord (VII) based on that tone.

subtonic VII   Major triad built on the natural minor form of $\hat{7}$; generally occurs as part of a modulation or in a sequence.

supertonic   The second note in a scale ($\hat{2}$); also, the name of the chord (ii) based on that tone.

suspension (SUS)   Accented embellishing tone that is approached by common tone from a note of the previous chord and resolves down by step.

symmetrical binary form   Binary form in which both parts are the same or nearly the same length.

symmetrical period   Period in which the antecedent and consequent are the same length.

syncopation   An accent on a metrically weak beat.

tendency tone   In four-part harmony, a tone with a strong tendency to move stepwise either up or down.

tenor clef   C clef (𝄡) indicating that the fourth line from the bottom of the staff is middle C; used for tenor range of cello, trombone, and bassoon.

ternary form   Three-part form of a movement or piece (**ABA**) characterized by contrast and return, in which a first section (**A**, generally ending with a perfect authentic cadence in the main key) is followed by a contrasting middle section (**B**, often in or modulating to V or the relative key), with a return of the first section or a variant of it (**A** or **A′**), in the main key. The middle section may end with a bridge that leads back to the main key.

theme and variations   Instrumental form that starts with the presentation of the theme followed by a series of variants of the entire theme, with most of the variants of the theme usually appearing in the home key.

third   Interval between two tones spanning three scale steps (letter names), as C–E or $\hat{1}$–$\hat{3}$; in a chord, the third above the root (in a triad, the middle note).

third inversion   Position of seventh chord in which the seventh is in the bass, indicated $^4_2$.

through-composed   Song form in which each verse of the text is set with different music. Compare *strophic form*.

tie   A curved sign between two noteheads indicating the addition of the time values; can be used to create durations that last across barlines or for which there is no single-note representation.

time signature   An indication of notated meter, generally in the form of two stacked numbers indicating the number of beats per measure and the type of note representing one beat.

tonic   The central organizing tone in a key, and the first note in a scale ($\hat{1}$).

tonic key   *Main key*.

tonicization   Momentary change of key, generally indicated by the use of an applied dominant chord but without a cadence to the new key.

Tonnetz   A map or chart of triads on which the triadic transformations can be easily read: within each row, triads are related by transposition at the minor third; within each column, triads are related by transposition at the major third.

transition   In sonata form, passage in the exposition that follows the primary theme and precedes the secondary theme; the transition usually concludes with a strong half cadence, either in the tonic or in the secondary key.

transposition   (1) To shift a scale, melody, or passage to another note while maintaining its pattern of whole and half steps. (2) An operation that moves the notes of a set or series by a certain ordered pitch-class interval. Abbreviated T_n, where n is the interval of transposition.

treble clef (G clef)   𝄞 symbol indicating that the second line from the bottom of the staff is G above middle C.

triad   Harmonic element consisting of three pitches: a root pitch and a third and fifth above it.

triad quality   Quality of a triad: major, minor, augmented, or diminished.

triadic transformation   Nontraditional way of relating one major or minor triad to another, involving a change of triad quality (major becomes minor, and vice versa), with one or two notes held in common and the remaining note or notes moving by semitone or whole tone. See *L, P, R, SLIDE*.

trichord   A pitch-class set containing three pitch classes.

trichord class   One of the twelve set classes for trichords.

triple meter   Meter with a three-beat grouping (one strong and two weak beats).

triplet   The division of a note value into three equal parts instead of two: for example, an eighth-note triplet consists of three notes equal in duration to one quarter note.

twelve-by-twelve matrix   Chart showing the forty-eight forms of a twelve-tone series (twelve Primes, twelve Inversions, twelve Retrogrades, twelve Retrograde-Inversions). P is read horizontally from left to right, RP horizontally from right to left, I vertically from top to bottom, and RI vertically from bottom to top.

twelve-count   The identification of the forms of the series with a label (for example, P_D or RI_F) and the use of numbers (1–12) to indicate the order position of each note within the series.

twelve-tone music   Style of music based on a twelve-tone series as a primary, referential structure.

twelve-tone series   An ordered presentation of the twelve pitch classes.

unaccented   Sounding on a relatively weak beat or part of the beat or appearing after (most of) the notes of the chord are sounded.

unison   Name of the interval between two notes at the same pitch level, as C–C or Î–Î.

unordered pitch interval (upi)   The number of semitones between two pitches without regard to their direction (up or down).

unordered pitch-class interval (upci)   The distance counted in semitones between two pitch classes, where the order of the pitch classes (first and second) is not specified. Also called *interval class*.

upper neighbor   Neighbor tone that is a step above the note it embellishes.

upper voice   In four-part harmony, the soprano, alto, or tenor (i.e., not the bass).

viola clef   *Alto clef.*

voice   In four-part harmony or other part writing, a single melodic part (such as the soprano, alto, tenor, or bass).

voice crossing   Harmonic writing in which a voice descends below the next lowest voice, or ascends above the next highest voice.

voice exchange   Voice leading in which two chord tones are traded between two voices, as when the bass moves from the root to the third of a chord at the same time that the soprano moves from the third to the root.

voice leading   The manner in which one chord, note, or interval moves to the next.

whole note   Note written as an open notehead with no stem, representing the duration twice as long as a half note.

whole step, whole tone   Distance of two half steps.

whole-tone collection   Combination of two augmented triads a whole-tone apart, arrangeable as a scale of whole tones. There are two content-distinct whole-tone collections.

Credits

Index of Music Examples

Index of Terms and Concepts

immobilized sentence, 440
imperfect authentic cadence(s) (IAC),
    68–69
    V^7 at, 108
    in binary form, 326
    within a period, 319–20
    in phrase pair, 318–19
imperfect consonances, 30
inclusion relationship between
    diatonic and pentatonic scales,
    359–60
incomplete neighbor tones (INT), 81,
    83, 121–22
index of inversion, 402–5, 409
interval(s), 24–32
    augmented, 26–27
    compound, 25–26
    consonant, 30
    defined, 24
    describing in post-tonal music, 393
    diminished, 26–27
    dissonant, 30
    enharmonic, 29–30, 384–85
    harmonic, 24
    inversion of, 28, 392–93
    in a key, 30–31
    major, 26–27
    measuring by semitones, 384–85
    melodic, 24
    minor, 26–27
    motion between, 58–59
    motives, 386–87
    natural (white-key), 28–29
    perfect, 27
    qualities, 26–30
    simple, 25–26
    size, 24–25
interval class (ic), 392–93
interval of transposition, 398–400, 409
interval ordering, 352
introduction (in sonata form), 347
invariance, 434–36
inversion(s)
    complements and, 401
    defined, 28
    index of, 402–5, 409, 426
    of intervals, 28, 392–93
    in keyboard format, 48
    of pitch-class sets, 401–5, 409
    Roman numerals and, 37, 40–41
    of seventh chords, 40–41
    of triads, 35–36
inversional axis. See axis of symmetry
inversional symmetry, 412–21
    defined, 412
    in pitch, 414–16
    in pitch class, 416–19
    wedge progressions, 412–14
Inversion (I) order of series, 424–28
Ionian mode, 352
Italian augmented sixth chord (It^{+6})

harmonic progressions, 276–77
harmonies preceding, 279–80
intervals in, 275

key(s)
    defined, 18
    intervals in, 30–31
    major, 18–19
    minor, 19–20
    parallel, 22
    relative, 21
    in ternary form, 334–35
keyboard format for four-part harmony,
    46–48
    figured bass for, 52
    inversions, 48
    notation, 46–47
    spacing, 48
key signature(s)
    defined, 18
    for major keys, 18–19
    for minor keys, 19–20
    notating, 19

lament bass, 222
leading tone
    in V chord, 98, 99–100
    in V^7, 104–5
    in V^6_5, 120
    in applied-chord descending fifth
        sequences, 293
    approaching in voice leading, 57–58
    doubled in sequences, 206–7
    doubling avoided for, 50, 99
    in minor-key harmonies, 37, 49, 98
    resolution of, 50, 61–62, 99–100,
        104, 351
    scale degree, 15
leading tone, secondary, 229
leading-tone seventh chord (vii^{o7}), 41,
    162–65
    as applied chord, 240, 271
    harmonic progressions, 163
    in modal mixture, 265
    moving to and from V^7, 163–64
    voice leading, 164–65
leading-tone seventh chord, first-
    inversion (vii$^{o6}_5$), 41, 163
    moving to and from V^7, 163–64
    voice leading, 164–65
leading-tone seventh chord, second-
    inversion (vii$^{o4}_3$), 41, 163
    moving to and from V^7, 163–64
    voice leading, 164–65
leading-tone seventh chord, third-
    inversion (vii$^{o4}_2$ or vii^{o2}), 41, 163
    moving to and from V^7, 163–64
    voice leading, 164–65
leading-tone seventh chord, half-
    diminished (vii^{ø7}), 40, 165–66

as applied chord, 240–41
inversions of, 40
leading-tone triad (vii^o), 36, 37
    avoiding in root position, 196
    tonicization impossible for, 237
leading-tone triad, first-inversion (vii^{o6}),
    37, 127–35
    alternating with other Dominant-to-
        Tonic progressions, 129–30
    as applied chord, 240
    in figured bass, 134
    harmonic progressions, 127–29
    moving to other Dominant harmonies
        from, 130
    as neighbor chord to I, 129
    as passing chord between I and I^6, 128
    Subdominant harmonies leading to,
        137, 139
    voice leading to I in four-part
        harmony, 131
leading-tone triad, second-inversion
    (vii$^{o6}_4$), 37
leading-tone triadic transformation (L),
    374–78, 381
    leading to subdominant chords, 177–78
    voice leading, 181–83
leaps
    in first-species counterpoint, 87
    in fourth-species counterpoint, 92
    in second-species counterpoint, 88, 89
    in upper voices, I–V chords, 100
    in voice leading, 56–58
ledger lines, 3
Locrian mode, 353
L–P chain, 376–78
Lydian mode, 352, 353, 354

main key (defined), 244
main theme. See primary theme (in
    sonata exposition)
major interval(s)
    in major keys, 30–31
    in minor keys, 31
    as quality, 26–27
major key(s)
    intervals in, 30–31
    key signatures for, 18–19
    modulations to closely related keys in,
        253–54, 257
    seventh chords in, 40
    triads in, 36–37
major pentatonic scale, 356
major scale(s)
    defined, 14
    order of whole tones and semitones,
        14–15
major seventh chord(s), 38
    in major keys, 40
major triad(s)
    in hexatonic collection, 366
    identification in post-tonal music, 375